LORDS OF THE SEA

D1570221

The John Whitney Hall Book Imprint
commemorates a pioneer in
the field of Japanese Studies
and one of the most respected
scholars of his generation.
This endowed book fund
enables the Center for
Japanese Studies to publish
works on Japan that
preserve the vision and
meticulous scholarship of a
distinguished and beloved historian.

LORDS OF THE SEA

Pirates, Violence, and Commerce
in Late Medieval Japan

Peter D. Shapinsky

This book was financed in part through generous grants from the
Dean's Office, College of Liberal Arts and Science,
University of Illinois at Springfield, and the
John Whitney Hall Book Imprint.

Center for Japanese Studies
The University of Michigan
Ann Arbor, 2014

Michigan Monograph Series in Japanese Stuudies, Number 76

Published by the Center for Japanese Studies,
The University of Michigan
1007 E. Huron St.
Ann Arbor, MI 48104-1690

Library of Congress Cataloging-in-Publication Data

Shapinsky, Peter D., 1974–
　　Lords of the sea : pirates, violence, and commerce in late medieval Japan / Peter D. Shapinsky.
　　　　pages cm. — (Michigan monograph series in Japanese studies ; number 76)
　　Summary: "Lords of the Sea revises our understanding of the epochal political, economic, and cultural transformations of Japan's late medieval period (1300–1600) by shifting the conventional land-based analytical framework to one centered on the perspectives of seafarers usually dismissed as 'pirates'"—Provided by publisher.
　　Includes bibliographical references and index.
　　ISBN 978-1-929280-80-3 (hardback : alkaline paper) — ISBN 978-1-929280-81-0 (paperback : alkaline paper) — ISBN 978-1-929280-82-7 (ebook)
　　1. Pirates—Japan—History.　2. Seafaring life—Japan—History.　3. Murakami family.　4. Social change—Japan—History.　5. Violence—Japan—History.　6. Japan—History—1185–1600.　7. Inland Sea (Japan)—History.　8. Japan—History, Naval—To 1868.　9. Japan—Commerce—History.　I. Title.

DS857.S49 2014
952'.023—dc23

2014016634

This book was set in Minion Pro.
The *kanji* were set in Hiragino Mincho Pro.

This publication meets the ANSI/NISO Standards for Permanence of Paper for Publications and Documents in Libraries and Archives (Z39.48—1992).

Contents

Illustrations

Tables

Preface

In terms of Romanization, I follow the Pinyin system for Chinese, the modi
fied Hepburn system for Japanese, and the modified McCune-Reischaue
system for Korean. I follow standard historiographical practice with regar
to East Asian names. Individuals in premodern Japan employed several dif
ferent types of names throughout their lives, including lineage names, fam
ily names, honorary titles, childhood names, and adult names. When pos
sible, I have simplified this usage for the sake of comprehension. Typicall
I will refer to individuals using their family name first, then adult persona
name, or the name by which they are most commonly known to historian
(e.g., Oda Nobunaga). Subsequent usage will simply supply the given nam
(Nobunaga). The surnames of warlords (daimyo) will also be used to identif
their war band or domain (i.e., the Mōri). It should not be assumed that in
dividuals who employed the same surname were necessarily blood relations
The several seafaring houses that went by the surname Murakami, who con
stitute some of the protagonists of this study, did not consider themselve
a single family or lineage in the medieval era. Much of the perception tha
they constituted a single lineage is a result of genealogical invention that oc
curred in later periods. I distinguish the various Murakami seafaring house
from each other by referring to them by the island upon which each base
itself, and by which they are often identified in the sources (e.g., Noshima
Murakami Takeyoshi, Kurushima Murakami Michifusa, Innoshima Mura
kami Sukeyasu). Chinese and Korean figures are typically identified first b
both surname and given name, while subsequent references typically giv
only their surname.

Part of the fun of doing medieval Japanese maritime history is work
ing around incomplete records and dealing with multiple calendrical sys
tems. I have converted the various Japanese, Korean, and Chinese years
which were tallied in era names assigned for propitious purposes during th
reign of a particular monarch, to their equivalent in the Western calenda
Months and days have been simply translated as they appear in the source
(e.g., eighth day of the seventh month, 1588). In citations, when known, th
date of the document will be given with the reign-era year first, followed b
the Western equivalent in parentheses or square brackets, followed by th

East Asian month and day. When the year is not given by the source but can be ascertained through context, a "?" will follow the suggested year (as in Tenshō 6? [1578] 6.23). Otherwise, these will be denoted with "no year" followed by the month and day. Intercalary months are notated with the prefix "int." When no date is known at all for the source, I employ the phrase, "no date." When citing Chinese and Korean sources that employed dates based on the sexagenary cycle, I transposed the ten heavenly stems and twelve earthly branches into ordinal numbers.

East Asian printed books were traditionally paginated differently from those produced in the West, with each numbered page referring to the front and back of a single leaf. In order to cite works written in that format, I follow standard usage and add "a" and "b" to refer to the front and back respectively (e.g., 1a-3b).

Although it is impossible to translate medieval Japanese weights and measures exactly, there is one measure that appears in the text for which an approximation will be useful. Japanese ships were typically categorized by the amount of cargo they could carry, measured in *koku*, which equaled approximately 0.3 cubic meters (300 liters). This measure of shipping volume should not be confused with the *koku* used to measure amounts of rice and to assess the productive capacity of territories. That *koku* measured approximately 180 liters of rice.

Currency in late medieval Japan often took the form of round copper coins cast with a square hole in the center. Most coins were imported from China. Japanese dealt in individual pieces of copper cash (*mon*), sets of ten coins (*hiki*), and strings of a thousand copper coins (*kanmon*). By the fourteenth century, these could be converted into paper bills of exchange for convenience.

Many of the place-names in this book refer to small islands and ports in Japan's Seto Inland Sea region. The book contains several maps for reference. In particular, it is hoped that figure 2, a map of the Inland Sea region (page 3) and figure 7, a map of the central Inland Sea region (page 72), will be helpful in this regard.

Unless otherwise noted, all translations are my own.

Acknowledgments

This book considers the perspectives of men and women who appear in historical sources as pirates as a way to explore several historical transformations of late medieval Japan from the waterline. Learning how to read, interpret, and craft narratives based on the wide variety of Japanese, Chinese, Korean, and European materials needed for this project required immeasurable assistance from teachers, colleagues, family, and friends. To you all I extend my heartfelt gratitude.

The project began as a dissertation at the University of Michigan, where I was fortunate to work with a group of extremely dedicated professors. I am grateful to my mentor, Hitomi Tonomura, who encouraged me to consider the perspectives of seafarers and who continues to ask the tough, but very helpful, questions. Leslie Pincus, Esperanza Ramirez-Christensen, and Victor Lieberman added invaluable guidance and assistance at the dissertation stage. I would also like to acknowledge the indispensable instruction of Professors Kondō Shigekazu and Kurushima Noriko of the Historiographical Institute at the University of Tokyo (Tokyo Daigaku Shiryō Hensanjo), who led *kanbun* workshops organized by Joan Piggott at Cornell University. I am particularly grateful to Professor Kurushima, who played a crucial role as my advisor during a year of research at the Historiographical Institute. She helped me make the most of my research time, invited me to participate in her seminars, and hosted me on later trips to Japan. In regular meetings, she shared her deep understanding of medieval sources and contexts and encouraged me not to let myself be distracted by the dominant voices of the authorities and institutions responsible for the creation of so many of the documents. Professors Murai Shōsuke, Gomi Fumihiko, and Ronald P. Toby also welcomed me into their graduate *zemi* and generously shared their vast knowledge. I also extend my appreciation to Igawa Kenji, Kikuchi Hiroyuki, and Mieda Akiko who tutored me in reading and interpreting many of the sources required for this project. In addition, the leading specialist on the history of the Murakami families, Yamauchi Yuzuru, now of Ehime University, generously provided me with copies of primary and secondary works, assisted me in interpreting and understanding some of the intricacies of Inland Sea history, and even took the time to help me navigate my way among pirate islands by bicycle and boat. Jennifer Manthei of the University of Illinois, Springfield assisted me with the translation of Portuguese sources.

Several scholars generously gave of their time to read and comment on all or parts of the manuscript at various stages, shaping my thinking on several aspects, including: Adam Clulow, Thomas D. Conlan, David Eason, Brian Goldsmith, Morgan Pitelka, Kenneth R. Robinson, David Spafford, Kenneth M. Swope, and Kären Wigen. I am also grateful for advice and ideas on the project I received from Philip C. Brown, Andrew Goble, Tomoko Kitagawa, Thomas Nelson, Ronald P. Toby, Umezawa Fumiko, Watanabe Miki, and Michael Wood. At the University of Illinois, Springfield, I would like to credit the helpful discussions I have enjoyed with my supportive colleagues, particularly in the Departments of History and English. I would also be remiss in overlooking the assistance provided by the interlibrary loan team at UIS, who help make doing medieval Japanese maritime history possible in central Illinois.

In transforming the dissertation into a book, I am grateful for the opportunities to present parts of this work as well as for the questions and feedback I received at several venues, including: the American Historical Association's Conference on Seascapes, Littoral Cultures, and Trans-Oceanic Exchanges (Washington, D.C., 2003); the Society for Military History Annual Conference (2006); Duke University's Asia/Pacific Studies Institute (2006); the Association for Asian Studies Annual Meetings (2007, 2008, 2009); the Japan's Natural Legacies Conference (University of Montana, Bozeman, 2007); the International Conference on Piracy and Maritime Security in the South China Sea (Hainan Island, People's Republic of China, 2008); Japan's Long Sixteenth Century: A Workshop (University of Southern California, 2008); Pieces of Sengoku: Interpreting Historical Sources and Objects from Japan's Long Sixteenth Century (Princeton University, 2009); Lost Strands from Japan's Sixteenth Century Conference (University of California, Berkeley, 2010); The Early Modern Medieval: Reconstructing Japanese Pasts (University of Michigan, 2011); Sea Rovers, Silk, and Samurai (Emory University, 2011); University of Illinois, Urbana-Champaign Center for East Asian and Pacific Studies (2012).

Executive Editor Bruce Willoughby at Center for Japanese Studies Publications patiently helped me to navigate the process from manuscript to book and produced a beautiful volume. An anonymous reviewer offered insightful, detailed critiques, which greatly facilitated revisions of the manuscript. Any errors are mine alone.

The financial support of several generous institutions made this work possible. Research and writing at the dissertation stage was made possible by a Fulbright/Institute of International Education Dissertation Grant for Japan as well as the University of Michigan Department of History and Center for Japanese Studies. Subsequent research was facilitated by a short-term travel grant from the Northeast Asia Council of the Association for Asian Studies; a University of Illinois, Springfield Summer Research Grant; and the University of Michigan Asia Library and Center for Japanese Studies. Completion of the manuscript was facilitated by receipt of a University of Illinois, Springfield College of Liberal Arts and Sciences Scholarship Enhancement Non-instructional Assignment Award. The book was finished during a semester of sabbatical leave granted by the University of Illinois, Springfield. Publication was generously supported by a subvention granted by the Dean's Office, College of Liberal Arts and Sciences, University of Illinois, Springfield.

Parts of this work have appeared previously. I am grateful to the following publishers and institutions for granting permission: "From Sea Bandits to Sea Lords: Nonstate Violence and Pirate Identities in Fifteenth- and Sixteenth-Century Japan," in *Elusive Pirates, Pervasive Smugglers: Violence and Clandestine Trade in the Greater China Seas*, edited by Robert J. Antony (Hong Kong: Hong Kong University Press, 2010), 27–41; "Protectors, Predators, and Purveyors: Pirates and Commerce in Late Medieval Japan," *Monumenta Nipponica* 64.2 (2009): 273–313; "With the Sea As Their Domain: Pirates and Maritime Lordship in Medieval Japan," in *Seascapes: Maritime Histories, Littoral Cultures, and Transoceanic Exchanges* edited by Jerry Bentley, Kären Wigen, and Renate Bridenthal (Honolulu: University of Hawai'i Press, 2007), 221–38.

I also wish to extend my gratitude to the several institutions who provided images and permissions for this book: the Historiographical Institute, University of Tokyo (Tokyo Daigaku Shiryō Hensanjo); the Kanagawa Prefectural Kanazawa Bunko Museum (Kanagawa Kenritsu Kanazawa Bunko) and the nearby temple of Shōmyōji; Konda Hachimangū in Osaka; the Kyoto Prefectural Archives and Museum (Kyoto Furitsu Sōgō Shiryōkan); the Newberry Library, Chicago; the Saga Prefectural Nagoya Castle Museum (Saga Kenritsu Nagoyajō Hakubutsukan); and the Yamaguchi Prefectural Archive (Yamaguchi-ken Monjokan).

Without the support of my family none of this would be possible. From my parents Eve and Gerald, brother Stephen, and sister Beth, I learned to appreciate curiosity, learning, and imagination. I am grateful for the love of my wife, Alicia, who has endured life with Japanese pirates for a long time. I dedicate this book to our sons, Alexander and Tristan, who are a constant inspiration.

Abbreviations

CCNSMJ   Chūgoku Chōsen no shiseki ni okeru Nihon shiryō shūsei: Min jitsuroku no bu. 6 vols. Kokusho Kankōkai, 1975.

CCNSS   *Chūgoku Chōsen no shiseki ni okeru Nihon shiryō shūsei: Seishi no bu.* 2 vols. Kokusho Kankōkai, 1975.

CWS   *Chosŏn wangjo sillok.* Edited by Kuksa P'yŏnch'an Wiwŏnhoe. 49 vols. Seoul: Tamgudang, 1986.

DNK   *Dai Nihon komonjo, iewake.* Compiled by Tokyo Teikoku Daigaku Shiryō Hensanjo. Tokyo Teikoku Daigaku Shuppankai, 1901–.

DNS   *Dai Nihon shiryō.* Compiled by Tokyo Teikoku Daigaku Shiryō Hensanjo. Tokyo Teikoku Daigaku Shuppankai, 1901–.

EK   *Ehime-ken shi shiryō-hen kodai chūsei.* Edited by Ehime-ken Shi Hensan Iinkai. Matsuyama-shi: Ehime-ken, 1983.

NET   *Nihon engyō taikei shiryō-hen kodai chūsei,* vol. 1. Edited by Nihon Engyō Taikei Henshū Iinkai. Nihon Engyō Kenkyūkai, 1982.

NKBT   *Nihon koten bungaku taikei.* 100 vols. Edited by Takagi Ichinosuke, Nishio Minoru, Hisamatsu Sen'ichi, Asō Isoji, and Tokieda Motoki. Iwanami Shoten, 1958–68.

NMKBS   *Nichimin kangō bōeki shiryō.* Compiled by Yutani Minoru. Kokusho Kankōkai, 1983.

YK   *Yamaguchi-ken shi shiryō-hen chūsei.* 4 vols. Yamaguchi-shi: Yamaguchi-ken, 1996–2008.

INTRODUCTION
Welcome to "The Pirate Isles"

> It is an ancient mariner,
> And he stoppeth one of three . . .
> He holds him with his skinny hand,
> "There was a ship," quoth he.
> "Hold off! Unhand me, grey-beard loon!" . . .
> He holds him with his glittering eye—
> The Wedding-Guest stood still,
> And listens like a three years' child:
> The Mariner hath his will.[1]

In the spring of 1420, with "the new willow leaves fresh and gold,"[2] a Korean ambassador named Song Hŭigyŏng (1376–1446) set off on a mission to Japan. He was prepared to fulfill his king's commission "to record and make poetry of everything that encountered my eyes and ears" on his journey to and from the Japanese capital of Kyoto.[3] In his poetic travelogue, Song devoted long passages to rendering the habits of Japanese pirates and the conditions of their maritime world. As he sailed through the region known today as the Seto Inland Sea (Setonaikai),[4] he passed through narrow channels surrounded by small, mountainous islands where people made their homes (see figures 1 and 2). His description of one island resonates through the work as a leitmotif for his perceptions of Japanese littoral life: "the island contains luxuriant woods and tall stands of bamboo; temples occupy the heights; the

---

1. Samuel Taylor Coleridge, "Rime of the Ancient Mariner," in *The Rime of the Ancient Mariner and other Poems* (New York: Dover, 1992), pp. 5–6.
2. Song Hŭigyŏng, *Nosongdang Ilbon haegnok* (*Rōshōdō Nihon kōroku: Chōsen shisetsu no mita chūsei Nihon*), edited by Murai Shōsuke (Iwanami Shoten, 1987), no. 1 (when citing this diary, I refer to the passage number).
3. Ibid., no. 196.
4. Premodern Japanese did not name any of their oceans, so any use of names for the seas is anachronistic.

1

Figure 1. Map of East Asia in the sixteenth century. Adapted from Conrad Totman, *A History of Japan*, 2nd ed. (Malden, Mass.: Blackwell Publishing, 2000), p. xxv.

people's homes lie down by the seashore, their fishing boats moored at the foot of a palisade."[5] Song noticed that many of these settlements harbored pirates, who established themselves as lords over the waterways. Describing one pair of islands in the Inland Sea, Song wrote, "In this region live hordes of pirates; the writ of the king [shogun] does not extend here."[6]

5. Ibid., no. 83.
6. Ibid., no. 162.

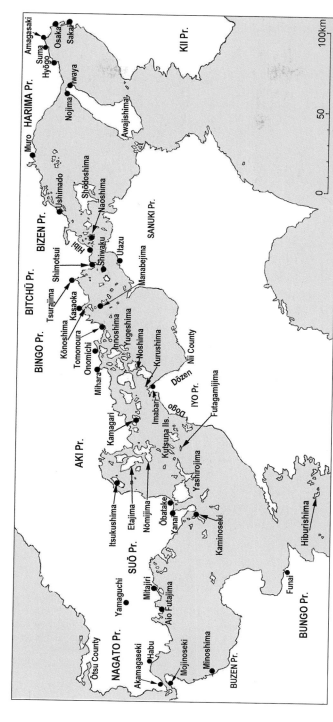

Figure 2. Map of the Inland Sea region in the late medieval period. Adapted from *Hyōgo Kitazeki irifune nōchō*, edited by Hayashiya Tatsusaburō (Chūō Kōron Bijutsu Shuppan, 1981), pp. 260–61.

By the mid-sixteenth century, accounts by Chinese and European visi
tors to Japan echoed Song Hŭigyŏng's description of autonomous pirate
dominions. In 1556, a self-proclaimed "plain clothed" man of no rank or
position from Ming China named Zheng Shun'gong voyaged to Japan in an
attempt to convince Japanese authorities to suppress pirates. He hoped that
his efforts in Japan would earn him a government post, and so he devoted
considerable attention to the Japanese littoral in his 1565 book, *Mirror on
Japan (Riben yijian)*.[7] He described parts of the Inland Sea as "criminals
islands, meaning a region of pirates. The inhabitants devote themselves to
traveling by sea and robbing pilgrimage ships. If the passenger ship is large
then the pirates board and take the large ship. If the ship is small, the pirates
board it, take it, and kill everyone. If they encounter monks, then they steal
the treasure but leave them alive."[8] One European navigator offered sail
ing directions that amplified the imagery of Zheng, his contemporary. He
warned that only with the permission and protection of local pirate leaders
could ships safely traverse the waterways of western Japan: "all the people
of this land . . . are not in any sort to be trusted" due to the prevalence
of "rovers, for they have many foists [oared vessels] wherewith they rove
and steale. . . . The ships and foists that desire to passe through it, asking
leave, they may pass without let or hindrance."[9] Some early European visi
tors to Japan even named parts of the archipelago "The Pirate Isles" (*Ilhas
dos Ladrones*). The major contemporary European cartographers imprinted
that piratical regionality in the minds of their readers, collectors, and navi
gators, as figure 3, part of a map by the Dutch mapmaker Arnold Florent van
Langren (1571–1644) shows.[10]

7. Zheng Shun'gong, *Riben yijian* (Beijing: Gushu Shiwen Diange, 1939), "Qionghe huahai," ch. 1, p. 1a
ch. 6, p. 11b.
8. Ibid., ch. 4, p. 20b.
9. Jan Huygen van Linschoten, *Iohn Huighen van Linschoten. His discours of voyages into ye Easte &
West Indies*, translated by John Wolfe (London: 1598; repr. Amsterdam: Theatrum Orbis Terrarum, Ltd. and Norwood, N.J.: Walter J. Johnson Inc., 1974), p. 377. For additional context, see
C. R. Boxer, *The Christian Century in Japan, 1549–1650* (Berkeley: University of California Press,
1951), pp. 127–28.
10. Arnold Florent van Langren was a Dutch cartographer who drafted maps used in Linschoten's collection of rutters, maps, and travelers' tales, which was widely known in Europe at the time. The
Arnold Florent van Langren map is oriented with East at the top. Always placing North at the top
is a modern Euro-American cartographical convention. Other cartographers who disseminated
the image of Japan as "pirate isles" include some of the most prominent and popular European
cartographers of the time: Gerardus Mercator (1512–94), Abraham Ortelius (1527–98), and Luis
Teixeira (ca. 1564–1604). João Rodrigues, *João Rodrigues's account of 16th c. Japan*, edited and
translated by Michael Cooper (London: Hakluyt Society, 2001), pp. 45–46.

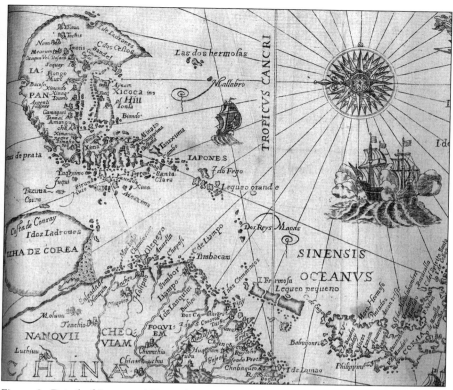

Figure 3. Detail of Japan and Korea from a 1598 map by Hendrik Florent van Langren of "the trew description of all the Coasts of China, Cauchinchina, Camboya, Sÿao, Malacm, Arraacn, and Pegu, together with all the Island's there abowts, both great and smale, with the cliffes, Breaches, Sands, Droughts and Shallowes, all perfectly drawne and examined with the most expert Cardes of the Portingales Pilots." In Jan Huygen Linschoten, *Iohn Huighen van Linschoten his Discours of Voyages into Ye Easte and Weste Indies*, map facing p. 32. Photo courtesy of the Newberry Library, Chicago, Case Folio G131.506, and used with their permission.

The notations for the pirate islands on the Langren map do not have any discernable correspondence with actual islands.[11] This lack of geographical specificity may signify that Portuguese navigators and cartographers perceived that pirate power was the defining feature of particular regions in the seas around Japan. In this vein, the western "Ilhas dos Ladrones" indicates

---

1. On occasion the name "Ilhas dos Ladrones" was also used to mark the Marianas Islands in this period.

the strength of pirates around Tsushima and the coasts of Kyushu and Korea; the location of the eastern inscription on the Kii Peninsula may represent the strength of pirates in the Kumano region and the Seto Inland Sea.

In late medieval Japan (ca. 1300–1590), although seafarers who received the appellation "pirate" inhabited much of the western littoral, some of the most dominant bands sailed the channels known today as the Seto Inland Sea. Among the most powerful and well known were a handful of tenuously associated families who went by the surname Murakami.[12] The indefatigable sixteenth-century Jesuit chronicler, Luis Frois (1532–97), wrote that one Murakami, Noshima Murakami Takeyoshi (ca. 1533–1604), "is the greatest pirate in all of Japan. He lives in a grand fortress and possesses many retainers, holdings, and ships that continually fly across the waves. His name is the Noshima Lord. He is so powerful that on these coasts as well as the coastal regions of other kingdoms [domains], all pay him annual tribute out of fear that he will destroy them."[13] Frois called him, along with Kurushima Murakami Michifusa (ca. 1561–97), "supreme captains of all the pirates of the seas."[14]

These images of Murakami and other "pirates" as lords of the sea transcended the hyperbole of travelers' tales.[15] Over the course of late medieval Japan, seafarers on the receiving end of the label "pirate" exploited the fact that waterways, not terrestrial roads, served as the dominant means of bulk and long-distance transport. They took advantage of favorable political and economic circumstances in order to establish themselves as lords of maritime production, distribution, exchange, and protection networks. Both land-based elites across the archipelago and visitors from overseas acknowledged and validated this pirate suzerainty.

Pirates constituted one of late medieval Japan's faces to the world. They were among the first Japanese that foreigners met, transporting, protecting

---

12. Although the various houses entered into marriage alliances and shared patrons on occasion, they were not a close-knit, single-family organization. That idea is a myth created and propagated in the Edo period by seafaring houses, their daimyo overlords, and domainal historians. Twentieth century ethnologists suggested that the name "Murakami" might derive from the title held by village headmen in the central Seto Inland Sea region (Miyamoto Tsune'ichi, *Setonaikai no kenkyū*, vol. 1 (Miraisha, 1965), p. 351. There is no need to assume familial connection based on surname alone.
13. Luis Frois, *Historia de Japam*, edited by José Wicki, S.J. (Lisbon: Presidência do Conselho de Ministros, Secretaria de Estado da Cultura, Direcção-Geral do Património cultural, Biblioteca Nacional de Lisboa, 1984), vol. 4, pp. 248–49.
14. Ibid., p. 282.
15. On the exaggeration and invention in Jesuit records, see Jeroen Lamers, *Japonius Tyrannus: The Japanese Warlord Oda Nobunaga Reconsidered* (Leiden: Hotei Publishing, 2000), pp. 217–24; Michael Cooper, *Rodrigues the Interpreter: An Early Jesuit in Japan and China* (New York: Weatherhill Press, 1974), pp. 163–65.

piloting, or attacking visitors from overseas.[16] They also helped integrate Japan into the global shipping networks that were beginning to twine around the earth. Furthermore, pirates represented one convergence of Japanese history with global maritime history. The idea of Japan as a space containing "pirate isles" epitomizes the situation along many of the shipping lanes beginning to connect the globe in this period. By the sixteenth century, almost any strategically situated, highly trafficked coastline, strait, or island around the world could reasonably have been labeled a piratical space.[17]

Many of the visitors to late medieval Japan recognized and accepted the strength and autonomy of Japanese pirates because of similar conditions in the waters surrounding their lands of origin. Land-based state officials attempted to transform the decks of ships into spaces juridically indistinguishable from national lands, but state power often attenuated once ships left sight of land.[18] In order to impress their will on far-flung parts of the globe, land-based rulers came to rely upon and tolerated the largely autonomous nature of seafaring individuals and organizations. From the wealthy shipping families of China's Fujian coast to the storm-tossed sailors aboard flimsy Iberian caravals, many of the seafarers responsible for establishing the first global maritime trade networks at one point or another received monikers that we translate as "pirate." In the channels of western Japan that fed the Japanese termini of regional and global maritime trade routes, seafarers labeled as pirates exemplified this global trend by establishing themselves as political authorities in particular littoral regions with the cognizance and recognition of land-based state governments. Song Hŭigyŏng's account of the early fifteenth century provides an example of limited dominion, whereas visitors in the sixteenth century found large portions of western Japan's maritime world under "pirate" control.

This book explores the social histories and perspectives of seafarers labeled pirate who brought parts of late medieval Japan's maritime world under their sway. It explores late medieval Japan from the waterline. During these three centuries, as a result of the actions of pirates, parts of the maritime world asserted their autonomy from the land and substantially affected the political, economic, military, and cultural histories of Japan before

---

16. Perhaps most famous is the case of Yajirō, who helped inspire and facilitate Francis Xavier's first trip to Japan in 1549 (Jurgis Elisonas, "Christianity and the Daimyo," in *The Cambridge History of Japan*, vol. 4: *Early Modern Japan*, edited by John W. Hall et al. [Cambridge: Cambridge University Press, 1991], p. 303).

17. Anne Pérotin-Dumon, "The Pirate and the Emperor," in *Bandits at Sea*, edited by C. R. Pennell (New York: New York University Press, 2001), pp. 25–26.

18. Lauren Benton, "Legal Spaces of Empire: Piracy and the Origins of Ocean Regionalism," *Comparative Studies in Society and History* 47.4 (2005): 700–724.

being reabsorbed into a land-centered, agricentric early modern regime. Dominant historiographies of late medieval Japan have focused almost exclusively on land-based forms of political economy and culture. This should not be surprising given that the majority of the population lived on the land and lived off the production of the land, and I do not mean to dispute the importance of the land-based political economy for the feeding and survival of much of the Japanese population. However, investigating seafarers labeled pirates from a waterline perspective shows how the premodern archive that scholars use for such projects needs to be understood as the product of authorities and institutions biased toward the land. The creation of written records represented an attempt to impose particular, self-serving perspectives on the world, obscuring alternative visions and agendas.[19] In addition, such a maritime perspective enables one to incorporate Japanese history into global maritime processes and other transnational frameworks. The sea blunts the continuing influence of scholarship that detaches Japan from Asia and sees the late medieval period as the decentralization, civil war, commercialization, and unification of an isolated, land-based island nation. Last, this book uses an exploration of pirates in order to illuminate the historiographically neglected lives, practices, and technologies of seafarers—from captains to sailors, from shipping merchants to salt makers, fisher folk, and migrant families of boat people.

WHAT IS A PIRATE?

The history of and meanings attached to terms for pirate lie at the heart of this investigation. There is no stable, objective category of pirate that can made comprehensible with a simple legal definition. The meaning of "pirate" shifts depending on the political and cultural contexts. Almost never did seafarers use the term to reference themselves. Much promising work has been done in crafting comparative, transnational models for pirate populations from various eras and locales by considering ideas such as economic impact, "social banditry," and "sea peoples." Nevertheless, the particular case of Japanese pirates suggests that much remains to be done to understand how pirates thought of themselves. They neither considered them

---

19. Thomas Keirstead argues for the importance of considering the exercise of power in the creation of medieval records in *The Geography of Power in Medieval Japan* (Stanford, Calif.: Stanford University Press, 1992).

selves engaged in resistance; nor did they feel that they had been co-opted; nor did they self-identify as sea people.[20]

In English-language studies of Japan, two words are usually translated as pirate: *wakō* and *kaizoku*, with some variants. The term *wakō* does not typically appear in medieval Japanese historical sources;[21] it is the modern Japanese pronunciation of a pejorative character compound that appears only in Korean and Chinese sources (pronounced *waegu* in Korean and *wokou* in Chinese). Usage and meaning of this phrase shifted depending on political circumstances inside China and Korea and the types of interaction occurring between Japan and its neighbors. In contrast, the term *kaizoku* is a Japanese historical one. Similar to its cousins, *wokou* and *waegu*, the usage of *kaizoku* changed over the premodern period. Each shift in usage reflected corresponding changes in the ways that land-based Japanese elites represented their ability to control the seas, nautical violence, seafarers, and licit and illicit maritime exchange. Nevertheless, even by the late medieval period, when Japanese land-based authorities utilized the concept of *kaizoku* to sponsor as well as condemn seafarers, mariners did not self-identify using that word.

Symptomatic of a pervasive land-centered bias in much of the historiography, scholars from Japan's early modern Edo period (1600–1867) through the twentieth century tended not to concern themselves with seafarers' perspectives or identities. They attempted to reconcile competing historical usages of *kaizoku* by adopting the perspectives of elite land-based authors and institutions and added new strata of meanings on top of medieval ones. Many employed the history of pirates as a means to promote other ideologies

---

20. For economic perspectives, see John L. Anderson, "Piracy and World History: An Economic Perspective on Maritime Predation," in *Bandits at Sea: A Pirates Reader*, edited by C. R. Pennell (New York: New York University Press, 2001), pp. 82–106; David J. Starkey, "Pirates and Markets," in *Bandits at Sea: A Pirates Reader*, edited by C. R. Pennell (New York: New York University Press, 2001), pp. 107–24. For social banditry and pirates, see Erik Hobsbawm, *Bandits* (New York: Delacorte Press, 1969); Marcus Rediker, *Between the Devil and the Deep Blue Sea: Merchant Seamen, Pirates and the Anglo-American Maritime World, 1700–1750* (Cambridge: Cambridge University Press, 1987); Robert Antony, *Like Froth Floating on the Sea: The World of Pirates and Seafarers in Late Imperial South China* (Berkeley: Institute of East Asian Studies, University of California Berkeley, 2003). Anton Blok critiques Hobsbawm's social bandit model by suggesting that many bandits ended up co-opted by state interests in the review essay "The Peasant and the Brigand: Social Banditry Reconsidered," *Comparative Studies in Society and History* 14.4 (1972): 494–503. For sea peoples, see Robert Ritchie, *Captain Kidd and the War Against the Pirates* (Cambridge, Mass.: Harvard University Press, 1986), ch.1.

21. It does appear in Edo-period compendia and studies of Ming texts on Japan. See, for example, Kasai Shigesuke's *Nankai tsūki*, in *Shintei zōho shiseki shūran*, vol. 20 (Kinugawa Shoten, 1967), p. 164.

and agendas—from Neo-Confucian moralizing to popular entertainment, from nationalism to Marxism. Edo-period moral models of history translated freewheeling, mercenary pirates who engaged in commerce, salt making, and fishing into "naval vassals" (*suigun*)—maritime analogues of land-based samurai—and bound their historical destinies to the lords they served in the Edo period.[22]

In the late nineteenth and early twentieth centuries, Japanese scholars built new historical models on early modern foundations and reinterpreted the history of *kaizoku* in ways that fed the interests of their new modern state. Some forced the history of Japanese pirates to fit Western historical patterns. Edo-period works that described how *kaizoku* led raids in China found a special place in the hearts and pages of those writers delving into the historical record in search of precedents for Japanese imperial expansion analogous to the European seafarers heralded as the vanguard of the Age of Exploration.[23] Prewar ethnologists understood *kaizoku* to have been part of populations of "sea people" (*ama*), one of several types of rural communities that retained elements of essential, traditional Japanese-ness.[24] Such projects contributed to global trends in patriotic historiography, as contemporary scholars in Europe and North America penned encomia to pirates like Francis Drake (1540–96), Henry Morgan (ca. 1635–88), and Jean Bart (1651–1702) as national heroes.[25]

In the postwar period, the dominant Japanese Marxist schools of historiography excoriated prewar scholars for their ahistoricity and co-option by wartime militarist ideologues.[26] However, despite rigorous reexaminations of the medieval source material, Marxist scholars attempted to reconcile competing usages of *kaizoku* by interpreting the history of pirates through

---

22. Kasai, *Nankai tsūki*, pp. 164–68.
23. For an examination of ties between colonialism and historiography in modern Japan, see Stephan Tanaka, *Japan's Orient: Rendering Pasts into History* (Berkeley: University of California Press, 1993). For histories claiming Japanese pirates as precedents for empire, see Yamada Nakaba, *Ghenkō: The Mongol Invasion of Japan* (London: Smith, Elder & Co., 1916); Takekoshi Yosaburō, *Wakō-ki* (Hakuyōsha, 1939); Takekoshi Yosaburō, *Story of the Wakō* (Kenkyūsha, 1940).
24. Hashimoto Mitsuru, "Chihō: Yanagita Kunio's Japan," in *Mirror of Modernity: Invented Traditions of Modern Japan*, edited by Stephen Vlastos (Berkeley: University of California Press, 1998), p. 138. Yanagita Kunio, *Kaijō no michi*, in *Yanagita Kunio zenshū*, vol. 21 (Chikuma Shobō, 1997), pp. 377–587. Miyamoto, *Setonaikai no kenkyū*.
25. C. R. Pennell, "Introduction," in *Bandits at Sea: A Pirates Reader*, edited by C. R. Pennell (New York: New York University Press, 2001), pp. 5–6.
26. Amino Yoshihiko, *Nihon chūsei no hinōgyōmin to tennō* (Iwanami Shoten, 1984), pp. 240–43. H. D. Harootunian, "Disciplinizing Native Knowledge and Producing Place: Yanagita Kunio, Origuchi Shinobu, Takata Yasuma," in *Culture and Identity: Japanese Intellectuals during the Interwar Years*, edited by J. Thomas Rimer (Princeton, N.J.: Princeton University Press, 1990), pp. 120–24.

the lens of a feudal, lord-vassal relationship. Such paradigms followed the grain of historical sources, took the regional warlord (daimyo) or other land-based elite sponsor as the historical subject, and treated *kaizoku* as either criminals or vassals. To identify the latter, scholars anachronistically applied the Edo-period term "naval vassals" (*suigun*).[27] Euro-American scholars largely accepted and reproduced these interpretations of Japanese pirates as they focused on questions related to land-centered state institutions and denizens of the land. English-language historiography has generally failed to interrogate the shifting meanings of *kaizoku*. Instead, it focuses predominantly on *wakō*, features Japanese pirates as a subset of Japan's international relations, and finds them generally predators and parasites—symptomatic of a lack of central control in the late medieval period.[28]

Much of the credit for bringing the sea back into Japanese history goes to Amino Yoshihiko (1928–2004). He argued that as a result of seventh-century reforms based on Chinese models, agricentrism remained a potent ideology throughout the premodern period. Amino criticized the dominant Marxist historians for presupposing that land-based modes of production constituted the foundation of Japanese society, because in doing so, they tacitly accepted and reproduced premodern agricentrist ideology.[29] By contrast, Amino worked to uncover the histories of peoples he labeled nonagriculturalists" (*hinōgyōmin*)—"those who engaged in occupations other than land-based agriculture; whose livelihoods occurred in spaces like mountains, fields, rivers, oceans, markets, ports, harbors, and thoroughfares; people who run the gamut from sea people and mountain people to merchants, artisans, artists, and entertainers."[30] While eschewing ethnologists'

---

27. For example, see Udagawa Takehisa, *Setouchi suigun* (Kyōikusha, 1981), but the term *suigun* is ubiquitous. Although the term *suigun* does not appear in medieval Japanese sources, it is possible that some medieval Japanese knew of the term as a result of their contacts with Koreans or Chinese who used the same character compound when referring to naval forces incorporated directly into a state-administrative structure (Hirase Naoki, "Shugo daimyo Ōuchi-shi to kaihen no busō seiryoku: kaizoku, keigo-shū, wakō," *Yamaguchi-ken chihōshi kenkyū* 71 (1994): 23, n. 6). The *Nihon kokugo daijiten* notes that in the ancient period, the term *suigun* meant a battle that took place on the water (*Nihon kokugo daijiten*, shukusatsu-ban [Shōgakukan, 1974], vol. 6, p. 293).

28. Important works include Benjamin H. Hazard, "The Formative Years of the Wakō, 1223–1263," *Monumenta Nipponica* 22.3 (1967): 260–77; Tanaka Takeo, "Japan's Relations with Overseas Countries," with Robert Sakai, in *Japan in the Muromachi Age*, edited by John W. Hall et al. (Berkeley: University of California Press, 1977), pp. 159–78; Jurgis Elisonas, "The Inseparable Trinity: Japan's Relations with China and Korea," in *The Cambridge History of Japan*, vol. 4: *Early Modern Japan*, edited by John W. Hall et al. (Cambridge: Cambridge University Press, 1991), pp. 235–300; Kenneth R. Robinson, "From Raiders to Traders: Border Security and Border Control in Early Chosŏn, 1392–1450," *Korean Studies* 16 (1992): 94–115.

29. Amino, *Nihon chūsei no hinōgyōmin to tennō*, pp. 27–31.

30. Ibid., p. 27.

11

essentialist nationalism, Amino embraced their concept of "sea people" as a way to portray the maritime dimensions of nonagricultural Japanese history.[31] Amino assumed that the historical term "sea people" encompassed the identities of the entire spectrum of maritime occupations, defining them as "[t]hose people who made a living on the surface of the water—whether lake, pond, river, or ocean—and engaged in a seamless continuum of occupations ranging from fishing to salt production, to shipping, to commerce, and that extended to raiding."[32] He categorized pirates as a subset of the sea people.[33] Amino's influence on the study of pirates can be seen in the works of some recent scholars, who embraced the concept of "sea people" to help unify the several seemingly contradictory faces of *kaizoku*: retainers, collectors of protection money, rebels, outlaws, and agents of intercultural exchange linking Japan and the rest of Eurasia.[34]

However, Japanese seafarers did not employ the term "sea people" (*ama*) any more than they used the term "pirate" when describing themselves. Like *kaizoku*, *ama* implicitly reflects the points of view of the land-based elites whose perspectives dominate extant source material. Instead of trying to reconcile competing usages for *kaizoku* or simply relativizing the term as a completely subjective epithet, this book reads the sources from the waterline and contends that the disparate historical usages of *kaizoku* bespeak the existence of a population of autonomous seafarers who became active, creative forces in late medieval history.

In the late medieval period, land-based elites depended on pirates in order to access the maritime environment and influence littoral populations. Patronage systems birthed by such dependence created opportunities for members of seafaring houses to participate in the production of written correspondence and contracts. Although written using the institutional, land-centered created codes that informed laws, diaries, memoirs, tales, edicts, and other texts from premodern Japan, patronage correspondence and contracts provided seafarers tools with which to present their perspectives. Because some seafaring houses, including the aforementioned Noshima Murakami, served the Mōri and other daimyo houses that survived into the Edo period, a relatively rich collection of pirate and patronage records has survived. These sources reveal that in late medieval Japan, many of the leaders of seafaring bands exploited the sponsorship oppor-

---

31. Ibid., pp. 240–41.
32. Ibid.
33. Ibid., pp. 259–65.
34. Saeki Kōji, "Kaizoku-ron," in *Ajia no naka no Nihonshi*, vol. 3: *Kaijō no michi*, edited by Arano Yasunori et al. (Tokyo Daigaku Shuppankai, 1992), pp. 35–62. Yamauchi Yuzuru, *Setouchi no kaizoku: Murakami Takeyoshi no tatakai* (Kōdansha, 2005), pp. 6–10.

tunities offered by land-based elites in order to present themselves and be recognized as sea lords.

SEA LORDS

Neither an explicitly historical phrase nor a presentist irruption into the past, the expression "sea lord" represents one way that seafarers portrayed themselves in historical sources and offers a way to give a sea-centered focus to narratives about local autonomy, commerce, lordship, warfare, and international relations in late medieval Japan. Some Japanese scholars have come to use variants of the term "sea lord" in order to understand the "pirates who ruled over the sea people" or to express the independence of and distinctive maritime institutions devised by "pirates."[35] I interpret the concept of sea lord more broadly to represent the agency of a type of lord who emerged from populations of seafarers and who sought to develop autonomous dominion over maritime networks of people, routes, and resources. They seem to have been particularly prevalent in the Inland Sea region. There, sea lords emerged from the ranks of local elites based in the littoral who specialized in maritime industries, naval warfare, and the administration of littoral holdings. Over the course of the late medieval period some of these maritime magnates came to wield significant autonomous political and economic power. They dedicated their energies to maintaining maritime power bases and to developing sea-based networks of production, distribution, exchange, and protection.

In order to do so, they embraced a culture of betweenness. Sea lords consistently sought to remain autonomous maritime powers by positioning themselves between land-based powers. Staying at sea kept them at a distance from land-based sponsors culturally as well as politically and militarily. Maintaining a maritime power base placed sea lords within the land-based cultural imaginary of "sea people," who were exotic and threatening but still sufficiently within the Japanese ecumene to owe services to land-based lords.

At the same time, sea lords chose to adopt land-based language and symbols of lordship when representing themselves. They felt that doing so would legitimize their autonomy and control over littoral areas by facilitating the receipt of recognition from higher status elite patrons who would see

35. Amino, *Nihon chūsei no hinōgyōmin to tennō*, p. 263. Amino uses the phrase *umi no ryōshu*. Kishida Hiroshi, *Daimyo ryōgoku no keizai kōzō* (Iwanami Shoten, 2001), p. 352. Kishida uses the phrase *umi no daimyo*.

sea lords as something familiar. They also sought to institutionalize their authority over and to help encourage acceptance by the inhabitants of their domains. In other words, sea lords worked to secure both internal and external validation of their lordship.[36]

For example, central and provincial authorities alike began to identify the Noshima Murakami seafaring house as *kaizoku* in the 1430s because of Noshima attempts at controlling the shipping of estates like Shiwaku and Yugeshima.[37] Jesuit records in particular show that this perception of the Noshima as pirates persisted through the sixteenth century.[38] By the sixteenth century, however, leaders of the family such as Noshima Murakami Takeyoshi commonly employed titles and names associated with the exercise of political, economic, and cultural authority by land-based elites in Japanese society. The Noshima closed many leaves of correspondence and negotiations with patrons and retainers with honorary titles tied to the imperial court like "Governor of Yamato Province" (Yamato no kami) and the imperial clan-name Minamoto—a name well respected in warrior circles. On occasion, they accepted rewards appropriate for land-based warrior lords, including swords with gold fittings and horses.[39]

Sea lords thus made conscious choices to use land-based forms of documents and to follow land-based cultural conventions. They engaged in "code switching"—they sought cultural, economic, or political advantage through the use of linguistic and other cultural forms associated by members of a society with a particular level of status, authority, or cachet.[40] Although the means by which sea lords acquired their titles too often remain unclear,[41]

36. For this understanding of lordship, I am drawing on a definition of sovereignty articulated by Janice E. Thomson, *Pirates, Mercenaries, and Sovereigns: State-Building and Extraterritorial Violence in Early Modern Europe* (Princeton, N.J.: Princeton University Press, 1994), ch. 1.
37. For Shiwaku, see "Ashikaga shogun gonaisho narabi ni hōsho dome," Eikyō 6? (1434) 7.4, quoted in Hashizume Shigeru, *Setonaikai chiiki shakai to Oda kenryoku* (Shibunkaku Shuppan, 2007), p. 183. For Yugeshima, see NET pp. 413–14, doc. 291:3, Kanshō 3 (1462) 5.17.
38. Luis Frois, *Historia de Japam*, vol. 4, pp. 248–49.
39. EK doc. 2102, Eiroku 13 (1570) 9.20; EK doc. 1846, Eiroku 5 (1562) 1.28; EK doc. 2294, Tenshō 10? (1582) 4.17.
40. Monica Heller, "Code-Switching and the Politics of Language," in *One Speaker, Two Languages: Cross-Disciplinary Perspectives on Code-Switching*, edited by Lesley Milroy and Pieter Muysken (Cambridge: Cambridge University Press, 1995), p. 160; Miriam Silverberg, *Erotic Grotesque Nonsense: The Mass Culture of Japanese Modern Times* (Berkeley: University of California Press, 2006), p. 33.
41. In the sixteenth century, powerful aristocrats, members of the imperial family, powerful warlords, and other elite patrons could request titles from the reigning emperor. See Asao Naohiro, "The Sixteenth-Century Unification," translated by Bernard Susser, in *The Cambridge History of Japan*, vol. 4: *Early Modern Japan*, edited by John W. Hall et al. (Cambridge: Cambridge University Press, 1992), p. 83.

the highest authorities in Japan recognized and accepted the usage of those titles and land-based written forms by pirates.

As a result of their code switching, sea lords appear in many records almost indistinguishable from land-based lords and samurai. However, any perception of sea lords as warriors is in part a discursive fiction. Accepting recognition as samurai did not make one necessarily a full-time warrior by trade. In the late medieval period, although warrior elites did call themselves samurai, many populations who only provided military services occasionally also used the term "samurai" self-referentially. Some of these commoners, including estate residents, villagers, merchants, and shrine-purveyors, embraced the original, wider, meaning of samurai: "one who serves."[42] Indeed, members of sea-lord bands engaged in a wide variety of nonviolent occupations, including shipping, fishing, and salt making.

The connections between sea lords and warriors are also a natural conclusion based on the fact that the patronage records that comprise the majority of extant sources for sea lords are often dedicated to discussions regarding the exercise of violence. Representations of seafarers as samurai followed a feedback loop: sea lords presented themselves as land-based samurai to make themselves more attractive to sponsors in official correspondence, and patrons then recognized the sea lords' self-designation out of need for sea-lord services in a period of strife. Over the course of the late medieval period, for sea lords to expect continued recognition as warrior lords by sponsors needing military performance increasingly required that sea-lord bands be successful in arms. Eventually, to a very large extent, the reputations of sea lords came to rise and fall on their martial prowess. At the end of the sixteenth century, when Toyotomi Hideyoshi (1537–98) unified Japan, he forced those who engaged in violence to choose either warrior or non-warrior status. In the early modern period, the term "samurai" lost other signification attached to it, and it became equated with a "warrior class." Changes in the usage of the term *kaizoku* corresponded to this change in the meaning of the term "samurai."[43]

The betweenness of sea lords extended beyond the confines of the archipelago. While firmly part of the Japanese cultural fabric, sea lords also drew on a wide array of practices with parallels across sea-based communities

---

42. Ikegami Hiroko, "Sengoku no sonraku," *Iwanami Kōza Nihon tsūshi*, vol. 10, *chūsei* 4, edited by Asao Naohiro et al. (Iwanami Shoten, 1994), pp. 102–7; Thomas D. Conlan, *State of War: The Violent Order of Fourteenth-Century Japan*, Michigan Monograph Series in Japanese Studies, no. 46 (Ann Arbor: Center for Japanese Studies, University of Michigan, 2003), pp. 112–23.
43. Katsumata Shizuo, *Sengoku jidairon* (Iwanami Shoten, 1996), pp. 280–84.

around the world. In Japan as well as other parts of the world, the dialectical interactions between seafarers and their natural environments[44] had an impact on the development of their livelihoods equal to that of the politics, economy, and culture out of which a particular pirate population emerged. This global perspective suggests that Japanese sea lords placed themselves politically, militarily, economically, and culturally between land-based authorities, which enabled them to establish an autonomy that it is useful to examine with a nonstate lens.

SEA LORDS AS NONSTATE AGENTS

James C. Scott usefully defines "nonstate spaces" as maritime, littoral, upland, and other "locations where, owing largely to geographical obstacles, the state has particular difficulty in establishing and maintaining its authority."[45] In particular, Scott emphasizes the impossibility of establishing "concentrated grain agriculture" in such spaces as a reason for both the lack of state control and the choice of people to inhabit such spaces.[46] Around the world in the premodern period, officials differentiated those who elected to live in nonstate spaces—from the steppe to the littoral—from the more agriculturally and ideologically suitable inhabitants of the state by deploying demonizing terminology such as barbarian, bandit, and, of course, pirate.[47]

In his analyses of medieval Japan, Amino Yoshihiko likewise focused on the nonagricultural aspects of places that he argued medieval Japanese considered free from proprietary attachment (a concept he called *muen*). To the mountains and seas, Amino added interstitial linkages such as bridges, crossroads, and ports. Such spaces proved conducive for pirates and "evil bands" who sought to develop commercial networks in resistance to established agricentric, state institutions.[48]

However, the case of late medieval Japan suggests that it was the ability of pirates (i.e., sea lords) to appropriate and demarcate littoral and maritime

---

44. See the discussion of historical ecology found in Peregrin Horden and Nicholas Purcell, *The Corrupting Sea: A Study of Mediterranean History* (Malden, Mass.: Blackwell Publishers, 2000), pp. 45–49.
45. James C. Scott, *The Art of Not Being Governed: An Anarchist History of Upland Southeast Asia* (New Haven, Conn.: Yale University Press, 2009), p. 13.
46. Ibid.
47. Ibid., pp. 28–31, 137.
48. Amino Yoshihiko, *Muen, kugai, raku: Nihon chūsei no jiyū to heiwa* (Heibonsha, 1978); Amino Yoshihiko, *Akutō to kaizoku: Nihon chūsei no shakai to seiji* (Hōsei Daigaku Shuppankyoku, 1995), pp. 364–66; Amino Yoshihiko, *Nihon chūsei no hinōgyōmin to tennō*, p. 27.

spaces and to take advantage of land-based elite perceptions of the sea as dangerous and uncontrollable that rendered the Japanese maritime world nonstate in the eyes of both Japanese and foreign observers. Interpreting the leaders of Japanese "pirates" as "sea lords" illuminates the degree to which Japanese state attempts at "enclosure"[49] of the sea at the rhetorical level gave way to the control of local seafarers at the level of actual practice in the late medieval period. The military might, economic power, political connections, and mobility of sea-lord bands enabled them to establish domains on the sea lanes that gradually rendered land-based claims to the sea illusory during this time.

In addition to the global parallels, the nonstate character of sea-lord autonomy in late medieval Japan had regional and domestic dimensions. In the wider East Asian maritime world, decentralization in Japan accompanied a weakening of control by Ming China over their littoral. This "pulse" of decentralization across the East Asian maritime world created opportunities for autonomous, sea-based, "piratical" organizations to take control of maritime thoroughfares.[50] In Japan, independent maritime powers represented just one facet of the autonomy that spread across Japan in the fifteenth and sixteenth centuries. In the fourteenth century, the balance of power collapsed among samurai in Kamakura, aristocrats and the emperor in Kyoto, and powerful temples and shrines that together constituted the state in early medieval times.[51] Initial successes first by Emperor Go-Daigo (r. 1333–36) and then by the Ashikaga shogunate (ca. 1336–1573) to centralize several aspects of state authority under their aegis failed in the long term.[52] By the 1440s the ability of Japanese central authorities such as imperial family members, aristocrats, and shoguns to project power in the provinces had weakened, and various largely self-determining local and regional organizations had come to fill this void.

Although sometimes characterized as a time of low overthrowing the high (*gekokujō*), this era from the mid-fifteenth through the late sixteenth centuries known as the Warring States period (Sengoku) witnessed significant administrative innovation and creative interpretations of past

49. Scott, *The Art of Not Being Governed*, pp. 4–9.
50. Arano Yasunori, Ishii Masatoshi, Murai Shōsuke, "Jiki kubunron," in *Ajia no naka no Nihonshi*, vol. 1: *Ajia to Nihon*, edited by Arano Yasunori et al. (Tokyo Daigaku Shuppankai, 1992), p. 11.
51. A phenomenon known to historians as the "Gates of Power" (*kenmon taisei*). For a good overview in English, see Mikael S. Adolphson, *The Gates of Power: Monks, Courtiers, and Warriors in Premodern Japan* (Honolulu: University of Hawai'i Press, 2000), pp. 10–20.
52. Andrew Edmund Goble; *Kenmu: Go-Daigo's Revolution* (Cambridge, Mass.: Harvard University Asia Center, 1996); Kenneth Grossberg, *Japan's Renaissance: The Politics of the Muromachi Bakufu* (Cambridge, Mass.: Harvard University Asia Center, 1981).

precedent. Competing groups sought stability and rule of law. Warrior provincial governors (*shugo*) and regional warlords (daimyo), villagers, merchant organizations, urban enclaves, port-city merchants, religious leagues, and seafarers labeled "pirates" all carved out spaces of political, economic, and cultural autonomy in this period.[53]

The Seto Inland Sea region played host to the nonstate autonomy of sea lords in two ways. First, sea lords territorialized its chokepoints and networks. Second, the Inland Sea came to be surrounded by semi-independent centers of authority that sea lords could play one against the other. These authorities included powerful temples and other religious institutions, the Muromachi bakufu, and warrior provincial governors, many of whom sought to establish themselves as autonomous regional warlords. By the sixteenth century, daimyo worked both inside and outside the existing political institutional and cultural frameworks of late medieval Japan to construct "an autonomous sphere of political control," consciously incorporating inhabitants within a public, domainal space controlled by the lord's family. They independently engaged in overseas diplomacy, unleashed their own dogs of war, and gave sanction to their own sponsored violence.[54] Jesuit observers went so far as to call these daimyo domains "kingdoms."[55]

Most of these land-based state agents failed to hold the sea space directly and thus depended on sea lords for a host of violent and nonviolent services from purveying, to salt manufacture, to fishing, to shipping, to fighting. Sea lords exploited this need and developed distinctive practices of patronage and mercenarism, moving between the various land-based authorities surrounding the Inland Sea.

53. Mary Elizabeth Berry, *The Culture of Civil War in Kyoto* (Berkeley: University of California Press, 1994); Hitomi Tonomura, *Community and Commerce in Late Medieval Japan: The Corporate Villages of Tokuchin-ho* (Stanford, Calif.: Stanford University Press, 1992); Carol Richmond Tsang, *War and Faith: Ikkō Ikki in Late Muromachi Japan* (Cambridge, Mass.: Harvard University Press, 2007); V. Dixon Morris, "The City of Sakai and Urban Autonomy," in *Warlords, Artists, and Commoners: Japan in the Sixteenth Century*, edited by George Elison and Bardwell L. Smith (Honolulu: University of Hawai'i Press, 1981), pp. 23–54; V. Dixon Morris, "Sakai: From Shōen to Port City," in *Japan in the Muromachi Age*, edited by John W. Hall et al. (Berkeley: University of California Press, 1977), pp. 145–58.
54. Katsumata Shizuo, "The Development of Sengoku Law," with Martin Collcutt, in *Japan Before Tokugawa: Political Consolidation and Economic Growth, 1500–1650,* edited by John Whitney Hall et al. (Princeton, N.J.: Princeton University Press, 1981), pp. 101–13. For all their autonomy, lords on sea and land all accepted the sacerdotal and calendrical sovereignty of the emperor, recognized the utility of titles derived from the imperial court and the Muromachi bakufu, and often accepted the superiority of classical aristocratic cultural forms to others. On the powers of the court in this period, see Lee Butler, *Emperor and Aristocracy in Japan, 1467–1680: Resilience and Renewal* (Cambridge, Mass.: Harvard University Press, 2002). On the relevance of the Muromachi bakufu, see Yata Toshifumi, *Nihon chūsei sengoku-ki kenryoku kōzō no kenkyū* (Hanawa Shobō, 1998), pp. 15–16.
55. Frois, *Historia de Japam*, vol. 4, pp. 248–49.

MERCENARISM

Although the term "mercenary" may connote soldiers of fortune who fight for those who offer the most money, I use the term to highlight the mobility of sea lords. Janice Thomson notes that a monetary component in and of itself does not sufficiently distinguish mercenaries from soldiers on a lord's payroll. She defines mercenarism as the characteristic of a nonstate organization that makes a living by "enlisting in and recruiting for a foreign army."[56] In other words, mercenaries are best understood as fighters who value the opportunities that accrue from maintaining the ability to proffer services across political borders and between distinct political entities. The competing political powers surrounding the Inland Sea in the late medieval period constituted such distinct entities.

Sea-lord mercenarism derived from entrepreneurial drive and ambitions for autonomy, not as backstabbing for political gain. Such maritime mercenarism was facilitated by the growth of a marketized service economy that emerged as Japan underwent a commercial revolution. Monetization, population growth, cash cropping, and other changes spread across the archipelago in the late medieval period. As central control over remote holdings declined, networks that linked privately administered estates (*shōen*) with land-based elite proprietors in the capital competed with, intersected with, and evolved into cash-based regional, transarchipelagic, overseas, and service-based commercial networks.[57] This commercialization occurred most dynamically in the western littoral, especially the Seto Inland Sea region,[58] where, not coincidentally, service-providing organizations also seem to have enjoyed more autonomy than in other parts of Japan.[59]

Although concentrated in western Japan, several groups on land and sea in the late medieval period developed entrepreneurial, mercenary operating

---

56. Thomson, *Pirates, Mercenaries, and Sovereigns*, p. 27.

57. Sakurai Eiji, "Chūsei no shōhin ichiba," in *Shintaikei Nihonshi*, vol. 12: *Ryūtsū keizaishi*, edited by Sakurai Eiji et al. (Yamakawa Shuppansha, 2002), pp. 199–234.

58. On commercialization, see Toyoda Takeshi and Sugiyama Hiroshi, "The Growth of Commerce and the Trades," with V. Dixon Morris, in *Japan in the Muromachi Age*, edited by John W. Hall et al. (Berkeley: University of California Press, 1977), pp. 129–44; Tonomura, *Community and Commerce*; Suzanne Gay, *The Moneylenders of Late Medieval Kyoto* (Honolulu: University of Hawai'i Press, 2001); William Wayne Farris, *Japan's Medieval Population: Famine, Fertility, and Warfare in a Transformative Age* (Honolulu: University of Hawai'i Press, 2006); and Ethan Isaac Segal, *Coins, Trade, and the State: Economic Growth in Early Medieval Japan* (Cambridge, Mass.: Harvard University Asian Center, 2011).

59. Yamamuro Kyōko, "Sengoku no chiikisei," *Iwanami kōza Nihon tsūshi*, vol. 10, *chūsei* 4, edited by Asao Naohiro et al. (Iwanami Shoten, 1994), pp. 177–78.

methods focused on movement.[60] Fujita Tatsuo uncovered populations of what he calls "peripatetic warriors" (*watari aruku bushi*) among sixteenth-century warrior families who served different lords in different locales.[61] Murai Shōsuke argued that the Korean and Japanese seafarers identified by Koreans as Japanese pirates in the fifteenth and sixteenth centuries were "marginal" figures who "lived in spaces two centers considered peripheries . . . but who could mediate with either."[62] The desire of sea lords to perform services autonomously is epitomized by one article in the bylaws of a sixteenth-century Inland Sea sea-lord band. This article makes it inadmissible for patrons to dictate the terms or forms of service: "when performing duties for patrons on sea and land, they are to be performed according to our bylaws."[63] Bands such as the Noshima Murakami certainly held a similar philosophy. Between 1540 and 1580, the Noshima Murakami switched their loci of employment over ten times among several competing patrons. They did so in order to receive forms of currency,[64] provisions, title to posts and holdings, and confirmation for their claims to components of maritime domains, such as ports, toll barriers, and fishing villages.

The effects of such widespread patronage can be seen in semantic changes in the meaning of words such as "pirate." Whereas in earlier periods usage of *kaizoku* spun variations on themes of criminal maritime violence, rebellion, and outlawry, in the late medieval period the term encompassed both perpetrators of illicit violence and sponsored seafarers.[65] This blurring of illegal and legal was characteristic of perceptions of seafarers across the maritime world at this time. In popular usage in states surrounding the Mediterranean and Atlantic worlds, terms like "corsair," "privateer," and "pirate" became interchangeable. Figures like the Maltese and Barbary Corsairs, Francis Drake, and Henry Morgan took advantage of their dominance in nonstate maritime space to straddle boundaries of perceived licit and illicit

---

60. For warriors who followed such a strategy, see the discussion of *tozama* in Conlan, *State of War*, ch. 5; for commercial agents (*toi*), see Usami Takayuki, *Nihon chūsei no ryūtsū to shōgyō* (Yoshikawa Kōbunkan, 1999), pp. 140–42; Sakurai, "Chūsei no shōhin ichiba," p. 208; for villagers and warriors, see Fujiki Hisashi, *Zōhyōtachi no senjō: chūsei no yōhei to doreigari* (Asahi Shinbunsha, 1995).

61. Fujita Tatsuo, *Nihon kinsei kokka seiritsushi no kenkyū* (Azekura Shobō, 2001), p. 297.

62. Murai Shōsuke, *Chūsei Wajinden* (Iwanami Shoten, 1993), p. 39.

63. EK doc. 2194, Tenshō 4 (1576) 11th month, auspicious day.

64. Currency (meaning items trusted by people to carry value across transactions or to hold value as payment for services rendered) in medieval Japan included valuable commodities such as silk and rice, in addition to precious metals in the form of coinage or bullion (Sakurai, "Chūsei no shōhin ichiba," pp. 203–7; Segal, *Coins, Trade, and the State*, pp. 8–10).

65. Mansai, *Mansai jugō nikki*, edited by Hanawa Hokinoichi and Ōta Toshirō, *Zoku gunsho ruijū hoi* 1 (Zoku Gunsho Ruijū Kanseikai, 1928), vol. 2, p. 546, Eikyō 6 (1434) 1.19; p. 553, Eikyō 6 (1434) 1.30. Tenyo Seikei, *Boshi nyūminki*, in NMKBS, p. 203.

behavior for personal gain.[66] A close observer of Japanese society in the late sixteenth century, the Jesuit Luis Frois, intermixed the terms "corsairs," "pirates," and "robbers" when describing sea lords.[67] The definition for *kaizoku* in the 1602 Japanese-Portuguese dictionary highlights this semantic overlap: "corsair or pirate" (*corsairo ou pirate*), or, in the legal terminology of the early modern Mediterranean, a unity of sponsored and unsponsored maritime predation.[68]

In addition to the autonomy of nonstate, mercenary seafaring bands, the integral nature of one particular service—that of violence—to any successful political or commercial maritime venture increased the semantic blurring of legal and illegal and the betweenness of seafaring bands like those of Japanese sea lords. In today's world in which the nation-state is the defining social, geopolitical unit of many people's identities, forms of nonstate, privatized violence are commonly perceived as transgressive behavior like terrorism and piracy. However, across the globe in the premodern period, states did not dictate a monopoly on legitimate violence. Instead, state and nonstate actors alike treated violence as a commodity—something "democratized, marketized, and internationalized."[69]

This commoditization of violence became particularly widespread in the maritime world in this period. Mariners and their sponsors perceived commerce and violence as parts of a continuum of seafaring identities and livelihoods, not as contradictory phenomena. Seafarers in commercial systems purveyed nonstate violence in the same ways that they exchanged luxury and subsistence commodities. Anne Pérotin-Dumon notes that across the premodern world, when states lacked powerful navies, the use of force "was not a trait of piracy but more broadly of the commerce of that age."[70] Sometimes mariners went armed to protect and raid, while at other times they sold their "protective" services to states and merchants and became licensed pirates.[71] In turning to pirates to extend their authority over

66. Alfred P. Rubin, *The Law of Piracy* (Newport, R.I.: Naval War College Press, 1988), pp. 14–15; Fernand Braudel, *The Mediterranean and the Mediterranean World in the Age of Philip II*, translated by Siân Reynolds, 2nd ed. (Berkeley: University of California Press, 1995), pp. 866–87. In European international law in the medieval and early modern periods, heads of states transformed seafarers into corsairs and privateers by issuing licenses to attack specific enemies, usually during a period of declared war. These licenses were known as letters of marque and letters of reprisal.
67. Frois, *Historia de Japam*, vol. 4, pp. 248–49.
68. *Vocabvlario da lingoa de Iapam*, edited by Doi Tadao (Iwanami Shoten, 1961), p. 67.
69. Thomson, *Pirates, Mercenaries, and Sovereigns*, pp. 3–4. Thomson here refers specifically to the premodern European experience, but I believe that, in this case, her conclusions warrant extension to a global context.
70. Anne Pérotin-Dumon, "The Pirate and the Emperor," in *Bandits at Sea*, pp. 29–30.
71. Ibid., p. 29.

the waves and authorizing them to deploy violence, land-based states further encouraged the rise of autonomous nonstate, sea-based organizations.[72] The history of Japanese sea lords illuminates the commoditization of maritime violence in Japan.

MARITIME LORDSHIP AND SEA TENURE

Japanese sea lords made their betweenness and mercenarism possible by maintaining a thalassocratic focus to their lordship, expanding their domains in the strategic, nautical chokepoints located between land-based authorities. It was through the manipulation of patronage relations that sea lords secured access to institutional and rhetorical tools for establishing autonomous dominion over maritime space. They used those tools in order to develop distinct forms of lordship characterized by the regulation of access to maritime spaces and resources. Such control can usefully be thought of as sea tenure.[73] Although often discussed in relation to fishing communities,[74] such a definition of sea tenure allows us to consider how Japanese sea lords transformed littoral and oceanic space and networks into "territory." Most studies of premodern Japan have tended to limit discussions of territory to tenurial practices of the terra firma, considering that political power stemmed from the ability to mobilize men and resources of the land, to control the distribution of land, and to determine the destiny of products of the land.[75] In addition, historical explorations of sea tenure have been constrained by modern preconceptions of the sea as a commons—a vast resource free for all to fish and an ungovernable plane of transport and conflict.[76]

However, in late medieval Japan as well as other parts of the world, both land- and sea-based populations considered the sea to be a space of contested possession and attempted to territorialize the sea as well as the land.[77]

72. Thomson describes this as an "unintended consequence" of the sponsorship of pirates and other nonstate groups (Thomson, *Pirates, Mercenaries, and Sovereigns,* ch. 3).
73. Arne Kalland, *Fishing Villages in Tokugawa Japan* (Honolulu: University of Hawai'i Press, 1995), p. 3.
74. Ibid.
75. See for example John W. Hall, *Government and Local Power, 500–1700: A Study Based on Bizen Province* (Princeton: Princeton University Press, 1966).
76. Philip Steinberg, *The Social Construction of the Ocean* (Cambridge: Cambridge University Press, 2001), p. 12; Kalland, *Fishing Villages in Tokugawa Japan,* p. 3.
77. Steinberg, *The Social Construction of the Ocean,* pp. 28–30.

Robert D. Sack helpfully defines territoriality as "[a]n attempt by an individual or group to affect, influence, or control people, phenomena, and relationships, by delimiting and asserting control over a geographic area."[78] For Sack, creating "territory" is a form of social action carried out by one individual or group communicated to others through symbolism, gestures, force, or other means indicating that one has the authority and ability to demarcate a particular region and then to control what goes on inside that space.[79]

Across premodern Japan, sea tenure practices emerged as a result of negotiations between state-level entities and local littoral inhabitants. Arne Kalland's explanation of sea tenure in the Edo period is also applicable to earlier times: "a matrix of institutions defined and enforced on many levels; from the formal rights and licenses issued by the state and local authorities, to more informal regulations made by the villagers."[80] As early as the fourteenth century, some sea lords sold their services as local managers for local littoral holdings to authorities in distant Kyoto. They learned from such experiences precedents for legitimizing control over rights to access maritime space, divisions of the harvests, and control over maritime industries, including shipping.

One chief way that sea lords restricted access was by operating protection businesses. Most often, they occupied, fortified, and established ship- and island-based toll barriers in chokepoints. From these installations, sea lords could administer the heavily trafficked narrow shipping channels that linked wider basins, bisected island chains, or propelled the sea toward ports. They regulated cargoes, crews, the movement of ships, and the use of maritime violence.

Chokepoint power bases and protection businesses exemplified sea-lord betweenness. These maritime culture elements of sea lords need to be understood as a combination of local Japanese practices and global responses to similar maritime environments. On the one hand, worldwide, chokepoints sometimes gave rise to "toll states."[81] Other pirate populations operated in similar ways, from relative contemporaries like corsairs in the Mediterranean and the Zheng organization in Taiwan, to pirates in the late twentieth and early twenty-first centuries in the straits of Melaka and Gulf of Aden. They all took advantage of control of narrow channels to establish sea-based

---

78. Robert David Sack, *Human Territoriality: Its Theory and History* (Cambridge: Cambridge University Press, 1986), p. 19. Steinberg introduces Sack's ideas in a wider theoretical exploration of territoriality at sea (*The Social Construction of the Ocean*, pp. 29–30).
79. Sack, *Human Territoriality*, pp. 20–23.
80. Kalland, *Fishing Villages in Tokugawa Japan*, p. 4.
81. Scott, *The Art of Not Being Governed*, p. 49.

political organizations founded on regulating the flow of maritime traffic in their regions.[82]

On the other hand, sea lords could also capitalize on the existence of analogues to chokepoints and protection businesses on land to make them selves seem familiar—and thus hirable—to potential sponsors. Land-based lords as well as sea-based lords administered commerce, controlled choke points and thoroughfares, and institutionalized toll barriers, lading fees and exemption systems. On land and sea, such practices helped lords receive recognition as legitimate rulers.[83]

An examination of one sea-lord domain, that of the Noshima Mu rakami at its height in the 1580s, vividly demonstrates how sea lords formed distinctly sea-based domains full of chokepoints, which facilitated the prac tice of sea tenure (see figures 2 and 7). They based themselves in a castle on Noshima, a tiny island less than a kilometer in circumference that occupied a chokepoint along major shipping lanes.[84] From this islet, the Noshima expanded out along the sea lanes to control major ports and toll barriers like Shiwaku, Kasaoka, and Kaminoseki, fishing villages, salt works, timber stands, harbors of the Kutsuna Islands and other places, and tiny island for tresses like Mushijima, Nakatoshima, and Minoshima. The Noshima and other sea lords developed these nodal points into interlocking, maritime networks of production, distribution, exchange, and protection. Such net works helped tie the archipelago together and helped link Japan with much of the rest of the world.

In domains such as these, sea lords administered a wide variety of maritime industries and peoples: sailors, navigators, fisher folk, and even families of boat people. The scale of the Noshima Murakami sea-lord band seems to have increased dramatically between the fifteenth and sixteenth centuries. The Noshima may have overseen a few hundred sailors in the fif teenth century. By the late sixteenth century, around a thousand mariners may have sailed for the Noshima Murakami.[85] Although it is impossible to

82. John H. Pryor, *Geography, Technology, and War: Studies in the Maritime History of the Mediter ranean, 649–1571* (Cambridge: Cambridge University Press, 1988), pp. 156–57; Patrizia Carioti "The Zheng's Maritime Power in the International Context of the 17th c. Far Eastern Seas," *Ming Qing yanjiu* 5 (1996): 29–67; Tonio Andrade, *Lost Colony: The Untold Story of China's Firs Great Victory over the West* (Princeton: Princeton University Press, 2011); Iwao Seiichi, *Shinper shuinsen bōekishi no kenkyū* (Yoshikawa Kōbunkan, 1985), pp. 108–9.

83. Yata, *Nihon chūsei sengoku-ki kenryoku kōzō no kenkyū*, pp. 62–64, 236–40.

84. Yamauchi Yuzuru, *Kaizoku to umijiro: Setouchi no sengokushi* (Heibonsha, 1997), pp. 17–19, 30– 31, 147–48.

85. I have used two methods to estimate sea-lord populations. First, by the fourteenth century mos vessels on average may have required one person per 20 to 25 *koku* of lading (Shinjō Tsunezō *Chūsei suiunshi no kenkyū* [Hanawa Shobō, 1995], p. 78). The *Hyōgo Kitazeki irifune nōchō* give

know for sure how many people lived in the domains of sea lords, because sea lords tended to establish domains and industries in the chokepoints of the archipelago, especially in the Seto Inland Sea, the main thoroughfare for goods and services in premodern Japan, they had a significance that outweighed their numbers.

SETTING: THE SETO INLAND SEA

Like the sea-lord bands that coursed its waves, the Seto Inland Sea region is perhaps best understood as both part of Japan and integrated into a global maritime world. This aortic salt-water channel links the three major islands of Honshu, Shikoku, and Kyushu. It runs some 450 kilometers long, reaches 55 kilometers across at its widest point, and 5 kilometers across at its narrowest.[86] Some seven hundred islands dot its channels, and they range in size from landmasses tens of kilometers wide, to islets less than a kilometer in circumference, to specks of rock, seaweed, and scrub vegetation.[87] Chains of these islands bind together Kyushu, Shikoku, and Honshu, dividing the Inland Sea into basins and creating a series of maritime chokepoints.

The Pacific pours into the Inland Sea at three points, its southeastern, western, and southwestern extremities, causing the narrow channels joining the Inland Sea's various basins to pulse with rushing rapids. Because tides

---

a snapshot of seaborne commerce from 1445–46; it records ships' port of registry, cargo, lading, and shipmaster among other information (*Hyōgo Kitazeki irifune nōchō*, edited by Hayashiya Tatsusaburō [Chūō Kōron Bijutsusha, 1981]). Using the numbers of ships and different shipmasters for each port of registry known to be controlled by a particular sea-lord family allows a general approximation of the number of sailors available to a particular family in the mid-fifteenth century. For the sixteenth century, the large paper trail from Toyotomi Hideyoshi's war in Korea provides some useful starting points. Major sea-lord houses such as the Noshima Murakami and Kurushima Murakami served in the invasion flotillas and led at times upwards of one thousand troops, respectively. For example, in the initial invasion's order of battle in 1592, the brothers Kurushima Michifusa and Tokui Michiyuki led a force of 700 in the fifth division (*Dai Nihon komonjo iewake 8, Mōri-ke monjo*, vol. 1, pp. 143–48, doc. 885, Tenshō 20 [1592] 3.13). In addition, using Korean war multipliers (daimyo generally had to supply five samurai/sailors, etc., per 100 *koku*) with other records of Noshima and Kurushima *kokudaka* information (Kurushima with 14,000 *koku* and Noshima with 18,000), we can estimate that the Kurushima could provide 700, the Noshima 900 (for *kokudaka* information, see Yamauchi, *Setouchi no kaizoku*, pp. 162–74). For numbers in the Korean campaign, see Miki Seiichirō, "Chōsen eki ni okeru gun'yaku taikei ni tsuite," *Shigaku zasshi* 75.2 (1966): 1–26. However, *kokudaka* only assessed rice productivity, which was not a useful indicator of production or wealth in the maritime world, so the actual numbers may be higher.

86. Okiura Kazuteru, *Setouchi no minzokushi: Kaiminshi no shinsō o tazunete* (Iwanami Shoten, 1998), p. 42.

87. Akimichi Tomoya, "Setouchi no seitaigaku—Setouchi no gyorō to seien," in *Setouchi no ama bunka*, edited by Amino Yoshihiko et al. (Shōgakukan, 1991), p. 52.

change direction every six hours and high and low tides differ by as much as two meters,[88] only expertly piloted, shallow-draft ships could safely traverse these waters.[89] Harbor settlements, including those of sea lords, often developed hostelries and grew into way stations for people waiting for the tides and winds to shift in their favor in order to continue their journeys.

Although most of the region's inhabitants devoted themselves to maritime livelihoods, grains still constituted an important food source, as they did for the rest of Japan. With the exception of a few large islands like Awaji and Yashirojima, meager amounts of arable land limited population growth in littoral areas and stimulated subsistence trade. Sponsorship in the Seto Inland Sea region often included rice or foodstuffs, suggesting ecological partnerships of maritime goods and services in exchange for food. Such partnerships highlight symbiotic connections between nonstate and state space and populations.[90]

In comparison to other coastal areas in Japan, the Inland Sea enjoys a relatively tranquil climate due to protective mountain ranges to the north and south. However, water surface temperature varies drastically in the Inland Sea depending on the season. Whereas the outer ocean only changes a few degrees over the course of the year, the surface temperatures of the Seto Inland Sea can differ as much as 20 degrees centigrade between summer and winter (8–28 degrees C). These temperature variations mean that a particular fishing season depends on the water temperature and that an unusually warm or cold season can spell disaster for both fish populations and the humans that depend on them.[91]

Furthermore, the degree of enclosure for each of the Inland Sea's subregional basins—attached to each other only by narrow straits—gives each subregion of the Inland Sea a distinctive environment. Water quality, salinity, depth, and type of sea bottom all differ slightly in each part.[92] The drastic swell and ebb of the tides occur at different times.[93] This variation spawned microecological diversity as different types of fish, seaweeds, and other living things established particular habitats in each basin.[94] This di

88. Ibid., p. 53.
89. The danger of not having an expert pilot in waters such as these is vividly illustrated by an account written by the Jesuit João Rodrigues. Rodrigues recorded that in November 1596, the navigator bringing the new Bishop for Japan, Pedro Martins, to the capital misjudged the currents off the coast of Iyo and smashed into the nearby ship of Terazawa Hirotaka, governor of Nagasaki. Cooper, *Rodrigues the Interpreter*, pp. 114–15.
90. Miyamoto, *Setonaikai no kenkyū*, p. 13. This topic will be taken up in detail in chapter 2. For nonstate and state symbioses, see Scott, *The Art of Not Being Governed*, pp. 26–27.
91. Akimichi, "Setouchi no seitaigaku—Setouchi no gyorō to seien," p. 52.
92. Ibid., p. 53.
93. Ibid., p. 59.
94. Ibid., p. 53. For microecologies, see Horden and Purcell, *The Corrupting Sea*.

late medieval warfare and Japan's so-called military revolution of the late sixteenth century. As leaders of naval mercenary bands who controlled how and when services were to be performed, sea lords developed techniques and technologies that both reflected their desire to make themselves familiar to sponsors but also echoed practices of the wider maritime world. Their autonomy meant that they, not their sponsors, determined the shape of the naval dimensions of the military revolution. Chapter 5 treats the effects sea-lord power had on the wider East Asian world. Sea lords contributed to evolving Chinese and Korean perceptions of maritime East Asia as a region united by the movements of "Japanese pirates." Encounters between sea-lord bands and Korean diplomats and sea-lord participation in tribute trade missions with China led Korean and Chinese scholar officials to incorporate the seafaring denizens of the Inland Sea into the category of Japanese pirates instead of limiting the category to those of Japan's coastal rim. Chapter 6 explores the transition from medieval to early modern Japan by examining unification and the outlawing of piracy from the perspective of sea lords. Sea lords managed to retain significant autonomy on the seas right up to unification, after which they no longer found it profitable or necessary to continue their Sengoku-era practices. They took advantage of the recognition they received as land-based type lords in order to negotiate positions as important members of the early modern elite. However, to do so meant surrendering maritime autonomy and transforming themselves into land-based lords, living up to their rhetoric of lordship. In doing so, they helped bridge divides between land and sea and incorporate the maritime world into a new terracentric early modern Japanese political order.

CHAPTER 1

Japanese Pirates and Seascapes

> I fear thee, ancient mariner!
>
> I fear thy skinny hand!
>
> And thou art long, and lank, and brown,
>
> As is the ribbed sea-sand[1]

For Japanese seafarers, the late medieval period (ca. 1300–1600) presented them a window of opportunity to escape and manipulate labels of "pirate" thrust upon them and to craft identities as autonomous political and economic powers, as sea lords. As part of that process, they adopted forms of writing and other modes of representation that land-based elites respected. In doing so, mariners could not avoid engaging with the concept of *kaizoku* as well as larger representations of the sea and sea people, which were saturated with land-based biases. It is useful to think of representations of the sea and sea people as seascapes.

The root meanings of the characters for *kaizoku* (sea + bandit) imply that it was a simple term signifying maritime criminality. However, the wide variety of meanings that *kaizoku* accumulated over time and the fact that Japanese seafarers never referred to themselves with the word suggest that it is more useful to interpret this concept as a barometer for changes in the ways in which land-based peoples regarded the contents of seascapes. Japanese elites considered *kaizoku* to be a subset of sea people, and they keyed their use of the term to the strength of the land-based state's hold on the sea lanes. The late medieval domains of sea lords both contributed to and became possible because of increasing perceptions of the sea and sea people as nonstate phenomena.

Historically, societies often constructed seascapes in ways that reflected their abilities and interests in controlling that space, in treating the space as "territory."[2] Complex confluences of social, political, economic, and cultural

---

1. Samuel Taylor Coleridge, "The Rime of the Ancient Mariner," in *The Rime of the Ancient Mariner and Other Poems* (New York: Dover, 1992), p. 12.
2. Philip Steinberg, *The Social Construction of the Ocean* (Cambridge: Cambridge University Press, 2001), pp. 28–29.

forces dictate the shape of natural-historical worldviews. Historical sources for environments and their denizens are encoded in culturally specific forms.[3] People with different political, economic, military, cultural, and territorial perspectives and objectives—even within the same political, geographical, or cultural unit—constructed the ocean differently in different places at different times. The sea is thus a "social space, a space of society" acted upon and represented by groups in society. But, in turn, to some degree the sea also acted on those representing the sea.[4] The dialectical representations that emerged as a result of those interactions had significant political consequences. These representations both reflected and helped determine the degree of influence wielded by state and nonstate authorities at sea.[5]

Earlier scholarship has characterized Japanese perceptions of the sea along lines reminiscent of debates that positioned the oceans more generally as either a free commons devoid of tenurial attachments or a space bounded by states.[6] Some have argued that Japanese divided the seas into proximal and distal: nearby seas were safe and could be known and controlled; distant ones were the converse.[7] However, in premodern Japan, seascape tapestries were woven of competing and overlapping threads of cultures and ideologies. Changes in seascape representations occurred not as a switch from one image to another but instead as cultural palimpsests: a gradual overlaying of more and more layers of representation, with earlier strata still partially visible and influential.

Two major worldviews influenced creators of seascapes. Land-centered representations dominated but did not completely overwhelm what people knew of the sea. Seafarers also impacted how others perceived them. Sailing, fishing, salt making, shipping, piracy, and other livelihoods cannot be accomplished in isolation. These practices provided opportunities for the creation of communal common cultures of work among some groups of littoral inhabitants. Seafarers' cultures of work derived from a different, more intimate form of knowledge about the relationship between the maritime

---

3. William Cronon, *Changes in the Land: Indians, Colonists, and the Ecology of New England* (New York: Hill and Wang, 1983), pp. 6–8, 19–22. Peregrine Horden and Nicholas Purcell, *The Corrupting Sea: A Study of Mediterranean History* (Oxford: Blackwell, 2000), pp. 1–29.

4. Steinberg, *The Social Construction of the Ocean*, pp. 6, 20–23.

5. Ibid., pp. 27–28.

6. Ibid., ch. 1, pp. 89–98. Amino Yoshihiko, *Muen, kugai, raku: Nihon chūsei no jiyū to heiwa* (Heibonsha, 1978), p. 188; Hotate Michihisa, "Chūsei zenki no gyogyō to shōensei: kaai ryōyū to gyomin o megutte," *Rekishi hyōron* 376 (1981): 15–43.

7. Marcia Yonemoto, "Maps and Metaphors of the 'Small Eastern Sea' in Tokugawa Japan (1603–1868)," *Geographical Review* 89.2 (1999): 170, 177–78.

environment and themselves separate from land-based representations.[8] Social scientists have detected sea-based identities and cultures that evolved as
a result of long periods of dangerous, communal shipboard work apart from
the land-based world.[9] Because of their dependence on seafarers for travel
and protection at sea, land-based voyagers and observers who encountered
seafarers transmitted aspects of this culture when crafting travelogues, poems, and other seascapes. Seascapes should thus be understood as fusions of
various types of land-centered representations and, on occasion, maritime
work cultures, as "heteroglossic" blends of various forms of knowledge and
representations.[10] The late medieval phenomenon of seafarers naming themselves sea lords can thus be thought of as an extension of the ways in which
littoral inhabitants had hitherto used work to impact their representations
in seascapes.

This chapter excavates different strata of representation from seascapes.
It traces the evolving meanings of *kaizoku* and pegs them to wider historical changes in seascape representations. Ancient representations of the sea
and seafarers depict a desire to incorporate the sea and seafarers into the
state, while also recognizing, fearing, and demonizing their alterity. The
importation of Chinese worldviews, the establishment of the Ritsuryō state
in the seventh century, and classical literary aesthetics deepened this land-
centeredness. These early constructions retained their potency throughout
the premodern period. For example, Ritsuryō legal precedents regarding
pirates as bandits and ruffians still had real meaning for land-based elite
lawmakers in the sixteenth century, even while those same lawmakers recognized the autonomous domains of sea lords.

However, cultural, economic, political, and religious transformations in
Japan caused land-based authorities to change expectations that they had for
the sea and seafarers and to overlay new seascapes atop the old. The Ritsuryō
state's centralized union of land and sea began to break down around the
tenth century as temples and shrines started to sponsor their own groups
of maritime purveyors, salt producers, and shippers, effectively marking

8. Richard White, "'Are You an Environmentalist or Do You Work For A Living?': Work and Nature,"
   in *Uncommon Ground: Rethinking the Human Place in Nature*, edited by William Cronon (New
   York: Norton and Co., 1995), p. 172.
9. Greg Dening, *Islands and Beaches: Discourse on a Silent Land: Marquesas, 1774–1880* (Melbourne,
   Australia: Melbourne University Press, 1980), pp. 157–58; Marcus Rediker, *Between the Devil and
   the Deep Blue Sea: Merchant Seamen, Pirates and the Anglo-American Maritime World, 1700–
   1750* (Cambridge: Cambridge University Press, 1987), ch. 4.
10. For "heteroglossia," see Mikhail Bakhtin, "Discourse in the Novel," in *The Dialogic Imagination:
   Four Essays*, edited by Michael Holquist, translated by Caryl Emerson and Michael Holquist
   (Austin: University of Texas Press, 1981), pp. 288–91.

the beginning of the end of imperial control of maritime production and distribution networks.[11] At the same time, Buddhist thinkers developed sophisticated cosmologies that reinforced older terracentric constructions. By the twelfth century, warriors had established themselves as one branch of government, effectively ending court control of the military, changing perceptions of violence in Japan. In the late medieval period, the rise of sea-lord power and the concomitant loss of central control over littoral regions led— as one might expect—to high anxieties among land-based elites regarding the sea in the late medieval period. By the time land-based elite dependence on sea-lord bands peaked in the sixteenth century, it was commonly perceived as unthinkable to attempt sea travel or other maritime operations without the aid of pirates. Sea lords exploited these perceptions when extending their holds over maritime networks.

TERRACENTRISM AND SEASCAPES

Although it is sometimes possible to read sea-based perspectives from historical sources, for most of the premodern period land-based representations of the sea predominated. Seascapes almost always contained land-centered biases that both extolled the virtues of land-based habitation and that treated the maritime world as "Other."[12] Terracentrism encompassed a continuum of representations stretched between the desire of the land-based court to incorporate the sea into state institutions and perceptions of the sea as a terrifying, unknowable, uncontrollable space.[13] Constructions of piracy in Japan, of *kaizoku*, need to be understood within that continuum.

The roots of terracentrism in late medieval Japan that shaped both representations of seafarers and the forms of written language appropriated by sea lords reach back to some of the earliest political and cultural formations in the archipelago. We must acknowledge the centrality of the sea for even the oldest communities in the archipelago. Excavations of the famous Jōmon shell mounds show peoples dependent on the sea for food and transport. During the Yayoi period (ca. 900 B.C.E.–250 C.E.), littoral chieftains incorporated parts of the Japanese archipelago into political formations

11. Amino Yoshihiko, *Nihon chūsei no hinōgyōmin to tennō* (Iwanami Shoten, 1984), pp. 247–49.
12. Marcia Yonemoto has made a similar argument for the Edo period, arguing that Edo-period writers tended to accept Chinese "geocentric" attitudes towards the sea (Yonemoto, "Maps and Metaphors," p. 178).
13. Yonemoto also identifies "fear" as one of the major Japanese experiences of the sea (ibid., pp. 171–72, 176).

based on the sea; some early polities even encompassed territories on both the Korean Peninsula and in the archipelago.[14] The fruits of the sea were part of the ritual economy of ancient Japan, among the four fundamental forms of production and four types of goods presented to the deities.[15]

However, ancient myths tell more ambivalent stories. One of the earliest extant attempts at inscribing official history by the Japanese state, the *Record of Ancient Matters* (*Kojiki*, ca. 712), reflects tensions between landed desires to incorporate the sea within a state framework and concomitant fears of the sea as a dangerous, terrifying space. One of the progenitor deities of the archipelago, Izanagi, bestowed the sea upon one of his offspring, the god Susano'o, to be his demesne.[16] Gods of the sea and channels were included in the pantheon,[17] ritually incorporating the sea within Japan.

On the other hand, the *Kojiki* also includes stories that represent the sea as a terrifying realm, a space not fully compatible with the Japanese state. The god Susano'o, though in charge of the sea, proved as uncontrollable as the waves, going on a rampage that resulted in his exile to the distant western province of Izumo.[18] In order to cross a stretch of sea safely, the indomitable warrior Yamato Takeru could only look on helplessly as his consort Oto Tachibana-hime felt compelled to sacrifice herself to appease the god of the sea,[19] highlighting the degree to which early Japanese elites perceived sea travel as perilous. Perhaps the most vivid depiction of the sea as an Other space incompatible with the land is the story of a daughter of the sea god named Toyo-Tama-Bime-no-Mikoto. After her human husband broke his word not to watch her give birth and stole a glimpse of her in the form of a crocodile, she grew angry and forever severed the paths between the worlds of land and sea.[20]

When the founders of the first centralized, bureaucratic state in Japan adapted Chinese imperial models of governance to craft government

14. Conrad Totman, *A History of Japan*, 2nd ed. (Malden, Mass.: Blackwell Publishing, 2005), pp. 42–43, 49–50.
15. Ancient Shinto prayers, known as *norito*, considered "that which lives in the blue ocean—the wide-finned and the narrow-finned fishes, the seaweeds of the deep and the seaweeds of the shore" as equal in significance to grains, liquors, and textiles. *Norito: A Translation of the Ancient Japanese Ritual Prayers*, edited and translated by Donald Philippi (The Institute for Japanese Culture and Classics, Kokugakuin University, 1959), pp. 17–31.
16. *Shinpen Nihon koten bungaku zenshū*, vol. 1: *Kojiki*, edited by Yamaguchi Yoshinori et al. (Shōgakukan, 1997); *Kojiki*, edited and translated by Donald Philippi (Tokyo University Press, 1968), Book 1, ch. 12.
17. Ibid., Book 1, chs. 7 and 15.
18. Ibid., Book 1, chs. 13 and 16.
19. Ibid., Book 2, ch. 84.
20. Ibid., Book 1, ch. 45.

institutions in the seventh century, they buttressed earlier forms of terracen trism with continental agricentric ideologies. These political and economic philosophies considered grain-based agricultural production to be the cen tral pillar supporting the state and held land dwelling and land production to be normative.[21] These continental cultural influences caused the founder of Japan's new Ritsuryō state to attempt to impose institutional, agricen tric, and land-centered worldviews on Japan's varied geographies. They es tablished enduring institutional precedents for assessing and representing the productive capacity of the archipelago in measures of rice production.[2] Poetic names for Japan coined in this period imagined Japan as a land o "fresh rice ears." Such poetic names persisted across the premodern period.[2]

The Ritsuryō reforms did not alter Japanese elites' fundamental para digm for representing the sea as a continuum of incorporation and fear Ritsuryō founders located "territorial waters," which extended to the borde with Korea,[24] and included both land and sea within the jurisdictions o provinces. They also borrowed Chinese definitions of the sea to help inte grate the inner sea world into their land-centered state. The classical Chinese term, *hai*, which corresponds to the Japanese word for sea, *umi*, not only referred to an aquatic body but also signified a terrestrial region of the world corresponding to a major compass direction.[25] Japanese officials in the Ritsuryō period reiterated this usage by incorporating the sea institutionally into the Western Sea (Saikaidō), Southern Sea (Nankaidō), and Eastern Sea (Tōkaidō) circuits.[26] They attempted to defend these waters with naval force installed in provincial capitals and other centers of state power.[27]

Such institutional incorporation enabled early lawmakers to perceive i as possible to regulate minutiae on both land and sea equally in law code

21. Amino Yoshihiko, "Emperor, Rice, and Commoners," in *Multicultural Japan: Paleolithic t Postmodern*, edited by Donald Denoon et al. (Cambridge: Cambridge University Press, 1996' pp. 235–39; Charles Holcombe, *Genesis of East Asia, 221 B.C.–A.D. 907* (Honolulu: University o Hawai'i Press, 2001), pp. 202–3.

22. Amino, *Nihon chūsei no hinōgyōmin to tennō*, pp. 30–31.

23. Kitabatake Chikafusa, *A Chronicle of Gods and Sovereigns: Jinnō Shōtōki of Kitabatake Chikafusa* edited and translated by H. Paul Varley (New York: Columbia University Press, 1980), p. 49.

24. Bruce L. Batten, *Gateway to Japan: Hakata in War and Peace, 500-1300* (Honolulu: University o Hawai'i Press, 2006), p. 98.

25. Unno Kazutaka, "Japan before the Introduction of the Global Theory of the Earth: In Search of Japanese Image of the Earth," *Memoirs of the Toyo Bunko* 38 (1980): 42.

26. Medieval Europeans also conceptualized seas as spaces representing points of the compas (Martin W. Lewis, "Dividing the Ocean Sea," *Geographical Review* 89.2 (4/1999): 188–214).

27. Shinjō Tsunezō, *Chūsei suiunshi no kenkyū* (Hanawa Shobō, 1995), pp. 5–6.

like the *Engi shiki*, which dictates limits on the amount of time that sea travel should take.[28] The court issued toll exemption passes (*kasho*) for purveyors on these sea lanes with the expectation that such passes would be respected.[29] Schematic, institutional models of the imperium such as can be found in a thirteenth-century encyclopedia, *Nichūreki*, depicted Japan as a collection of sea and land routes (figure 4). Only the sea lanes required special designation—representing their perceived Otherness—but, using the same lines for land and sea also signified an expectation that travel from land to sea and back again should be seamless.

Land-based authorities reflected both their own expectations of service from littoral inhabitants and the work cultures of maritime communities by classifying particular sea spaces by function. Writers employed shorthand

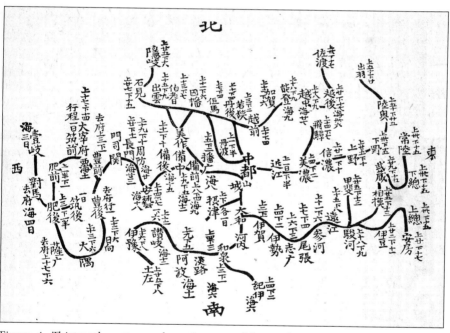

Figure 4. Thirteenth-century schematic map of Japan from *Nichūreki*. Adapted from *Nichūreki* in *Kaitei shiseki shūran*, vol. 23, edited by Kondō Heijō (Kondō Shuppanbu, 1903), p. 190.

28. Iida Yoshirō, *Nihon kōkaijutsushi: kodai kara bakumatsu made* (Hara Shobō, 1980), pp. 5–6.
29. Amino, *Nihon chūsei no hinōgyōmin to tennō*, pp. 96–97.

terms that defined the sea through the act of crossing it.[30] Authorities
designated several categories of coastal settlements as territories that provided services and produced maritime goods forwarded to the capital as
nonagricultural tax (*nie*): "bay" (*ura*), "harbor" (*tsu*), "anchorage" (*tomari*),
"island" (*shima*), and even "sea" (*umi*). Although some of these categories
retained currency into late medieval times, others were absorbed into institutional language related to estates (*shōen*) and provincial and state lands
(*kokugaryō*).[31] In the medieval period, maritime as well as terrestrial thoroughfares, crossroads, and markets continued to be perceived of as having
close ties to the emperor, and thus as inherently public spaces.[32]

Nevertheless, as was the case in other parts of the world,[33] however much
they wanted to control the sea, many Japanese elites also represented the sea
as a nameless, unknown, dangerous, and uncontrollable "Other space." For
all of the institutional organization that occurred in the Ritsuryō period, the
architects of those institutions did not leave us records of names for the seas
aside from vague directional nomenclature. Lack of a name suggests perceptions of unknowability. Even though provincial borders extended onto
the waves, lack of knowledge and control over the sea rendered maritime
borders vague and placed boundary zones in dispute. By the late medieval
period, Japanese elite writers recognized that seas had become free-floating
spaces detached from the land and subject to the whims of whatever authority could enforce its sense of the border.[34] In 1371, the warlord and poet
Imagawa Ryōshun (ca. 1326–1420), found it "strange to think of crossing
provincial boundaries at sea."[35]

30. One of the most common verbs one finds in late medieval documents regarding the sea in pre
    modern Japan is "cross the sea" (*tokai*). A crossing was known as a *watari*. For example, in 148?
    the Ōuchi attempted to regulate the crossing from Akamagaseki to various sites: see, *Ōuchi-sh
    okitegaki*, nos. 108–15, *Chūsei hōsei shiryōshū*, vol. 3, *Buke kahō* 1, edited by Satō Shin'ichi et al
    (1965), pp. 77–79.
31. Amino, *Nihon chūsei no hinōgyōmin to tennō*, p. 282; Amino Yoshihiko, "Kodai, chūsei, kinse
    shoki no gyorō to kaisanbutsu no ryūtsū," in *Kōza Nihon gijutsu no shakaishi*, vol. 2: *Engyo
    gyogyō*, edited by Nagahara Keiji et al. (Nihon Hyōronsha, 1985), pp. 216–17, 240–41.
32. Amino, *Nihon chūsei no hinōgyōmin to tennō*, pp. 37, 97–98.
33. For the case of Europe, see Alain Corbin, *The Lure of the Sea: The Discovery of the Seaside in th
    Western World, 1750-1840*, translated by Jocelyn Phelps (Oxford, U.K.: Polity Press, 1994), ch. 1
    for Arab and Indian Ocean views of the sea, see Steinberg, *The Social Construction of the Ocean
    pp. 45–49.
34. Yamauchi Yuzuru, *Setouchi no kaizoku: Murakami Takeyoshi no tatakai* (Kōdansha, 2005)
    pp. 22–23.
35. Imagawa Ryōshun, *Michiyukiburi*, in *Shinpen Nihon koten bungaku zenshū*, vol. 48: *Chūsei nikk
    kikōshū*, edited by Nagasaki Ken et al. (Shōgakukan, 1994), p. 406.

Associations of the sea with danger also came to Japan embedded within the foundations of classical Chinese culture. One well-known Chinese saying popularized by the early Confucian philosopher Xunzi (ca. 312–230 B.C.E.) used vivid imagery of ships and the sea as a metaphor to represent the potential menace of ineffective governance: "the lord is the ship, the people the water; the water is that which supports the ship, but also that which can overturn the ship."[36] This metaphor found wide currency among medieval Japanese writers. They encountered it in various other Chinese texts and continued to reproduce the phrase in warrior chronicles and everyday correspondence through the sixteenth century.[37] The fourteenth-century *Tale of the Heike* and other versions of the Heike story employed Xunzi's expression to symbolize the overthrow of imperial rule by the overweening warrior Taira no Kiyomori (1118–81) at the end of the Heian period (ca. 794–1181).[38] A natural extension of Xunzi's dictum then would equate calm seas with a peaceful state and rough seas with political turmoil. Writing about the pilgrimage of Former Emperor Takakura (1161–81) to Itsukushima Shrine during the time of disorder that arose after the ascendancy of Taira no Kiyomori, one court writer tied the fear inspired by storms and rough seas to the terrifying, potential violence of the disorders wrought by Kiyomori's authority: "people despaired, wondering what reason there was for the Retired Emperor to unexpectedly have to fight the waves to make a Pilgrimage to the ends of the sea. But no one dared stick their neck out in protest in this climate of rough seas and unceasing tempest."[39]

36. See ch. 9 of Xunzi, "Wangzhi," in Xunzi, *The Works of Hsüntze*, edited and translated by Homer H. Dubs (Taipei: Confucius Publishing Co., 1972), pp. 182–83. For the power of metaphors in society, see Victor Turner, *Dramas, Fields, and Metaphors: Symbolic Action in Human Society* (Ithaca, N.Y.: Cornell University Press, 1974), ch. 1.
37. In addition to the text of the *Xunzi* itself, the phrase can be found in a book on politics in the age of the Tang Emperor Taizong, Wu Jing's *Zhen'guan zhengyao*, which had reached Japan by the Heian period. Wu Jing, *Zhen'guan zhengyao* [Jōgan Seiyo], edited and translated by Harada Taneshige, *Shinyaku Kanbun taikei*, vols. 95–96 (Meiji Shoin, 1978), p. 778. The term also appears in *Baishōron* (Shuzo Uyenaka, "A Study of Baishōron: A Source for the Ideology of Imperial Loyalism in Medieval Japan," Ph.D. Diss., University of Toronto, 1976, p. 120); in the 1526 military chronicle *Kashima chiranki* (*Gunsho ruijū*, vol. 21: *Kassenbu* [Zoku Gunsho Ruijū Kanseikai, 1930], p. 49), and a letter from the general Shiji Hiroyoshi (1467–1557) (DNK 8, *Mōri-ke monjo*, vol. 2, doc. 593, no year.5.28).
38. *Heike monogatari*, NKBT 32, p. 265; *Tale of the Heike*, edited and translated by Helen C. McCullough (Stanford, Calif.: Stanford University Press, 1988), p. 128; *Genpei jōsuiki*, edited by Ichiko Teiji et al. (Miyai Shoten, 1991), vol. 2, ch. 12, p. 212.
39. Minamoto Michichika, *Takakura-in Itsukushima gokōki*, in *Shin Nihon koten bungaku taikei*, vol. 51: *Chūsei nikki kikōshū*, edited by Kawazoe Shōji et al. (Iwanami Shoten, 1990), pp. 5–6; *Four Japanese Travel Diaries of the Middle Ages*, edited and translated by Herbert Plutschow and Hideichi Fukuda (Ithaca, N.Y.: China-Japan Program, Cornell University, 1981), p. 28.

Much of the fear of the sea stemmed from the dangers associated with sea travel. Early seascapes depict sea travel as a terrifying experience. In the *Tosa Diary*, a tenth-century progenitor of Japanese travel narratives, Ki no Tsurayuki (872–945) related how the sense of helplessness on a sea voyage paralyzed travelers with fear: "As for the weather, all we could do was depend on the captain and crew. For men unused to these journeys, it was a great source of worry. Women lay their heads on the floor of the ship and cried."[40] As in many places across the premodern world, safe passage in Japan often required divine intervention. Those embarking on sea voyages in Japanese ports commonly worshipped both Buddhist deities, especially Avalokiteśvara (Jp. *Kannon*), and Shinto deities (*kami*) related to the sea at shrines such as Sumiyoshi and Itsukushima that dotted the coastline. By the fifteenth and sixteenth centuries, Japanese seafarers had added the worship of Tianfei (also known as Mazu), Chinese goddess of the sea, and Christianity to the array of religious practices available for propitiating a safe voyage.[41]

SEA PEOPLE

Sea lords also had to engage with land-based representations of littoral inhabitants as "Other." If most literate elites living in the capital in early Japan could scarce conceive of the life of a farmer,[42] they found those who plowed the waves to be a different breed entirely. Seascapes served these Japanese elites as a way to bolster their land-centered and agricentric ideologies by marking littoral inhabitants and maritime workers as "Other," as "sea people." To do so, they used two seemingly interchangeable expressions, *ama* and *kaijin*, written using a variety of character combinations.[43] Regardless if Inland Sea sea-lord bands saw themselves as part of a larger Japanese or circum-China Sea population of ocean-going peoples, such subjectivities are obscured by the cultural imaginary of "sea people" that land-based elites

40. Ki no Tsurayuki, *Tosa nikki*, NKBT 20, p. 36. In English, see *Classical Japanese Prose: An Anthology*, compiled and edited by Helen Craig McCullough (Stanford, Calif.: Stanford University Press, 1990), pp. 73–102.
41. Ki, *Tosa nikki*, p. 27; Ennin, *Ennin's Diary: The Record of a Pilgrimage to China in Search of the Law*, edited and translated by Edwin O. Reischauer (New York: Ronald Press Co., 1955), pp. 2, 6, 94, 125; Peter D. Shapinsky, "Polyvocal Portolans: Nautical Charts and Hybrid Maritime Cultures in Early Modern East Asia," *Early Modern Japan* 14 (2006): 22–23; Murai Shōsuke, *Ajia no naka no chūsei Nihon* (Azekura Shobō, 1988), p. 111. Worship of Mazu thrived among seafarers of China's southeast coast during the Ming Dynasty.
42. Hitomi Tonomura, *Community and Commerce in Late Medieval Japan: The Corporate Villages of Tokuchin-ho* (Stanford, Calif.: Stanford University Press, 1992), pp. 189–90.
43. See glossary.

used to marginalize littoral populations. As a historical term, *ama* neither embodied the collective voice of maritime experience nor reflected the identities of seafarers and littoral inhabitants.

Instead, landed elites in the premodern period utilized the term *ama* in ways similar to early twentieth-century ethnologists: to denote the perceived experiential divide between "normal" landed lives and "abnormal" or "special" sea-based lives. As Bruce Batten has argued, the Ritsuryō state promoted an "ethnic" ideology of normal "Japanese" as "rice farmers" that "spread outward and downward through Japanese society throughout the remainder of the premodern period."[44] Land-based elites defined themselves as normal people by designating an antithesis—sea people.[45]

The paragons of classical Japanese literary and historical writing constructed durable images of sea people along a continuum similar to that by which they understood the marine environment. Some seascapes simply identified "sea people" as a different category of person, some focused on the need for maritime services, especially in the contexts of naval protection and the sex trade,[46] whereas others highlighted the fear-inspiring, destructive capacity of pirates. The premodern practice of delegating maritime responsibilities away to "sea people" may have heightened the feeling of powerlessness of dealing not only with the ocean and weather but also with seafarers themselves.

Land-based writers might identify sea people as Other by evoking a sense of awe inspired by the experience gap that they perceived about the sea. While the author of *The Tosa Diary* related how fear of the sea and dependence on seafarers made men "worry" and women prostrate, he also expressed wonder at how sea people's maritime lifestyle enabled them to comprehend and deal with the nautical environment:

Kumo mo mina	The clouds resemble
Nami to zo mieru	White-capped waves to our eyes
Ama mo ga na	Only sea people

44. Bruce L. Batten, *To the Ends of Japan: Premodern Frontiers, Boundaries, and Interactions* (Honolulu: University of Hawai'i Press, 2003), pp. 118–19.

45. Jacqueline Pigeot, *Femmes galantes, femmes artistes dans le Japon ancien (XIe - XIIIe siècle)* (Paris: Gallimard, 2003), p. 74. Usage similar to the concept of "sea people" in premodern Japan occurred in early modern China, where land-based people commonly used the epithet, "water people" (*suishangren*) to identify Hokkien and Dan boat people (Robert J. Antony, *Like Froth Floating on the Sea: The World of Pirates and Seafarers in Late Imperial South China* [Berkeley: University of California, Berkeley Institute of East Asian Studies, 2003], pp. 9–10).

46. Janet Goodwin, *Selling Songs and Smiles: The Sex Trade in Heian and Kamakura Japan* (Honolulu: University of Hawai'i Press, 2007).

| Izure ka umi to | Can readily discern the |
| Toite shiru beku | Separation of sea and sky[47] |

Such sentiments pervade the classical canon[48] and established archetypical models of sea people that remained relevant well into the medieval period. The well-traveled linked-verse master poet Sōgi (ca. 1421–1502) wrote in one travelogue of the awe that struck him watching fisher folk calmly and deftly handle their small craft in tossing billows outside the bay of Habu in Nagato: "The winds grew fierce. Everyone moaned to each other in fear. Seeing how the sea people in their little fishing smacks acclimated to the pitching waves was amazing."[49]

Such descriptions of an experiential separation between seafarers and land dwellers are also the result of the observations of travelers who, however much they may have disliked the uncouth sailors,[50] could not avoid contact with them. These seascapes may then highlight the work-based knowledge of the environment, the navigational expertise of pilots and other mariners who, being able to "read" the nautical environment, perceived it differently from those who could not.

The dependence of land-based elites on seafarers to provide services heightened the sense of sea people as alien. The earliest extant representations of sea people highlight expectations of service. In the *Kojiki*, "sea people [*ama*]" are depicted as a distinct category of people who serve the Yamato Court and present nonagricultural tax goods to the sovereign.[51] By the Heian and early medieval periods, *ama* had been incorporated into status classifications used across Japan, including artisans and other specialists (*shokunin*), commoners, unfree persons, and pirates.[52]

The term *kaizoku* (pirate) originally denoted those sea people whom Japanese authorities perceived as both threatening and existing outside of

47. Ki, *Tosa nikki*, p. 38.
48. See for example the *Pillow Book* (*Makura no sōshi*) of Sei Shōnagon (ca. 966–1017): "There's no one so impressive and downright awe-inspiring as men who go about in boats. Even if the water's not particularly deep, how can they go rowing off so nonchalantly in such a frail and unreliable thing? Let alone when there are unfathomable depths of water below" (Sei Shōnagon, *The Pillow Book*, edited and translated by Meredith McKinney [New York: Penguin, 2006], p. 242).
49. Sōgi, *Tsukushi no michi no ki*, in *Shin Nihon koten bungaku taikei*, vol. 51: *Chūsei nikki kikōshū*, edited by Fukuda Hideichi et al. (Iwanami Shoten, 1990), p. 411. For an English version, see Eileen Kato, "Pilgrimage to Dazaifu: Sogi's *Tsukushi no Michi no Ki*," *Monumenta Nipponica* 34.3 (1979): 344–45.
50. Ki no Tsurayuki described his ship's captain as "an insensitive lout" for barging in and breaking up a farewell feast, "insistent that we go soon, declaring 'the tide is full, the wind blowing fair'" (Ki, *Tosa nikki*, p. 30).
51. *Kojiki*, Book 2, ch. 105.
52. Amino, *Nihon chūsei no hinōgyōmin to tennō*, pp. 242–69.

the Japanese state, symbolizing the dangerous, uncontrollable aspect of the sea. In other words, the early meanings of pirates hewed closely to the root meaning of the two characters: "sea" and "bandit." Legal decisions based on Ritsuryō codes outlawed pirates as ruffians, who harassed travelers just as bandits did on land, and as manifestations of rebellion.[53] However, actual usage of words for "pirate" pointed to a much wider range of mobile mariners, who either existed outside or refused to recognize the state's writ. Heian-period elites identified Korean refugees, the rebel Fujiwara no Sumitomo (d. 941), and foreign invaders all equally as pirates.[54] Early Japanese authorities condemned other seafarers as pirates for resisting the state's regulation of access to sea lanes (i.e., its sea tenure) by perpetrating "habitual illegal crossings" and refusing to acquire "check station passes."[55] Based largely on Chinese sources, the early tenth-century Japanese dictionary *Wamyō ruijushō* places pirates—along with boat-based female entertainers—in the category of "beggars and thieves," suggesting that for some Heian elites such peripatetic figures represented a constant threat to the social order.[56] Or, as one Heian-period history records, pirates "drifted north and south like floating grasses . . . yearning naught for their homes."[57] Such constructions have parallels in the distrust of many sedentary societies toward nomadic populations, from Chinese perceptions of their steppe neighbors to Mediterranean representations of forms of "transhumance."[58]

Elite writers compounded pirates' ostracism from the political order by equating pirates with the dangers of sea travel. Pirates defied imperial commands for the safe return of subjects. Ki no Tsurayuki caught wind that pirates had threatened revenge (probably due to his pirate-suppressing obligations as governor), and he bemoaned his fate: "I dwell on rumors of pirates

---

53. *Ruijū sandaikyaku,* in *Kokushi taikei,* vol. 25: *Ruijū sandaikyaku, Kōnin kyakushō* (Yoshikawa Kōbunkan, 1965), p. 614.
54. Batten, *Gateway to Japan,* ch. 3.
55. *Ruijū sandaikyaku,* quoted in Batten, *Gateway to Japan,* p. 93.
56. As Janet Goodwin shows, *Wamyō ruijushō* definitions were not universally accepted in Heian Japan (Goodwin, *Selling Songs and Smiles,* pp. 21, 38–39). Nevertheless, the dictionary does present a powerful example of how the Chinese influence on the perception of "sea peoples" affected perceptions in premodern Japan. In compiling the *Wamyō ruijushō,* Minamoto Shigatō included definitions of entertainers and pirates that he drew from the *History of the Latter Han Dynasty* (*Hohanshu*) (Goodwin, *Selling Songs and Smiles,* p. 135). The *Wamyō ruijushō* definition for pirate (*kaizoku*) reads: "the Hohanshu relates that the pirate Zhang Bolu attacked nine coastal provinces" (Minamoto Shitagō, *Wamyō ruijushō,* edited by Masamune Atsuo [Kazama Shobō, 1962], p. 12b).
57. *Nihon sandai jitsuroku,* 867.11.10, quoted in Karl Friday, *The First Samurai: The Life and Legend of the Warrior Rebel, Taira Masakado* (Hoboken, N.J.: John Wiley & Sons, 2008), p. 111.
58. Fernand Braudel, *The Mediterranean and the Mediterranean World in the Age of Philip II,* translated by Siân Reynolds (Berkeley: University of California Press, 1995), p. 94.

planning revenge. The sea has grown even more frightening; it is enough to turn one's hair white."[59]

The identification of pirates as a type of sea people continued throughout the medieval period. The thirteenth-century didactic tale "How a Pirate Converted and Became a Monk" turns the simple act of seafaring into potential piracy with the phrase "passing my life floating on the waves day and night."[60] Well into the sixteenth century, patrons who sponsored sea lords to perform nautical violence associated those seafarers directly with the marine environment. The Ōuchi family knew some of their most oft-sponsored sea lords—those from the islands of Kure, Kamagari, and Nōmi—collectively as the "three islander gang" (*mikajima-shū*).[61] The Kurushima Murakami family of sea lords received the appellation "the offshore family" (*oki-ke*) from their Mōri patrons.[62]

AESTHETICS: SONGS AND THE SEA

For land-based elite Japanese writers, poetry and songs constituted some of the most ancient and hallowed of all literary forms. For much of the premodern period, Japanese poets attempted to tame the waves by inscribing the seas and seafarers into court-centered, terracentric seascapes. Classical writers marked inspiring natural features and famous places on land and sea as places of historical and literary significance by recognizing the name as poem-worthy, deeming it a "poetic pillow" (*utamakura*).[63] Later writers found significance in spaces that could be embedded in seascapes and landscapes with poetic pillows. These poetic devices forever colored the perceptions of writers and readers, prefiguring their experiences with physical environments. Sites with *utamakura* precedent could only be viewed as an *utamakura*, and those places without such precedents lacked value.[64] Refer-

59. Ki, *Tosa nikki*, p. 43.
60. "Kaizoku hosshin shukke no koto," in *Shinpen Nihon koten bungaku zenshū*, vol. 10: *Uji shūi monogatari*, edited by Kobayashi Yasuharu et al. (Shōgakukan, 1996), no. 123; "How a Pirate Was Converted and Became a Priest," in *A Collection of Tales from Uji: A Study and Translation of Uji Shūi Monogatari*, edited and translated by D. E. Mills (Cambridge: Cambridge University Press, 1970), pp. 333–36.
61. Sagara Shōjin, *Shōjinki*, 10.26 in YK, vol. 1, p. 356.
62. EK doc. 2404, Tenshō 11? (1583) 11.26; Tanamori Fusaaki, *Fusaaki oboegaki*, in *Hiroshima kenshi kodai chūsei shiryō hen*, vol. 3 (Hiroshima-shi: Hiroshima-ken, 1978), p. 1120.
63. Herbert Plutschow, "Introduction," in *Four Japanese Travel Diaries of the Middle Ages*, edited and translated by Herbert Plutschow and Hideichi Fukuda (Ithaca, N.Y.: China-Japan Program, 1981), p. 4.
64. Ibid., p. 5.

encing earlier *utamakura* precedents or recording the image in more permanent media such as calligraphy and painting further transformed particular places into emotion-laden seascapes and landscapes.

By referencing preceding travelers and *utamakura*, poets also bridged temporal divides and made the alluded-to object one with the poet in time as well as space, imposing a sense of timeless permanence on parts of the environment, including the maritime world.[65] With such allusions, writers could suggest that everything should be as it was when the progenitor image existed. For example, poetically inclined Seto Inland Sea voyagers found the beach at Suma significant because it was an *utamakura* associated with court icons Ariwara no Yukihira (818–93) and Genji.[66] Centuries after these characters supposedly lived, Imagawa Ryōshun felt disillusioned that nothing remained of those earlier two literary heroes of the Suma strand. The dismay he felt in his present reimagined Genji's "golden age" when the sea would have been a tame part of the Ritsuryō provincial system: "We reached Suma, and although there was nothing particularly eye-catching about the place . . . I thought of the scene when, all those years ago, He [Genji] lived here. . . . Now, there is not even the dilapidated shack of the barrier or anyone to staff it."[67]

At the same time, writers steeped in the culture of the court used *utamakura* and other poetic devices to objectify sea people as part of the environment. They expected sea people to embody certain poetic ideals but not to be able to give voice to them. For countless writers glorifying Japanese court aesthetics, sea people, female divers, boats, ships, the smoke from salt making, gathering seaweed, and fishing might be employed to represent the transience of life, the desire for love, the evanescence of love, and countless other feelings. However, such artists concomitantly refused to grant that those same sea people might be capable of similar humanity. They treated sea people as poetic props, little different from boats, waves, sand, salt, or fish. Off the coast of today's Mukaishima in Hiroshima Prefecture, Imagawa Ryōshun contemplated the inhabitants of the islands stretching before his gaze, rhetorically asking, "I wonder if the sea people there even understand human emotions."[68] Similarly, a fifteenth-century noh play entitled *Ama*

---

65. Ibid.
66. Genji referenced Yukihira when pondering his impending exile to Suma: "While someone lived there long ago, he gathered that the place was now extremely isolated and that there was hardly a fisherman's [*ama*] hut to be seen there." (Murasaki Shikibu, *The Tale of Genji*, edited and translated by Royall Tyler [London: Penguin, 2001], p. 229; *Genji monogatari*, edited by Abe Akio, *Shinpen Nihon koten bungaku zenshū*, vol. 21 [Shōgakukan, 1995], p. 161).
67. Imagawa, *Michiyukiburi*, p. 394.
68. Ibid., p. 399.

repeatedly has its female lead—the ghost *shite* role—identify herself as a sea person without the capacity to understand true emotions.[69]

However, seafarers did on occasion shape poetic discourse. By building their domains in chokepoints, one of the nonstate littoral spaces of late medieval Japan, sea lords caused travelers to perceive those spaces as "piratical"— transforming both the geographical perceptions of medieval Japanese and how we understand the medieval maritime environment through extant sources. For example, the frothy whitewater of the rushing rapids in a narrow channel became a metaphor for the power of "pirates" in those spaces. Writers tied the image of those whitecaps to a hotbed of banditry in the Han Dynasty known as "White Waves" (Paipo, in Shanxi Province).[70] Imagawa described one such locale as "narrow channels . . . where pirates rise up in assault like the white waves."[71] For those who knew the allusion, the narrow channels with fast currents that caused white-capped swells became ever more tied to those potentially fearsome, service-providing, alien, violent pirates with each passing wave.

ESTATES, COMMERCE, AND THE MARITIME ECONOMY

In the Heian period, state-run systems of maritime procurement gave way to patron-client systems and privately administered estates (*shōen*) under the proprietorship of powerful families and temples. Centrally based estate proprietors extended their reach into regions once solely the preserve of state authority such as harbors, ports, beaches, and rivers. Proprietors and estate residents extended the boundaries of the estate offshore.[72] A proprietor's agent stated in 1315, "Regarding Your Bay and connected lands, be sure to administer Your Sea."[73] Kamo shrines claimed the "inner seas" (*naikai*) of the provinces of Iyo and Sanuki as part of their estates.[74] Historian Hotate Michihisa has identified several specific ways by which estate inhabitants and proprietors sought to demarcate such inner sea space, including the use of nearby islands and offshore rocks as landmarks, the designation of set

69. *Ama*, in *Shinpen Nihon koten bungaku zenshū*, vol. 59: *Yōkyokushū*, vol. 2, edited by Koyama Hiroshi et al. (Shōgakukan, 1998), pp. 535, 539; *Ama: The Diver*, in *Japanese Nō Dramas*, edited and translated by Royall Tyler (London: Penguin, 1992), p. 27.
70. Imagawa, *Michiyukiburi*, pp. 394–95.
71. Imagawa Ryōshun, *Rokuon'indono Itsukushima mōdeki*, in *Gunsho ruijū*, vol. 18: *Nikki-bu, kikō-bu* (Zoku Gunsho Ruijū Kanseikai, 1899–), p. 1106.
72. For a discussion of estates constituting a "system," see Thomas Keirstead, *The Geography of Power in Medieval Japan* (Stanford, Calif.: Stanford University Press, 1992).
73. Quoted in Hotate, "Chūsei zenki no gyogyō to shōensei," p. 23.
74. Amino, *Nihon chūsei no hinōgyōmin to tennō*, p. 276, nn. 92 and 95.

distances offshore, by line of sight, and the delimiting of boundaries in relation to shipping lanes.[75] Residents, managers, and proprietors of the Inland Sea island estate of Yugeshima considered that it encompassed the shipping lanes and net-fishing sites some five kilometers offshore. Competing proprietary agents—including nascent sea lords—felt no contradictions in disputing and regulating such spaces.[76]

Beginning in the tenth century, authorities sponsored sea people to collect and transport goods that once fell under the category of the Ritsuryō nonagricultural tax system. By the eleventh century, ruling authorities had begun to settle many of these populations in littoral estates and to enroll them as service organizations by granting them tax and toll exemptions.[77] These authorities drew on Ritsuryō precedents when devising institutional language, and they continued to conceptualize the sea as part of the land.[78] Aristocrats, imperial family members, officials of religious institutions, and other proprietary officials employed the term "sea people" to refer to the seafaring producers and purveyors who inhabited their littoral estates.[79] For example, a 1231 letter of appointment from the harbor settlement of Tagarasunoura on the Japan Sea coast defines the responsibilities of "the village chief" (*tone*) as "the administration of the sites of sea people" (*ama*), including their divisions of the harbor for fishing.[80] Littoral counties, villages, and estates bearing the name "sea people" (*ama*) dotted the premodern landscape.[81] However, as later chapters will show, the institutional language of estates and other structures often required modification when applying them to maritime peoples and geographies, giving rise to hybrid categories.

For estate proprietors, pirates represented the antithesis of the incorporated sea person, serious threats to the safe delivery of rents from distant holdings. However, as the medieval period progressed, estate proprietors came to rely more and more on locals for estate management, especially after the Kamakura bakufu proved unable to restrain its retainers from attempting to take control of parts of estates. Some estate proprietors took a fatalistic view of piracy, treating it as a natural disaster, but one that did not release estate residents from responsibility to pay dues. One directive from

---

75. Hotate, "Chūsei zenki no gyogyō to shōensei," pp. 21–23.

76. NET 169 "Yugeshima no shō ryōke jitō sōbun ezu," no date. Yugeshima is taken up in greater detail in chapter 2.

77. Amino, *Nihon chūsei no hinōgyōmin to tennō*, pp. 240–60.

78. Ibid., pp. 30–31.

79. Ibid., p. 284.

80. *Hata monjo*, doc. 2, Kangi 3 (1231) 1.21 in *Wakasa gyoson shiryō*, edited by Fukui Kenritsu Toshokan and Fukui-ken Gōdoshi Kondankai (Fukui: Fukui-ken Gōdoshi Kondankai, 1964), p. 295.

81. DNK 11, *Kobayakawa-ke monjo* vol. 2, pp. 230, doc. 392, no year.10.4; Amino, "Kodai, chūsei, kinsei shoki no gyorō to kaisanbutsu no ryūtsū," p. 199.

the proprietor Tōji to its agents on the estate of Yugeshima in 1313 reads: "in cases of pirates, capsizing, or other natural disasters [*furyo no sainan*], [dues are to be paid according to precedent."[82] One could not anticipate or defend against pirate attacks, just make preparations for the aftermath—and hold residents responsible for delivery of rents to stop them from using piracy as an excuse for not paying. At the same time, proprietors also began realizing that pirates could help ensure the security of estates and the safe delivery of rents. Many *kaizoku* bands competed for titles to manage littoral estates like Yugeshima. As later chapters will show, it was opportunities like these that enabled local sea-based magnates to transform themselves into sea lords. Representing themselves in forms familiar to land-based elites made them hirable while retaining a maritime element reminded land-based sponsors of the potential for fear-instilling violence. The use of land-based written forms, titles, and tools of lordship by sea lords should be seen in this vein.

EFFECTS OF BUDDHISM

The introduction of Buddhism to Japan began in the sixth century but continued throughout the premodern period; it began to significantly impact perceptions of the sea and seafarers from the medieval period onward. Buddhist cultures added further terracentric dimensions to Japanese perceptions of the sea. Eschatological formulations consistently depicted the sea as an "otherworldly space," tied to both death and salvation.[83] Some Esoteric schools developed complex cosmological models that melded Shinto ideas with Buddhist and situated Japan at the center of the Buddhist cosmos with the emperor as the focal point of purity in the world. In these models, the sea lanes connecting Japan to foreign Others grew ever more polluted the further from Kyoto and closer to the foreign they became; oceans carried potentially demonic foreigners who carried contagion or who were bent on conquest.[84] Such constructions persisted through much of the premodern period. Records for the 735–37 smallpox epidemic blame the disease on overseas barbarians.[85] The 1274 and 1281 invasions of Japan dispatched by

---

82. NET pp. 294, doc. 173:5, Shōwa 2 (1313) 9.8. Shinjō Tsunezō, *Chūsei suiunshi no kenkyū* (Hanawa Shobō, 1995), pp. 500, 513, 776.

83. Max Moerman, "Passage to Fudaraku: Suicide and Salvation in Premodern Japanese Buddhism," in *The Buddhist Dead: Practices, Discourses, Representations*, edited by Bryan J. Cuevas and Jacqeline I. Stone (Honolulu: University of Hawai'i Press, 2007), pp. 266–96.

84. Murai, *Ajia no naka no chūsei Nihon*, pp. 109–11.

85. William Wayne Farris, *Population, Disease, and Land in Early Japan, 645–900* (Cambridge, Mass.: Harvard University Press, 1985), pp. 53–55.

Khubilai Khan remained vivid threats in Japanese elite consciousness for centuries after.[86]

Another way of charting the long-lasting impact of Buddhist cosmologies is by exploring extant maps from the medieval period. One major form of premodern Japanese cartography, Gyōki maps, depicts the land of Japan in the shape of a *vajra* (Jp. *dokko*).[87] A *vajra* (lit. diamond scepter or thunderbolt) is an important ritual implement connected to worship of the Cosmic Buddha, Mahāvairocana (Jp. Dainichi Nyōrai).[88] As figure 5, an early fourteenth-century map, shows, Gyōki maps can impose a particularly land-centered interpretation of Japan on readers. The representation of the land of Japan clearly demarcates the ancient Ritsuryō provincial divisions, with denotations of the quality of the grain yield for each. Surrounding this terracentric Japan is a scaly ring, thought to be part of a dragon protecting Japan.[89] Within the dragon's coils lie seas and islands, suggesting that the mapmaker considered some parts of the maritime world to be part of Japan. However, these maps, like other premodern representations of the sea, leave the sea nameless; only lands warranted labels. Beyond the bounds of the dragon lie the Japanese border islands of Tsushima[90] and Oki standing guard over the seas leading to premodern Japan's foreign Others: a panoply of human and inhuman creatures such as the bird-headed people of Ryūkyū, the demonic women (Rakshasas) of Rasetsu, and the inhabitants of the island Gandō, who, "although they build walled cities, are not human," as well as the more familiar inhabitants of China, Korea, and the Mongol empire.[91] Some of these composite Esoteric Buddhist cosmological and geographical visions showed not only the outer seas, but also the inner seas—the water worlds at the very heart of the archipelago—as border zones.[92] These

---

86. See, for example, Gosukōin, *Kanmon nikki* (Kunaichō Shōryōbu, 2002), Ōei 26 (1419) 8.13; Mansai, *Mansai jugō nikki*, edited by Hanawa Hokinoichi and Ōta Toshirō, *Zoku gunsho ruijū hoi* 1 (Zoku Gunsho Ruijū Kanseikai, 1928), vol. 1, p. 157, Ōei 26 (1419) 7.23.

87. Kuroda Hideo, "Gyokishiki 'Nihon-zu' to wa nanika," in *Chizu to ezu no seiji bunkashi*, edited by Kuroda Hideo et al. (Tokyo Daigaku Shuppankai, 2001), pp. 54–57. The name Gyōki derives from an ascription on some medieval maps that Gyōki (668–749), a Buddhist priest, and eventually a boddhisatva, supposedly created the first maps of Japan using this design.

88. Lucia Dolce, "Mapping the 'Divine Country': Sacred Geography and International Concerns in Mediaeval Japan," in *Korea in the Middle: Korean Studies and Area Studies: Essays in Honour of Boudewijn Walraven*, edited by Remco E. Breuker (Leiden: CNWS Publications, 2007), p. 289.

89. Ōji Toshiaki, *Echizu no sekaizō* (Iwanami Shoten, 1996), pp. 21–23.

90. Possibly indicative of the ambiguous status of Tsushima's sovereignty in the medieval period as both Japan and Korea exercised political and economic influence over the island.

91. Ōji, *Echizu no sekaizō*, pp. 27–29; Kuroda, "Gyokishiki 'Nihon-zu' to wa nanika," p. 45. Kuroda argues that the lack in specificity of the shape of these alien isles stands in direct opposition to Japan's very specific *vajra* shape (p. 44).

92. Kuroda, "Gyokishiki 'Nihon-zu' to wa nanika," p. 27.

51

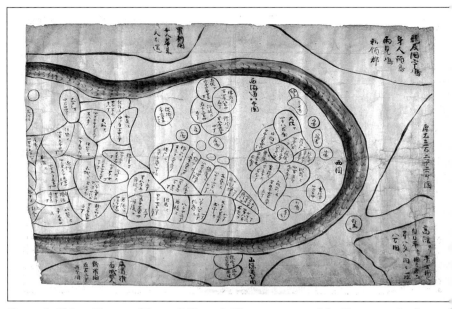

Figure 5. Shōmyōji map of Japan (*Nihonzu*). Photo courtesy of the Kanagawa Prefectural Kanazawa Bunko Museum (Kanagawa Kenritsu Kanazawa Bunko) and used with permission of Kanazawa Bunko and Shōmyōji.

boundary regions both separated Japan from and connected it to polluted, demonic, pestilential foreign Others.[93]

Buddhism also provided ways of incorporating the sea into Japan. The Shōmyōji map inscribes proximal seas within the provinces of Japan and within the serpent's ring. In addition, some texts and diagrams depicting Japan as a *vajra* include coastal waters as part of Japan. One Tendai version of the Esoteric Buddhist cosmography identifies three bodies of water at the heart of the archipelago—Lake Biwa, Ise Bay, and Tsuruga Bay—as "goblins' eyes" (*kimoku*).[94] Goblins' eyes are decorative circles on the handle at the center of the *vajra*;[95] by identifying the bodies of water as parts of the *vajra*, those maritime reaches become part of the Japanese "land of the gods." In addition, Esoteric Buddhist cosmologies prevalent in premodern Japan further used the concept of "inner sea" to describe the waters surrounding the pillar of the universe, Mt. Sumeru. Some medieval Japanese Esoteric sects

93. Ibid., pp. 26–27; Murai, *Ajia no naka no Chūsei Nihon*, p. 110.
94. Quoted in Dolce, "Mapping the 'Divine Country,'" p. 290.
95. Ibid., pp. 290–91, n. 4.

believed that various places in Japan corresponded to Mt. Sumeru, making the waters surrounding Japan, "inner seas."[96]

Such cosmographical visions could not but impact how land-based Japanese perceived seafarers as well as seas. Perceptions that sea people made a living by fishing, piracy, and other forms of potentially deadly violence encouraged landed elites to place *ama* within categories of the Buddhist damned.[97] And, if mariners were intermediaries between the polluted foreign Other and the pure center at the heart of the archipelago, the role of littoral peoples as intercessor with foreign Others may have further encouraged landed elites to regard littoral inhabitants as at least partly foreign Others.

Indeed, some early sources identified sea people as foreign. Although it is unclear if the information came from Japanese emissaries to China or Chinese visitors to Japan, the chapter on Japan in the seventh-century Chinese *History of the Southern Dynasties* (*Nan shi*) contains a description using iconography of hair, skin color, clothing, and customs to mark "sea people" as foreigners: "Ten thousand miles (*li*) to the southwest [of the land of Wo (Japan)] live the sea people [*hairen*] who have black skin, white eyes, are naked, and ugly. They like to eat meat and will shoot and devour passing travelers."[98] A late fifteenth-century genealogy of one powerful family named Kōno based in Shikoku relates a story of how one ancestor defeated invaders from overseas and turned them into "sea people" who served the Kōno: "He severed the leg tendons of those who surrendered and released them in the regions of Suma and Tarumi. Many of the descendants of [these captives] became mariners and boat people. It is said that later the sea people of the western seas became servants of the Kōno."[99]

Buddhism also inspired a number of tales in which sea people as *kaizoku* become stock villains and foils standing against the triumphs of the virtuous[100] and which show the benefits that accrue with Buddhist piety. In

96. John M. Rosenfield et al., *The Courtly Tradition in Japanese Art and Literature: Selections from the Hofer and Hyde Collections* (Cambridge, Mass.: The Fogg Art Museum, Harvard University, 1973), pp. 104–9.

97. The *Sarugakunō* play, *Akogi*, relates how a group of *ama* went fishing and broke an interdiction on killing, thus condemning themselves to hell (though through the intercession of Buddha's mercy they were saved in the end) (Okiura Kazuteru, *Setouchi no minzokushi: Kaiminshi no shinsō o tazunete* (Iwanami Shoten, 1998), pp. 131–32).

98. "Woguochuan," *Nan shi*, ch. 79, in *CCNSS*, vol. 1 (Kokusho Kankōkai, 1975), p. 25.

99. *Yoshōki Jōzōinbon*, in *Yoshōki, suiri gengi, Kōno bungenroku, kaiteiban*, edited by Kageura Tsutomu and Yamauchi Yuzuru (Matsuyama-shi: Iyo Shidankai, 1994), p. 11.

100. "Harima no kuni in'yōshi Chitoku Hōshi no koto," *Konjaku monogatarishū*, in NKBT 24, no. 19; "The Story of Chitoku Hōshi, the Yin-Yang Master of Harima," in *Japanese Tales*, edited and translated by Royall Tyler (New York: Pantheon Books, 1987), no. 61.

the story, "How a Pirate Was Converted and Became a Priest," the harsh acts of piracy—stealing goods, throwing people into the sea to drown—serve to contrast with the salvation that accrued when the pirate converted.[101]

However, Buddhism also contributed to the growing social acceptability of piracy. Sea people became servants of both Shinto and Buddhist religious institutions. Some accepted positions as licensed purveyors (*jinin, kugonin, gusainin*) of specific commodities for which they received tax-exemption passes from those religious institutions for their oceangoing voyages.[102] Other seafarers based themselves in narrow sea channels and mountain passes and earned a livelihood by ensuring the safety of travelers. In return for providing safe passage, they charged tolls that they presented to the deities of the sea or mountains as a portion of the first harvest of the year (*hatsuo*). Both of these populations became linked in the popular consciousness of medieval Japan to piracy, as can be seen in a tale included in the 1254 collection, *Stories Heard from Writers Old and New* by Tachibana Narisue (fl. mid-thirteenth century).[103]

This tale tells of pirates (*kaizoku*) affiliated with Kumano Shrine who intercept a Kumano abbot delivering some rice to be presented to the gods of Kumano. Not recognizing their abbot, the pirates attempt to take the rice to present it themselves to the deity. Using his magical powers to enhance his martial prowess, the abbot Gyōkai subdues the pirates and then promptly forgives them, recognizing that they are only doing their job.

> There was an abbot of Kumano named Gyōkai who was a great archer. Once when he was young, he crossed from Mikawa Province to Kumano. At the Ise Irago crossing he encountered some pirates [*kaizoku*].
>
> The outlaws [*akutō*] approached by ship and said, "Hand over your rice!" Gyōkai replied, "This is holy rice to be donated to Kumano. You bandits should not seek after it." Hearing this, the bandits [*akujū*] replied, "It is because it is rice for Kumano that the issue is not open for debate, and you cannot stop us. If you resist, we will see what becomes of your words."
>
> Gyōkai then pulled on his cuirass. He prepared one screaming-bulb arrow and one broad-headed arrow, set his shield in the prow of the boat, and said, "There is absolutely no way that I can permit you bandits to do as you desire. As for being able to stop you, because

101. "Kaizoku hosshin shukke no koto"; "How a Pirate Was Converted and Became a Priest," p. 333.
102. Amino, *Nihon chūsei no hinōgyōmin to tennō*, pp. 97–98.
103. Katsumata Shizuo, *Sengoku jidairon* (Iwanami Shoten, 1996), pp. 280–83; Sakurai Eiji, *Nihon chūsei no keizai kōzō* (Iwanami Shoten, 1996), pp. 279–80. Amino, *Nihon chūsei no hinōgyōmin to tennō*, pp. 245–46, 259.

this is holy rice, have no illusions that I cannot stop you." ... Gyōkai first loaded a screaming-bulb arrow and shot; the pirates all ducked and the arrow flew over their heads. When the arrow had sped past, echoing in their ears, immediately one pirate stood up, and in no time at all, it seemed that [Gyōkai] had drawn and nocked another arrow. Using the broad-headed arrow, he shot the standing pirate between the eyes. The pirate then fell flat on his face.

The speed of his archery astounded the pirates, and they asked, "Who are you?" He said, "You don't recognize me? I am the abbot Gyōkai! Well, knowing that all the pirates around here all grew up around Kumano, I forgive you, now that you acknowledge me and my skills."

The pirates replied, "Well, you did not say something at the beginning, so we made that extraordinary mistake."[104]

WARRIOR RULE, PIRATES, AND THE SEA

By the time Tachibana Narisue had begun assembling his story collection, responsibility for security on land and sea in the archipelago had been taken over by warriors. The large-scale sponsorship of war bands by authorities in the capital caused many to equate pirates with the exercising of military violence and samurai war bands. This trend is perhaps most visible in the literary transformations of the tenth-century pirate Fujiwara no Sumitomo. A court aristocrat appointed to suppress pirates in Iyo Province in Shikoku, Sumitomo chose not to help the court further incorporate the sea into the Heian state; instead, he became the chief of a "pirate" band that threatened the capital by seizing ships and centers of maritime production and distribution. Later writers appropriated Sumitomo's history for their own ends. Perhaps most famous is the version in the eleventh-century collection, *Tales of Times Now Past (Konjaku monogatari)*, "How Fujiwara no Sumitomo Was Killed for Being a Pirate." In that version, the author draws explicitly on samurai imagery to describe Sumitomo's acts[105]: "[Sumitomo] gathered many brave warriors to be his companions. They all girded themselves with bow and arrow and boarded ships. Sailing out into the sea, they intercepted

---

104. Tachibana Narisue, *Kokon chomonjū*, 2 vols., edited by Nishio Kōichi et al. (Shinchōsha, 1983), no. 435; Katsumata, *Sengoku jidairon*, pp. 280–82.
105. Saeki Kōji, "Kaizoku-ron," in *Ajia no naka no Nihonshi*, vol. 3: *Kaijō no michi*, edited by Arano Yasunori et al. (Tokyo Daigaku Shuppankai, 1992), pp. 38–39; "Fujiwara no Sumitomo kaizoku ni yorite korosaretaru koto," *Konjaku monogatarishū*, in NKBT 25, no. 2, pp. 366–68; William R. Wilson, "The Way of the Bow and Arrow: The Japanese Warrior in *Konjaku monogatari*," *Monumenta Nipponica* 28.2 (1973): 195–97.

any ships heading to the capital from the western provinces and pillaged the ships and killed the crews. By these means, they made their living."[106]

The story of Sumitomo is also the story of those who defeated Sumitomo. Warrior families transmitted histories of Sumitomo in order to prove their family's bona fides as warriors. By the fifteenth century, the Kōno, a warrior provincial governor family of Shikoku, used the tale of Sumitomo to reinforce the notion that they should control pirates and sea lords. Their version of the story details how the Kōno helped to defeat Sumitomo by incorporating into their band "an incredibly strong man named Murakami" who "in sea battles . . . was worth a thousand men."[107]

With the establishment of Japan's first warrior government, the Kamakura bakufu (ca. 1183–1333), and the ascendancy of the Hōjō regents, warriors took charge of defining and suppressing piracy. With its legitimacy tied to keeping peace in the archipelago, Kamakura lawmakers modified Ritsuryō definitions and focused on specific spaces rife with the potential for illicit violence.[108] Kamakura identified both seas and mountains as two environments particularly problematic in that regard, and often conjoined sea bandits (i.e., pirates, *kaizoku*) with mountain bandits (*sanzoku*). One article of a collection of judicial decisions from 1232, the Jōei Formulary, restricts the ability of provincial constables to raise forces except in "cases like rebellion, murder . . . night attacks, armed robbery, mountain banditry, and piracy."[109] For much of the thirteenth century, strategies implemented by the Kamakura bakufu kept the seas relatively secure. The bakufu inserted warrior stewards (*jitō*) into many of Japan's estates and established new provincial-level constabularies (*shugo*).[110] In order to secure the littoral, Kamakura counted on retainers (*gokenin*) drawn from sea-specialist families such as the Kutsuna and Matsura.[111] Sponsorship of such figures may have led to the popular recognition that seafarers labeled pirates could also bear titles and hold official positions, or that they might use such titles to add an aura of re-

106. "Fujiwara no Sumitomo kaizoku ni yorite korosaretaru koto," pp. 366–67.
107. *Yoshōki Jōzōinbon*, p. 16. For more on the appropriation of the Sumitomo story, see Matsubara Hironobu, *Fujiwara no Sumitomo* (Yoshikawa Kōbunkan, 1999), ch. 10.
108. Kasamatsu Hiroshi, "Youchi," in *Chūsei no tsumi to batsu*, edited by Amino Yoshihiko et al. (Tokyo Daigaku Shuppankai, 1983), p. 98.
109. *Goseibai shikimoku*, Article 3, "Shokoku no shugonin bugyō no koto," in *Chūsei hōsei shiryōshū*, vol. 1: *Kamakura bakufu hō*, edited by Satō Shin'ichi et al. (Iwanami Shoten, 1955), pp. 4–5.
110. Amino Yoshihiko, *Akutō to kaizoku: Nihon chūsei no shakai to seiji* (Hōsei Daigaku Shuppankyoku, 1995), pp. 246–72.
111. For the Kutsuna, see Yamauchi Yuzuru, *Chūsei Setonaikai chiikishi no kenkyū* (Hōsei Daigaku Shuppankyoku, 1998), pp. 94–99; for the Matsura, see Hyungsub Moon, "The Matsura Pirate-Warriors of Northwestern Kyushu in the Kamakura Age," in *Currents in Medieval Japanese History: Essays in Honor of Jeffrey P. Mass* (Los Angeles: Figueroa Press, 2009), pp. 363–99.

spectability to their actions. The eponymous subject of an early thirteenth-century didactic tale, "How a Pirate Converted and Became a Priest," is a *kaizoku* named Awaji no Rokurō, the "Imperial Punitive Agent."[112]

In the late Kamakura and Muromachi periods, vocabularies of licit and illicit violence became ambiguous, setting the stage for an equation of pirates with nonstate betweenness. The balances of power among the various blocs of warrior, court, and religious power tottered. Those with sufficient patronage or the military strength to enforce their will created justice, defined the meaning of licit and illicit, and used the rhetoric of defense to add justification for their cause, especially in local regions outside the grasp of shogunal or other central authorities.[113] These changes can be marked by tracing the evolution of the term "pirate," which more and more enhanced images of the sea and sea people as existing beyond the reach of the state and civilization.

By the late thirteenth century, the word *kaizoku* had become subsumed in a larger category of "outlawry," that of "evil bands" (*akutō*). Producers, purveyors, and fighters based in mountains and seas, people Amino Yoshihiko called "nonagriculturalists," appeared more and more in complaints as outlaws operating outside the purview of the traditional medieval institutional authorities.[114] Scholars commonly identify the rising tides of commercialization, disputes over provincial estates, dissatisfaction with the Kamakura bakufu, assertion of local control, and an increased recourse to violence as causes for the rise of "evil bands."[115] Others urge us to consider the word's use as a "rhetorical strategy designed to provoke a certain response from the recipients of complaints and suits."[116]

---

112. "Kaizoku no hosshin shukke no koto"; "How a Pirate Was Converted and Became a Priest," pp. 333–36.
113. As Thomas Conlan explains, terminology for criminal violence such as committing an outrage (*rōzeki*) overlapped with that for fighting a battle (*kassen*). The new Muromachi bakufu sanctioned offensive warfare (*kōsen*) if proved justifiable. Such justification might be framed in the discourse of righteous defense—fighting defensive warfare (*bōsen*) against an "unjust aggressor" (Thomas D. Conlan, *State of War: The Violent Order of Fourteenth-Century Japan*, Michigan Monograph Series in Japanese Studies, no. 46 (Ann Arbor: Center for Japanese Studies, The University of Michigan, 2003), pp. 213–19.
114. Amino Yoshihiko, *Nihon chūsei no hinōgyōmin to tennō*, p. 27; Amino, *Akutō to kaizoku*, pp. 365–66.
115. Lorraine F. Harrington, "Social Control and the Significance of Akutō," in *Court and Bakufu in Japan: Essays in Kamakura History*, edited by Jeffrey P. Mass (Stanford, Calif.: Stanford University Press, 1982), pp. 221–50; Jeffrey P. Mass, "Of Hierarchy and Authority at the End of Kamakura," in *The Origins of Japan's Medieval World: Courtiers, Clerics, Warriors, and Peasants in the Fourteenth Century*, edited by Jeffrey P. Mass (Stanford, Calif.: Stanford University Press, 1997), p. 31; Arai Takashige, *Akutō no seiki* (Yoshikawa Kōbunkan, 1997).
116. Morton Oxenboell, "Images of Akutō," *Monumenta Nipponica* 60.2 (2006): 259.

An oft-cited fourteenth-century account entitled *Mineaiki* exemplifies the ties between the new languages and constructions of violence of the fourteenth century and the contextualization of pirates within the category of evil bands. The anonymous monk who authored the account castigates evil bands—inclusive of pirates—for their violence, which had grown worse over time, causing the loss of estate revenue and rising political chaos: "In the Shōan and Kengen periods [1299–1303], outlaws filled people's gazes and overflowed their ears with the spectacles and sounds of depredations: various places ravaged, harbors assaulted by pirates [*kaizoku*], thieving, robbery, mountain banditry, and people driven from their homes without respite. . . . Since the Shōchū and Karyaku reign eras [1324–29], their behavior has transcended that of previous years, shocking the eyes and ears of the world."[117]

Mineaiki's author encodes pirates and evil bands—and by extension the regions from which they emerged—as Other. He ties them to the threat of violence emerging from peripheral, "nonagricultural"[118] regions like mountains and the coasts. According to *Mineaiki*, *akutō* did not dedicate themselves to the horseback archery or infantry skills of Kamakura samurai and their followers; they specialized in the forms of violence necessary for their home environments, became experts in siege warfare, and manufactured shields by sewing animal skins.[119] The anonymous author also used religious iconography to paint "evil bands" as "alien, inhuman beings." "They attire themselves in persimmon-colored cloth and women's hats. They wear neither *eboshi* nor *hakama*."[120]

The account shows shifting representations of "pirates" and other "evil bands." Beginning as those who charged protection monies to guide people over mountain passes (or through sea channels), they found employment both in self-aggrandizing missions, during which they used violent force to establish their own dominion, and as mercenary bands, who contracted out to feuding centers of power: "Some ten to twenty of them might fortify themselves in a castle, joining the resident forces as mercenaries. Or they might switch sides and let in the enemy. They do not forge lasting agreements. . . . They are found not only on battlefields, but also—claiming to be the allies of local lords—in holdings that they occupy and from which

---

117. *Mineaiki*, in *Hyōgo-ken shi, shiryō-hen chūsei*, vol. 4 (Kōbe-shi: Hyōgo-ken, 1989), pp. 64–65.
118. For *akutō* as nonagriculturalists, see Amino, *Akutō to kaizoku*, pp. 365–66.
119. *Mineaiki*, p. 65.
120. Ibid., p. 64. According to Amino Yoshihiko, the phrase *irui igyō* shifted its meaning in the late medieval period from a positively perceived "holiness" to a negatively perceived "inhumanity," possibly because outlaws and other violent bands appropriated the symbolic markers of holiness—especially clothes—to demonstrate their power. See Amino Yoshihiko, *Igyō no ōken* (Heibonsha, 1986), pp. 96–111.

they plunder hither and yon. Once they collected gratuities for what they called 'mountain crossing.' In these latter days, they call their extortions 'contracts.'"[121] The author also blames the Kamakura bakufu for failing to suppress outlawry and actually causing discontent by not living up to an ideal of virtuous government. In place of rule by the bakufu, local inhabitants joined with evil bands and pirates. *Mineaiki* sees *akutō*—including pirates—as bands that both helped to tear down old authorities and that created new centers of power like sea-lord domains: "Despite authorization for the provincial constabulary [*shugo*] to eradicate them, day after day, their numbers have multiplied. . . . Even the provincial constables are afraid of their authority, and the warriors sent to hunt them down return in fear. . . . Shogunal orders for punishment bear no fruit. The bakufu's communiqués recruit and recruit, casting nets that come up empty. As a result, the majority of the people in the provinces are the allies of the evil bands. . . . It is all because the warriors have lost the way of virtuous governance."[122]

The perception that traditional authorities such as warrior patrons bore some of the responsibility meant that accusations and evidence of piracy no longer sufficed to condemn someone, as they had in earlier periods. Instead, patronage connections came to supersede particular labels when assigning guilt. For example, in 1320, monks belonging to the temple complex on Mt. Kōya, Kongōbuji, submitted a complaint to the Kamakura bakufu that agents of the provincial constable of Bingo Province had invaded the important Inland Sea port of Onomichi. Onomichi occupied part of an estate governed by Kongōbuji, which had been "declared out of bounds for warriors" by the Kamakura shogunate. Kongōbuji identifies the provincial constable's agents as "evildoers" and "pirates."

> As the location of the estate's storehouses and harbor, Onomichi is a port for ships. As a result of the many ships that dock here, residents have prospered. For that reason, the provincial constable Nagai Sadashige assiduously made plans to invade and capture it when he had the opportunity. Thus, it came to pass that on the fifth day of the twelfth month of last year [1319], he sent in his deputy . . . and some hundred other evildoers [*akutō*]. They forced their way into the harbor and committed various evil acts, such as murder, cutting people down, arson, and driving people away. They burnt down a thousand buildings, including several shrine and temple halls, offices, and people's homes. Their evil acts transcend the great crimes of mountain bandits and pirates. . . . They readied several tens of

121. *Mineaiki*, p. 64-65.
122. Ibid.

large ships and loaded onto them objects belonging to religious centers and residents.[123]

The Kongōbuji monks contended that, under the guise of hunting pirates, the constable's forces became pirates themselves: "Claiming to be after notorious pirates [akutō] of this harbor, they captured the new managerial agents without investigation. . . . Although notorious pirates of the west, Ishi Hyōe nyūdō, Shinkaku Kō'ō taifu, Yoshimura Magojirō Sukeyuki, and others, are resident here, it is the provincial constable's agent here . . . who supports these bandits."[124]

As patronage loci multiplied, the Kamakura bakufu collapsed, and successive regimes—including the Muromachi bakufu (ca. 1336–1573)—failed to solve incidents like that of Onomichi in 1320. No government could enforce a position as universal arbiter of sanctioned violence in the archipelago, and meanings attached to piracy and other forms of violence multiplied. Even after the establishment of the Muromachi bakufu, the strife of the Northern and Southern Court conflicts, internecine provincial feuds, and succession struggles meant that viable, alternative sources of legitimization for the exercise of violence persistently made themselves available to seafarers. The perception that pirates enjoyed elite patronage permeated late medieval Japanese society to such an extent that, by the fifteenth century, one band of Inland Sea seafarers could use the threat of a patron to bluff one island's residents into acceding to their control. Their actions closely resembled those described in the aforementioned *Mineaiki* account. The nominal lord of the island complained: "pirates [kaizoku] calling themselves retainers have invaded and extorted in my holdings."[125] The establishment of longstanding connections between pirates and patrons cast shadows of doubt on practices of military sponsorship, including the system by which the Ashikaga recruited local warriors into their personal shogunal guards.[126]

The Muromachi bakufu's own laws encouraged subjective interpretations of violence, allowing "the legitimacy of violence" when framed as "defensive warfare."[127] Shifts and multiplications of meaning along similar lines abounded for words relating to violence in the maritime world. The concept of "protection" (keigo), underwent particularly extensive changes in usage. The term originally signified a variety of legitimate, sanctioned, and even

123. *Kongōbuji monjo*, vol. 2, doc. 17, Gen'ō 2 (1320) 8th month, *Kōya-san monjo*, vol. 2 (Kyoto: Kōya-san Monjo Kankōkai, 1937).
124. Ibid. For more on this incident, see Amino, *Akutō to kaizoku*, pp. 258–59.
125. EK doc. 1128, Ōei 7 (1400) 11.19.
126. NET pp. 413–14, doc. 291:3, Kanshō 3 (1462) 5.17.
127. Conlan, *State of War*, p. 216.

meritorious acts: guard service in Kyushu, a vigil before a temple, and the suppression of pirates.[128] By the sixteenth century, the term could be used to designate the inherently illicit violence of enemies[129] as well as the variety of violent services—including protection business—engaged in by sea lords.[130]

Late medieval shifts in the meaning of *keigo* corresponded to changes in the meanings attached to the Japanese term for "pirate" (*kaizoku*) itself. *Kaizoku* came to reference activities both licit and illicit, sponsored as well as unsponsored. In other words, in the late medieval period, the term *kaizoku* and affiliated words heightened and replicated the ambivalent, dual expectations of service and terror held by land-based elites towards the sea and seafarers. For example, during the fifteenth century, the Muromachi shogunate sponsored seafarers they labeled "pirates" (*kaizoku*) to protect their specially licensed trading vessels sailing to and from Ming China.[131] But even shogun-sanctioned piratical violence instilled fear. At the height of his power, having just ended the Northern and Southern Court conflict, Ashikaga Yoshimitsu traveled to western Japan in order to impress the great families there with his authority. Yet even Yoshimitsu relied on pirates to perform maritime protection. This dependence on pirates made one narrator apprehensive: "Pirates [*kaizoku*] in a line of warships protect the shogunal ship. What was there to be afraid of? And yet, despite the fact that the shogun's authority had grown to overawe the four seas, it seemed everyone was tremulous."[132]

Such ambivalence towards pirates continued through the sixteenth century, as is evidenced by the seemingly contradictory behavior of regional warlords (daimyo) who replaced the shogun as executive authorities in many parts of Japan. Many of these figures employed the term *kaizoku* to identify those seafarers they sponsored. In 1571, a powerful eastern warlord, Takeda Shingen (1521–73), ordered a subordinate to recruit "pirates [*kaizoku*]" from Ise Province.[133] However, at the same time, many of these same daimyo continued to outlaw piracy. They drew from a variety of older sources in the drafting of law codes, including classical Chinese and Ritsuryō law, the Kamakura Jōei Formulary and addenda, and medieval league contract law.

128. For *keigo* and the suppression of pirates, see EK doc. 406, Tokuji 2 (1307) 3.25.
129. EK doc. 1417, Kanshō 6? (1465) 9.3.
130. See chapters 3 and 4.
131. See, for example, *Mansai jugō nikki*, vol. 2, p. 547, Eikyō 6 (1434), 1.20; Tenyo Seikei, *Boshi nyūminki*, in NMKBS, p. 203.
132. *Rokuon'in saigoku gekōki*, in Shinjō Tsunezō, ed., *Shintō taikei bungaku hen,* vol. 5: *Sankeiki* (Shintō Taikei Hensankai, 1984), pp. 153–54.
133. *Mie-ken shi shiryō-hen kinsei,* vol. 1 (Tsu-shi: Mie-ken, 1993), p. 141, doc. 169, Genki 2 (1571) 11.20.

In these codes, regional warlords sought to restrict the free use of violence to their command.[134] Many condemned piracy as among the most serious violent crimes. For example, another eastern warlord house, the Date, replicated the Kamakura bakufu's construction of criminal piracy in their house code *Jinkaishū* by placing it in a category with covert theft, violent theft, and mountain banditry.[135]

The types of services pirates performed for sponsors may have heightened warlords' level of discomfort with them. Fujiki Hisashi includes pirates (*kaizoku*) in his analysis of "mercenary irregulars" (*zōhyō*), villagers who left their homes to sell their services to sponsors in order to make a living in war-performing services that daimyo found distasteful: arson, slave taking, rapine, and looting.[136] Slave taking seems to have inspired particularly negative connotations. Some Japanese believed that rules governing purity and impurity rendered slaves, slave takers, and slave traders—including pirates—as "outcastes."[137]

EFFECTS OF INCREASED MARITIME EXCHANGE

The increased dependence by land-based elites on seafarers they knew as "pirates" in the late medieval period coincided with increased levels of seaborne exchange among the countries of East Asia. Some of this domestic and international exchange occurred as a result of the autonomous control of shipping networks established by sea lords. This rise in international interaction and dependence on seafarers, including sea-lord bands, inspired new worldviews. New models of regional interaction coexisted with and in some cases replaced older ways of seeing the sea. In the new worldviews, mariners, including pirates, came to be seen as the means by which Japanese participated in wider Eurasian trading networks; seafarers symbolized the new commercial shipping connections linking the archipelago together and joining Japan to the world.[138]

134. Kobayashi Hiroshi, "Domain Laws (*Bunkoku-hō*) in the Sengoku Period: With Special Emphasis on the Date House Code, the *Jinkaishū*." *Acta Asiatica* 35 (1978): 39; Katsumata Shizuo, "The Development of Sengoku Law," with Martin Collcutt, in *Japan Before Tokugawa: Political Consolidation and Economic Growth, 1500 to 1650*, edited by John W. Hall et al. (Princeton, N.J.: Princeton University Press, 1981), pp. 103–4.

135. *Jinkaishū*, in *Chūsei hōsei shiryōshū*, vol. 3, *Buke kahō* 1, p. 146, no. 41 "Settō, gōtō, kaizoku, yamaotoshi no koto," Tenbun 5 (1535) 4.14.

136. Fujiki Hisashi, *Zōhyōtachi no senjō: chūsei no yōhei to doreigari* (Asahi Shinbunsha, 1995).

137. Michele Marra, *Representations of Power: The Literary Politics of Medieval Japan* (Honolulu: University of Hawai'i Press, 1993), pp. 78–82.

138. Murai, *Ajia no naka no chūsei Nihon*, pp. 125–31.

Increased maritime connectivity reinforced stylings in classical literary travelogues that depicted sea voyages as linear itineraries from port to port. It has been suggested that representations of sea routes hugging the coastline might be attempts by land-based elites to "subdue the sea's uncontrollable power."[139] However, the degree of land-based fear of the sea and dependence on seafarers in the premodern period meant that coastal itineraries probably reflected the shipping practices dictated by seafarers as well as the imaginations of land-based elites. Travelers experienced the inability of late medieval Japanese ships to tack into the wind (the structure of their sails meant that they always had to wait for a tailwind or row). Ships generally tramped from one port on to the next during the day, spending the night safely anchored in a harbor. Stopping points varied from journey to journey depending on the vagaries of wind and travel plans, but the routes consistently followed the coastlines.[140]

From the fourteenth century, increased movements of commercial commodities and passengers further encouraged the conceptualization of interconnected sea space in Japan. One late medieval compendium of common shipping bylaws makes claims to universality in Japan by listing signatories from the ports of Hyōgo, Urado in Tosa, and Bōnotsu in Satsuma,[141] leaving unstated but understood that the laws were applicable along the maritime networks connecting the three ports. A graphic representation of Japan as a collection of islands linked by coastal shipping corridors can be found in a Korean copy of a late thirteenth-, early fourteenth-century Japanese map, which a Japanese envoy presented to the Korean court. Figure 6 details the sea lanes binding western Japan together.[142]

Visions of Japan as an archipelago connected by commercial shipping lanes coexisted and competed with earlier cosmological models. Crucial interstices of these maritime networks were not only Buddhist "goblins' eyes" of the archipelago, but also major entrepôts. Ise Bay linked the Seto Inland Sea to eastern Japan; Tsuruga Bay held important ports in the Japan Sea network that tied Japan to Korea; Lake Biwa contained important shipping networks in its own right and connected the capital to the Japan Sea coast.

139. Yonemoto, "Maps and Metaphors," p. 174.

140. Yamauchi Yuzuru, *Chūsei Setonaikai no tabibitotachi* (Yoshikawa Kōbunkan, 2004), pp. 161–69; Ki, *Tosa nikki*, p. 47; Okiura, *Setouchi no minzokushi*, p. 120.

141. *Kaisen shikimoku*, in *Kaiji shiryō sōsho*, vol. 1, edited by Sumita Masa'ichi (Genshōdō, 1929), p. 6.

142. Shin Sukchu, *Haedong chegukki* (*Kaitō shokokuki: Chōsenjin no mita chūsei no Nihon to Ryūkyū*), edited by Tanaka Takeo (Iwanami Shoten, 1991). The origin of the *Haedong chegukki* maps is a matter of some debate. See Ōji, *Echizu no sekaizō*, pp. 84–105; Kenneth R. Robinson, "The *Haedong chegukki* (1471) and Korean-Ryūkyūan Relations, 1389-1471: Part 1," *Acta Koreana* 3 (2000): 94.

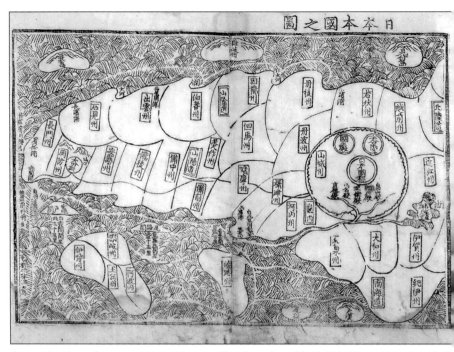

Figure 6. Map of western Japan from the *Haedong chegukki* (1471). Photo courtesy of the Historiographical Institute, University of Tokyo (Tokyo Daigaku Shiryōhensanjo), and used with their permission.

At the same time however, increased interaction brought increased knowledge of the wider maritime world, which both amplified older ideas about the sea and sea people and inspired new assessments. Land-based authorities increasingly came to the conclusion that the late medieval maritime world had become nonstate space that lay in the hands of pirates. Across the late medieval period, foreign governments complained about Japanese pirate raids. In response, Japanese authorities revived ancient conceptions derived from China that characterized pirates (and their mountain-bandit brethren) as a consequence of political disorder and fused them with accusations painting Japanese pirates as a scourge of the East Asian littoral. The *Chronicle of Great Peace* (*Taiheiki*), a late medieval war tale recounting the 1336–92 wars between the Northern and Southern Courts, condemned the conflict for enabling piracy to spread over sea lanes at home and abroad. They borrowed the poetic allusion of white waves for pirates in order to evoke these sentiments: "On the seas, pirates [*kaizoku*] abounded; it was impossible to avoid disasters stemming from *the white waves*. Lustful, wild outlaws gathered together, and these pirates pillaged many harbors and islands

On the post roads, post-station chiefs disappeared; barrier wardens rotated out. At last, these pirates assembled several thousand ships and assaulted the ports and anchorages of Yuan China and Koryŏ Korea. They stole treasures from [the port cities] Mingzhou and Fuzhou and burned offices and temples to the ground."[143]

Increased connectivity renewed fears of piracy as inevitable and unstoppable. Like estate proprietors, commercial shipping organizations treated pirates like naturally occurring phenomena. The aforementioned compendium of regulations for shipping merchants, *Kaisen shikimoku*, treats pirate attacks as acts of nature for which there is no defense. One can only make preparations to respond afterwards. So shipping organizations across Japan supposedly placed ships on standby in each other's regions to help those who fell afoul of pirates: "Regarding boat thieves and being taken by pirates. Northern provincial offices have placed boats in the west, and western provinces have placed boats in the north. Although these boats can be bought, they should not be used for commercial shipping."[144] There is no discussion of fighting off the pirates or that pirates might not strike, only the dour premonition that merchant ships would likely encounter pirates and that provisions had to be made for the aftermath.

Increases in foreign contacts also heightened preexisting perceptions of sea people and pirates as alien, even foreign, Others. A Zen monk and diarist, Kikō Daishuku (1421–87), recorded a conversation he had had with an elderly Chinese man about similarities among Japanese and Chinese populations of a subset of sea people Daishuku called "boat people": "In Kyushu there are many things more or less as they are in China. In China, boat people [*funabito*] live, ride, and beg for food on broken-down boats. They survive by receiving things from people on boats passing to and fro. . . . The Kyushu [boat] people spend their whole lives aboard ship, where many live with wives and children."[145] Late medieval authorities recognized a potential for piracy in this "boat people" population. In a letter to the Korean court in 1395, Imagawa Ryōshun bragged of suppressing "pirates [*kaichū kōzoku*] who live in their ships, follow the wind, and have no set abode."[146] Some Japanese equated such boat-people pirates with foreignness directly, suggesting that they possessed a culture different from normal Japanese. Similar to the seventh-century *Nan shi* description of sea people, a Japanese informer's report to the Korean court from 1510 uses descriptions of hair,

143. *Taiheiki*, NKBT 36, edited by Gotō Tanji et al., p. 450; Nakamura Hidetaka, *Nissen kankeishi* (Yoshikawa Kōbunkan, 1973), vol. 1, p. 248 (emphasis mine).
144. *Kaisen shikimoku*, p. 4.
145. Kikō Daishuku, *Shoken nichiroku*, Bunmei 18 (1486) 3.20, in NMKBS, 281–82.
146. CWS, *Taesong sillok*, vol. 8, pp. 2a-b, Taesong 4 (1395) 7.10; Saeki, "Kaizoku-ron," p. 46.

skin color, language, clothing, and other cultural markers to identify how *kaizoku* are different. But the informer's report also illustrates an awareness of the range of littoral livelihoods engaged in by littoral inhabitants: "They normally sail and raid with women and children in their ships. Their faces are tanned, their hair bleached. Their language and clothes differ from those of ordinary Japanese. They are adept at archery and skilled at wielding swords. They dive deep into the ocean and drill holes in ships."[147]

At the same time, in the late medieval period, land-based delegation to and dependence on nonstate seafarers—especially sea-lord bands—peaked. It became commonly perceived that without the assistance of pirates, safe passage of goods and passengers was difficult. Japanese came to commonly equate pirates and the toll barriers at which they sold and performed protection with sea travel in general. The centrality of protection practice to sixteenth-century sea lords can be seen in the ascription of the title "Toll-barrier Captain" to a sea lord named Ugashima who reputedly led a fleet of "fifteen pirate ships [*zokusen*]" in the 1550s.[148]

These perceptions amplified older images of travelers dependent on sea people and pirates as inevitable as natural disasters. Late medieval travelers willingly relinquished all responsibility for dealing with pirates to shipmasters, as if safety resided only in the capabilities of the captain and crew. The travelogue of the sixteenth-century daimyo scion Shimazu Iehisa (1547–87) relates that he encountered pirate-operated toll barriers at several Inland Sea ports. In all cases Iehisa noted that it was the responsibility of the shipmaster to handle such affairs.[149] Perceiving pirates as part of the seascape allowed landed elites to leave piratical matters to experts, perpetuating older ideas of sea people as service providers. Sea-lord bands like the Noshima Murakami also profited from such dependence, which facilitated acceptance of their protection businesses and enhanced their reputations. As will be seen, popular perceptions of pirates as agents indispensable for safe passage persisted through the sixteenth century and impeded Hideyoshi's pacification of the realm.

CONCLUSION

The category of "pirate" in premodern Japan was neither an objective legal definition, nor reflective of seafarers' identity. Instead, it was a subjective

---

147. CWS, *Chungjong sillok*, vol. 12, p. 12b, Chungjong 5 (1510) 8.24.
148. Bairin Shuryū, *Bairin Shuryū Suō gekō nikki*, in YK, vol. 1, p. 471, Tenbun 20 (1551) 4.1.
149. Shimazu Iehisa, *Chūsho Iehisa-kō Gojōkyō nikki*, in *Shintō taikei bungaku-hen*, vol. 5: *Sankeiki*, edited by Shinjō Tsunezō (Shintō Taikei Hensankai, 1984), p. 290; Yamauchi, *Setonaikai no*

representation of elites' perceptions of control over the sea. It can thus be read as a bellwether for how the attitudes of land-based elites toward the sea and seafarers changed over time. The history of the word's usage provides a key to reading seascapes, representations of the sea and its inhabitants, the only way of understanding how late medieval Japanese perceived the maritime environment. Even though elites encoded seascapes with land-centered ideological markers, these representations reveal overlapping and competing influences. Terracentrism tethered the sea and sea people to a continuum of representations stretching between fear and a desire to incorporate the sea and to harness its bounty. Land centeredness drew on a wide variety of sources, including ancient myths, Chinese philosophies, institutional cultures, court aesthetics, and Esoteric Buddhism. This continuum mixed and coexisted with impressions left by the work-based cultures of seafarers on the psyches of elite writers. Although they recognized sea people as Other, they also stood in awe of their uncanny abilities. Over time, the movements of ships and people on the sea etched images of connectivity that competed with inscriptions of sea as alteric and apart.

Each period's new representations did not erase earlier images in the collective imagination. Instead, new representations of the sea overlaid and interacted with previous ones, juxtaposing conflicting precedents. It may be that, by the late medieval period, the weight of such juxtapositions softened elite forms of representation. Recognizing the prestige attached to written, institutional discourse, local littoral magnates may have perceived sufficient flexibility in these written forms to fit their needs for tools for self-representation, communication, and dominion, further loosening the bounds of acceptable representation in elite discourse. Seascapes depicting the perspectives of seafarers thus become especially visible in the late medieval period, when perceptions of the sea as nonstate space, the dependence of land-based elites on autonomous seafaring bands, and the autonomy of sea lords all reached their apex. By this period, any attempt at institutional incorporation of the sea had to rely on autonomous maritime organizations such as those that land-based peoples denoted "pirates."

In the next chapter I discuss some of the first stirrings of maritime autonomy, of sea-based deployment of institutional language of patronage and lordship, and of concomitant land-based recognition of that autonomy that occurred in the context of maritime estates. Land-based elites increasingly turned to local elites to manage and protect those littoral holdings, even while denoting them as "pirates."

---

tabibitotachi, pp. 124–125. The ports were Naoshima in Sanuki, Hibinoseki in Bizen, and Ushimado in Bizen.

CHAPTER 2

Pirates and Purveyors: Commerce, Lordship, and Maritime Estates in Late Medieval Japan

In the Seto Inland Sea region during the fourteenth and fifteenth centuries, local littoral magnates, who often appear in the sources labeled as pirates (*kaizoku*) transformed themselves into sea lords. These figures expanded out from bases on tiny islands and coastal communities that occupied strategic positions in chokepoints along the sea lanes. Sea lords established domains consisting of maritime networks of production, distribution, exchange, and protection. They became entrepreneurs who independently, and often with the blessings of central and provincial authorities who became their patrons, invested resources into developing enterprises focused on exploiting connections between commerce and violence. In so doing, they played integral roles in two of the important historical processes of late medieval Japan: the growth of local lordship and commercialization.

Much of the local lordship and commerce at sea, as on land, emerged from territories known as estates (*shōen*), collections of holdings governed by elites through an elaborate system of titles to privileges and responsibilities known as *shiki*. Overly focused on land, cities, and land tenure as the keys to political power and commercial growth, earlier scholars disregarded littoral estates as possessing too little arable to support lordship or to spark significant commercial growth.[1] However, this chapter traces the origins of sea-lord domains, sea tenure practices, and maritime commercial networks to the interactions between seafarers labeled "pirates" and maritime *shōen* in the fourteenth and fifteenth centuries.

The histories of interaction between seafarers and estates reveal a trend in which the scope of commercialization increased as sea-lord authority did. In the late thirteenth and early fourteenth centuries, some local maritime magnates on the receiving end of the label "pirate" hired themselves out as mercenary guards and estate managers. They adapted estate-based methods of sea tenure, overseeing littoral estate residents and regulating access to

1. Watanabe Norifumi argued that Yugeshima contained insufficient arable for lordship in "Chūsei ni okeru naikai tōsho no seikatsu: Iyo no kuni Yugeshima o chūshin toshite," in *Setonaikai chiiki no shakaishiteki kenkyū*, edited by Uozumi Sōgorō (Kyoto: Yanagihara Shoten, 1952), pp. 81–108. See also the critique by Amino Yoshihiko in *Chūsei Tōji to Tōjiryō shōen* (Tokyo Daigaku Shuppankai, 1978), pp. 329–30.

resources.[2] They used the *shiki* system to legitimize their growing influence over estate residents, maritime industries, and local exchange networks. As they did so, these magnates made themselves invaluable to estate residents and proprietors, the administrators who held ultimate authority over estates. For residents, magnates provided access to routes of social mobility and new local networks of commercial exchange. For proprietors, local littoral elites offered expertise in settling disputes (especially with warrior stewards—*jitō*—appointed by the Kamakura bakufu), securing the integrity of the estate, and ensuring the safety of rent shipments.

Gradually these local littoral magnates became sea lords. They displaced traditional estate-proprietor vectors of exchange, turned estates into bases for services both violent and peaceful that they sold to sponsors in order to legitimize their growing maritime dominion, and represented themselves in ways that land-based elites recognized as characteristic of lordship. Early sea-lord domains tended to be limited in scale (generally consisting of intra-regional exchange networks), in terms of generational continuity, and in the number of patrons (generally limited to estate proprietors).

By the mid fifteenth century, more and more sea lords developed transgenerational control over domains. They fought with other local maritime magnates, using sea-based toll barriers to protect their shipping and to intercept the shipping of competitors. At the same time, just as the estate system allowed for compound, shared proprietorship, on occasion sea lords made agreements and shared as well as competed for control over maritime space and resources. Instead of estate proprietors, sponsorship increasingly meant dealing with officials of the Muromachi shogunate and warrior provincial governors (*shugo*), many of whom sought to increase their own power and to become regional warlords (daimyo). Sea lords competed to parlay mercenary naval and estate managerial services among these several sponsors into legitimacy for dominion over former estates. They helped transform former estates into transregional centers of maritime production and commercial shipping. By the fifteenth century, the Inland Sea commercial shipping economy had developed to the point that annually thousands of vessels carried commercial cargoes back and forth across the length of the Seto-naikai. As the real powers on many littoral estates and shipping centers, sea lords managed, promoted, developed, and protected much of this shipping.

Sea lords proved adept at understanding and exploiting the confluence of political decentralization, military strife, and commercial growth in late

2. See introduction and Arne Kalland, *Fishing Villages in Tokugawa Japan* (Honolulu: University of Hawai'i Press, 1995), pp. 2–7.

medieval Japan. In the late medieval period, as potential sponsors proliferated, no central authority proved capable of enforcing a decision on whether a particular act of violence was licit or not. In the context of late medieval estates, the label of pirate lost any essential meaning as a criminal category and became subject to the power of patronage and military muscle. Sea lords positioned themselves on the sea lanes between land-based centers of legitimacy as mercenaries. Many of the attempts by local littoral elites to transform themselves into sea lords included threats of and promises of protection from violence. They took advantage of land-based authorities' inability to project power at sea in the late medieval period. In order to explain the emergence of sea lords and the integral role they played in the commercialization of the littoral, this chapter will focus on the history of interaction between local maritime magnates and the few well-documented littoral estates in the fourteenth and fifteenth centuries—particularly the island estate of Yugeshima.

YUGESHIMA AND MARITIME ESTATES

The history of Yugeshima shows that geography matters. Commerce and lordship developed differently at sea than on land. Although Yugeshima was a poor candidate for a regime based on land tenure, sea lords found it ideal. Yugeshima is a small, kidney-shaped island measuring around 8.8 square kilometers in area and some 20 kilometers in circumference.[3] It lies at the northeastern end of an island chain rich in chokepoints, harbors, and shipping lanes that spans the Inland Sea between Onomichi in the north and Imabari in the south (see figure 7). Its geography resembles that of many other Inland Sea islands. Flat arable land is scarce on Yugeshima. The island consists of two mountainous regions connected by a small patch of level lowland in the center and ringed by flat beaches (see figure 8). So, its residents sought livelihoods from the sea.

Yugeshima is unusual because of its large number of surviving documents (a product of its history as an estate belonging to Tōji). In fact, estates dedicated to maritime production abounded in Japan. As a result of the Ritsuryō reforms of the seventh century, the state nominally had administrative control over all land in Japan. However, in the Nara period (ca. 710–84), the imperial court authorized mechanisms for privatizing land

---

3. Yamauchi Yuzuru, *Yugeshima no shō no rekishi* (Yugeshima-chō, Ehime-ken: Yugeshima-chō, 1985), p. 1.

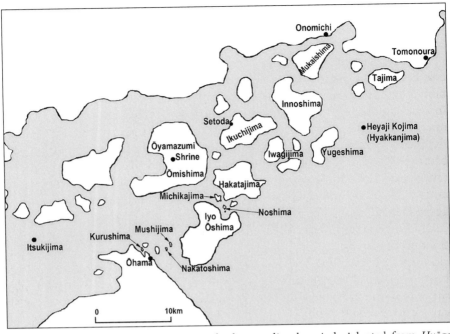

Figure 7. Central Inland Sea region in the late medieval period. Adapted from *Hyōgo Kitazeki irifune nōchō*, edited by Hayashiya Tatsusaburō (Chūō Kōron Bijutsu Shuppan, 1981), pp. 260–61.

Figure 8. The island of Yugeshima. Photo by the author.

ownership (i.e., estates), often in order to promote land reclamation efforts and to help religious institutions.[4] At that time, powerful Buddhist temples like Hōryūji and Tōdaiji established *shōen* on islands in the Inland Sea.[5]

By the tenth century, central authorities such as the retired emperor's court, religious institutions, and aristocratic families avidly worked to establish head proprietary control over privatized parcels of sea as well as land in order to secure specific resources. They settled bands of roving purveyors on holdings to produce and carry exclusively for them.[6] Local magnates fed these ambitions by commending administrative control over territory to central authorities in exchange for protection from state regulation and entry, inclusive of state taxation. In return for the protections that these central authorities could guarantee as head proprietors, local lords and residents agreed to pay a portion of their harvest to the head proprietors. In the so-called estate system,[7] every position in the estate hierarchy accrued institutional title (*shiki*) to a portion of the harvest from the particular estate, including workers and residents as well as managers, sub-proprietors, and the head proprietor. These shares in the estate were movable and alienable. The *shiki* mechanism became an important engine of medieval Japanese political economy. Even regions still subject to state tax came to be administered in some ways indistinguishable from estates.

Yugeshima first appears in records from 1135 that indicate that the retired emperor's court may have first held head proprietorship over the island. In 1239, the imperial princess Sen'yōmon'in (1181–1252), who had inherited the estate from her father Go-Shirakawa (1127–92), donated the estate to Tōji.[8] Indicative of the degree to which Japanese attempted to territorialize the seas with estates, Sen'yōmon'in also held proprietary title to several estates near Yugeshima: Aio Futajima in Suō, Innoshima in Bingo Province, Kitanoshō on Ikuchijima in Aki Province, and Kutsuna and Ōmishima in

4. Elizabeth Sato, "The Early Development of the Shōen," in *Medieval Japan: Essays in Institutional History*, edited by John W. Hall et al. (Stanford: Stanford University Press, 1974), pp. 91–108.
5. Yamauchi, *Yugeshima no shō no rekishi*, p. 11.
6. Amino Yoshihiko, *Nihon chūsei no hinōgyōmin to tennō* (Iwanami Shoten, 1984), pp. 240–60.
7. For ways of thinking of medieval estates as a system, see Thomas Keirstead, *The Geography of Power in Medieval Japan* (Stanford, Calif.: Stanford University Press, 1992), ch. 1.
8. NET pp. 1–2, doc. 1, Hōen 1 (1135) 6.3, NET doc. 2, Hōen 1 (1135) 9.13. Sen'yōmon'in details part of Yugeshima's history of bequests within the retired emperor's court in her letter of donation to Tōji (NET pp. 88–90, doc. 23, En'ō 1 [1239] 12th month). The Tōji monk Gyōhen (1181–1265) convinced Sen'yōmon'in to donate the estate to him in order to help resuscitate the fortunes of Tōji. For an explanation of this history, see Yamauchi, *Yugeshima no shō no rekishi*, p. 19.

Iyo.[9] Once part of the vast portfolio of Tōji, for the next two and a half centuries, Yugeshima's head proprietor was the Assembly of Eighteen (*jūhakku gusō*), one of the ruling bodies of monks of the Tōji temple complex.[10]

From the time of its earliest extant records, Yugeshima residents specialized in maritime industries: "salt works" (*shiohama*), shipping, and large-scale cooperative fishing using "net sites" (*amiba / aminiwa*). Wet and dry fields seem to have been only for subsistence. To administer this maritime production, proprietors and managers attempted to adapt estate-system institutions to the littoral environment. The island's proprietors and managers organized the estate by dividing groups of holdings administratively into production units (*myō*).[11] Agricentric ideologies caused the earliest surveyors to define the production units by wet fields (i.e., rice), dry fields, and mulberry, revealing the maritime production only by denoting occasions when dues drawn from these categories were replaced with salt.[12] However, according to a series of surveys of holdings and catalogs of rents owed completed between 1311 and 1313, each production unit contained "salt works," "upland timber stands," as well as "wet and dry fields."[13] Fishing installations were not included in the production unit according to these cataloging operations. Production-unit chiefs (*myōshu*) oversaw the residents (*hyakushō*)[14] and unfree laborers (*genin*) attached to each production unit, and took responsibility for the remittance of "goods from the mountains and seas"[15] to proprietors, meaning salt-filled straw sacks of various sizes and weights and "net goods,"[16] a term used to denote fruits of the sea.

9. NET pp. 83–87, doc. 21, no date; NET pp. 387–402, doc. 283, Ōei 14 (1407), 3rd month.

10. After Gyōhen's death, the Assembly of Eighteen wrested Yugeshima and other estates away from Gyōhen's faction (Amino, *Chūsei Tōji to Tōjiryō shōen*, pp. 315–17).

11. For interpretations of *myō*, see Keirstead, *The Geography of Power in Medieval Japan*, p. 50.

12. NET pp. 14–29, docs. 14–17, dated from Bunji 4 (1188) 9.29 to Bunji 5 (1189) 5th month; Yamauchi, *Yugeshima no shō no rekishi*, pp. 45–49; Amino Yoshihiko, *Rethinking Japanese History*, translated and with an introduction by Alan S. Christy, preface and afterword by Hitomi Tonomura, Michigan Monograph Series in Japanese Studies, no. 74 (Ann Arbor: Center for Japanese Studies, University of Michigan, 2012), p. 67.

13. NET pp. 243–86, docs. 165–68, dated from Ōchō 1 (1311) 7th month to Shōwa 2 (1313) 4th month.

14. As a status label, the term *hyakushō* has meant many things in different periods. In the estate setting, I will translate it as "resident" since the word refers specifically to those who possess rights and obligations as a result of their being recognized as official residents and producers on the estate. This status identity overlapped with other meanings of *hyakushō* as commoners who also possessed certain rights and obligations (Keirstead, *The Geography of Power in Medieval Japan*, ch. 2). *Hyakushō* were also considered to owe taxes and "were obligated through custom to act collectively," but they could also wield weapons, fight in battle, and become warrior retainers (Thomas Conlan, *State of War: The Violent Order of Fourteenth-Century Japan*, Michigan Monograph Series in Japanese Studies, no. 46 [Ann Arbor: Center for Japanese Studies, University of Michigan, 2003], pp. 111–21, quote from p. 113).

15. NET pp. 97–98 doc. 30, Shōka 3 (1259) 2.22.

16. NET pp. 97–98, doc. 30, Shōka 3 (1259) 2.22; NET p. 129, doc. 63, Kenji 1? (1275) 3.17.

The Assembly of Eighteen tasked the production-unit chiefs and an awk-wardly worded category of "shipmaster residents" (*kandori ken hyakushō*) with shipping the salt and other goods to the capital via the port of Yodo.[17] In addition to representing an adaption of terminology to the maritime environment, the combination of the two terms suggests that shipmasters or estate proprietors may have attempted to replicate the estate hierarchy aboard ship: the sailors sailing under the shipmaster would have been other *hyakushō* or unfree labor attached to particular production units.[18] Yugeshima *hyakushō* sailors may also have been responsible for fighting off pirates and engaging in other sorts of violence, as was common on other estates.[19]

Much of the maritime work required the cooperative labor of large numbers of residents, and the production units were attached to particular villages in which those residents lived. Many of the hamlets' names sug-gest that residents organized the large-scale fishing operations that do not appear in production-unit registers by village: Tsurihama (Fishing Beach), Kujira (Whale), and Kushi (Pole—used for marking net sites and bound-aries).[20] Customary practices in the littoral also seem to have shaped the implementation of the production-unit institution in that production-unit chiefs seem to have attempted to divide responsibilities for dues equitably among themselves.[21]

The inclusion of "upland timber" in the aforementioned surveys illus-trates the significant amounts of lumber required for sustaining maritime industries like salt production and shipping—let alone building houses, temples, and shrines and burning wood to keep warm. A 1311 survey reveals that each production unit was allotted a share of contiguous upland stands (*yama*) of woodland.[22] Like other salt-production centers throughout the Japanese archipelago in this period, Yugeshima residents made salt by col-lecting salt-encrusted sand in "salt wells" (*shio ana*), washing the salt crystals

17. NET pp. 291–93, doc. 173.1, NET p. 293, doc. 173.2 both dated Shōwa 2 (1313) 9.8.
18. Shinjō Tsunezō, *Chūsei suiunshi no kenkyū* (Hanawa Shobō, 1995), p. 71.
19. Usami Takayuki. *Nihon chūsei no ryūtsū to shōgyō* (Yoshikawa Kōbunkan, 1999), pp. 140–41.
20. NET pp. 243–61, docs. 165–66, Ōchō 1 (1311) 7th month. For the use of poles as boundary markers, see Hotate Michihisa, "Chūsei zenki no gyogyō to shōensei: kakai ryōyū to gyomin o megutte," *Rekishi hyōron* 376 (1981): 26–27. For growth of permanent villages in this period, see Kristina Kade Troost, "Peasants, Elites, and Villages in the Fourteenth Century," in *The Origins of Japan's Medieval World: Courtiers, Clerics, Warriors, and Peasants in the Fourteenth Century*, edited by Jeffrey P. Mass (Stanford, Calif.: Stanford University Press, 1997), p. 93.
21. Amino Yoshihiko, "Kodai chūsei kinsei shoki no gyorō to kaisanbutsu no ryūtsū," in *Kōza Nihon gijutsu no shakaishi*, vol. 2: *Engyō, gyogyō*, edited by Amino Yoshihiko et al. (Nihon Hyōronsha, 1985), p. 250; Yamauchi, *Yugeshima no shō no rekishi*, p. 52.
22. NET pp. 243–61, docs. 165–66, Ōchō 1 (1311) 7th month.

off the sand by pouring more seawater into the wells, and then boiling the resulting "brine" (*tare shio*) in cauldrons over a wood fire.[23] In addition to the salt-making equipment, *myōshu* and other wealthy residents owned and captained the ships used for delivering rents, so the production unit-based timber stands probably also supplied Yugeshima's shipping industry. By the fourteenth century, hollowed-out log vessels had given way to partially planked and fully planked ships capable of carrying several hundred *koku* in lading.[24] Given such heavy demand for wood, it is possible that the organized division of upland stands by production units and their inclusion in a survey may indicate planning to maintain a sufficient tree population.[25] Yugeshima's inhabitants continued to make salt by burning wood for hundreds of years.

The aforementioned fourteenth-century surveys occurred as a result of changes in the proprietorship of Yugeshima that occurred at that time. As a maritime estate remote from the capital, Yugeshima was vulnerable to incursions from local powers, and the introduction of Kamakura warrior stewards onto the island from the late twelfth century created additional tensions. Over the course of the thirteenth century, warrior stewards such as the Komiya family and their deputies attempted to force Tōji to accede to successive acts of aggrandizement. To neutralize the power of warrior stewards on Yugeshima and to fight them in the courts of the Kamakura bakufu, the Assembly of Eighteen ceased relying on its own officials dispatched from Kyoto to manage the estate. Instead, Tōji hired local littoral elites expert in estate management.[26] In an ensuing compromise that divided the estate

23. NET pp. 125–26, doc. 60, no date; NET pp. 302–9, doc.179, Shōwa 3 (1314) 12.3. Scholars think that Yugeshima residents in this period practiced an intermediate form of salt production between "raised beach" (*agehama*) and "channeled beach" (*irihama*). In the labor-intensive *age hama* method, salt makers repeatedly poured seawater over a prepared area of beach. In *irihama* tidal forces channeled seawater directly into sand beds. In both methods, the salinized sand was collected into central vats where additional seawater was poured over it to create the final brine. The resulting brine was then boiled away to produce the salt. Many salt-producing centers began developing *irihama* technology in the late medieval period. Other Yugeshima records indicate that residents used cattle to ease the burdens of transporting seawater, salt, wood, and other products. NET pp. 288–90, doc. 170, Shōwa 2 (1313) 7th month; NET pp. 243–61, docs. 165–66, Ōchō 1 (1311) 7th month; Yamauchi, *Yugeshima no shō no rekishi*, pp. 78–79.
24. Ishii Kenji suggested that the decrease in large girth trees due to deforestation may have stimulated this transition in methods of ship construction (Ishii Kenji, *Zusetsu wasen shiwa* [Shiseido, 1983], p. 44).
25. For more on commoners and timber management in the medieval period, see Conrad Totman, *The Green Archipelago: Forestry in Pre-Industrial Japan* (Berkeley: University of California Press, 1989), pp. 37–43.
26. The Komiya family held the *jitō shiki* for Yugeshima from around 1239 until 1296. Tōji hired estate manager experts who took the Komiya to suit in Kamakura where Komiya eventually lost their holdings on Yugeshima and were replaced by another *jitō* family (name unknown). Yamauchi

(*shitaji chūbun*) in 1303, Tōji retained proprietary authority over two-thirds of the estate, with the warrior steward gaining one-third.[27]

Such conflicts represented opportunities for local littoral elites to expand their role within the estate. The 1303 division constituted a partial victory for Tōji in that it led to a gradual diminution of Kamakura warrior power on the island. The title accruing to the warrior steward position (*jitō shiki*) became simply one proprietary title among others. However, the local littoral magnates hired to counter the warrior stewards ended up gaining significant influence over the island and its maritime industries.

Figures 9 and 10, an early fourteenth-century chart of the island and its translation, detail in-process negotiations among representatives of the Assembly of Eighteen (designated as the proprietor, *ryōke*), the local administrator appointed by Tōji (*azukari dokoro*), and the warrior steward related to the division of the estate. The map reveals that these entities valued Yugeshima for its maritime production, not rice paddies.[28] The graphic and text delineate the boundaries of the estate through explanations of the locations of various net sites for large-scale fishing operations. The ambiguity of the actual location of net-site installations hints at limitations in land-based institutions and forms of documentation for sea tenure. Nevertheless, according to this chart, proprietors, managers, and residents all agreed that Yugeshima estate extended some five kilometers offshore to the small island of Heyaji Kojima (probably present-day Hyakkanjima), meaning that they considered Heyaji Kojima, the island of Yugeshima, offshore fishing sites, and the interstitial sea space and sea lanes all to constitute part of the estate. The case of Yugeshima closely fits the pattern of other littoral estates in extending boundaries across water to shipping lanes, fishing grounds, and islands, mountains, points, and other landmarks.[29]

The inscriptions of net sites in particular epitomize the possibilities for sea tenure on Yugeshima. They extended from the shoreline out to sea, were subject to administrative regulation (such as temporary prohibitions against killing[30]), and became objects of dispute. Warrior stewards and other

Yuzuru, *Chūsei Setonaikai chiikishi no kenkyū* (Hōsei Daigaku Shuppankyoku, 1998), pp. 5–6; Yamauchi, *Yugeshima no shō no rekishi*, pp. 97–100).

27. NET pp. 210–11, doc. 139, Kengen 2 (1303) 1.18. Jeffrey Mass argued that this division was not an optimal outcome for most stewards and that the receipt of a one-third fraction by the *jitō* would point to a weak *jitō* presence (Jeffrey P. Mass, "Jitō Land Possession in the Thirteenth Century: The Case of *Shitaji Chūbun*," in *Medieval Japan: Essays in Institutional History*, edited by John W. Hall et al. [Stanford, Calif.: Stanford University Press, 1974], p. 171).

28. Amino, *Chūsei Tōji to Tōjiryō shōen*, pp. 335–36.

29. Hotate, "Chūsei zenki no gyogyō to shōensei," pp. 21–22

30. NET p. 131, doc. 66, no date.

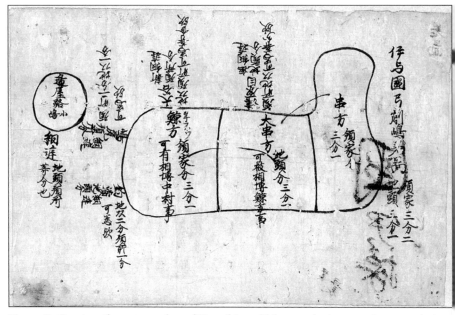

Figure 9. Fourteenth-century plan of Yugeshima. This map depicts ongoing negotiations over the division of Yugeshima between the warrior steward and proprietor. The document is from the Tōji collection of documents known as *Tōji hyakugō monjo*, と box, doc. 153. Photo courtesy of Kyoto Prefectural Archives and Museum (Kyoto Furitsu Sōgō Shiryōkan) and used with their permission.

littoral magnates exploited the large-scale net fishing operations in order to strengthen sea tenurial dominion. They helped residents defend their fishing territories from interlopers beyond the strand, but also tended to appropriate control over the nets, ships, and other tools of large-scale fishing and to extract portions of the catch as tribute.[31]

The chart's depiction of an extension of estate boundaries offshore onto shipping lanes also intimates the participation of Yugeshima residents in wider networks of exchange. Many estates traded for necessities on land and sea, opening up contacts with other locales.[32] Yugeshima's shipmaster residents established particularly close relations with residents on nearby Innoshima,[33] and they sold fish in nearby markets.[34]

31. Hyungsub Moon, "The Matsura Pirate-Warriors of Northwestern Kyushu in the Kamakura Age," in *Currents in Medieval Japanese History: Essays in Honor of Jeffrey P. Mass*, edited by Gordon M. Berger et al. (Los Angeles: Figueroa Press, 2009), p. 377.
32. Keirstead, *The Geography of Power in Medieval Japan*, p. 56.
33. NET pp. 288–90, doc. 170, Shōwa 2 (1313) 6th month.
34. NET p. 293, doc. 173.2, Shōwa 2 (1313) 9.8.

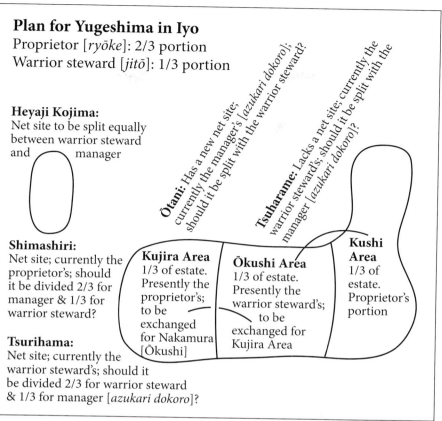

Plan for Yugeshima in Iyo
Proprietor [*ryōke*]: 2/3 portion
Warrior steward [*jitō*]: 1/3 portion

Heyaji Kojima:
Net site to be split equally
between warrior steward
and ⟋‾‾⟍ manager

Ōtani: Has a new net site; currently the manager's [*azukari dokoro*]; should it be split with the warrior steward?

Tsuharame: Lacks a net site; currently the warrior steward's; should it be split with the manager [*azukari dokoro*]?

Shimashiri:
Net site; currently the
proprietor's; should
it be divided 2/3 for
manager & 1/3 for
warrior steward?

Kujira Area
1/3 of estate.
Presently the
proprietor's;
to be
exchanged
for Nakamura
[Ōkushi]

Ōkushi Area
1/3 of estate.
Presently the
warrior steward's.
to be
exchanged for
Kujira Area

Kushi Area
1/3 of
estate.
Proprietor's
portion

Tsurihama:
Net site; currently the
warrior steward's; should it
be divided 2/3 for warrior steward
& 1/3 for manager [*azukari dokoro*]?

Figure 10. Translation of figure 9. Adapted from NET pp. 286–87, doc. 169.

By the early 1300s, Yugeshima shipmasters began expanding their local exchange networks by embezzling parts of the dues they carried and selling them on their own. At this time, the Assembly of Eighteen issued edicts against "nonpayment by shipmasters,"[35] specifically singling out shipmasters as culprits—sometimes by name as in the case of the "resident and shipmaster Gyōbunojō Shigehiro, who owed nine sacks [*hyō*] worth of salt."[36] Shipmasters may have felt justified in expropriating the salt and other dues in ways Tōji considered illegal for several reasons. More than one resident had to submit contracts promising family members as collateral for unpaid dues.[37]

35. NET p. 294, doc. 173.5, Shōwa 2 (1313) 9.8.
36. NET pp. 291–93, doc. 173.1 Shōwa 2 (1313) 9.8.
37. Amino Yoshihiko, "Mishin to minoshiro," in *Chūsei no tsumi no batsu*, edited by Amino Yoshihiko et al. (Tokyo Daigaku Shuppankai, 1983), pp. 134–42.

Drought, disease, and dearth struck regularly in this period.[38] Moreover, in contrast to many other littoral estates near Yugeshima, where proprietors provided shipmasters with tax-exempt fields and other grants, Tōji does not seem to have compensated Yugeshima shipmasters for the expenses they incurred shipping the salt and other goods to the capital.[39] Yugeshima residents thus had to outfit and maintain the ships themselves, pay for their own food and lodgings, and arrange their own protection.[40] Some scholars believe that the lack of sufficient arable land on Yugeshima may have contributed to the Assembly of Eighteen's policy.[41] However, no surviving account shows Tōji allowing Yugeshima shipmasters to augment their income by contracting their services to other estates or by paying in cash as other estate proprietors permitted in this period,[42] though Yugeshima shippers engaged in both practices in later periods.

Given the contacts possible in regional ports like Onomichi and central ports like Hyōgo or Yodo, it would be naïve to think that shipmasters from these nearby estates did not communicate with one another. Such entrepôt also gave Yugeshima shipmasters access to shipping agents (*toi*), who, in being responsible for the transport of dues from port to Tōji, had ready access to their own networks of carriers and dealers. Some of these *toi* evinced significant interest in marketing Yugeshima salt commercially and seem to have been aware of the profits to be made in the commoditization of certain dues paid in kind. In 1291, one shipping agent reputedly embezzled Yugeshima salt, "sold it to one merchant at a rate of 200 copper coins per sack of salt," which a Kyoto salt dealer bought "two or three days later for 400 coins per sack of salt," doubling the first merchant's profit.[43]

In any case, since receiving exempt fields or cash payments did not stop other estates' shipmasters from engaging in extracurricular commercial activities, it is doubtful that extra payments from Tōji would have done much to dampen the entrepreneurial spirit of Yugeshima shipmasters. Nevertheless, the absence of compensation undoubtedly encouraged the expropriation and marketing of some of the salt meant as dues. In response, Tōji

---

38. NET p. 102, doc. 38, Bun'ō 1 (1260), 7th month; NET pp. 125–26, doc. 60, no date; William Wayne Farris, *Japan's Medieval Population: Famine, Fertility, and Warfare in a Transformative Age* (Honolulu: University of Hawai'i Press, 2006), pp. 100–117.

39. Shipmasters from Yanai estate in Suō, Ōta estate by Onomichi, and Ōmishima in Iyo all seem to have received extra compensation (Shinjō, *Chūsei suiunshi no kenkyū*, pp. 40–42).

40. Ibid., pp. 75–76.

41. Ibid., pp. 41–42.

42. Ise Shrine permitted its shipmasters to contract out their shipping, and Mt. Kōya rewarded shipmasters on Minabe estate with cash (Fujimoto Yorihito, "Chūsei zenki no kandori to chiikikan no kōryū," *Nihon rekishi* 678 [2004.11]: 22, 27).

43. NET p. 178, doc. 117, Shō'ō 5 (1292) 10.14.

held all, "residents [*hyakushō*] and others," liable for the actions of the ship-masters[44] and required its on-site managers to enforce the payment of dues in arrears.[45]

Tōji monks actively resisted the commercialization of Yugeshima's salt because they used salt in religious ceremonies and because of the increasingly large number of tolls being applied to commercial shipments. Priests used salt as a purifier and presented it to the gods and buddhas.[46] Beginning in the late thirteenth century, various authorities—shoguns and their wives, temples and shrines, the imperial court, and local elites—all began to assess tolls on cargoes as ways to raise revenue.[47] To contest such actions, especially in the Yodo ports where Yugeshima ships offloaded cargoes, beginning around 1305 Tōji issued repeated orders that tax shipments be labeled with religious toll-exemption passes they called "umbrella tallies" (*kasafuda*) denoting their holy and noncommercial purpose.[48] The assertion that the salt sacks submitted by Yugeshima were, as one monk put it, "most assuredly not worldly, salable goods" and thus should be immune from tolls availed the Assembly little.[49]

Tōji blamed Yugeshima's shipmasters for increased perceptions of Yugeshima salt as a commercial commodity upon which tolls could be assessed. In 1307, the Assembly requested that "administrators" of one temple's barrier at the Yodo port of Watanabe "report shipmasters" who sought to sell salt, reiterating that Yugeshima's salt "has been decreed to be a non-salable item."[50] The growing number of toll barriers provided shipmasters one excuse for the missing dues, and it seems likely that they also may have blamed attacks from "pirates" and the ravages of "storms." As part of its attempts to stop "unpayment by shipmasters" in 1313, the Assembly ordered that "even in cases of pirates [*kaizoku*], capsizing [*nyūkai*], or other natural disasters, [dues] are to be paid according to precedent."[51] Tōji's strict policies regarding Yugeshima salt likely made shipmasters willing to join in the attempts by early sea lords to carve out autonomous commercial shipping networks.

44. NET pp. 291–93, doc. 173.1, Shōwa 2 (1313) 9.8.
45. NET p. 293 doc. 173.2, Shōwa 2 (1313) 9.8.
46. Amino Yoshihiko, *Chūsei no hinin to yūjo* (Akashi Shoten, 1994), pp. 56–58.
47. Aida Nirō noted early on that this function of medieval barriers makes them qualitatively different from those of the ancient and early modern periods (Aida Nirō, *Chūsei no sekisho* [Unebi Shobō, 1943, republished Yoshikawa Kōbunkan, 1983], ch. 1).
48. NET pp. 223–25, doc. 148, Kagen 4 (1306) 9.11.
49. NET p. 226, doc. 150, no year.3.5.
50. NET p. 233, doc. 153, Tokuji 2 (1307) 10.29. The temple was the Yasaka Hōkanji.
51. NET pp. 291–93, doc. 173.1, Shōwa 2 (1313) 9.8.

INITIAL STAGES OF SEA LORDSHIP:
THE CASE OF BEN NO BŌ SHŌYO AND YUGESHIMA

The local magnates Tōji hired succeeded in reducing the power of Kama-kura warrior stewards, but they failed in carrying out another of the tem-ple's aims: suppression of shipmasters' entrepreneurial activities. Some of the magnates, coming into the estate from the outside, extended their own influence over Yugeshima's maritime industries and shipmasters. Gradually they supplanted the estate-proprietor nexus with wider regional exchange networks, which they sought to bring under their sway. In the process, they established themselves as sea lords.

Amino characterizes this kind of nascent sea lord as a type of profes-sional estate manager who knew the local sea lanes and possessed the nauti-cal and military skills necessary to protect seaboard holdings from incur-sions and estate rents from extortion and embezzlement. They sometimes concurrently held positions in several estates, which enabled them to in-crease connections among estates and thus engage in commercial activi-ties.[52] Such figures did not always work against the proprietor. As the power of Kyoto and Kamakura waned in the early fourteenth century, proprietors increasingly looked to local maritime magnates to secure control over lit-toral space and populations and were sometimes willing to make common cause with them in order to continue the flow of rents. Such collaboration reflected a degree of flexibility on both sides, but tensions bespoke the tenu-ous nature of central authorities' control over local hires.

One of the earliest and best-documented of these outside estate officials who sought to use Yugeshima as a stepping-stone to sea lordship was a cer-tain Ben no Bō Shōyo. Based in Oyama in Iyo, Shōyo accepted a manage-rial appointment (*azukari dokoro shiki*) on Yugeshima from the Assembly of Eighteen around 1313, and he soon acquired title to the warrior stew-ard's portion as well.[53] Although his actions on Yugeshima caused some Tōji officials eventually to label him "[that] infamous pirate, Shōyo,"[54] he consistently emphasized his possession of officially recognized managerial posts.[55] Shōyo took advantage of these managerial positions to appropriate Yugeshima rents along with forwarding them to Tōji. But Shōyo was less in-

---

52. Amino Yoshihiko, *Kaimin to Nihon shakai: These Are What Japan Has Raised in its History* (Shin Jinbutsu Ōraisha, 1998), p. 236.
53. NET pp. 302–9, doc. 179, Shōwa 3 (1314) 12.3. Beyond its provincial locus, the location of Oyama is unknown.
54. NET p. 327 doc. 204, Genkyō 4? (1324) 4.19.
55. In one letter, possibly seeking to strike a sympathetic chord with his religious sponsors, he also identified himself as a "monk" (*sō*) (NET pp. 322–23, doc. 199, Genkyō 4 [1324] 1st month).

erested in establishing dominion over one island than in using his posts and
itles for the purposes of integrating Yugeshima into networks of production
nd exchange across sea lanes. He treated the sea channels as thoroughfares
nstead of boundaries and linked the estate with his Oyama base. In absorb-
ng Yugeshima into a wider domain, he extended its sea-tenurial boundar-
es beyond net sites and the island of Heyaji Kojima south to the Shikoku
nainland. Shōyo was not unique in these efforts. His contemporaries, the
Matsura of Northwest Kyushu laid claim to a maritime domain extending
•eyond fishing grounds and harbors to the trade routes with Korea.[56]

Shōyo also recruited Yugeshima shipmasters into his band and burgeon-
ng commercial dealings. Evidence for Shōyo's commercial activities exists
nostly in the form of complaints by Yugeshima residents, requiring that we
ead them against the grain. The information that can be culled from peti-
ions submitted to Tōji by Yugeshima residents shows that, on the one hand,
hōyo employed new methods of sea tenure and coercion to keep Yugeshi-
na's shippers under his sway, while, on the other, he lured them with ways to
void higher toll costs in the Yodo estuary by selling salt for cash in regional
narkets. He thus may have been partly responsible for Yugeshima residents
ubmitting dues in cash and as bills of exchange instead of, as hitherto, in
ind. In effect, he used at least some of what he appropriated to develop
ommercial enterprises.

Shōyo created the foundations for networks linking Yugeshima across
he seas to his base at Oyama by drawing on the precedent of warrior stew-
rds and forcibly exacting corvée labor to augment his maritime workforce.[57]
ome residents complained: "Lord Ben claimed that it was imperative for
umbers of people to be at his home in Oyama in Iyo; he crossed over with
rom four or five to seven or eight or ten at a time. Then he forced them to
vork for several days."[58]

By 1324, his labor pool and shipping networks established, Shōyo
ried to gain control over ships on Yugeshima by purchasing and borrow-
ng them, a practice that contradicted the existing arrangements in which
hipmasters owned and outfitted their own ships. Shōyo's new business
•ractices expanded the scope of Yugeshima's shipping by including ships
nd sailors from ports in other provinces: "Although he did buy ships, he
lso forcibly borrowed our ships without compensation as well as those from
³ingo and Aki."[59]

6. Moon, "The Matsura Pirate-Warriors of Northwestern Kyushu in the Kamakura Age," pp. 363–64.
7. NET pp. 302–9, doc. 179, Shōwa 3 (1314) 12.3.
8. NET pp. 297–300, doc. 176, Shōwa 3 (1314) 9th month.
9. NET pp. 328–29, doc. 205, Genkyō 4 (1324) 9th month. The nearby ports were most likely Onomichi
   or Innoshima in Bingo and Setoda or Mihara in Aki.

83

Shōyo captained these ships carrying goods including Yugeshima due to regional entrepôt such as the port of Dōgo, where he used his connection to exchange Yugeshima salt for cash at a better rate than at other ports: "H forced us to give him the dues for next year. . . . For sixty or seventy days he loaded our goods and shipped them away. . . . Regarding the dues for thi year . . . instead of taking them from Your Domain to Kyoto, he transporte the dues in a borrowed ship to a place called Dōgo in Iyo. At that place cash costs less salt than it does in Kyoto."[60] Through such maneuvers Shōy made a tidy profit. But he also sent dues to Tōji to meet his obligations to th proprietors. In a 1324 letter, Shōyo bragged that, unlike others appointe manager to Yugeshima, only he possessed the requisite skills to delive rents: "In Shōwa 4 [1315], I was appointed manager [shomu shiki]. . . . I cor respondingly forwarded the requisite thirty-five kanmon and fulfilled m managerial obligations. To the best of my ability, I left not one grain of th yearly rents and other duties unpaid. Next, Nasu Gorō nyūdō [Rengan]– who sought illicit gain—was named to be a manager [azukari dokoro shiki] Over the course of two short years, he had trouble controlling the island an failed to deliver the rents, whereas I loyally performed services."[61]

Some at Tōji regarded Shōyo's dealings dubiously, but his continue delivery of rents led the Assembly of Eighteen to at least initially overlool his perhaps overzealous exactions and unorthodox practices. The Assembl responded to many of the residents' complaints, at least early on, by issuin platitudes to Shōyo like "stop being excessive in your various manageria duties and cherish the people."[62]

Similarly, although on the surface Shōyo's new sea tenurial practice evidently awakened stiff resistance among some Yugeshima resident others seem to have welcomed Shōyo's ventures. In the third month of 1324 some residents came together and formed a league against Shōyo, imbibin a "holy elixir of common cause" containing the ashes of their sworn oath. However, knowing that Tōji was already wary of shipmasters selling sal some residents must have used these complaints to hide their own com plicity and commercial dealings under rhetoric of victimization. A petitio six months later admits that "some, both high and low, went with Shōy

60. Ibid.
61. NET pp. 322–23, doc. 199, Genkyō 4 (1324) 1st month.
62. NET pp. 300–1, doc. 177, Shōwa 3 (1314) 10.15; Yamauchi, Chūsei Setonaikai chiikishi no kenky pp. 10–11.
63. NET p. 326, doc. 203, Genkyō 4 (1324) 3rd month. For more on the process of building a leagu (ikki) and drinking the ashes of the sworn oath (ichimi shinsui), see Katsumata Shizuo, Ikki (Iw nami Shoten, 1982); Keirstead, The Geography of Power in Medieval Japan, ch. 4.

for about a hundred days."[64] Residents also concealed their own entrepreneurial activities by playing on Tōji's limited knowledge of maritime matters and geography. They portrayed Shōyo's commercial voyages to Dōgo
as harrowing expeditions as opposed to the safe, well-known routes to the
ports of the capital region. In doing so, they alluded to a common perception among land-based elites that calm seas represented political stability,
and rough ones chaos:[65] "Dōgo is a place difficult to reach and a place of
limitless evil. Compared to the sea route to the capital, the route to Dōgo is
much more dangerous."[66] In this formulation, Dōgo equaled illegality, thus
dangerous seas and pirates. By extension, Kyoto represented a legal vector
of exchange and placid waters. By describing the situation in this way, they
hid the fact that Shōyo probably chose Dōgo because it lay near his power
base of Oyama. If this were the case, he could probably ensure security on
the interstitial sea lanes between Dōgo and Yugeshima. In any case, the trip
to Dōgo took less time than sailing to the capital and consisted entirely of
coastal tramping.

Shōyo's independent, entrepreneurial endeavors may well have extended
to actions that Tōji officials interpreted as fencing stolen goods. In 1318, on
Shōyo's watch, Tōji ordered investigations into Yugeshima's managers and
warrior stewards because, as Assembly officials described it, "pirates [*kaizoku*] had stored stolen goods on Yugeshima."[67] Shōyo's connections to
other markets, links with Yugeshima shipmasters eager for additional cash,
and ability to exploit patronage by Tōji all point to Shōyo's complicity.

In addition, Shōyo clearly understood the commoditization of violence.
He recognized that members of the Assembly of Eighteen valued him because of his ability to protect Yugeshima. In a report to Tōji in the first
month of 1324, he emphasized his indispensability to Tōji by employing
the rhetoric of "evil bands" that so flourished in the late Kamakura period.[68] He characterized the lawlessness that he defended their island from

64. NET pp. 328–29, doc. 205, Genkyō 4 (1324) 9th month. Available information is insufficient to
    come to any firm conclusion as to the identity of those who sailed with Shōyo. Because there is
    no extant list of signatories to this petition, it is not clear how many of the residents either both
    signed and sailed with Shōyo or signed out of real distress.
65. See chapter 1.
66. NET pp. 328–29, doc. 205, Genkyō 4 (1324) 9th month. Tōji did recognize the possibility for
    duplicity in the accounts. In one case, they sent the residents' petition back for a sworn list of
    signatories (NET p. 291, doc. 172, Shōwa 2 [1313] 7.22). On another occasion, Tōji had Yugeshima
    residents send representatives to Kyoto to testify against Shōyo in person (NET pp. 302–9,
    doc. 179, Shōwa 3 [1314] 12.3).
67. NET pp. 315–16, doc. 189, no date.
68. See chapter 1.

as "evildoers from Sanuki . . . [who] forced their way onto the island and performed all sorts of evil deeds and committed outrages."[69] In describing his defense of the island, Shōyo showed how he sought out those willing to engage in nautical violence to help protect the island and forged them into a band. The ability to protect the island would also have attracted him to Yugeshima's shipmasters and other residents: "Using my own resources, personally led a force of several hundred. Heedless of our own lives, we gave battle and drove the evildoers away, performing loyal service."[70]

But the same ability to forge a band out of those willing to engage in nautical violence could also be used against him. When Shōyo rallied Yugeshima residents and members of his band against representatives of those factions who sought to displace him as manager, residents and opposing officials turned rhetoric of victimization and "evil doers"[71] against him. Shōyo complained to Tōji of having been slandered as an "evildoer."[7] Competitors condemned him as a "pirate" (*kaizoku*) and accused him of turning Yugeshima into a "haven for pirates."[73] Residents and official claimed that Shōyo and other "evildoers conspired to assemble a force of several hundred people from here and other provinces, and on [1324] 2.20 he pushed his way onto" Yugeshima.[74] Such actions illustrate the autonomy sought by nascent sea lords; Shōyo would protect the ships he had gained control of, networks he had developed, and potential profits available through control of Yugeshima from even his patrons and proprietor if necessary.

Shōyo disappears from recorded history after 1324, possibly indicating that he failed to retain the island by force or to acquire patronage sufficient to ensure his hold on it. The presence of Shōyo and other maritime magnates did have a lasting impact, however. After Shōyo's tenure, Tōji permitted Yugeshima residents to continue submitting dues in cash and as bills of exchange instead of in kind.[75] Perhaps it had little choice, but by acquiescing to the growing commercialized nature of Yugeshima's maritime industries and growing autonomy of the island's local magnate managers the Assembly of Eighteen retained a modicum of influence over the island

69. NET pp. 322–23, doc. 199, Genkyō 4 (1324) 1st month.
70. Ibid.
71. Morton Oxenboell, "Images of 'Akutō,'" *Monumenta Nipponica* 60.2 (2006): pp. 245–50.
72. NET pp. 322–23, doc. 199, Genkyō 4 (1324) 1st month.
73. NET p. 326, doc. 204, Genkyō 4? (1324) 4.19.
74. NET p. 327, doc. 203, Genkyō 4 (1324), 3rd month.
75. Yamauchi, *Chūsei Setonaikai chiikishi no kenkyū*, p. 31.

TRANSGENERATIONAL SEA LORDSHIP, PROTECTION, AND SEA TENURE IN THE MUROMACHI PERIOD

In the Muromachi period, sea lords continued to follow Shōyo's precedents, but they also began to establish themselves as transgenerational masters of maritime networks. Learning to code switch in order to represent themselves favorably to several constituencies, sea lords amassed trappings generally associated with lordship on land, such as the use of surnames and land-based honorary titles. They consolidated their authority at sea and sought to elevate themselves in the eyes of patrons who might otherwise see them merely as sea people and pirates. They also increasingly adopted the warrior-house model of organization.

Sea lordship became more possible as opportunities grew for performing violence-related services for a growing number of competing patrons: estate proprietors, warrior provincial governors, shogunal officials, and other authorities. With the collapse of the Kamakura bakufu, the eruption of the long-running civil war (1336-1392) between partisans of imperial claimants belonging to Northern and Southern Courts, and the weakening of Muromachi bakufu control after the 1440s, both the level and acceptability of violence and the scope of commercial trade increased. Sea lords took advantage of this environment to dictate how and when their services would be performed and to use mercenarism to expand their dominion over estates and the commercial networks centered on those estates.

The proliferation of conflict also meant that sea tenure more and more depended on restricting access to maritime spaces and populations by force, especially the forms of violence included within the category of "protection" (*keigo*). As chapter one explained, this term's meanings multiplied to encompass perceptions of both licit and illicit violence. The case of Yugeshima suggests that the increased scope of commercial trade from the time of Shōyo led to heightened competition for Yugeshima's marine resources and shipping networks, making it necessary for Tōji to grant its estate managers leeway in determining the degree of force required to retain control over the island and its industries. The ambiguities inherent in the term *keigo* created spaces for both sea lords and patrons to negotiate, for both to insert their perspectives on what protection entailed.

Tōji hoped that the term *keigo*—meaning violence performed legitimately in defense—would help rein in the freewheeling adventuring of sea lords under their control. Sea lords understood the term differently, perceiving it as a service that they provided how and when they wished. These competing interpretations are visible in a 1340 contract (*ukebumi*) forged between Tōji and a sea-lord estate manager on Yugeshima. The Assembly of Eighteen at first attempted to stem the tide of growing managerial autonomy by requiring its permission based on investigation of the circumstances and evidence from estate residents for any significant performance of "protection." Such strictures suggest that Tōji considered that local littoral magnates hired as managers were becoming notorious for using violence without Tōji's consent. By contrast, sea-lord managers tried to maximize their freedom of movement: "Regarding protection [keigo]: If it is a small matter, it falls under my purview. If a large matter that requires tens of troops and large amounts of provisions, I will send an express messenger and a report signed by the residents [hyakushō] within three days to report the incident to the temple. At that time, the temple will dispatch an agent to determine the veracity and extent of the incident."[76] In this contract, by leaving "small matters" undefined, Tōji monks acquiesced to sea lords who sought permission to engage in small-scale activity free of oversight. Unfortunately for Tōji, even these arrangements proved unworkable. By 1348, the contract for one new manager on Yugeshima permitted immediate action when there was not sufficient time to wait for the messenger to go and return,[77] providing aspiring sea-lord estate managers loopholes to freely engage in violence.

Usage of keigo sometimes signified symbiotic, ecological partnerships between sea lord and sponsor. Estate proprietors, warrior provincial governors, and other patrons paid for "protection," the provisioning of seafood and salt,[78] and other maritime services with foodstuffs and cash as well as shiki. These payments were sometimes known as "gifts" (shukōryō), a term whose meaning encompassed bribes, wine, or food. The Noshima Murakami first appear in extant sources as the recipients of such "gifts," recompense disbursed by Tōji for carrying out guard duty for Yugeshima estate.[79] By the sixteenth century, some sea lords accepted protection payments actually called "protection rice" (keigomai),[80] whereas others might receive salaries known as "floating rice" (ukimai), cash and kind payments in lieu of confirmation of new holdings or protection businesses.[81]

---

76. NET pp. 334–35, doc. 214, Ryakuō 3 (1340) 1.23.
77. NET pp. 343–44, doc. 230, Jōwa 4 (1348) 12.6.
78. EK doc. 2245, Tenshō 8? (1580) 3.28. Some types of fish, like bonito and sea bream (one of the most extensively harvested fish in the Inland Sea), had symbolic value in the late medieval Japanese gift economy (Morimoto Masahiro, "GoHōjō-shi no suisanbutsu jōnōsei no tenkai," *Nihonshi kenkyū* 359.7 [1992], pp. 35–36).
79. NET pp. 210–11, doc. 139, Jōwa 5 (1349) 12th month.
80. EK doc. 1733, Tenbun 12? (1543) 9.16.
81. See for example *Miyakubo-chō shi* (Miyakubo-chō, Ehime-ken: Miyakubo-chō, 1994), pp. 1111–12, doc. 121, Tenshō 11? (1583) 2.6; *Miyakubo-chō shi* p. 1123, doc. 155, Tenshō 11? (1583) 2.27. The

By the fourteenth and fifteenth centuries, *keigo* often meant protective escort for ships. Sea lords forced these payments on travelers or contracted to provide protective escort. They established private ship-based, fortress-based, and port-based toll barriers from which they provided protection. These barriers sometimes became hubs regulating traffic in shipping networks. Local maritime magnates seeking to become sea lords increasingly used maritime toll barrier-based protection as a way to compete for and extend influence over commercial networks.

During the wars of the Northern and Southern Courts both sides actively sought to control transportation arteries.[82] Sea lords perceived such warfare as entrepreneurial opportunities. Some geared their protection businesses to the scale of shipping involved, larger, more valuable vessels being worth more than smaller ones. For example, in 1340 Ashikaga Takauji authorized bands from the Kumano region to utilize control of chokepoint-based toll barriers in order to protect ships across a wide swath of the Inland Sea: "Regarding the chastisement of The Throne's enemies, as per your petition, the Taiji and Shiozaki families should carry out protection [*keigo*] for vessels carrying dues and commercial goods between Kamadonoseki [Kaminoseki] in Suō Province and Amagasaki in Settsu [today's Kōbe] and collect a fee of one hundred coppers [*mon*] per oar as payment."[83]

The impact of such practices can be seen in the popularization of variants on the terms "barrier erectors" (*sekidachi*)[84] and "barrier masters" (*sekikata*) as synonyms for sea lords by this period. Under the head proprietorship of Tōji, Yugeshima residents nominally participated on the side of the Northern Court in the civil war.[85] Although details remain unknown, sea lords based on Yugeshima developed sufficient reputation for providing protection and commerce raiding that after Ashikaga Yoshimitsu brought the civil war to a close in 1392 and initiated tribute trade with China, "barrier masters" (*sekikata*) from Yugeshima were among those he called on first to guard his China trade fleets.[86]

By the fifteenth century, the intercepting of ships and charging of protection monies at sea-based toll barriers situated in chokepoints constituted

---

ukimai system was not limited to patronage of sea lords; it was also used by the Mōri to reward land-based *bushi* as well. Kariyama Mototoshi, "Sengoku daimyo Mōri-shi ryōnai no ukimai ni tsuite," *Kōgakkan ronsō* 22.6 (1989.12): 50–57.

82. Conlan, *State of War*, pp. 93–94.

83. *Mera monjo* in *Kumano Nachi Taisha monjo*, vol. 3 (Zoku Gunsho Ruijū Kanseikai, 1974) doc. 1048, Ryakuō 3 (1340) 3.14.

84. For *sekidachi*, see EK doc. 1582, Bunki 1? (1501) 12.13; Yamauchi Yuzuru, *Kaizoku to umijiro: Setouchi no sengokushi* (Heibonsha, 1997), p. 150.

85. Yamauchi, *Yugeshima no shō no rekishi*, pp. 149–50.

86. NET pp. 384–85, doc. 278, no year.8.18.

one primary method by which sea lords established sway over maritime networks; protection businesses became a principal tool of sea tenure. Sea-lord bands competed to establish protection businesses in the channels surrounding Yugeshima. In the mid 1460s, a sea lord named Kurushima Murakami Zushonosuke, whom Tōji had hired to administer Yugeshima, submitted a report in the form of a letter to his patrons that vividly illustrates conflicts over maritime toll barriers that would enable aspiring sea lords to establish domains over maritime networks connecting contiguous islands and shipping lanes to Yugeshima. Some competing sea lords used estate titles as Shōyo had, whereas others fought over and fortified themselves in strongholds that overlooked chokepoints where barriers could be established. Zushunosuke labeled these latter figures "barrier erectors".[87] "The clerk [kumon] of Iwagijima [a nearby island] allied himself with barrier-erector pirates. They fortified themselves in Iwagijima fort, but this month he and all around him were killed by pirates [kaizoku] who then holed up in the fort. . . . This island [of Yugeshima] especially has constantly been a target of pirate [kaizoku] incursions. In the past two or three years, the residents have fled, and the dues from this place have not been delivered."[88] Iwagijima lies close to Yugeshima. By the fifteenth century, it had become a commercial shipping center, specializing in carrying the same products as Yugeshima—salt and soybeans—to Hyōgo port, where these goods were offloaded.[89] For one sea-lord band to control both Iwagijima and Yugeshima would enable it to combine both shipping organizations.

Successfully establishing toll barrier-based control had significant implications for both victor and vanquished. Economically, protection practices raised the protection costs of competitors and made it comparatively cheaper for the toll operators to send commercial shipments.[90] Sea lords who triumphed in these conflicts attempted to stabilize their authority across generations and began to consider rights to exercise violence and to extort protection in exchange for safe passage to be hereditary. For example, in 1483, the head of the Innoshima Murakami family, based on an island and littoral estate next to Yugeshima, bequeathed rights to charge protection monies called "harbor tolls" (sappo) to his heir.[91] Patrons accepted and con-

87. Yamauchi, Kaizoku to umijiro, ch. 1.
88. NET pp. 416–17, doc. 297, no year.5.26.
89. Hyōgo Kitazeki irifune nōchō, edited by Hayashiya Tatsusaburō (Chūō Kōron Bijutsu Shuppan 1981).
90. Frederic Lane, "Economic Consequences of Organized Violence," The Journal of Economic History 18.4 (1958): 409.
91. EK doc. 1519, Bunmei 15 (1483) 11.15.

irmed such inheritances.[92] Once such practices became hereditary, sea-lord)ands could institutionalize protection enterprises and add to and take ad-ʻantage of the multiplicity of meanings, constructive as well as baneful, that)rotection and toll barriers had for the people of fifteenth-century Japan)n land and sea. It is traditionally accepted that the widespread erection of)arriers increased protection costs and hindered commerce,[93] and indeed Murakami Zushonosuke's letter paints a grim picture. However, tolls and)rotection businesses commonly would be accepted if perceived as having ʻegitimate precedent.[94] Such tolls might be understood or portrayed as trans-ıction costs, religious piety, temple reconstruction funds, and salaries, as vell as protection.[95] Profits from such endeavors were often reinvested into naintaining and improving docks, warehouses, and other facilities.[96] Chap-er 1 showed how maritime toll taking became closely linked with pirates in he late medieval imagination. Furthermore, such escort was not only about ʻiolence or the protection from violence. Sea lords could also offer valu-ıble navigational services. The 1420 Korean ambassador Song Hŭigyŏng re-:orded occasions when "pirates" providing protection also guided his ships nto harbors.[97]

In addition, sea lords found toll barriers an especially effective means)f collecting income without destroying the source because—as in many)ther pirate communities around the world—sea lords lived in a symbiotic ʻelationship with merchant shipping; if they sank too many ships, their live-ihood would disappear.[98] Only if the ships refused to pay would sea lords ıormally attack. For example, Song Hŭigyŏng records the history of one of ıis predecessor ambassadors to Japan who ran afoul of "pirates." "All the

2. *Shirai monjo*, doc. 1, Meiō 4 (1495) 10.17, in *Buke monjo no kenkyū to mokuroku*, edited by Akutagawa Tatsuo (Ishikawa Bunka Jigyō Zaidan, Ochanomizu Toshokan, 1988), p. 190.

3. Hitomi Tonomura, *Community and Commerce in Late Medieval Japan: The Corporate Villages of Tokuchin-ho* (Stanford, Calif.: Stanford University Press, 1992), pp. 98–101; Suzanne Gay, *The Moneylenders of Late Medieval Kyoto* (Honolulu: University of Hawaiʻi Press, 2001), pp. 164–65; Farris, *Japan's Medieval Population*, pp. 146–47, 237.

4. Usami, *Nihon chūsei no ryūtsū to shōgyō*, pp. 20–21.

5. Aida, *Chūsei no sekisho*, ch. 1; Usami, *Nihon chūsei no ryūtsū to shōgyō*, pp. 29–42.

6. Wakita Haruko, "Ports, Markets, and Medieval Urbanism in the Osaka Region," translated by Gary P. Leupp and James L. McClain, in *Osaka: The Merchants' Capital of Early Modern Japan*, edited by James L. McClain et al. (Ithaca, N.Y.: Cornell University Press, 1999), pp. 30–31.

7. Song Hŭigyŏng, *Nosongdang Ilbon haengnok* (*Rōshōdō Nihon kōroku: Chōsen shisetsu no mita chūsei Nihon*), edited by Murai Shōsuke (Iwanami Shoten, 1987), no. 154. A seventeenth-century chronicle of sea-lord activities echoes Song's observations. "*Bukebandaiki: Santō kaizoku-ke ikusa nikki*, hoi no maki," *Suminoe* 230 (Fall 1998): 49.

8. Peregrine Horden and Nicholas Purcell, *The Corrupting Sea: A Study of Mediterranean History* (Oxford: Blackwell Publishers, 2000), p. 57.

gifts, naval stores, and even clothes were taken, though the ambassador and all his troops emerged unscathed."[99] The seizing of cargo while leaving the passengers and crew alive allowed pirates and sea lords to plunder the ship on future occasions and the passengers to spread word of the pirates, increasing their reputation.

PATRONAGE, ESTATES, AND SEA LORDS
IN THE FIFTEENTH CENTURY

In contrast to Shōyo, who limited his patronage connections to Tōji and estate *shiki*, sea lords in the fifteenth century sustained authority across generations and bolstered claims to littoral holdings like Yugeshima by securing multiple, often competing channels of patronage, including warrior provincial governors and the Muromachi bakufu. If accused of piracy or some other crime, those who had secured sufficiently transcendent sponsorship could counteract suits by Tōji and other aggrieved authorities. Multiple patrons also helped because, as the letter by Kurushima Murakami Zushunosuke quoted above intimates, violent competition for valuable littoral holdings like Yugeshima intensified in the fifteenth century. As a result of several protection business-based conflicts sanctioned by multiple patrons, the Assembly of Eighteen lost its already tenuous grip on the island.

The effects of compound patronage and competition among sea lords on Yugeshima and other littoral estates are visible in a rare, lengthy letter written by a sea lord to his patron. From the 1420s through the 1460s, Tōji officials relied heavily on the Kurushima Murakami sea-lord band to manage the island and protect rent shipments.[100] In 1456, Kurushima Murakami Jibunoshin reported to Tōji regarding the situation on Yugeshima. In his letter, Jibunoshin boasts of his local expertise, demonstrating the continuing importance to Tōji of having such figures take charge of remote estates and the ability of sea lords to exploit that need. Jibunoshin lays out the array of competing interests on Yugeshima: "Regarding Yugeshima . . . it is located close to my home, so I am well aware of the situation. . . . Koizumi

---

99. Song, no. 85.
100. It is probable that Jibunoshin belonged to the Kurushima Murakami for two reasons. In 1456 Murakami Jibunoshin defended Yugeshima against the Noshima Murakami and the titles for the Innoshima Murakami in this period tended to be very different (e.g., Murakami Bitchū no kami Yoshisuke; see EK doc. 1297, Bun'an 6 [1449] 6.14). Because both Jibunoshin and Tōji make reference to the precedent of a Murakami Uemonnojō who held a post on Yugeshima in 1420, we can assume that the Kurushima Murakami exercised some authority over Yugeshima from 1420 (NET p. 402, doc. 284, Ōei 27 [1420] 8.1; NET pp. 407–8, doc. 287.9, Kanshō 2 [1456] 9.21).

Kobayakawa, Yamaji . . . and both villages of Noshima all hold [some part of Yugeshima]."[101] To demonstrate this expertise meant knowing the important patrons in the region, being aware of the patronage connections between various sea-lord bands and land-based sponsors, having contacts with a wide array of sea lords, and being able to mediate among patrons and sea lords. Some of this expertise derived from shared patronage. In the mid fifteenth century, several, including the Kurushima Murakami, supplemented manager titles on Yugeshima with sponsorship by the Hosokawa family—powerful provincial governors and shogunal officials: "The Koizumi Kobayakawa and Yamaji are each in the employ of my lord Hosokawa. . . . Regarding Noshima . . . If you were to order that dues were to be paid, even a little, I would be willing to mediate."[102] Identifying Hosokawa as "my lord" also illustrates the commodified, mercenary nature of sea-lord violence as the Kurushima simultaneously served Kōno Norimichi, who at times fought against the Hosokawa, especially after the outbreak of the Ōnin War in 1467.[103] As was the case with Shōyo, management of Yugeshima, payment of rents, and negotiations with other sea lords also seem to have entailed additional commercial dealings that other factions in Tōji or other sea lords might label illicit. In order to allay suspicion that the Kurushima Murakami sought to expropriate part of Yugeshima's commercial wealth, Jibunoshin wrote in a postscript: "Previously, we have undertaken these mediating roles, and it has seemed to others that we are arrogating the profit for ourselves, not dealing with the profits as dues."[104]

In 1462, an explanation by a Tōji official to his superiors further demonstrates how sea lords, including the Koizumi Kobayakawa family, capitalized on having multiple patrons to assert their claims to sea-based dominion. The author wrote regarding those the Kurushima were supposed to protect Yugeshima from: "those engaged in extortion [ōryō] on Yugeshima: the Koizumi Kobayakawa (members of the shogunal guard [hōkōshū]), Noshima (pirates [kaizoku]), and Yamaji (the same [pirates]). Of these three extorting gangs, the Koizumi are the most nefarious."[105] Parts of the extensive Kobayakawa family had held some degree of proprietary title to Yugeshima

101. NET pp. 402–4, doc. 285, Kōshō 2 (1456) 5.8. The island of Noshima itself only had one settlement, but the Noshima also based family members on nearby islands like Mushijima and Nakatoshima.
102. Ibid.
103. For the Kurushima and Kōno Norimichi during the Kōno feud of the mid fifteenth century, see EK doc. 1304, Hōtoku 3? (1451) 2.23; NET pp. 402–4, doc. 285, Kōshō 2 (1456) 5.8; Sagara Shōjin, *Shōjinki*, YK, vol. 1, p. 350, Bunmei 10 (1478), 10.18. For the Hosokawa and Kōno, see Yamauchi, *Setonaikai no chiikishi no kenkyū*, pp. 294–95.
104. NET pp. 402–4, doc. 285, Kōshō 2 (1456) 5.8.
105. NET p. 414, doc. 291.3, Kanshō 3 (1462) 5.17.

since the 1370s at the latest[106] and, as we saw in Kurushima Murakami Jibunoshin's 1456 letter above, could call at times upon Hosokawa patronage to protect their holdings. The 1462 attribution of the Koizumi Kobayakawa as members of the shogunal guard suggests that the Koizumi had attempted to use that status and the patronage that came with it to legitimize attempts to exert control over Yugeshima. The Koizumi also operated in concert as a league (*ikki*) with other Kobayakawa branch families,[107] giving them extra resources potentially to call upon. In contrast, Tōji recognized the Yamaji and Noshima as no more than service-providing local maritime magnates ("pirates"). The Noshima Murakami had as late as 1349 begun to sell their maritime protection services to Yugeshima's managers and proprietors.[108] The Yamaji were sea lords from Sanuki who contracted to perform protection and other services for the Hosokawa.[109]

SHARED LORDSHIP

The fate of Yugeshima after the 1460s remains unclear until it appears as a holding of the Kurushima Murakami over a century later,[110] meaning that at some point the Kurushima Murakami eventually wrested control of the island from competitors. One distinctive characteristic of the situation on Yugeshima in the centuries between Shōyo and sole Kurushima control is the existence of multiple claimants to parts of Yugeshima. Sometimes this situation evolved into an unstable balance of shared authority. In the aforementioned 1456 letter by Kurushima Murakami Jibunoshin, the Koizumi Kobayakawa and Yamaji shared control of Yugeshima in their alliance against the Kurushima Murakami and perhaps the Noshima Murakami. The situation on Yugeshima grew even more complex in 1460 when the Assembly of Eighteen dispatched a monk, Eison Shōnin, to Yugeshima to represent and enforce Tōji's interests in person. Eison had previously handled Yugeshima affairs in Kyoto, and Tōji monks thought that in person he could apply his expertise to rectify Tōji's weakening hold on the island.[111] To some

---

106. NET pp. 368–69, doc. 266, Ōan 4 (1371) 7.19.
107. DNK 11, *Kobayakawa-ke monjo* vol. 1, pp. 83–85, no. 109, Hōtoku 3 (1451) 9th month, auspicious day.
108. EK doc. 747, Jōwa 5 (1349), 10th month.
109. Hashizume Shigeru, *Setonaikai chiiki shakai to Oda kenryoku* (Shibunkaku Shuppan, 2007), pp. 140–41.
110. EK doc. 2333, Tenshō 10? (1582) 9.1.
111. NET p. 411, doc. 289, Chōroku 4 (1460), 9th month.

extent, this compound governance resulted from the existence of several hamlets on the island as well as legacies of the estate system that enabled multiple levels of proprietorship and managerial posts. In addition, warrior provincial governors also sometimes assigned local strongmen to administrative posts to ensure the flow of tax revenues.[112]

Although it is unclear how this compound sea-lord governance worked on Yugeshima, it is possible to extrapolate from arrangements made for shared sea tenure on the island of Futagami, some fifty kilometers to the southwest of Yugeshima in the Kutsuna island chain. During much of the sixteenth century, the Kōno, a warrior provincial governor family in Iyo (*shugo*), sought to maintain control over the island by licensing at least three sea-lord families—the Kurushima Murakami, the Noshima Murakami, and the Imaoka—as tax farmers and administrators. These sea lords gradually incorporated parts of the island and its inhabitants into their respective domains. The situation of compound lordships continued until the Noshima Murakami conquered the island in 1582.[113]

As on Yugeshima and other littoral communities in Japan, the Futagami population lived in settlements defined by maritime function—bay (*ura*) and harbor (*tomari*)—as well as by the estate production unit (*myō*). Inhabitants of Futagami also engaged in violence for their sea-lord overlords. The Kurushima Murakami, for example, recruited the Futagami family to provide protection for merchant and pilgrimage ships bound for seasonal festivals and markets at the religious centers on the island of Itsukushima.[114] When sea lords did not require actual corvée labor as fighters, sailors, and shippers, they imposed corvée substitution taxes.[115]

Sea lords like the Kurushima, Noshima, and Imaoka all extracted allotments of timber, wheat harvests, and marine products and oversaw the disposal of Futagami commodities. These bands all dispatched agents to administer their interests on the island and included privileges for these agents as part of their taxation apportionment arrangements. For example, the Kurushima Murakami agents received rights to sea cucumbers collected by the harbor and bay villagers. Futagami also possessed bountiful stands of

---

112. Yata Toshifumi, *Nihon chūsei sengoku-ki kenryoku kōzō no kenkyū* (Hanawa Shobō, 1998), pp. 106–7.

113. EK doc. 1577, Bunki 1 (1501) 8.6; *Futagami monjo*, doc. 46, Eiroku 1 (1558) 10th month, auspicious day, in Amino Yoshihiko, "Iyo no kuni Futagamijima o megutte: Futagami-shi to Futagami monjo," *Nihon chūsei shiryōgaku no kadai: Keizu, gimonjo, monjo* (Kōbundō, 1996), pp. 272–74.

114. EK doc. 1732, Tenbun 12? (1543) 9.14; Suzuki Atsuko, *Nihon chūsei shakai no ryūtsū kōzō* (Azekura Shobō, 2000), p. 85.

115. *Futagami monjo*, doc. 40, Eishō 2 (1505) 8.6; doc. 41, Eiroku 2 (1559) 8th month, auspicious day.

timber. Yearly it sent firewood to the Kurushima Murakami and other sea lords as tax in kind.[116] The wood harvested on Futagami would have helped the Kurushima and other sea lords who managed saliculture and shipbuilding centers like Yugeshima. The Noshima called on Futagami residents to help provision their band and to provide fruits of the sea for gifts.[117]

Shared maritime lordship also extended to sea tenurial practices such as the assessing of protection fees at toll barriers and the concomitant providing of protection. Although sea lords used maritime toll barrier-based protection as a way to compete for and to extend influence over commercial networks, they also granted each other legitimacy by recognizing each other's right to charge protection monies. By recognizing each other's boundaries and protection businesses, they also stabilized the borders between sea-lord domains, allowing them to devote resources to other ends. Such an agreement can be seen vividly in the travelogue of Song Hŭigyŏng, Korean ambassador to Japan in 1420, as he passed through the Kamagari region of the Inland Sea: "In this region, there are pirates [i.e., sea lords] of the east and west. If a ship coming from the east has an eastern pirate on board, then the western pirates will not harm it. If a ship coming from the west has a western pirate on board, then the eastern pirates will not harm it."[118] Two sea-lord bands concerned with Yugeshima and Futagami, the Noshima Murakami and Kurushima Murakami, forged marriage alliances with each other in the late fifteenth and early sixteenth centuries.[119] If successful, such unions had several potential benefits. Alliances facilitated shared lordship situations like that of Futagami and other cooperative activities. Maritime borders near each other's home base could be secured, which facilitated the growth of local exchange networks and could awaken a perception that the small region between Kurushima and Noshima constituted a single, unified space.[120]

Song Hŭigyŏng's account of Kamagari is also notable for its description of one main method by which sea-lord bands provided protection. The Kamagari sea lords would send members of their bands to physically travel aboard the same ship as those who paid for protection. Phrases translated as "riding along" (*uwanori, nakanori*) became common euphemisms for sea-

116. *Futagami monjo* doc. 40, Eishō 2 (1505) 8.6; ibid., doc. 41, Eiroku 2 (1559) 8th month, auspicious day; ibid., doc. 48, Eiroku 12 (1569) 9th month, auspicious day.
117. For example, in return for Noshima Murakami Takeyoshi's entrusting the victualing of his band to the Futagami lord Taneyasu, Taneyasu sent Takeyoshi nineteen rockfish as a gift (EK doc. 2245, no year.3.28).
118. Song no. 162; Amino, *Rethinking Japanese History*, p. 94.
119. EK doc. 1645, Daiei 4 (1524) 8.14.
120. Miyamoto Tsune'ichi, *Setonaikai no kenkyū*, vol. 1 (Mirai Shakan, 1965), pp. 34–35.

lord protection businesses as practiced by bands concerned with Yugeshima like the Noshima Murakami and Kurushima Murakami in the sixteenth century.[121] In other cases, sea lords would dispatch ships to escort vessels.[122]

SEA LORDS AND COMMERCIAL SHIPPING IN THE FIFTEENTH CENTURY

Although the records of Tōji give an image of unceasing strife among pirates battling for control, the various sea lords associated with the island— the Yamaji, Koizumi Kobayakawa, Noshima Murakami, and Kurushima Murakami—were also entrepreneurs who actively participated in regional trade networks. They helped develop Yugeshima into a major commercial shipping center by administering and protecting shipping and other maritime industries. Between the first month of 1445 and the first month of 1446, in the midst of the turmoil over Yugeshima's management, twenty-six ships claiming Yugeshima registry passed through the northern barrier of Hyōgo port carrying mostly salt to be sold commercially.

An extant log, kept by Tōdaiji, the wealthy, powerful temple that administered the northern toll barrier of Hyōgo port, provides details about all the ships that passed through that barrier over the course of thirteenth months, from 1445.1 through 1446.1. This log, the *Hyōgo Northern Toll Barrier Shipping Register* (*Hyōgo Kitazeki irifune nōchō*), presents the reader with a snapshot of late medieval commercial shipping in the Seto Inland Sea. It records, in over 1,900 entries, arrivals in Hyōgo port, 106 ports of registry, shipmasters, cargoes, barrier fees, and the designated commercial agents (*toi*) for each ship. Ships ranged in size from small craft carrying a few tens of *koku* to huge dromonds capable of carrying upward of a thousand *koku*.[123] Scholars have identified two types of networks from the data in the Hyōgo register: smaller, intraregional shipping and larger, transregional shipping.[124]

---

121. EK doc. 1709, no year.9.26; EK doc. 1897, no year.11.26; EK doc. 1978, no year.6.15; Udagawa Takehisa, *Nihon no kaizoku* (Seibundō Shinkōsha, 1983), pp. 138–40.

122. Mansai, *Mansai jugō nikki*, edited by Hanawa Hokinoichi and Ōta Toshirō, *Zoku gunsho ruijū hoi* 1 (Zoku Gunsho Ruijū Kanseikai, 1928), vol. 2, p. 553, Eikyō 6 (1434) 1.30.

123. *Hyōgo Kitazeki irifune nōchō*. It is worth mentioning that 1445 seems to have been a slow year for the Japanese economy. Bakufu-sanctioned violence against the Akamatsu of Harima had thrown the surrounding provinces into chaos (Imatani Akira, "Setouchi seikaiken no suii to irifune nōchō," in *Hyōgo Kitazeki irifune nōchō*, edited by Hayashiya Tatsusaburō [Chūō Kōron Bijutsu Shuppan, 1981], p. 282). And of course there were untold ships that did not pass through the Hyōgo barrier.

124. Mutō Tadashi, "Chūsei no Hyōgo no tsu to Setonaikai suiun," in *Hyōgo Kitazeki irifune nōchō*, edited by Hayashiya Tatsusaburō (Chūō Kōron Bijutsu Shuppan, 1981), pp. 246–54.

CHAPTER 2

Yugeshima shipmasters participated in both networks. Some shipmasters made several runs over the course of a year, indicated by the repetition of certain shipmasters' names in the log. That these shipmasters always carried similar amounts and types of cargo indicates that shipmasters based on Yugeshima owned or at least captained particular ships.[125] In total, Yugeshima ships carried 3,713 *koku* of salt in 1445, ten times the largest estate shipment to Tōji.[126] Not all of the salt carried to Hyōgo then came from Yugeshima. Rather, the Yugeshima shippers seem to have acquired and transported these amounts as professional, commercial sea merchants.

First, Yugeshima shippers carried Yugeshima salt to a port, probably Onomichi, where they sold it for cash. By the fourteenth century, Onomichi had become one of the largest and busiest ports in the region in Japan, with reportedly over one thousand structures, including residences, temples, the warehouses of Ōta estate, and docks capable of handling tens of ships at once.[127] Yugeshima shippers next transported loads of salt obtained at Onomichi to Hyōgo. The Hyōgo log's authors referred to this cargo as "Bingo," alluding to the province in which Onomichi was located. Ships registered to ports on islands surrounding Yugeshima also carried products identified as "Bingo."[128] Such evidence suggests that various producing centers transported salt to Onomichi and sold the local salt to wholesalers for cash (which was then sent to estate proprietors as dues). The wholesalers then hired shippers such as Yugeshima's, who carried amalgamated bundles of salt to Hyōgo.

Information from the log also points to Yugeshima shippers having developed commercial links to other estates and ports in the region. According to the Hyōgo register, one Yugeshima shipmaster named Shirōzaemon captained ships carrying 180 and 200 koku of salt, and a "Shirōzaemon of Yugeshima" also appears in a record from nearby Ōta estate as master of a ship of similar size traveling from Onomichi to Sakai in the eleventh month of 1444. Ōta estate sometimes hired shipmasters from the surround-

125. For example, the Yugeshima shipmaster Hyōetarō captained a ship five times through the Hyōgo barrier carrying between 160 and 180 *koku*. Tarōemon transported seven shipments of between 150 and 170 *koku* (*Hyōgo Kitazeki irifune nōchō*; Yamauchi, *Chūsei Setonaikai chiikishi no kenkyū*, p. 36)

126. At its height as an estate, Yugeshima only sent a few hundred *koku* of salt to Tōji in dues (Yamauchi, *Chūsei Setonaikai chiikishi no kenkyū*, pp. 31–32).

127. *Kongōbuji monjo*, vol. 2, doc. 17, Gen'ō 2 (1320), 8th month in *Kōya-san monjo*, vol. 2 (Kyoto: Kōya-san Monjo Kankōkai, 1937). Historian Yamauchi Yuzuru suggested that Onomichi was the site of transshipment because of the inclusion of soybeans on one Yugeshima ship in the Hyōgo register (11.26 entry). Yugeshima did not produce soybeans, but Ōta no shō produced soybeans in large quantities (Yamauchi, *Chūsei Setonaikai chiikishi no kenkyū*, pp. 32–33).

128. *Hyōgo Kitazeki irifune nōchō*.

ing region to ship dues.[129] Yugeshima shippers' experiences with protection businesses and their extensive commercial connections may well have made them attractive to other estate proprietors and residents as carriers. Networks of commercial agents (*toi*) had also grown more sophisticated by the fifteenth century, and those in Hyōgo also provided another set of connections. The agent who handled all of Yugeshima's shipmasters, Dōyū, handled around 20 percent of all shipments through the port, dealing with ships registered at ports both proximate to and distant from Yugeshima.[130]

The significant presence of sea lords on Yugeshima makes it probable that they provided management and protection for these sophisticated long- and short-range shipping networks. One way that sea lords won the allegiance of shipmasters and promoted commerce was by using patronage connections to win toll-barrier immunities (*kasho*). Some sea lords expanded their influence by combining patronage and toll immunity privileges with the ability to deploy violence in the defense of their shipping and to hinder competitors. The Ikuchi Kobayakawa, who based themselves in the port of Setoda on Ikuchijima, west of Yugeshima, exemplified this type of organization.

The Ikuchi Kobayakawa belonged to the aforementioned Kobayakawa league, an extensive family-based network of land- and sea-based lords that included the Koizumi Kobayakawa and other branches that sought influence over Yugeshima. By the fourteenth century, branches of the Kobayakawa had extended their power over several littoral estates in the central Inland Sea region, including Ikuchijima.[131] At various times, the Ikuchi Kobayakawa sought to conquer neighboring islands, actions that easily could have earned them the label "pirate." In 1343, Tōji labeled them "evil bands" (*akutō*) for "invading temple lands" and "constructing fortifications" on Innoshima (located just to the north of Yugeshima).[132] In the 1460s, Kurushima Murakami Zushonosuke reported that he defeated residents of Ikuchijima seeking to conquer Yugeshima itself.[133] However, the Ikuchi Kobayakawa escaped significant punishment because they, like the Koizumi and other members of the Kobayakawa league, could invoke patronage by the Ashikaga shoguns. Such sponsorship gave them a certain leeway in their actions and made their organization very attractive to shipping organizations

129. See the entry for Bun'an 1 (1444) 4.15 in the *Bingo Ōta no shō nengu hikitsuke*, in *Kongōbuji monjo*, vol. 2, doc. 164.

130. Usami, *Nihon chūsei no ryūtsū to shōgyō*, pp. 158–61.

131. Kawai Masaharu, "Kobayakawa-shi no hatten to Setonaikai," in *Setonaikai chiiki no shakaishiteki kenkyū*, edited by Uozumi Sōgorō (Kyōto: Yanagihara Shoten, 1952), pp. 121–25.

132. NET, pp. 440–41, doc. 20, Ryakuō 4 (1341) 3.28; NET p. 441, doc. 21, Ryakuō 4 (1341) 3.28.

133. NET pp. 416–17, doc. 297, no year.5.26.

seeking protection. Shogunal sanction also may have alleviated anxieties of merchants and residents regarding Ikuchi dominion. In 1422, the Muromachi bakufu bestowed upon the Ikuchi Kobayakawa toll immunities (*kasho*) for ships registered at the port of Setoda. These *kasho* enabled their ships to "be passed through all seaborne tolls, river tolls, and Hyōgo tolls without incident."[134]

Pursuit of profit led to an abuse of these privileges. A flood of ships claimed Setoda registry to demand immunity at Hyōgo, reflecting, perhaps, a combination of Kobayakawa-sponsored shipping and other merchants seeking the protection and immunity available by flying a Setoda flag. After only four months the Muromachi bakufu retracted the pass in the face of complaints by the operators of both the northern and southern barriers of Hyōgo and their religious proprietors, Tōdaiji and Kōfukuji. The shogunal edict explained, "Last year, we issued an edict to Kobayakawa Ikuchi Inaba nyūdō exempting Ikuchi ships from toll-barrier fees. As a result, extremely large numbers of merchant ships from Setoda and other places rushed to pass through calling themselves Setoda ships."[135]

Even without such passes, the Ikuchi Kobayakawa had transformed the port of Setoda into the sixth busiest port listed in the Hyōgo register. Sixty-nine ships in the log claimed Setoda registry. Of these, eighteen exceeded four hundred *koku* of lading, the largest number of ships in that range of any port in the register. Several of these shipmasters owned their own ships and made repeated trips. Setoda's prominence attracted seafaring merchants from other parts of the Inland Sea region. One shipmaster claiming Setoda registry came from Sanuki Province.[136] Among the most important ports in Sanuki were those belonging to the islands of Shiwaku, located east of Yugeshima in a chokepoint between Honshu and Shikoku.

Documents pertaining to Shiwaku offer further evidence for connections between sea lords, violence, and the expansion of commercial shipping in the Inland Sea in this period. Similar to Yugeshima, Shiwaku enters history as a littoral estate specializing in salt production. The Fujiwara regents held the head proprietorship of Shiwaku through the thirteenth century, after which the title passed into the hands of the Ogasawara family, *shugo* of Shinano.[137] By the fifteenth century, one of the deputy provincial gover-

134. *Setoda-chō shi shiryō-hen* (Setoda-chō, Hiroshima-ken: Setoda-chō Kyōikuiinkai, 1997), doc. 13, Ōei 29 (1422) 12.2.
135. Ibid., doc. 14, Ōei 30 (1423) 3.17.
136. *Hyōgo Kitazeki irifune nōchō.*
137. *Shinpen Marugame-shi shi*, vol. 4: *Shiryō-hen* (Marugame-shi, Kagawa-ken: *Marugame-shi shi* Hensan Iinkai, 1994), doc. 17; ibid., doc. 18, Hōgen 1 (1156), 7th month; ibid., doc. 43, Kenchō 5 (1253) 10.21; ibid., doc. 87, Eitoku 3 (1383) 2.12.

nor families for Sanuki, the Yasutomi, administered the island on behalf of the Hosokawa, powerful shogunal officials and warrior governors of Sanuki Province. The Yasutomi also oversaw the port of Utazu, giving them control over both sides of an important Inland Sea chokepoint.[138]

Shiwaku had a long history as a provincial commercial and shipping center and had become one of the busiest ports in Japan by the fifteenth century. As early as the twelfth century, the island had acquired a reputation as a busy regional market and port. The monk and poet Saigyō (1118–90) described how merchants—not estate officials—from Kyoto island-hopped between Shiwaku and nearby Manabe, located off the coast of Bitchū Province. "There is an island called Manabe. Merchants from Kyoto travel there heavily laden with goods ready to deal. They also cross to Shiwaku, where I have heard they engage in commerce."[139]

The 1445–46 Hyōgo register contains thirty-seven entries with ships claiming Shiwaku as port of registry, making it the fifteenth most often claimed. The wide range of goods carried in Shiwaku vessels suggests that Shiwaku had become a major entrepôt where smaller intraregional carriers brought and transshipped goods to be delivered by long-distance Shiwaku shippers. One Shiwaku shipmaster hired himself out as an exclusive carrier of perilla for the Ōyamazaki lamp-oil merchants; others carried salt, dried fish, rice, wheat, barley, soybeans, and paper, among other goods.[140] Shiwaku's status as an important port can also be deduced from the fact that ships registered at other ports carried goods labeled with the shorthand term "Shiwaku," similar to the label "Bingo" on salt carried by Yugeshima shippers, though which particular product the term "Shiwaku" refers to is not clear.[141] Like Yugeshima and Setoda, Shiwaku shipmasters owned their ships—some more than one—and made repeated voyages carrying similar amounts of lading.

Shiwaku mariners both sought patronage and evinced a willingness to engage in violence and other activities that central authorities might consider illicit in order to enhance Shiwaku's commercial position, to acquire resources for improving the port's infrastructure, and to acquire and keep toll-exemption passes. Shiwaku seafarers enjoyed the patronage of powerful

138. Hashizume, *Setonaikai chiiki shakai to Oda kenryoku*, pp. 140–41.
139. Saigyō, *Sankashū*, quoted in *Kasaoka-shi shi* (Kasaoka-shi, Okayama-ken: Kasaoka-shi, 1983), p. 435. Saigyō traveled to Shikoku in 1168, and this anecdote may date from that trip.
140. *Hyōgo Kitazeki irifune nōchō*; Hashizume, *Setonaikai chiiki shakai to Oda kenryoku*, p. 69; for Ōyamazaki merchants, see Suzanne Gay, "The Lamp-oil Merchants of Iwashimizu Shrine: Transregional Commerce in Medieval Japan," *Monumenta Nipponica* 64.1 (2009): 1–51.
141. For example the *Hyōgo Kitazeki irifune nōchō* entry for 1445.3.6 records a ship registered to the port of Tsurajima passing the Hyōgo barrier carrying "200 *koku* of Shiwaku."

figures in the Muromachi bakufu and established connections with important commercial and religious centers such as the Ōyamazaki lamp-oil merchants, who could appeal to Iwashimizu Shrine, the imperial court, and Muromachi bakufu for toll exemptions.[142] Eleven (out of thirty-seven) Shiwaku ships with passes for Yodo barriers appear in the Hyōgo register.[143] By 1478, the Kōfukuji temple complex, proprietors of Hyōgo port's southern barrier, complained that, "the barrier is one in name only,"[144] suggesting that, much as with the case of the Ikuchi Kobayakawa's *kasho*, shipmasters may have abused exemption privileges. The monks of Kōfukuji took advantage of a close relationship with members of the Hosokawa family and other bakufu administrators in order to arrange the cancelation of the exemptions. Shiwaku seafarers protested this cancelation: a "local administrator" (*zasshō*) of Shiwaku named "Dōkō Genzaemon, initiated a suit about the exemption passes . . . and, together with allies from [Shiwaku's] various harbors, he traveled up to the Hosokawa in Kyoto bringing various folded paper edicts [i.e., *kasho*] and other documents and gifts."[145] The seafarers were also willing to engage in violence in order to demonstrate their displeasure, a fact Kōfukuji took advantage of in order to counter Dōkō Genzaemon's legal actions. A Kōfukuji operative known as the "samurai monk Tōshun no Bō enticed Yasutomi soldiers and others [from Shiwaku] into seizing ten ships from the capital." Kōfukuji then reported the piracy to the Hosokawa, causing Genzaemon to "lose face" and his suit.[146] The Hosokawa retracted the exemption pass and ordered the Yasutomi to ensure that the barrier fees were paid. The Yasutomi thereupon forwarded the instructions to the shipmasters of Shiwaku.[147]

Like the Hosokawa and Yasutomi, littoral magnates recognized the immense strategic and economic value of Shiwaku's chokepoints, harbors, and shipping industries and contended for dominion over the island. By the 1430s, accusations spread through the capital that the Noshima Murakami had established toll barriers without official sanction in the region around Shiwaku, an attempt to use a protection business to exert some authority over the Shiwaku shipping industry. To mitigate what the Hosokawa and other central authorities perceived as the damage from these advances by the Noshima, one shogunal official called on the Kobayakawa, seeking their

142. Gay, "The Lamp-oil Merchants of Iwashimizu Shrine," pp. 1–2.
143. *Hyōgo Kitazeki irifune nōchō*, entries for 1445.6.12, 1445.11.2, and 1445.12.19.
144. *Tamon'in nikki*, edited by Tsuji Zennosuke (Kadokawa Shoten, 1968), Bunmei 10 (1478) 2.27; Hashizume, *Setonaikai chiiki shakai to Oda kenryoku*, p. 141.
145. *Tamon'in nikki*, Bunmei 10 (1478) 2.27.
146. Ibid.
147. *Tamon'in nikki*, Bunmei 10 (1478) 4.4.

seafaring expertise in order to avoid or break through the Noshima protection racket: "We would be grateful for your help with the Shiwaku matter as we will be leaving from Shiwaku in Sanuki soon, and the Noshima barrier-erector pirates (*sekidachi*) . . . have been perpetrating illicit acts."[148] These Noshima efforts toward securing Shiwaku as part of their domain occurred roughly contemporaneously with their attempts to take control of Yugeshima, each part of a larger plan to expand Noshima maritime dominion in territories of strategic and commercial significance.

CONCLUSION

This chapter has presented sea-based narratives about the transition from an economy dominated by estate networks to one dominated by commercial networks and the emergence of local lordship, two stories usually limited to the terra firma. The histories of maritime estates like Yugeshima, Innoshima, Ikuchijima, and Shiwaku have shown the ubiquity of attempts to territorialize the seas. Local littoral magnates transformed themselves into sea lords by becoming entrepreneurs who devoted resources to developing enterprises at the intersections of commerce and violence. In the fourteenth century, figures like Shōyo exploited patrons' needs for violent and nonviolent services related to estate management, defended the estate from those who sought to challenge his supremacy there—sanctioned by the proprietor or not—and attracted estate residents by providing safe access to burgeoning local and regional exchange networks. From one perspective, like local lords on land, sea lords hastened the demise of the estate institution by inserting themselves as the key mediating figure between proprietors, residents, and the surrounding locales; from another, they kept estates viable as institutions by ensuring the transmission of rents commuted into coins.

By the fifteenth century, sea lords appear more and more as transgenerational masters of maritime networks. They specialized in forms of violence that were categorized and commodified as "protection." These services included managing estates and ensuring the security of rent transports and other ships at toll barriers installed in and around chokepoints. Such barriers became the focal points of conflicts between sea lords competing for control of littoral holdings and installations integral to the regulation of maritime traffic—sea tenure. It is arguable that the need for the services of and competition among sea lords like the Koizumi Kobayakawa, Yamaji,

<hr>

148. "Ashikaga shogun gonaisho narabi ni hōsho dome" Eikyō 6? (1434).7.4, quoted in Hashizume, *Setonaikai chiiki shakai to Oda kenryoku*, p. 183.

Kurushima Murakami, and Noshima Murakami hindered commercial development by increasing protection costs. However, it would be anachronistic to consider the possibility of having commercial shipping or secure littoral estates without the protection that sea lords could provide during the strife that was endemic to much of the late medieval period. Under the control of sea lords, maritime estates became some of the most active and profitable commercial shipping centers in Japan, dominating both local and long haul networks in the Inland Sea region. Sea-lord families legitimized their aggrandizement of littoral holdings by seeking patronage at the highest levels of provincial and central authority. Among the most helpful fruits of this patronage were toll exemption passes that enabled further growth of sea-lord commercial networks. Chapter 3 carries this history of sea lordship and commerce forward by focusing on one of the sea-lord bands that competed for Yugeshima, the Noshima Murakami, in the sixteenth century, when sea-lord dominion reached its apogee.

CHAPTER 3

With the Sea As Their Domain:
The Noshima Murakami in the Sixteenth Century

It is, it is a glorious thing
To be a pirate king![1]

In the sixteenth century, some sea lords expanded the dominion of their forebears to unprecedented degrees, not just in terms of geography, but also to the degree that the maritime domain increasingly fell under the unitary control of a single sea-lord family. The swathes of maritime space that constituted their domains became recognized as an integral part of the patchwork tapestry of autonomous, regional political and economic powers of sixteenth-century Japan. Among the sea lords identified as the most formidable in this regard was the Noshima Murakami family, who in less than a century transformed themselves from minor, local powers into figures whose power, durability, and standing inspired the Jesuit chronicler Luis Frois (1532–97) to dub the head of the band, Noshima Murakami Takeyoshi (ca. 1533–1604), "The greatest pirate in all of Japan."[2] They owed such an ascent to shrewdly combining autonomous aggrandizement with code switching and tactical choices in patrons across much of the sixteenth century. Based on his long experience with the Japanese maritime world, Frois offered this précis of the process: it was because the Noshima Murakami were of a "house that had endured for many years, had accrued a reputation as great lords [*senhores grandes*], and are treated and served as such" that they could "maintain their preeminence as supreme pirates in all of Japan."[3]

To elaborate—the further that the Noshima extended their reach over the sea lanes, the more their potential worth to a sponsor increased and the greater their latitude of movement. The greater the extent of the patronage, the further they sailed and the greater their domains and reputations grew.

---

1. W. S. Gilbert and Arthur Sullivan, *Pirates of Penzance*, 1879.
2. Luis Frois, *Historia de Japam*, edited by José Wicki, S. J. (Lisbon: Ministério da Cultura e Coordenação Científica Secretaria de Estado da Cultura, Biblioteca Nacional, 1984), vol. 4, p. 248.
3. Ibid., p. 249.

The wider the Noshima's perceived influence, the more travelers sought their protection, and ultimately, the lower protection costs went, promoting further commercial expansion. At the height of their authority in the latter half of the sixteenth century, sea lords like the Noshima became powerful enough to transcend the need for patronage. They developed specific tools of dominion that reflected the distinctly maritime nature of their power: protection businesses, ships, and "sea castles"[4] located in chokepoints. They also took advantage of patronage, borrowed extensively from land-based tools of lordship, and regulated the human elements of their domains by issuing codes of laws and other practices. Travelers and authorities across Japan recognized their domains and treated the Noshima as the equivalent of central authorities in their ability to guarantee safety on the seas through the issuance of protection passes. Frois adumbrated these elements crucial to sea-lord dominion: "He lives in a grand fortress and possesses many retainers, holdings, and ships that continually fly across the waves. . . . He is so powerful that on these coasts as well as the coastal regions of other kingdoms [reinos], all pay him annual tribute out of fear that he will destroy them."[5]

The Noshima understood how to take advantage of military and political changes in sixteenth-century Japan. During this time, the scale and intensity of warfare grew. Warrior provincial governors (shugo) competed with local rivals for advantage; winners transformed themselves into regional warlords (daimyo) who consolidated autonomous domains.[6] Power blocs led by particularly powerful daimyo families emerged; other daimyo jockeyed for position within those and shifted allegiances among them. The Noshima correspondingly shifted their loci of service to these warlords. Although patrons had some leverage in negotiating with sea lords, sea lords still controlled how, when, and to whom services would be provided and dictated how payment was to be rendered. Sea lords like the Noshima were aware that their warlord patrons needed the services and resources sea lords could bring them: fighting sea battles, operating protection businesses, directing commercial shipping organizations, managing maritime produc-

4. For phrase "sea castle," see Yamauchi Yuzuru, *Kaizoku to umijiro: Setouchi no sengokushi* (Heibonsha, 1997).
5. Frois, *Historia de Japam*, vol. 4, p. 248.
6. Although it is common to distinguish between *shugo* daimyo and the more autonomous daimyo of the Sengoku period, during the sixteenth century even the most powerful autonomous lords continued to secure the *shugo* title from the shogun as one means of justifying their authority, and Muromachi bakufu institutional practices and cultures continued to have currency across Japan (Yata Toshifumi, *Nihon chūsei sengoku-ki kenryoku kōzō no kenkyū* [Hanawa Shobō, 1998]; Yamamuro Kyōko, "Sengoku no chiikisei," in *Iwanami Kōza Nihon tsūshi*, vol. 10, *chūsei* 4, edited by Asao Naohiro et al. [Iwanami Shoten, 1994], 162–91).

tion, and governing multiple ports. These aspiring regional hegemons desired to harness the engines of Inland Sea commercial networks, tether them to their domains, and deny them to competitors. Patrons attempted to use marriages, oaths, supplies of food, extensive rewards, and other means to bind sea-lord families closer to them, but to little avail. Mercenary sea lords like the Noshima switched service among competing warlords in order to maximize rewards. After all, many daimyo could issue edicts in support of sea-lord interests. For the Noshima and other sea lords, one patron was as good as another, and two were better than one.

However, such autonomy had limits. Economically, sea-lord power depended on controlling maritime linkages. Only through continued operation of networks of maritime violence and commerce could sea-lord domains continue to function. Such networks thus required the Noshima to maintain patronage relations and to attract customers through force of reputation. Each addition to the Noshima domain reflected a strategic choice that increased the scope of Noshima commercial enterprises, particularly their shipping and protection concerns. As an integral part of the sixteenth-century Japanese "war economy,"[7] the Noshima Murakami profited greatly from this strife because they could both provide mercenary naval services and defend shippers from potential overspill from those mercenary naval operations.

In addition, as the Noshima gained power and wealth, they more and more accepted aspects of land-based elite culture as markers of status and power. The code switching that enabled them to portray themselves in ways attractive to land-based lords increasingly made them indistinguishable from those lords as they began practicing cultural pursuits consonant with land-based elite status. Patronage thus brought the Noshima culturally more and more within the sphere of land-based elite society.

It is thus possible to narrate the expansion of the Noshima in the sixteenth century by charting the intersections of their patronage, their acquisition of holdings and privileges, their expansion of maritime commercial networks, and their development of distinctive tools, practices, and trappings of lordship and status. At the dawn of the sixteenth century, Noshima territories consisted of their home island and stronghold of Noshima and small, nearby holdings governed by relatives such as the harbor of Ōhama (in modern-day Imabari) and islet fastnesses like Mushijima and Nakatoshima (see figure 7);[8] they also held a partial claim to Futagamijima and Kutsuna Island.[9]

7. Wayne Farris, *Japan's Medieval Population: Famine, Fertility, and Warfare in a Transformative Age* (Honolulu: University of Hawai'i Press, 2006), p. 235.
8. EK doc. 1645, Daiei 4 (1524) 8.14; Yamauchi Yuzuru, *Chūsei Setonaikai chiikishi no kenkyū* (Hōsei Daigaku Shuppankyoku, 1998), pp. 120–32.
9. EK doc. 1151, Ōei 12 (1405) 9.21.

Between the 1520s and 1580s, the Noshima switched their services back and forth among several blocs of warlord families, sometimes serving multiple sponsors concurrently: the Hosokawa, the Kōno in Iyo, the Ōuchi and Mōri in western Honshu, the Miyoshi of Sanuki, the Ōtomo of northern Kyushu, and the "first unifier," Oda Nobunaga (see table 1 and figure 11). At the peak of their power in the 1580s, the Noshima Murakami domain encompassed a sprawling network of chokepoints, ports, island fortresses, and fishing villages that stretched along shipping corridors across much of the Seto Inland Sea, from Minoshima and Kaminoseki in the west to Shiwaku and Kasaoka in the east (see figure 2). They developed, promoted, protected, and administered extensive commercial shipping networks beyond those centered on Hyōgo explored in chapter 2, with connections both within and beyond the archipelago.

TABLE 1

Timeline of patrons competing to sponsor the Noshima Murakami

Dates	Patron bloc 1	Patron bloc 2
1520s	Hosokawa Takakuni (1484–1531) & Ōuchi Yoshioki (1477–1528)	Hosokawa Sumimoto (1489–1520) & Hosokawa Harumoto (1514–63)
1532–51	Ōuchi Yoshitaka (1507–51)	Kōno, Ōtomo, Amako, Itsukushima Shrine
1555–57	Mōri Motonari (1497–1571)	Sue Harukata (1521–55), Ōuchi Yoshinaga (ca. 1532–57)
1560s–1570s	Mōri, Kobayakawa, Kōno	Ōtomo, Amako, Miyoshi
1570–80	Mōri, Kobayakawa, Kōno, Ikkō Ikki, Ashikaga Yoshiaki (1537–97)	Oda Nobunaga (1534–82)
1580s	Mōri, Kobayakawa, Kōno	Oda Nobunaga, Hashiba (later Toyotomi) Hideyoshi (1536–98)

SIXTEENTH-CENTURY PATRONAGE AND DOMAINAL EXPANSION

In the early sixteenth century, the Noshima reaped significant reward from their long-standing service relations with the Hosokawa, a family of powerful warrior provincial governors and shogunal officials. During the mid-fifteenth century, the Noshima had pressed claims to and established protection businesses in the waters around the island estates of Yugeshima and Shiwaku, where the Hosokawa exerted significant influence. They sought

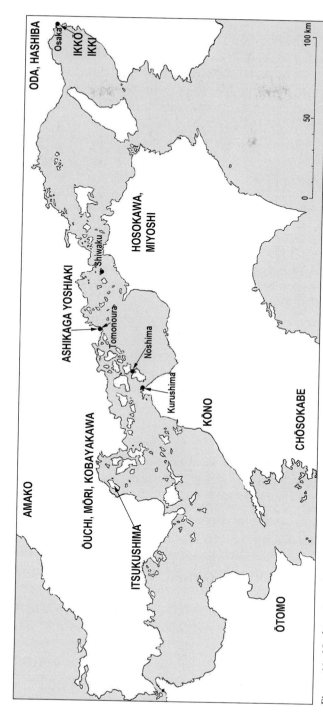

Figure 11. Noshima Murakami patrons during the sixteenth century. Adapted from *Hyōgo Kitazeki irifune nōchō*, edited by Hayashiya Tatsusaburō (Chūō Kōron Bijutsu Shuppan, 1981), pp. 260–61.

Hosokawa patronage to enhance those claims.[10] In the late fifteenth century, one member of the Noshima, Murakami Yoshikata, "married the daughter of the Hosokawa retainer Kodama Yajirō." This union also gained the Noshima access to the resources and commercial connections of Shigi estate in Settsu where the Kodama resided.[11] In the 1520s, the Hosokawa officially recognized Noshima control over the island-based estate and port of Shiwaku. Because of earlier Noshima ambitions toward Shiwaku, it is likely that when Hosokawa Takakuni deeded the Noshima "the administrator post for the Sanuki provincial holding of Shiwaku,"[12] the Hosokawa were acquiescing to a Noshima fait accompli. Hosokawa Takakuni held little actual sway over the Noshima, who accepted the sponsorship of Takakuni's nephew, Hosokawa Harumoto, to fight against Takakuni in 1531.[13]

Noshima control over the island of Shiwaku provides a clear example of how sea lords capitalized on the ability to exert unitary authority in order to expand shipping concerns that provided ships, violence, and protection from violence. The Noshima administered a large organization of shippers, known as *kaisen*, residing on Shiwaku.[14] Together, they developed the port of Shiwaku into a way station where travelers could stop for the night, take lodgings, change ships, wait for favorable winds, and arrange with the Noshima for protection. In the fall of 1566, an estate agent from the western Honshu province of Bitchū sailed to Shiwaku and took lodgings for twelve days before taking another ship to the port of Sakai.[15] Around the same time, the powerful regional warlord of western Honshu, Mōri Motonari, and his son Takamoto jointly requested the Noshima Murakami's "best efforts" in the "hiring of naval escort [*uwanori*]" to Shiwaku.[16] Jesuits frequently stopped over on Shiwaku when traveling between the capital and Kyushu; there the Noshima could provide them with protection, ships, and lodgings.[17] The presence of Jesuits and other foreigners in ports like Shiwaku gave the Noshima lords expertise in cross-cultural negotiation and exchange.

10. See chapter 2.
11. EK doc. 1645, Daiei 4 (1524) 8.14.
12. EK doc. 1663, no year.4.13. The document probably dates from between 1521 and 1525. Takakuni was *shugo* of Sanuki from 1508–31 and deputy shogun (*kanrei*) from 1521–31. He took the tonsure in 1525, after which he probably used a different name. Takakuni sought to enthrone Ashikaga Yoshiharu (1511–50) as shogun and needed significant naval forces.
13. Hashizume Shigeru, *Setonaikai chiiki shakai to Oda kenryoku* (Kyoto: Shibunkaku Shuppan, 2007), p. 183.
14. EK doc. 2086, Genki 1? (1570), 6.15.
15. *Shinpen Marugame-shi shi*, vol. 4: *Shiryō-hen* (Marugame-shi, Kagawa-ken: Marugame-shi shi Hensan Iinkai, 1994), doc.134, Eiroku 9 (1566) 9.21.
16. EK doc. 1897, no year.11.26.
17. Frois, *Historia de Japam*, vol. 2, pp. 4–5, 481–82; vol. 3, pp. 246–47; vol. 4, pp. 219, 461.

By 1532, the Noshima Murakami had shifted their patronage, performing "maritime services"[18] for two warlords in western Japan, the Ōtomo and Kōno, who were fighting against a third, Ōuchi Yoshitaka. For example, the Noshima assembled "a huge naval protection force" to attack the bases of sea lords in the service of the Ōuchi, including harbors in the Kamagari Islands.[19] By the end of the decade, however, the Noshima also agreed to serve the Ōuchi, it seems in return for greater license for their protection businesses. The Ōuchi granted them sanction "to escort ships [*uwanori*] as far as Hiroshima Bay."[20]

The Noshima aspired to unitary possession of that protection business, and they "issued repeated complaints" when other sea lords conducted protection operations in what the Noshima considered their space.[21] The inability of the Ōuchi to ensure such exclusivity by reining in the activities of other sea lords under their sponsorship may have driven the Noshima to seek alternate patronage with the Kōno of Iyo. When, in 1540, Ōuchi Yoshitaka authorized another sea-lord band known as the Shirai, as well as others in his employ, to sail "protection ships" to attack the Kutsuna Islands of Iyo because of Kōno participation in wars against the Ōuchi,[22] the Noshima initially came in on the side of the Kōno.[23] The Kurushima Murakami, the Innoshima Murakami, and other bands joined the Noshima Murakami in this conflict. As a coalition of perhaps "twenty or thirty ships," they fought a naval campaign that reputedly included a picturesque engagement in front of the great Torii gate of Itsukushima.[24] However, such a decision made their home islands a target. In the summer of 1541, Ōuchi-sponsored sea lords led by the Shirai family retaliated by carrying the battle back into the home waters of the Noshima, Kurushima, and Innoshima, including a battle at the island of Noshima itself.[25]

By the end of 1541, however, the Noshima Murakami, Kurushima Murakami, and Innoshima Murakami succeeded in fighting the sea-lord forces sponsored by the Ōuchi to a standstill. Such a performance inspired Ōuchi

18. EK doc. 1665, Tenbun 1? (1532) 7.20.

19. EK doc. 1708, no year.7.13.

20. EK doc. 1709, no year.9.26.

21. Ibid.

22. EK doc. 1705, Tenbun 9 (1540) 8.20; EK doc. 1706, Tenbun 9 (1540) 8.21.

23. The Noshima may have entered into this campaign at the behest of the head priest of Itsukushima Shrine, Tomoda Okifuji, who rebelled against Ōuchi Yoshitaka at the instigation of Amako Haruhisa in the first month of 1541 (Tanamori Fusaaki, *Fusaaki oboegaki*, in *Hiroshima-ken shi kodai chūsei shiryō-hen*, vol. 3 (Hiroshima-shi: Hiroshima-ken, 1978), p. 1120).

24. Ibid.

25. EK doc. 1713, Tenbun 10 (1541) 7.28.

CHAPTER 3

Yoshitaka to rehire the Noshima, Kurushima, and Innoshima. However, these sea lords set the terms of service and seem to have been able to apply considerable leverage during negotiations. In a letter to retainers, Ōuchi Yoshitaka acknowledged that "the Kurushima's request differs from their original message; however, as we really need them, this [change] should be permitted."[26] The Innoshima switched sides in exchange for rights to administer part of the valuable port of Tomonoura.[27] As a major port close to Innoshima and a strategic point where sea lanes from the southwest and the west converged,[28] Tomonoura would have been of inestimable value to the Innoshima, while it would have been in the interest of daimyo patrons not to allow sponsored parties to establish power bases consisting of such strategic, contiguous holdings.

The Noshima Murakami (together with the Imaoka band) wrangled perhaps the most significant reward. In exchange for switching to Ōuchi sponsorship, the Noshima Murakami lord, Takashige, won the right to operate a protection business for international trade based at the shrine and market island of Itsukushima.[29] Takashige negotiated the rights to intercept and "examine at Itsukushima and other inlets and bays" trading vessels and to assess "protection money [dabetsu yakusen] according to a ship's lading of goods related to trade with the continent [karani]."[30]

Both the Noshima Murakami and the Ōuchi benefitted from this sponsorship agreement. The Noshima Murakami gained a lucrative, legal protection business and access to overseas trade networks. Ōuchi Yoshitaka acquired a way both to hurt the shipping of his competitors and to protect his own shipping, thus increasing protection costs for the opposition. Yoshitaka confirmed Noshima privileges even after merchants from the entrepôt of Sakai (a chief port for the China trade in the sixteenth century) brought complaints against the Noshima Murakami for infringing on their traditional preserve of taxing overseas trade ships. Sakai merchants were in league with Yoshitaka's rivals, the Hosokawa, so Yoshitaka continued to back the Noshima. In the final decision, Yoshitaka authorized the Noshima to charge protection money based on the lading of all China trade ships except for those from the provinces of Hyūga and Satsuma (under control

26. YK, vol. 2, p. 946 doc. 12, Tenbun 10? (1541) 11.15.
27. EK doc. 1741, Tenbun 13 (1544) 7.3.
28. Fujiwara Seika, Nankō nikki zankan, in Fujiwara Seika-shū, edited by Kokumin Seishin Bunka Kenkyūjo (Kyoto: Shibunkaku Shuppan, 1941), vol. 2, p. 379.
29. EK doc. 1770, Tenbun 21? (1552) 4.20.
30. EK doc. 1730, Tenbun 11? (1542) 5.21.

of the Shimazu family and located in southern Kyushu), which traditionally were the preserve of Sakai merchants to tax.[31]

This Noshima protection enterprise stimulated further development of the island of Itsukushima as a commercial center. The Noshima did not simply intercept overseas trading ships but actually directed them to make anchorage at Itsukushima,[32] which indirectly fostered the growth of enterprises to deal with the increased traffic of commercial vessels. By the mid sixteenth century, Itsukushima had become a nexus of archipelagic and overseas commerce and a way station for foreign and domestic travelers. Its periodic markets teemed with merchants selling medicines, silks, and other goods from the continent.[33]

With their control of several chokepoints, especially those of the port of Shiwaku, the Noshima were perfectly situated to regulate this traffic, as is evidenced by Noshima retaliation to the abrogation of their rights to tax China trade ships. Under pressure from Sakai merchants who helped fund his coup d'état against Ōuchi Yoshitaka in 1551 with a grant of 10,000 *hiki* in copper coins, Sue Harukata cancelled the Noshima's rights to tax and protect the China trade ships in 1552.[34] Shortly thereafter, officials close to Harukata reported on reprisals launched by the Noshima and other aggrieved bands: "pirate ships [*zokusen*] are on the increase, and those from Muro and Shiwaku repeatedly have been causing unforeseen incidents that create difficulties for the Kyoto and Sakai merchants."[35]

The main line of the Noshima Murakami also invoked Ōuchi sponsorship in order to consolidate their domain by suppressing a rival line. In the late 1540s the Noshima house split when a branch family based on the nearby island of Nakatoshima challenged the main line over the house headship.[36] Sponsorship by the Ōuchi and a marriage alliance gained the main line access to additional resources, which enabled the main line to subdue the branch family. The Ōuchi dispatched the Shirai sea-lord family to help the Noshima by attacking Nakatoshima in 1546.[37] In addition, because

31. Ibid.
32. EK doc. 1770, Tenbun 21? (1552) 4.20; *Daiganji monjo*, doc. 65, Tenbun 21 (1552) 2.28, in *Hiroshima-ken shi kodai chūsei shiryō-hen*, vol. 3 (Hiroshima-shi: Hiroshima-ken, 1978), pp. 1221–22.
33. Suzuki Atsuko, *Nihon chūsei shakai no ryūtsū kōzō* (Azekura Shobō, 2000), pp. 86–90.
34. EK doc. 1770, Tenbun 21? (1552) 4.20. *Daiganji monjo*, doc. 69, Tenbun 21? (1552) 9.3.
35. *Daiganji monjo* doc. 68, Tenbun 21? (1552) 8.26.
36. For an alternate interpretation of the feud, see Yamauchi, *Chūsei Setonaikai chiikishi no kenkyū*, pp. 127–32.
37. EK doc. 1756, Tenbun 15 (1546) 9.13.

Noshima Murakami Takeyoshi (ca. 1533–1604) had married a daughter of Kurushima Murakami Michiyasu (1519–67),[38] the Noshima could call on the Ōuchi to pressure the Kurushima Murakami to help the Noshima Murakami by stopping "pirate" raids by Nakatoshima. As Ōuchi officials wrote to the Kurushima: "Lately, we have received several orders regarding the conflict between Noshima and Nakatoshima. The orders specify that the two should restore peaceful relations. Nevertheless, the Nakatoshima band is incessantly sending pirate ships [zokusen] to the bays of Suō Province [where the Ōuchi were based]. We expect to receive an edict that . . . as in previous years, we will hire you."[39] In return for such services, the Kurushima Murakami requested and received "toll immunities [kasho] for Suō Province,"[40] which made Kurushima shipping more profitable. As a result of this assistance, by 1552, Noshima Murakami Takeyoshi had assumed command of the Noshima band.[41]

The Noshima main line was aware of the dangers that their fratricidal feud and their naval mercenarism on behalf of the Ōuchi and the Kōno posed for shipping. From ports like Shiwaku, they offered to escort customers safely through the war zones, and their reputations as purveyors of protection won them customers. In 1546, the temple of Hōsenji in Suō Province (a branch of the powerful Daitokuji Zen temple complex) hired Shiwaku shippers to transport cash dues and monk passengers to Sakai.[42]

In 1551, a major locus of sea-lord patronage changed when Sue Harutaka assassinated Ōuchi Yoshitaka. In 1555, a former Ōuchi retainer named Mōri Motonari (1497–1571) went to war with the Sue, most famously defeating them at the battle of Itsukushima. Before this battle, each side scrambled to secure sea-lord assistance, sending flurries of correspondence, the remnants of which illustrate the advantages held by maritime service providers over patrons. To secure sea-lord assistance, the Mōri had no qualms about arranging marriage alliances with "pirates," but even such an alliance secured with the Kurushima Murakami in 1554 did not guarantee participation by the Kurushima in the battle.[43] The Kurushima delayed entering the conflict as long as possible, and the Mōri sent incessant requests up to the night be-

38. Yamauchi Yuzuru, *Setouchi no kaizoku: Murakami Takeyoshi no tatakai* (Kōdansha, 2005), p. 54.
39. EK doc. 1768, no year.9.20.
40. Ibid.
41. Yamauchi, *Chūsei Setonaikai no chiikishi no kenkyū*, p. 132; EK doc. 1770, Tenbun 21? (1552) 4.20.
42. DNK 17, *Daitokuji monjo*, vol. 6, p. 329, doc. 2298, Tenbun 15? (1546) 2.14.
43. Nishio Kazumi, *Sengoku-ki no kenryoku to kon'in* (Seibundō, 2005), pp. 19–26. Motonari's fourth son, Hoida Motokiyo, also married a daughter of Kurushima Murakami Michiyasu. See also Yamauchi, *Setouchi no kaizoku*, pp. 54–55.

fore the battle.[44] The Noshima Murakami also took advantage of such convulsions to play both sides, entertaining offers from both the Mōri[45] and the Sue,[46] though they ultimately seem to have declined to fight for either.

By the late 1550s, it had become clear to the Noshima and other sea lords that the Mōri were becoming an important power in western Honshu, and they soon accepted Mōri offers of sponsorship. Initially, the Mōri did not have much experience or influence in the maritime world and relied heavily on "pirates" for maritime functions. So the Mōri lost little in granting littoral holdings to sea lords, and in fact may have gained some indirect influence at sea.[47] Records of sea-lord sponsorship from this period reveal both the extent to which land-based written forms had permeated sea lords' negotiations for recompense and the degree to which sea lords dictated the terms of service. After the defeat of Sue Harukata's forces, sea lords who had formerly acted under Sue sponsorship accepted offers of service from Mōri Motonari, but only after Motonari acceded to their terms. One such group of sea-lord bands submitted a "catalog of desired lands" recorded in terms of land-based productive capacity in *koku*. Of course, by the term "lands," the sea lords specified places like "628 *koku* in three harbors" or "original holdings augmented by 130 *koku* on the island."[48]

True to this pattern, the Noshima Murakami pushed the Mōri to grant them title to specific maritime locations and other privileges that would enhance their sea-based dominion, while rejecting inland locations. In the early 1560s, the Mōri wanted the Noshima to aid them in an attack on the port of Tsurajima (in today's Okayama Prefecture) but had only a small amount of inland territory available for recompense, a reward that the Mōri admitted "was nothing special, especially as we had promised it to them before."[49] Instead, the Noshima eventually extracted from the Mōri confirmation of

---

44. EK doc. 1800, Tenbun 24? (1555) 9.27; EK doc. 1801, no date.

45. EK doc. 1797, Tenbun 24? (1555) 5.28. Only chronicles and forgeries written long after the battle document participation by the Noshima Murakami, Kurushima Murakami, and Innoshima Murakami on the side of the Mōri in the battle of Itsukushima. The weight of evidence from 1555 clearly documents Mōri desires for the services of these sea lords, but some or all of them probably declined. However, as the battle assumed greater importance in the mythology of the Mōri rise to power, it became necessary for sea lords and others to place themselves on the correct side of history. For a discussion of the battle and its sources, see Yamauchi, *Chūsei Setonaikai chiikishi no kenkyū*, pp. 160–82.

46. EK doc. 1769, no year.4.20.

47. Yamauchi, *Setouchi no kaizoku*, p. 23.

48. Quoted in Udagawa Takehisa, "Ōuchi-shi keigo-shū no shōchō to Mōri-shi no suigun hensei," in *Mōri-shi no kenkyū*, edited by Fujiki Hisashi (Yoshikawa Kōbunkan, 1984), pp. 440–41. For another example of "lands" used this way, see EK doc. 2300, Tenshō 10? (1582) 4.20.

49. EK doc. 1900, no date.

Noshima interests in Kasaoka,[50] an important commercial shipping port.[51] Kasaoka represented an important strategic position for the Noshima in particular: it is connected via a chain of islands to the Noshima commercial center of Shiwaku. Indeed, in addition to the port of Kasaoka, the Noshima acquired the salt-producing island of Kōnoshima, which protects the harbor of Kasaoka (see figure 2), and which also creates a chokepoint along the access routes to the port.[52] But Kasaoka also lay on the frontier of Mōri territories, and Noshima control gave the Mōri indirect influence over that region.

The Noshima both exploited their patronage connections with the Mōri and played the Mōri off against other daimyo in order to expand unitary control over maritime networks. Between 1561 and 1571, the Noshima participated in a proxy war over the straits of Shimonoseki fought on behalf of the Mōri and the Ōtomo. From the Mōri, the Noshima gained some control over Kaminoseki,[53] an important port and toll barrier in the Inland Sea, and Minoshima,[54] a tiny island on the Kyushu coast. Minoshima commanded approaches to the straits of Shimonoseki and lucrative trade routes that both encircled Kyushu and extended out toward China and Korea.

After inflicting several defeats on Ōtomo-sponsored sea-lord forces, the Noshima could demand significant reward from the Ōtomo lord, Sōrin, in exchange for switching sides. Ōtomo Sōrin granted the Noshima permission to expand their protection business over an entire Kyushu province's coastline: "harbor tallies [sappo] for Chikuzen Province."[55] The Noshima became such a fixture on the Kyushu coastline in this period that local "pirates" impersonated them, borrowing the aura of Noshima might to intimidate passing shipping.[56] Ōtomo Sōrin was an attractive patron for the Noshima because he hosted Chinese and Portuguese merchants and so could offer the Noshima connections with overseas raiding and trading networks and stable supplies of important overseas products like saltpeter, an essential ingredient in black powder for firearms.[57] It may have been in order to support

50. *Kasaoka-shi shi shiryō-hen*, vol. 2 (Kasaoka-shi, Okayama-ken: Kasaoka-shi, 2001), doc. 116, no year.11.23.
51. Kasaoka sent three ships through the Hyōgo barrier in 1445 (*Hyōgo Kitazeki irifune nōchō*, edited by Hayashiya Tatsusaburō (Chūō Kōron Bijutsu Shuppan, 1981).
52. Yamauchi, *Setouchi no kaizoku*, pp. 149–51; YK, vol. 3, p. 578, doc. 190, Bunroku 2 (1593) 9.28.
53. EK doc. 2053, Eiroku 11? (1568) 10.18; YK, vol. 4, pp. 275, doc. 6, Tenshō 2 (1574) 11.3; Kishida Hiroshi, *Daimyō ryōgoku no keizai kōzō* (Iwanami Shoten, 2001), p. 198.
54. EK doc. 2176, Tenshō 4? (1576) 3.2.
55. EK doc. 2075, Eiroku 12? (1569) 9.22.
56. EK doc. 2091, Eiroku 13? (1570) 7.24.
57. Kishida, *Daimyō ryōgoku no keizai kōzō*, pp. 4–5.

such merchants that Sōrin requested that Takeyoshi "mobilize protection on the sea lanes for travelers I am sending to the port of Sakai" and to "waive the tolls to be paid at Shiwaku harbor" in 1570.[58]

During this period of strife between Ōtomo and Mōri, the Noshima continued to provide protection services for those seeking safe passage through war zones. Their reputation as naval protection experts and figures who operated between the warring factions (maintaining their autonomy) attracted customers and patrons of the highest status. In 1569, the shogun, Ashikaga Yoshiaki, and Oda Nobunaga entrusted a Shiwaku shipmaster with the safe transport of an envoy being sent to broker a peace deal between the warring rivals.[59]

The documents from the negotiations between the Mōri and the Noshima Murakami in this period illustrate the practices of self-representation that sea lords used when pondering patronage offers. In order to smooth their return to Mōri patronage in 1570, Noshima Murakami Takeyoshi exchanged oaths with Mōri Motonari and Motonari's heir Terumoto (1553–1625). The two oaths integrate a set of reciprocal responsibilities into a sacred contract. Takeyoshi agreed to serve the Mōri exclusively and the Mōri agreed to treat Noshima as promised in negotiations. A clause on investigation indicates the instability of the relationship, which the Mōri may have hoped could be fortified with a sacred oath. Both sides agreed on a mechanism for keeping lines of communication and arbitration open in any circumstance in which one side felt a distance growing between them. To demonstrate his sincerity, Takeyoshi signed his oath in blood.

Sworn Oath

- I swear that unswervingly, I will perform services for Motonari and Terumoto alone [*muni*].
- If in the course of duty, a distance grows between us, there will be an investigation.

If I have belied the above, I will suffer the holy wrath and punishment of Bonten and Taishakuten, Shitennō, all the gods of the sixty-some provinces of Japan, major and minor, especially Mishima Daimyōjin, Hachiman Daibosatsu, Tenmandaijizai Tenjin, and all associated and related deities. Thus my sworn oath as above.

---

58. EK doc. 2087, Eiroku 13? (1570) 2.13.
59. *Zōtei Oda Nobunaga monjo no kenkyū*, edited by Okuno Takahiro (Yoshikawa Kōbunkan, 1988), vol. 2, *hoi*, doc. 21, Eiroku 12? (1569) 10.26.

Eiroku 13 [1570] 9.20

Murakami Kamon no kami Minamoto Takeyoshi

[sealed in blood and signed]

[To:] Mōri Shōyūtarō [Terumoto], Mōri Uma no tō [Motonari], and Company[60]

Mōri Motonari, Kobayakawa Takakage (1533-1597), and Mōri Terumoto swore in return:

Sworn Oath

- As before, it is our infinite wish manifest that we forever accept your single-hearted, generous service.
- If in the course of things, a distance comes between us, it is understood that we agree to an investigation.
- On our part, we will without disagreement behave as has been discussed since the beginning.

If we have belied the above, we will suffer the holy punishments and wrath of Bonten, Tenshakuten, Shidaitennō, and especially Both Great Deities of Itsukushima, and Tenmandaijizai Tenjin. Thus the oath is as above.

Eiroku 13 [1570] 9.25

[Signed], Mōri Terumoto, Kobayakawa Takakage, [Mōri] Uma no tō Motonari

[To:] Murakami Kamon no kami Takeyoshi[61]

The language used by Takeyoshi resounds with hybridity that developed in documents joining land and sea. The Mōri accepted Takeyoshi's claims to titles steeped in a history of terracentrism. The honorary rank *Kamon no kami* originated in titles from the Ritsuryō period, and the name Minamoto is an imperial clan name favored by warriors. But Takeyoshi also swore by Mishima Daimyōjin, a sea god whom the Noshima Murakami and other sea

60. EK doc. 2102, Eiroku 13 (1570) 9.20.
61. EK doc. 2103, Eiroku 13 (1570) 9.25. Both Takeyoshi and the Mōri wrote their oaths on the back of paper talismans from the Nachi waterfall deity of Kumano (Satō Shin'ichi, *Shinpen komonjogaku nyūmon* [Hōsei Daigaku Shuppankyoku, 1997], pp. 229–35). Such seals were commonly used for oaths in the Sengoku period and were carried around Japan by Kumano nuns (*bikuni*). See Barbara Ruch, "Woman to Woman: Kumano Bikuni Proselytizers in Medieval and Early Modern Japan," in *Engendering Faith: Women and Buddhism in Premodern Japan*, edited by Barbara Ruch, Michigan Monograph Series in Japanese Studies, no. 43 (Ann Arbor: Center for Japanese Studies, University of Michigan, 2002), p. 557.

lords from Iyo propitiated frequently and to whom they dedicated territory, weapons, and other valuables.[62]

In addition, neither side specified the duration of service, which created ambiguity that worked for both sides. The Mōri could claim that the oath held for longer than perhaps the Noshima wanted, whereas the Noshima interpreted his oaths as having no contradiction with mercenarism. Less than a year after submitting his blood-sealed oath, Takeyoshi accepted concomitant offers from the Miyoshi—at that time engaged in a struggle against the Mōri.[63] In response, Mōri Terumoto sponsored a group of sea lords to lay siege to Noshima, after which he took hostages from the Noshima in exchange for lifting the siege. However, in spite of any misgivings Terumoto had regarding the Noshima's continued mercenary behavior, Terumoto continued to rely on the commercial and protection expertise of the Noshima. And the Noshima took advantage of continued Mōri sponsorship to expand their domains and commercial networks.

Between 1573 and 1582, the Noshima Murakami completed their final set of strategic pivots. They maneuvered themselves between unprecedentedly puissant power blocs and received extremely lucrative patronage opportunities in return. An aspiring hegemon named Oda Nobunaga had begun to push west of Kyoto. He also recruited allies in Kyushu and evicted the last Ashikaga shogun from Kyoto. The ousted Ashikaga Yoshiaki eventually sought refuge with Mōri Terumoto and assembled what historians have called an anti-Nobunaga coalition that consisted of daimyo like the Mōri and the Ikkō Ikki Pure Land Buddhist sectarians.[64] Yoshiaki used these connections to recruit the Noshima Murakami and other sea lords.

The Noshima Murakami participated in several naval and amphibious operations against the Oda. In 1576, the Noshima helped lead an expedition that broke an Oda blockade and delivered provisions to the Ikkō Ikki citadel in Osaka. To do so, the Noshima defeated a fleet led by Oda-sponsored sea lords.[65] The next year, the Noshima seized a castle that enabled them to control part of the harbor of Utazu,[66] an important port near Shiwaku.[67] Then,

---

62. For example, see a dedication by an ancestor of Takeyoshi to the shrine: EK doc. 1525, Bunmei 17 (1485) 8.23.

63. EK doc. 2114, Genki 2? (1571) 5.7; EK doc. 2116, Genki 2? (1571) 7.27.

64. Jeroen Lamers, *Japonius Tyrannus: The Japanese Warlord Oda Nobunaga Reconsidered* (Leiden: Hotei Publishing, 2000), p. 165. This campaign will be examined in detail in chapter 4.

65. EK doc. 2183, Tenshō 4? (1576) 7.15.

66. EK doc. 2213, Tenshō 5? (1577), int. 7.20; EK doc. 2214, Tenshō 5? (1577) int. 7.24.

67. Forty-seven ships carrying mostly salt claimed Utazu as port of registry in the *Hyōgo Kitazeki irifune nōchō*; Hashizume, *Setonaikai chiiki shakai to Oda kenryoku*, pp. 233–34.

between 1579 and 1582, the Noshima joined a coalition of Mōri-sponsored sea lords to cordon the Inland Sea against the commercial and military shipping of Nobunaga and his allies. Mōri Terumoto authorized the Noshima to legitimately seize any ships heading to or from the capital region at toll-barrier ports including Shiwaku and Kaminoseki.[68]

However, the Noshima Murakami also entered into negotiations to provide naval services for the Oda. At one point, the Noshima sent Nobunaga a baby hawk, which symbolically signified loyal service to Nobunaga. In his thank you note for the hawk, Nobunaga assumed that the Noshima would soon be providing naval services for him and promised the Noshima that "because it will become time to exert ourselves again in battle, if there is anything that you desire, there should be no problem providing it."[69] The Noshima requested safe access to the port of Sakai for their shipping merchants. The possibility of acquiring the Noshima's services in general and the trade and resources available through the port of Shiwaku in particular seems to have overcome any resentment on the part of Nobunaga about the Noshima's prominent role in the 1576 defeat. In the third month of 1577, Nobunaga issued an edict to his magistrate for the port of Sakai that instructed him to ensure the safe passage of Shiwaku ships seeking to enter that port. Regardless of the ongoing military conflict, Shiwaku ships (and by extension the Noshima) had acquired safe, unrestricted access to the capital markets through the port of Sakai: "Regarding ships from Shiwaku traveling to and from the port of Sakai. As before, there is to be no interference. If by some chance, there are those who cause conflict, they will be punished."[70] In addition, sea lords did not always scrupulously follow the Mōri law on stopping ships from the capital and often found it profitable to smuggle goods to and from the Oda zone of control. Such smuggling is explicitly condemned in a letter from Mōri officials to a sea lord named Takai Tōemonnojō: "Although it has been the policy of this house to intercept all ships from the capital, word has also reached us of captains and others from our domain taking on the cargoes of bands from the capital."[71]

68. *Hagi-han batsuetsuroku*, edited by Nagata Masazumi (Yamaguchi-shi: Yamaguchi-ken Monjokan 1967), vol. 3, p. 840, doc. 15, Tenshō 7? (1579) 2.30; Kishida, *Daimyo ryōgoku no keizai kōzō* pp. 52–53.

69. EK doc. 2272, no year.11.26; Yamauchi, *Setouchi no kaizoku*, p. 111. Nobunaga was famous for being an avid falconer (J. S. A. Elisonas and J. P. Lamers, "Introduction," in Ōta Gyūichi, *The Chronicle of Lord Nobunaga* [Leiden: Brill, 2010], p. 18).

70. *Zōtei Oda Nobunaga monjo no kenkyū*, doc. 704, Tenshō 5? (1577) 3.26. Some scholars have even speculated that this red-seal letter operated as a type of toll-exemption and protection pass and that the line "as before" may reference the toll-exemption privileges enjoyed by Shiwaku in the fifteenth century (Hashizume, *Setonaikai chiiki shakai to Oda kenryoku*, p. 322).

71. *Hagi-han batsuetsuroku*, vol. 3, pp. 842–43, doc. 30, Tenshō 7? (1579) 2.25.

For powerful sea lords to join the Oda seriously imperiled Mōri ambitions, which gave significant leverage to sea lords in negotiations with sponsors. In 1582, when the Kurushima Murakami accepted Nobunaga's offer of patronage, the Noshima Murakami took advantage of the desperation of the Mōri for naval services. They secured legitimate title to several former Kurushima Murakami holdings and raided Kurushima Murakami shipping with impunity.[72] By doing so, the Noshima expanded their domain to its greatest extent and exerted unitary control over spaces where they had once had to share governance. For example, the Noshima lost no time in forcibly evicting the Kurushima Murakami from the Kutsuna Islands and imposing their will on the residents of that chain of islands, including the island of Futagamijima.[73]

TOOLS OF SEA LORDSHIP IN THE SIXTEENTH CENTURY

In establishing unitary control over their growing domain in the sixteenth century, the Noshima innovated several distinctive sea tenurial and commercial practices. These drew on wider Japanese practices, took advantage of their control over maritime space, and enabled the Noshima to control access to domainal maritime space and to regulate what happened in that space. In particular, the Noshima designed protection operations, ships, and castles as tools of sea lordship and adapted land-based, warrior institutions to the maritime world in order to help administer the human elements of their domain.

Protection Operations

By the sixteenth century, the transportation infrastructure of the archipelago consisted of a patchwork of fractured, overlapping interests.[74] Carrying and protecting passengers and trade constituted one of the chief livelihoods of the Noshima Murakami. The Noshima also depended on these enterprises to convince domainal inhabitants, travelers, and representatives of land-based authorities (shogunal officials, aristocrats, religious institutions, and regional warlords) that the Noshima Murakami constituted legitimate

72. The post-1582 interactions between the Noshima and Kurushima will be explored in chapter 6.
73. EK doc. 2302, Tenshō 10 (1582) 4.25.
74. Kitai Toshio, "Sengoku makki Honganji no kōtsū taisaku," *Nihonshi kenkyū* 294 (1987): 1; Hitomi Tonomura, *Community and Commerce in Late Medieval Japan: The Corporate Villages of Tokuchin-ho* (Stanford, Calif.: Stanford University Press, 1992), p. 98.

authorities and vital parts of the seascape. In translating the extortion of protection money into perceptions of legitimacy, the Noshima faced challenges similar to daimyo on land who sought to control thoroughfares and shipping, to fortify strategic road intersections, and to charge lading and protection fees on cargoes passing through regions under their control,[75] or who allowed their armies to charge villages half their harvest to "ensure their safety."[76] Sea lords like the Noshima Murakami designed protection enterprises to encourage perceptions of legitimacy in this period in several ways. They connected their tools and practices of protection to the definition of stable maritime domainal boundaries, economic incentives, and the performance of lordship. They institutionalized and routinized protection practices. And they wrapped themselves in a nimbus of legitimacy by drawing on hallowed precedents of land-based authorities.

The Noshima used protection businesses to define stable boundaries, which helped them to consolidate and unify their domain. Toll barriers set in chokepoints enabled the Noshima to regulate access to domainal maritime space. For example, the Noshima fixed their eastern boundary at the port and chokepoint of Shiwaku. Shiwaku's history as a prominent commercial port inspired perception of it as a place where one encountered a change in itinerary and thus a boundary between regions. As we have seen, Shiwaku appears frequently as a port where merchants transshipped goods, where travelers changed charters and waited for a favorable wind, and where patrons requested protection. The Noshima enhanced this perception by treating the waters around Shiwaku as the entryway into a space in which all protection businesses had to have their approval. They directed their captains to engage in combat in order to prevent competitors from assessing protection tolls there. In the summer of 1550, one "Genzo of Shiwaku was captain" of a ship "packed to the scuppers carrying three hundred passengers" traveling westward from the port of Sakai. One passenger on Genzo's ship, a monk named Bairin Shuryū, recorded how an unknown vessel approached their ship. Bairin labeled this new ship a "pirate [*zokusen*]" because after "engaging in negotiations," probably over a toll, "they shot arrows at our [Genzo's] ship." In sailing close to the port of Shiwaku, Genzo had entered Noshima domainal waters, where he could not be subject to the tolls of others, hence the epithet, "pirate." So Genzo and other members of the crew used firearms to drive the "pirates" away.[77]

---

75. Yata, *Nihon chūsei sengoku-ki kenryoku kōzō no kenkyū*, pp. 63–64, 239–40.

76. Fujiki Hisashi, *Zōhyōtachi no senjō: chūsei no yohei to doreigari* (Asahi Shinbunsha, 1995), p. 178.

77. Bairin Shuryū, *Bairin Shuryū Suō gekō nikki*, in YK, vol. 1, p. 467, entries for Tenbun 19 (1550) 10.14, 10.19.

vored the Fathers they did not need his [Takeyoshi's] favor. Nonetheless, he returned to the Brother and fulfilled his request, commanding then that he be bestowed with a banner of silk with his [Noshima Murakami Takeyoshi's] sigil in order that when they encountered a suspicious ship, they could show it to them."[88] However, the crest pennants only guaranteed safety inside the maritime networks under Noshima control. Frois explained that "in other regions, there were pirates who did not recognize his [Noshima] suzerainty or respect him."[89] In other words, after leaving the Noshima domain, travelers potentially entered networks under the control of other sea lords.

A close reading of figure 12, a reproduction of one of only two Noshima crest pennants still extant, helps us understand how the flag-based protection system functioned. The name of the recipient is inscribed on the right. In figure 12, it is the Monomōshi of Itsukushima in Aki, high-ranking shrine officials, who requested a pass.[90] On the left, the Noshima wrote the date of issue (Tenshō 9 [1581], 4.28). Because much communication in sixteenth-century Japan took place via messenger[91] and because the recipient would want the flag bearer to return safely, the flag likely took effect on this date. The Noshima lord (in this case Takeyoshi) signed his name under the date to activate the pass. The effective duration of the passes is not known. The condition of the Monomōshi flag suggests that it hung from a pole outside the ship—perhaps from the masthead—to make it clear to any approaching ship that the bearer sailed under the paid protection of the Noshima Murakami and was immune from any other toll barrier or other "piratical" interference in what the Noshima considered their domain.

The character read *kami* dominates the center of the flag and explicitly denotes the Noshima Murakami as the source of authority and protection. The *kami* character is the second half of the name Murakami and served as the family crest. In addition, the character is also read *ue*, a word that in late medieval Japan signified figures and institutions of the highest authority. The pennant would thus cause observers to equate the Noshima Murakami with legitimate maritime dominion.

The Noshima Murakami crest-pennant protection business heralded their sea lordship by taking advantage of the meanings attached to flags flown on ships and by their ability to make the promise of protection a reality. Seafarers flew flags in late medieval Japan chiefly to display connections with

---

88. Frois, *Historia de Japam*, vol. 4, pp. 248–49.
89. Ibid., p. 249.
90. Takahashi, "Shinshutsu no 'Murakami Takeyoshi kashoki ni tsuite,'" jō, p. 43; Kanaya, *Kaizoku-tachi no chūsei*, p. 65.
91. Yamada Kuniaki, *Sengoku no komyunikēshon: jōhō to tsūshin* (Yoshikawa Kōbunkan, 2002).

authorities. In the fifteenth and sixteenth centuries, imperial and daimyo patrons who sponsored the outfitting of ships marked their patronage by providing the ship a flag with their crest on it.[92] Seafarers also commonly flew pennants on which were inscribed the names of deities such as Hachiman Daibosatsu, Mishima Daimyōjin, and Amaterasu Ōmikami, invoking the heavenly realm to ensure safe passage.[93]

The practice of dictating how and which flags were to be flown on ships drew on symbolism associated with sea tenure in medieval Japan. From their time as managers on estates like Yugeshima and Shiwaku, the Noshima learned that residents and proprietors laid claim to and sought to administer maritime space by planting poles (*sao*) in the sea. Poles marked sites where ships moored and nets hung, actively extending tenure into the water by connecting deeper and shallower seas to the work done in those spaces.[94] But sea lords realized that sea tenure necessitated mobility. As a medium in constant flux, the sea could only be pinned down by sailing on top of it and presenting a visible symbol of dominion: showing the flag. The iconography on the flag represented to all who saw it the identity of the power that planted the pole.

The crest-pennant system also enhanced the public character of Noshima Murakami domainal authority. Because both the Noshima and recipients of crest pennants perceived the flags as a guarantee against a wide variety of forms of maritime hindrances—from marauders to the assessment of lading fees and other tolls—it is likely that they interpreted crest pennants as a form of pass granting immunity from tolls, as *kasho*. However, for the Noshima to issue *kasho* represented a fundamental appropriation of privileges traditionally understood as the preserve of the highest-status, land-based authorities.

The practice of issuing such passes began in the Ritsuryō period as one power of the imperial court. By the medieval period, imperial, aristocratic, religious, and warrior authorities had acquired rights to issue *kasho*.[95] For example, in the thirteenth century, the Hōjō, shogunal regents and leaders of the Kamakura bakufu, issued *kasho* in the forms of flags that displayed the pyramid crest of the Hōjō family. Text on the flag granted immunity from "barriers in ports and harbors of the various provinces" written on them.[96]

92. Tenyo Seikei, *Boshi nyūminki*, NMKBS, p. 202; Zheng Shun'gong, *Riben yijian* (Peking: Gushu Shiwen Diange, 1939), "Qionghe huahai," ch. 9, p. 7b.
93. Tanaka Takeo, *Wakō: umi no rekishi* (Kyōikusha, 1982), pp. 175–76.
94. Hotate Michihisa, "Chūsei zenki no gyogyō to shōensei: kakai ryōyū to gyomin mibun o megutte," *Rekishi hyōron* 376 (1981.8): 26–28.
95. Amino Yoshihiko, *Nihon chūsei hinōgyōmin to tennō* (Iwanami Shoten, 1984), pp. 96–97.
96. *Hata monjo*, in *Wakasa gyoson shiryō* (Fukui: Fukui-ken Gōdoshi Kondankai, 1963), p. 306, doc. 19, Bun'ei 9 (1272) 2nd month; *Wakasa gyoson shiryō*, pl. 25. The shogunal regent Hōjō Tokimune issued the flag for a ship registered to the Japan Sea harbor of Tagarasunoura.

Although it is unclear if the Noshima knew of the Hōjō example, the Noshima Murakami had ties to both recipients and targets identified in a variety of *kasho* that circulated in late medieval Japan. The Noshima drew on these earlier examples in order to develop the crest-pennant system. In the fourteenth and fifteenth centuries they competed for managerial positions to legitimize their hold on part of the island estate of Yugeshima. Yugeshima's proprietor, Tōji, issued *kasho* in the visible, iconographic form of "umbrella tallies" (*kasafuda*) to Yugeshima shippers in order to emphasize the religious, "nonsalable" nature of Yugeshima salt.[97] The Noshima were among those whom Tōji hired to protect Yugeshima shipping, but who instead expropriated the salt to sell commercially.[98] The Noshima also likely learned significant *kasho* lore from Shiwaku shippers and others in their domain who had received passes from the Muromachi shogunate. Muromachi bakufu passes also had a visual component, a stamped document to be carried by the recipient's agents and shown to the barrier authorities.[99] In addition, the Noshima practice of issuing documents in the format of "folded paper edicts" (*origami gechijō*) to accompany crest pennants[100] matches the practice of bakufu administrators, who issued *kasho* in the form of "folded paper edicts."[101] However, the Noshima expanded the scope of the exemption promised by traditional *kasho*. Whereas the Hōjō regents and Muromachi bakufu administrators usually targeted barriers (*seki*) on seas, rivers, ports, and crossings,[102] the Noshima guaranteed crest-pennant recipients a much wider form of protection. They promised "to ensure that nothing untoward occurs as you travel to and fro on the seas."[103]

The links of the Noshima crest-pennant system to *kasho* enabled the Noshima Murakami to lay claim to having established a transcendent, unitary, and legitimate authority tied to providing "public good" (*kōgi*). In doing so, they paralleled the efforts of regional warlords on land, who sought to attract popular acceptance and recognition of supreme territorial authority by demonstrating their ability to regulate and support their domainal economy. The public character of this domainal authority may have been enhanced by the choice of the Noshima and other sea lords to base themselves in maritime thoroughfares and ports, spaces traditionally understood as having

97. NET pp. 223–25, doc. 148, Kagen 4 (1306) 9.1; NET p. 226, doc. 150, no year.3.5.
98. See chapter 2; NET pp. 402–4, doc. 285, Kōshō 2 (1456) 5.8; NET p. 414, doc. 291:3, Kanshō 3 (1462) 5.17.
99. Arima Kaori, "Muromachi bakufu bugyōnin hakkyū kasho ni tsuite no ichi kōsatsu," *Komonjo kenkyū* 48 (1998.10): 61–62.
100. YK, vol. 4, pp. 275–76, doc. 7, Tenshō 13 (1585) 3.10.
101. Arima, "Muromachi bakufu bugyōnin hakkyū kasho ni tsuite no ichi kōsatsu," p. 56.
102. Ibid., pp. 57–59.
103. YK, vol. 4, pp. 275–76, doc. 7, Tenshō 13 (1585) 3.10.

connections to the highest public authority, the emperor.[104] Furthermore, it is also possible that both the Noshima and crest-pennant recipients may have understood the systemic nature of the protection system as a variety of free-market policies (*rakuichi-rakuza*) that warlords across Japan were implementing in that period to stimulate commerce within their domains by eliminating guilds, barriers, and other commercial restrictions.[105]

Although quantitative data does not exist, the Noshima Murakami crest-pennant system likely stimulated commerce by reducing protection costs and the number of proprietary jurisdictions through which commerce had to pass.[106] On the Noshima's sprawling domainal sea lanes, for the cost of the crest pennant, commercial shippers only had to deal with the Noshima's commercial jurisdiction. The reputation and public character of the Noshima as protection providers and sea lords eased concerns over requesting a crest pennant. At the same time, the ability of Noshima to select recipients enabled them to shape commerce by selecting those merchants who and cargoes which would receive the reduction in protection costs.[107] With this system, the Noshima probably attracted increased business and thus received further external validation of their dominion.

The use of a flag-based protection system to represent the dominion over aquatic space in Japan was not limited to the Noshima Murakami. During the fifteenth and sixteenth centuries, lacustrine pirates of Lake Biwa extended their authority over a domain of "forty-nine harbors." They regularized protection in the form of escort (*uwanori*) conducted in return for payment and then systematized it into a practice of selling "banners" (*hirahira*) with their insignia as symbols of safe passage.[108] Although there

---

104. Sasaki Junnosuke, "The Changing Rationale of Daimyo Control in the Emergence of the Bakuhan State," with Ronald P. Toby, in *Japan Before Tokugawa: Political Consolidation and Economic Growth, 1500 to 1650*, edited by John W. Hall et al. (Princeton, N.J.: Princeton University Press, 1981), p. 280; Asao Naohiro, "Shogun and Tennō," with Marius B. Jansen in *Japan Before Tokugawa: Political Consolidation and Economic Growth, 1500 to 1650*, edited by John W. Hall et al. (Princeton, N.J.: Princeton University Press, 1981), pp. 251–54. The Mōri among other Noshima patrons, employed the rhetoric of *kōgi* (Herman Ooms, *Tokugawa Ideology: Early Constructs, 1570–1680* [Princeton, N.J.: Princeton University Press, 1985] p. 27)

105. Sasaki Gin'ya, "Sengoku Daimyo Rule and Commerce," with William B. Hauser, in *Japan Before Tokugawa: Political Consolidation and Economic Growth, 1500 to 1650*, edited by John W. Hall et al. (Princeton, N.J.: Princeton University Press, 1981), pp. 142–45.

106. Frederic Lane, "Economic Consequences of Organized Violence," *The Journal of Economic History* 18.4 (December 1958): 401–17.

107. The Noshima are here engaging in a similar practice to that of Enryakuji, which controlled barriers in the Lake Biwa region and gave exemptions to client merchants (Tonomura, *Community and Commerce*, pp. 99–100).

108. Sakurai Eiji, *Nihon chūsei no keizai kōzō* (Iwanami Shoten, 1996), pp. 287–89. The quotes are from Myōsei, *Honpukuji atogaki*, a detailed account of goings on in and around the Lake Biwa port

is no documentation connecting the two systems, travelers accustomed to one might accept the other without complaint, giving further legitimacy to both systems.

Such sea-lord innovations and applications of the protection business contributed to transformations in the meaning and function of barriers. In the late medieval period, barriers seem to have been chiefly for profit. By recognizing barriers as boundaries instead of simple moneymakers, sea lords were participating in a shift to a practice characteristic of early modern Japan in which bakufu and domainal authorities used barriers to restrict the movements of people and goods.[109]

Ships

As was suggested by the mounting of crest pennants on the masts, in the sixteenth century, sea lords designed ships as instruments of disciplinary power and dynamic symbols and tools of lordship.[110] Sea lords used ships to shape seafarers into crews and domainal inhabitants into parts of a band. Officers disciplined sailors to life and work at sea, a world of motion: sails went up and down, oars went back and forth, watches rotated, and crews moved from station to station propelling their craft through the waves.[111] Lordship at sea—as on land—divides space into "us and them." On a vessel, such a division enabled violence against Others located outside the ship. Ships provided havens for mariners and a space for their social world, outside of which lay the lethal world of storms, sharks, enemies, and prey.[112] When viewed from inside the hull, fighting to defend one's ship, fighting for a sponsor, and fighting for the maritime domain all blended into the same thing. If crews saw their vessel as a home, then defending that home provided sanction for violence perpetrated against the outside. In creating

of Katata. Also see Amino Yoshihiko, *Rethinking Japanese History*, translated and with an introduction by Alan S. Christy, preface and afterword by Hitomi Tonomura, Michigan Monograph Series in Japanese Studies, no. 74 (Ann Arbor: Center for Japanese Studies, University of Michigan, 2012), p. 94.

109. Sakurai Eiji, "Chūsei no shōhin ichiba," in *Shintaikei Nihonshi*, vol. 12: *Ryūtsū keizaishi*, edited by Sakurai Eiji and Nakanishi Satoru (Yamakawa Shuppan, 2002), p. 229.

110. Marcus Rediker, *The Slave Ship: A Human History* (New York: Viking, 2007), pp. 44–45.

111. Greg Dening, *Mr. Bligh's Bad Language: Passion, Power and Theatre on the Bounty* (Cambridge: Cambridge University Press, 1992), pp. 5–6, 19; Hans Konrad von Tilburg, "Vessels of Exchange: The Global Shipwright in the Pacific," in *Seascapes: Maritime Histories, Littoral Cultures, and Transoceanic Exchanges*, edited by Jerry H. Bentley et al. (Honolulu: University of Hawai'i Press, 2007), p. 38.

112. Greg Dening, *Islands and Beaches: Discourse on a Silent Land: Marquesas, 1774–1880* (Melbourne: Melbourne University Press, 1980), pp. 158–59.

crews and bands by taking them out onto the waves, sea lords could trans
form chokepoints into territorial linchpins from which they could extend
their power over maritime networks.

The ability to construct fleets also reflects the effort that sea lords put
into developing well-sinewed domainal institutions. To assemble a ship re
quired marshaling a host of human and material resources: ritual specialists
and implements necessary for implanting the "soul of the ship" (*funadama*)
in the step for the base of the mast, a labor force composed of carpenters
(*daiku*) and commoners (*hyakushō*), and timber and other naval stores. At
times sea lords bought lumber, iron, and other necessities in markets selling
materials from all across Japan.[113] Patrons were also a good source of ma
teriel.[114] Ideally, however, sea lords would rely on domainal timber stands.
For example, the Noshima Murakami, Tokui, and Kurushima Murakami all
exacted timber allotments from Futagami.[115] Shipwrights and patrons held
specific species of trees in high regard for crafting especially seaworthy ves
sels in late medieval Japan: Japanese cypress (*hinoki*), camphor (*kusunoki*),
cryptomeria (*sugi*), elm (*muku*), and pine (*matsu*). Cypress and cryptome
ria strengthened against rotting and getting waterlogged, while shipwrights
used pine for those parts of the ship that needed to withstand the force of
waves striking them.[116]

Sea lords constructed two types of ships in the sixteenth century that
facilitated the establishment and maintenance of domains. Small, fast inter
ceptors known as "barrier ships"[117] enabled them to police domainal bound
aries and to carry out ship-based protection businesses. For their flagships,
sea lords devised heavily armed and armored dreadnoughts (*atakebune*).[118]
Dreadnoughts were not fast or nimble like the barrier ships. Instead, the

113. Much of this information is drawn from a series of documents written by the sea lord Kuki
Moritaka (1573–1632). *Mie-ken shi shiryō-hen kinsei*, vol. 1 (Tsu-shi, Mie-ken: Mie-ken, 1993),
pp. 661–62, doc. 260, no year.1.12; ibid., pp. 663–64, doc. 264, no year.2.18. The compilers date
these documents to a period between 1600 and 1605 based on Moritaka's signature.
114. *Zōtei Oda Nobunaga monjo no kenkyū*, doc. 771, Tenshō 6? (1578) 7.10.
115. See chapter 2; EK doc. 2239, Tenshō 7? (1579) 6.3.
116. DNK 2, *Asano-ke monjo*, vol. 1, pp. 215–17, doc. 178, Tenshō 19? (1591) 9.13; *Mie-ken shi shiryō-
hen kinsei*, vol. 1, pp. 663–64, doc. 264 no year.2.18; Conrad Totman, *The Green Archipelago:
Forestry in Pre-Industrial Japan* (Berkeley: University of California Press, 1989), pp. 15, 20, 143;
Ishii Kenji, "*Nagoya-jō zu* no atakebune ni tsuite," *Kokka* 915 (1968.6): 33.
117. On *sekibune*, see Ishii Kenji, *Wasen II* (Hōsei Daigaku Shuppankyoku, 1995), pp. 127–131.
118. The term "dreadnought" is admittedly an unorthodox translation, given that the word became
known as a class of warship in the early twentieth-century Atlantic World. I selected it in order
to reflect the innovative and heavily armed and armored nature of the *atakebune* (see chapter 4).
"Dreadnought" is also a creative translation of the characters for *atakebune* (lit., a "safe-house
vessel," in which one would fear nothing). Thus, the term also reflects the importance of the

resembled nothing so much as massive floating fortresses. In addition to military purposes,[119] sea lords employed dreadnoughts as awesome displays of power and authority, borrowing in particular from the pageantry and spectacle associated with castles on land.

Atakebune were some of the largest ships built in sixteenth-century Japan. They measured upwards of 30 meters in length and 13 meters across the beam; they could carry hundreds of *koku* in lading (some approached a thousand *koku*). Their hulls were composed of planks erected atop a keel. A steering oar maneuvered the ship. Propulsion came from one or two massive sails mounted on removable masts and from as many as one hundred rowers stroking with massive oars that required two people to operate. *Atakebune* had crossbeams that extended outside the hull of the ship to support shelves. Atop the shelves and beams shipwrights erected elaborate superstructures known as "turrets" (*yagura*). In earlier periods, turrets on ships were temporary constructions erected for specific battles, but with the dreadnought, sea lords integrated into the ship turrets that might run the length of the ship, all covered with four or five centimeters of wooden armor plating—or even iron plates in strategic locations. It was these turrets that inspired Edo-period chroniclers to designate *atakebune* as "castles of the sea."[120]

Dreadnoughts' turrets closely resembled castle turrets on land. Korean records describe Japanese flagships from the 1592–98 Japanese invasions as "ships with castle turrets on them."[121] Figure 13, a detail of an Edo-period screen painting depicting Hizen Nagoya Castle during Hideyoshi's invasion of Korea,[122] shows clear similarities between *atakebune* turrets and castle turrets. On land citadels transcended simple fortifications and came to

---

protection business for sea lords. Ishii Kenji identified two types of *atakebune,* the *Isesengata* of central Japan and the *Futanarigata* of western Japan (including the Setonaikai) (Ishii, "*Nagoya-jō zu no atakebune ni tsuite*," pp. 32–33).

119. Military dimensions are explored in chapter 4.

120. *Mie-ken shi shiryō-hen kinsei*, vol. 1, pp. 661–62, doc. 260, no year.1.12; ibid., pp. 663–64, doc. 264, no year.2.18; Ishii, *Wasen* II, pp. 120–26; Ishii, "*Nagoya-jō zu no atakebune ni tsuite*," pp. 32–36; Ishii Kenji, *Zusetsu wasen shiwa* (Shiseidō, 1983), pp. 50, 62–65. William Wayne Farris, "Shipbuilding and Nautical Technology in Japanese Maritime History: Origins to 1600," *Mariner's Mirror* 95.3 (2009.8): 275–77. Quotation from Ishii, *Wasen* II, p. 122.

21. Yi Sunsin, *Nanjung ilgi (ranchū nikki)*, edited by Kitajima Manji (Tōyō Bunko, 2001), 1592.6.2; *Nanjung Ilgi: War Diary of Admiral Yi Sun-sin*, translated by Ha Tae-hung, edited by Sohn Powkey (Seoul: Yonsei University Press, 1977), p. 6.

22. This screen is thought to be a copy of a depiction of Hizen Nagoya Castle by Kanō Mitsunobu (1565–1608) (Narisawa Katsushi, "Nanban byōbu no tenkai," in *Tokubetsuten Nanban kenbunroku: Momoyama kaiga ni miru seiyō to no deai*, edited by Kōbe Shiritsu Hakubutsukan [Kōbeshi: Kōbe-shi Supōtsu Kyōiku Kōsha, 1992], p. 81).

Figure 13. Image of *atakebune*. Detail from the *Screen Painting of Nagoya Castle in Hizen* (*Hizen Nagoya-jō zu byōbu*). Photo courtesy of the Saga Prefectural Nagoya Castle Museum (Saga Kenritsu Nagoya-jō Hakubutsukan) and used with their permission.

symbolize the political authority of a particular daimyo, especially when heavily decorated with politically charged symbolic iconography.[123] Decorations on dreadnoughts played similar roles.

Sea lords planned the decorations and fittings of the ships' "castles" in order to dazzle the eye and to impress on observers their power as masters of the seas. In 1578, Kuki Yoshitaka (1542–1600), a sea lord from Shima, near Ise, built and fitted out six iron-plated *atakebune* for Oda Nobunaga. According to a Jesuit eyewitness, these ships were the "best and largest in Japan, being about the size of [Portuguese] royal carracks."[124] The vessels "shocked the eyes and ears of those who came to sightsee" at Sakai.[125] When Nobunaga came to view the ships, Kuki Yoshitaka "fitted out the great ships in grand style with flags, pennants, and curtains wrapped around the hull."[126] Similarly, an early Edo-period chronicle written by sea-lord descendants brags that one mid-sixteenth-century Noshima Murakami flotilla consisted of "around one hundred ships decorated more beautifully than even the shogun could have managed."[127] Access to the services of artisans necessary for creating such a spectacle was one benefit of sea lords accepting daimyo patronage. After the Noshima accepted Ōuchi sponsorship in the middle of the sixteenth century, skilled woodworkers and other artisans of Itsukushima actually came to reside on Noshima for a time.[128] Oda Nobunaga at times ordered castle artisans to help shipwrights.[129]

Dreadnoughts also represented the intersections of sea-lord bands with the wider East Asian maritime world. Contacts with seafarers from overseas brought sea lords cannons and, in order to increase seaworthiness, the knowledge to fit dreadnought hulls with watertight bulkheads in the Chinese manner.[130] Evidence for Chinese ships in sixteenth-century Japan reveals close connections to sea lords. Kuki Yoshitaka's 1578 flotilla of iron-plated dreadnoughts also included a Chinese junk.[131] A Chinese expatriate

123. William Coaldrake, *Architecture and Authority in Japan* (London: Routledge, 1996), ch. 5; Carolyn Wheelwright, "A Visualization of Eitoku's Lost Paintings at Azuchi," in *Warlords, Artists, and Commoners: Japan in the Sixteenth Century*, edited by George Elison and Bardwell L. Smith (Honolulu: University of Hawai'i Press, 1981), pp. 87–111.
124. Letter by Organtino Gnecchi-Soldo SJ (1530–1609), quoted in Lamers, *Japonius Tyrannus*, p. 155.
125. Ōta Gyūichi, *Shinchō-Kō ki*, edited by Okuno Takahiro (Kadokawa Shoten 1969), p. 248.
126. Ibid., p. 252.
127. "*Bukebandaiki: Santō kaizoku-ke ikusa nikki*, hoi no maki," *Suminoe* 230 (Fall 1998): 49.
128. EK doc. 1760, Tenbun 16? (1547) 4.25.
129. Ōta, *Shinchō-Kō ki*, p. 149.
130. Ishii, *Wasen* II, pp. 124–27; Ishii, "*Nagoya-jō zu* no atakebune ni tsuite," pp. 31–39; Ishii, *Zusetsu wasen shiwa*, pp. 62–64.
131. Ōta, *Shinchō-Kō ki*, p. 248.

merchant pirate, Wang Zhi (d. 1557), who repeatedly visited Noshima Murakami patrons like the Ōuchi and Ōtomo and who reputedly included Inland Sea "pirates" in his band, is also credited with constructing gigantic,
turreted vessels.[132]

Sea-Lord Castles

In addition to the castles on their ships, sea lords ordered the construction of
island- and peninsula-based castles especially designed to command chokepoints. Sea lords based themselves on two major categories of islands: tiny
islands like Noshima, sometimes less than a kilometer in circumference,
and larger islands like Yugeshima and Shiwaku that contained repositories
of resources, populations, and large ports. Many sea lords constructed their
home castles and headquarters on the former. Today, Noshima slumbers,
uninhabited, across from the small town of Miyakubo-chō on the larger island of Iyo Ōshima. However, examination of this island reveals how sea
lords developed a distinctly maritime style of fortification and residence
that turned entire islets into sea castles[133] (figure 14) from which they ruled
over domainal networks that sprawled across much of the Inland Sea. Despite their small size, these sea-lord strongholds contained permanent
settlements and anchorages fully capable of harboring even the largest of
the late sixteenth-century turreted sea-lord dreadnoughts.[134] The heights of
Noshima and surrounding islands offer sightlines over the busy channels
of the Inland Sea extending for tens of kilometers, rendering approaching
ships visible and the establishment of toll barriers easy.[135] To make the castle,
Noshima workers leveled off the peaks on the island and turned the entire
island into a fortified citadel; they even extended a bridge to an adjacent
islet.[136] Postholes bored into the rocky outcrops surrounding the island indicate placements of boardwalks, wharfs, and possibly even battlements that
once rimmed the shoreline.[137] Noshima's proximity to Iyo Ōshima and other
islands was of crucial importance. The larger islands housed other settle-

---

132. Zheng Ruozeng, *Chouhai tubian* (Beijing: Zhonghua Shuju, 2007), p. 620; CWS, *Myŏngjong sillok*
   vol. 20, pp. 28a-b, Myŏngjong 11 (1556) 4.1.
133. Yamauchi, *Kaizoku to umijiro*, p. 14.
134. Ibid., p. 50; EK doc. 2241, Tenshō 7? (1579) 12.7.
135. Yamauchi, *Kaizoku to umijiro*, p. 147.
136. Yamauchi, *Setouchi no kaizoku*, p. 26; *Miyakubo-chō shi* (Miyakubo-chō, Ehime-ken: Miyakubo
   chō, 1994), p. 93.
137. In the early twentieth century, archaeologists found the remains of wood in many of the post
   holes, adding further credence to these theories (Yamauchi, *Kaizoku to umijiro*, pp. 25, 32).

Figure 14. The Island of Noshima. Photo by the author.

ments and markets, helping ensure that the Noshima had secure access to sufficient resources.[138] This location made Noshima a chokepoint. These waters became heavily traveled in the late medieval period. They contain fast currents that made these channels difficult to navigate safely without expert piloting.[139] Such channels were not suitable for large-scale fishing operations that required calm waters.[140] As a result, alternate subsistence strategies were necessary. Sea lords chose to operate protection businesses with which they could intercept ships, charge protection money, provide valuable escort and navigational services, and transform maritime space into territory.[141]

Archaeological investigation of Noshima and surrounding islands has revealed significant commonalities with the castles of daimyo on land. Warlords on land and sea lords both situated their home castle at the center of a

138. Ibid., pp. 31–33.

139. Ibid., pp. 17–18.

140. Akimichi Tomoya, "Setouchi no seitaigaku—Setouchi no gyorō to seien," in *Umi to rettō bunka,* vol. 9: *Setouchi no ama bunka,* edited by Amino Yoshihiko et al. (Shōgakukan, 1991), pp. 52–53, 61–62.

141. Pirates on Lake Biwa used sea castles and barriers in similar ways (Sakurai, *Nihon chūsei no keizai kōzō,* p. 287).

web of subsidiary strongholds and villages.[142] As a maritime domain, Noshima's ancillary fortifications and settlements lay on surrounding islands connected by sea lanes instead of roads. Branches of the Noshima family lived on Mushijima and Nakatoshima, where remains of castle enceintes have been found. Additional ruins have been found on Michikajima to the north of Noshima and on the Iyo Ōshima coast opposite Noshima (see figure 7).[143]

Archaeological evidence reinforces the idea that the Noshima Murakami integrated their domain into extensive commercial networks. Comparisons of amounts and types of materiel excavated from sea-lord castles, residences, and other ports in the Inland Sea region has led one archaeologist to suggest that the strength of "pirates" rerouted trade routes as "pirate" castles became new centers of consumption and exchange.[144] These networks provided access to both luxury and everyday-use items. Over ten thousand pieces of pottery dating from the thirteenth through sixteenth centuries were unearthed on Michikajima, including some seven thousand domestically produced pots, jars, flasks, mortars, and other pieces of utilitarian Bizen ware. Excavations also revealed significant amounts of overseas trade pottery: Chinese, Korean, and Vietnamese bowls, plates, serving implements, celadon jars, dishes, and censers. On Noshima itself, over 1,100 pieces have been unearthed to date, including Bizen ware, Chinese celadon, and Tenmoku bowls. Chinese coins from the Song and Ming dynasties that circulated as currency in late medieval Japan were unearthed in conjunction with the trade pottery.[145]

The presence of Tenmoku bowls and celadon suggests that the Noshima Murakami were aware of tea-bowl classification schema that attributed high value to particular styles of Tenmoku bowls and foreign ceramics,[146] and that they even may have partaken in tea ceremony. This suggests that as sea lord bands grew in political and economic power, they also sought out opportunities to prove their bona fides as lords by engaging in elite, land-based

142. David Spafford, *A Sense of Place: The Political Landscape in Late Medieval Japan* (Cambridge Mass.: Harvard University Press, 2013), pp. 243–48.

143. *Miyakubo-chō shi*, pp. 101–3.

144. Shibata Keiko, "Kaizoku no iseki to ryūtsū," in *Chūsei Setouchi no ryūtsū to kōryū*, edited by Shibagaki Isao (Hanawa Shobō, 2005), pp. 267–69.

145. *Miyakubo-chō shi*, pp. 97–100; Shibata, "Kaizoku no iseki to ryūtsū," pp. 262–64. For Chinese coins, see Ethan I. Segal, *Coins, Trade, and the State: Economic Growth in Early Medieval Japan* (Cambridge, Mass.: Harvard University Press, 2011).

146. Saeki Kōji, "Chinese Trade Ceramics in Medieval Japan," translated and adapted by Peter D Shapinsky, in *Tools of Culture: Japan's Cultural, Intellectual, Medical, and Technological Contact in East Asia, 1000s-1500s*, edited by Andrew E. Goble et al. (Ann Arbor, Mich.: Association for Asian Studies, 2009), pp. 178–79.

cultural forms. They turned their residences in their fortifications into the stages upon which they performed lordship culturally.

Some members of sea-lord bands attempted to partake in classical, aristocratic pastimes. A scion of a powerful regional warlord family from southern Kyushu named Shimazu Iehisa (1547–87) stopped over in Shiwaku on a 1575 voyage. He snobbishly derided attempts by a group of Noshima retainers who had taken up kickball (*kemari*): "We went to the mansion of Shiwaku resident Fukuda Matajirō, where we played kickball. It was unappealing and without quality, nothing but legs flying in the air. And that was not the only thing that looked bad."[147]

Sea lords may have received better receptions for their linked verse (*renga*). Many, including Noshima Murakami Takeyoshi and Motoyoshi, participated in the performance of votive linked-verse (*hōraku renga*) marathons of up to ten thousand verses presented regularly to the sea god enshrined at Ōyamazumi Jinja on Ōmishima, northwest of Noshima.[148] In order to participate, sea lords had to be well versed in the allusions, traditions, and rules of *renga* composition. Such training required cultivation of a land-centered, Kyoto-based sensibility, further intimating a growing education in and acceptance of elite culture.[149] Poems composed by Noshima Murakami sea lords show such an aesthetic transformation, as in this stanza by Noshima Murakami Motoyoshi from 1576.5, with nary a word from the waterline:

From tree to tree my gaze	Kigi o mishi
alighted on new flowers,	Hana wa Taisan
Taisan's sprouting leaves	no wakaba ya[150]

Likely, patronage connections with powerful warlords brought the Noshima and other sea lords into contact with itinerant *renga* masters. In the late medieval period several such poets scattered to the provinces in response to the decline of central authority and the invitations of regional warlords who

147. Shimazu Iehisa, *Chūsho Iehisa-kō gojōkyō nikki*, in *Shintō taikei Bungaku-hen*, vol. 5: *Sankeiki*, edited by Shinjō Tsunezō (Shintō Taikei Hensankai, 1984), p. 290. For more on *kemari* in Sengoku society, see Lee Butler, *Emperor and Aristocracy in Japan, 1467–1680: Resilience and Renewal* (Cambridge, Mass.: Harvard University Press, 2002), pp. 74–75.
148. Yamauchi, *Setouchi no kaizoku*, pp. 155–56.
149. Esperanza Ramirez-Christensen, *Heart's Flower: The Life and Poetry of Shinkei* (Stanford, Calif.: Stanford University Press, 1994), pp. 122–23.
150. Quoted in Yamauchi, *Setouchi no kaizoku*, p. 158. Taisan may refer to the temple-topped hill in today's Matsuyama whose origin story is featured in the introduction.

cherished ambitions to transform their capitals into cultural centers. Patrons appreciated poets both as teachers of the arts and operatives with political connections.[151] Among Noshima patrons, the Ōuchi, for example, became a sponsor of the *renga* master Sōgi (1421–1502).[152] Participation in votive *renga* performance also helped to cement domainal unity among the higher echelon sea-lord band members and to forge bonds among representatives from various sea-lord bands. Each had to surrender his individual ego to the larger goal of creating a unified collection of linked verse.[153]

Governing the Human Element

The practices commonly engaged in by sea-lord bands could not be performed by an individual.[154] As their domains reached their apogee of extent power, and influence, sea lords worked to carefully oversee the shipmasters, sailors, fighters, and other domainal residents, male and female, in their domains. Although some scholars have portrayed *kaizoku* as a single class of armed, village-based mariners,[155] sea lords of the Inland Sea organized their bands hierarchically; the Noshima Murakami and others adapted land-based institutional structures of regional warlord houses and domain to fit the maritime world.

Inland Sea littoral lords like the Noshima Murakami expanded from a family-based operation into a band (*shū*). By the sixteenth century they had adapted land-based discourses and trappings of warrior lordship in order to structure their family and band as a "house" (*ie*) that ruled over the larger corporate structure of a domain (*ryō*). Such structures united the head sea lord family with agnatic relations, subsidiary bands, port workers, shipping organizations, fishing and salt-producing villages, merchants, and other groups of littoral inhabitants all ostensibly tied together by hierarchical, familial bonds.[156]

---

151. Ramirez-Christensen, *Heart's Flower*; H. Mack Horton, "Renga Unbound: Performative Aspect of Japanese Linked Verse," *Harvard Journal of Asiatic Studies* 53.2 (December 1993): 443–51; Donald Keene, "Jōha, a Sixteenth-Century Poet of Linked Verse," in *Warlords, Artists, and Commoners: Japan in the Sixteenth Century*, edited by George Elison and Bardwell L. Smith (Honolulu: University of Hawai'i Press, 1981), 113–32.

152. Eileen Katō, "Pilgrimage to Dazaifu: Sōgi's Tsukushi no michi no ki," *Monumenta Nipponica* 34. (Autumn 1979): 333–67.

153. Horton, "Renga Unbound," pp. 478–79.

154. Yamauchi, *Chūsei Setonaikai chiikishi no kenkyū*, p. 8.

155. Fujiki, *Zōhyōtachi no senjō*, pp. 18–19, 133–34.

156. Bitō Masahide, "Thought and Religion: 1550–1700," in *The Cambridge History of Japan*, vol. Early Modern Japan, edited by John W. Hall et al. (Cambridge: Cambridge University Press, 1991), pp. 373–78. For a discussion of the Ōuchi and Mōri, two frequent patrons whose house structure could have served as a model, see Matsuoka Hisato, "The Sengoku Daimyo of Western

The Noshima Murakami lords delegated the administration of specific enterprises and locales to trusted family members and officers by treating them as retainers. They and other sea lords appropriated the forms of written documents that patrons used to reward them in order to appoint and confirm family members and followers to positions and holdings. Murakami Takeyoshi gave a son, Takemitsu, responsibility for the important port and barrier of Kaminoseki.[157] Other relatives controlled places like the fortress island of Mushijima and the port of Kasaoka.[158] In 1583, the Noshima made one retainer family, the Toshinari, responsible for the "harbor taxes" (*urazeni*) and "protection rice" (*satsumai*) for Aio in Suō Province.[159] The Toshinari and other retainers would have also borne responsibilities for ensuring that local villages provided enough sailors and fighters. To support the Toshinari, Noshima Murakami Takeyoshi granted them holdings like the island and port of Iwagijima and "Toshinari-myō on Kutsuna Island worth 1,250 *kanmon*."[160]

Similarly, sea lords organized members of their domain by using both maritime occupational terminology and land-based institutional or status labels. Sea lords had a wide array of hierarchical, purely maritime titles from which to choose: commodore (*sōsendō*), captain (*sendō, funabito*), shipmaster (*kandori*), vice-captain (*wakisendō*), clerk (*kakitsuke*), officer (*shikan*), ropesmen (*itten, niten, santen*), "head sailor" (*kaburi kako*), and sailor (*funako, kako*).[161] During the Korean invasion of 1592, for example, the Noshima Murakami selected eleven "head sailors" to lead the other sailors on the ships under the officers.[162]

Sea lords could fuse professional categories with warrior status titles in order to organize band members hierarchically as well. Doing so made their bands appear familiar to sponsors. For example, in 1541, the sea lord Shirai Fusatane submitted to his patron, the daimyo Ōuchi Yoshitaka, an injury

Japan: The Case of the Ōuchi," with Peter Arnesen, in *Japan Before Tokugawa: Political Consolidation and Economic Growth, 1500 to 1650*, edited by John W. Hall et al. (Princeton, N.J.: Princeton University Press, 1981), pp. 95–100.

157. *Hagi-han batsuetsuroku*, vol. 3, pp. 840, doc. 15; Kishida, *Daimyo ryōgoku no keizai kōzō*, pp. 198–99.

158. Yamauchi, *Kaizoku to umijiro*, ch. 4; Yamauchi, *Chūsei Setonaikai chiikishi no kenkyū*, pp. 115–36.

159. YK, vol. 2, pp. 116–17, doc. 2, Tenshō 11 (1583) 12.30.

160. YK, vol. 2, pp. 116–17, doc. 3, Tenshō 12 (1584) 10.6. For other examples, see EK doc. 2343, Tenshō 10 (1582) 10.23; EK doc. 2405, Tenshō 11 (1583) 12.30.

161. Tenyo, *Boshi nyūminki*, pp. 208–9; *Tokubei Tenjiku monogatari*, in *Edo hyōryūki sōshū*, vol. 1, edited by Yamashita Tsuneo (Hyōronsha, 1992), p. 503; *The English Factory in Japan, 1613–1623*, edited and compiled by Anthony Farrington (London: The British Library, 1991), doc. 409, p. 1061; Kawabuchi Kyūzaemon, *Ruson oboegaki*, in *Kaihyō sōsho*, vol. 6 (Kōseikaku, 1928), pp. 14–15. *Miyakubo-chō shi*, p. 1104, doc. 101, Tenshō 20 (1592) 6.19.

162. *Miyakubo-chō shi*, p. 1104, doc. 101, Tenshō 20 (1592) 6.19.

report recounting deeds accomplished during a sea battle against a coalition of sea lords that included the Noshima Murakami. Use of warrior status categories and forms of documentation allowed sea lords to seek recognition, reward, and compensation from patrons for injuries suffered by their soldiers and crews. To highlight the nautical nature of services provided, sometimes the sea lord might modify the status categories with maritime occupational categories. Following the standard format for such reports, Fusatane appended a list of the injured "followers and servants," arranged from highest to lowest rank. Those figures that patrons would recognize as *samurai* with surnames top the list. These included other sea lords and retainers fighting under the standard of the Shirai such as the Kuwahara and Kodama. Next came "servants" (*bokujū*) and "sailors" (*kako*) from seaside villages in the Shirai domain.[163]

Boat people and slaves inhabited the lowest rungs of the class structure of littoral society. Itinerant groups of boat people (*ebune*) are thought to have been ubiquitous in the medieval and early modern Kyushu and Inland Sea littorals. Entire families, men, women, and children, made their homes aboard small fishing boats propelled by a single steering oar and perhaps a sail.[164] Such nomadic populations were not bound by traditional political boundaries and so possessed expert knowledge of local currents and conditions. They would have been attractive agents for sea lords. The 1420 Korean ambassador to Japan, Song Hŭigyŏng, wrote a poem describing how such people he encountered off the coast of Tsushima engaged in a continuum of occupations that included fishing and raiding:

The child flicks a short rod, over the crest of each wave he gambols

Father wields the bamboo fish trap with quick casts and hauls

The old mother inside cooks and cares for the children

From catching fish to catching ships, one little boat does it all![165]

Connections with sea-lord bands gave boat people access to markets and patrons. Slaves, meaning unfree persons who could be bought, sold, and inherited, also existed in sea-lord society, as they did across medieval Japan.

163. EK doc. 1713, Tenbun 10 (1541) 7.28. Other wound reports use the term *chūgen* to identify "servants" (*Hagi-han batsuetsuroku*, vol. 4, pp. 300–301, doc. 7, Daiei 4 [1524] 7.3).
164. Okiura Kazuteru, *Setouchi no minzokushi: Kaiminshi no shinsō o tazunete* (Iwanami Shoten 1998), ch.6.
165. Song Hŭigyŏng, *Nosongdang Ilbon Haegnok* (*Rōshōdō Nihon kōroku: Chōsen shisetsu no mita chūsei Nihon*), edited by Murai Shōsuke (Iwanami Shoten, 1987), no. 36.

Raids on the continent brought back Chinese and Korean captives to sell in Japan, and sea lords sold captives taken in battle.[166]

In addition to using land-based status language to enforce hierarchies in their bands, sea lords also followed the example of land-based lords and issued written case-by-case decisions and codes. Such edicts and laws reinforced the unitary nature of their authority, helped them to administer parts of their domains, and perpetuated the idea that the Noshima ruled for the good of the inhabitants of the domain. In particular, sea lords sought to restrict subordinates' abilities to exploit the very intersections of commerce and violence that had abetted the formation of sea-lord domains.[167]

Part of administering the shippers and other inhabitants of their domain entailed preventing quarrels and violent self-redress (*jiriki kyūsai*), a common problem on land and sea. By doing so, they encouraged loyalty among followers by enhancing perceptions that they fell under the authority of the Noshima lord.[168] Noshima Murakami Takeyoshi admonished "shippers of Shiwaku" in a 1570 letter that "[t]here should be no dispute regarding the passenger service" of a sponsor's agent to the port of Sakai.[169]

The Noshima Murakami found written codes of laws helpful for securing unitary authority over newly conquered holdings and incorporating them into their domain. After conquering the Kutsuna Islands in 1582, the Noshima Murakami issued regulations for their residents. The Noshima were fully aware that islands in that chain, such as Futagami and Kutsuna, contained populations of seafarers formerly under the dominion of multiple overlords like their rivals the Kurushima Murakami. Some of the Futagami fought naval battles alongside the Kurushima against the Noshima in 1582, for instance.[170] This code demonstrates an awareness among the Noshima Murakami of the centrality to their sea lordship of both the actions and rhetoric attached to the concept of "protection" (*keigo*). The Noshima here invoke the term, but leave it undefined, restricting to themselves and trusted agents the rights to engage in violence and the panoply of protection practices that regulated maritime spaces and populations. In doing so, they

---

166. EK doc. 509, Genkyō 4 (1324) 7.3; Amino Yoshihiko, "Kodai, chūsei, kinsei shoki no gyorō to kaisanbutsu no ryūtsū," in *Kōza Nihon gijutsu no shakaishi*, vol. 2: *Engyō gyogyō*, edited by Amino Yoshihiko et al. (Nihon Hyōronsha, 1985), p. 254; Thomas Nelson, "Slavery in Medieval Japan," *Monumenta Nipponica* 59 (2004): 470–72; Fujiki, *Zōhyōtachi no senjō*, pp. 31–33, 134.
167. Katsumata Shizuo, "The Development of Sengoku Law," with Martin Collcutt, in *Japan Before Tokugawa: Political Consolidation and Economic Growth, 1500 to 1650*, edited by John W. Hall et al. (Princeton: Princeton University Press, 1981), pp. 101–24.
168. Katsumata, "The Development of Sengoku Law," pp. 106–8.
169. EK doc. 2086, Genki 1? (1570), 6.15.
170. EK doc. 2440:3, Tenshō 10 (1582) 5.19; doc. 2440:4, Tenshō 10 (1582) 6.30.

hoped to restrict these new domainal inhabitants solely to activities related to maritime production and to avert any possibility of the islands' inhabitants either working with other sea-lord bands or striking out on their own as sea lords. The Noshima further limited possibilities for conflict and unlicensed piracy by dictating the routes for transport and shipping vessels.

Laws for the Kutsuna Seven Islands:
- The islands' inhabitants are not to engage in protection [*keigo*].
- Coming and going by commoners [*hyakushō*] in the service of retainers with holdings here is forbidden.
- Even in regular sea crossings in any direction, if by chance they take ship with retainers, it will be ruinous, so it is forbidden for residents to do so.
- When making crossings by ship to perform services, servants and retainers of the various islands are to go as far as Ōshima and Tsushima, both coming and going.

There are to be no violations of the aforementioned laws.
Tenshō 10 [1582] 4.25 Murakami Motoyoshi
To: Kutsuna temples, shrines, and commoners and [the residents of]
Nuwa, Tsuwaji, Futagami, and Muzuki Islands[171]

The Tsushima-Ōshima shipping routes to and from Noshima denoted in the fourth clause forced a detour away from the enemy base of Kurushima, pushing the Kutsuna inhabitants away from the temptations of former Kurushima overlords.

While recognizing the need for retainers to control private holdings and to administer parts of the Noshima domain, this code shows that the Noshima also resembled warlords on land who attempted to assert transcendent, unitary authority (*kōgi*) by bypassing retainers and addressing commoners directly. By restricting the ability of Kutsuna islanders to join together with Noshima retainers, the Noshima lords weakened potential centrifugal tendencies among their retainers and may have enabled the Noshima to bind their retainers closer to them instead of their village power bases. The Noshima also recognized that they depended on taxes, labor, and military services that villagers provided, and thus that they needed to regularize and appease that labor source.[172] When engaging in large-scale

171. EK doc. 2302, Tenshō 10 (1582) 4.25.
172. Sasaki, "The Changing Rationale of Daimyo Control in the Emergence of the Bakuhan State," pp. 276–82; Michael Birt, "Samurai in Passage: The Transformation of the Sixteenth-Century Kanto," *Journal of Japanese Studies* 11.2 (1985): 376–86.

activities, sea lords would augment the ranks of their crews by conscript-ing or hiring volunteers from among littoral villagers under their influence, sometimes known as "local protection forces" (*jige keigo*).[173]

However, similar to the case of daimyo on land, not all sea lords wielded transcendent authority. Sometimes sea-lord band members and other do-mainal inhabitants could temper the authority of sea lords and force the lord to share power with a select group of retainers. In some cases, retainers could draw on the legacy of leagues of common cause (*ikki*).[174] As befit their joint maritime power base, these retainers focused on the nautical activi-ties of the domain. For example, in 1576, Hoketsu Norinobu, a sea lord on a much smaller scale than the Noshima Murakami, issued a set of bylaws for the population of the sinuous island of Hiburishima, located off the south-west coast of Iyo, that reflects a power-sharing agreement between sea lord and band. First, the bylaws required that the sea lord and select members of the band (identified as the harbor council), not the patron, collectively dic-tated the performance of piratical activities.

- When performing duties for patrons on sea and land, they are to be per-formed according to our bylaws.

Second, the council directed that they—not Norinobu—regulated the com-mercial intercourse of the island.

- Commerce with ships entering or leaving the harbor is to be decided collectively by the island council.

The third item regulated the disposition of salvage. Coastal communi-ties could be torn apart by competition over the possession of shipwrecks, whales, driftwood, castaway vessels, and other valuable goods that washed ashore.[175]

- Objects that are spotted adrift or that wash ashore are to be reported to the harbor council.[176]

173. EK doc. 1564, no year.6.8; YK, vol. 4, p. 274, doc. 2, no year.5.8.
174. Katsumata, "The Development of Sengoku Law," pp. 103, 117–18. For examples of *ikki* involving seafarers, see DNK 11, *Kobayakawa-ke monjo*, vol. 1, p. 83, doc. 109, Hōtoku 3 (1451) 9th month, auspicious day; Hyungsub Moon, "The Matsura Pirate-Warriors of Northwestern Kyushu in the Kamakura Age," in *Currents in Medieval Japanese History: Essays in Honor of Jeffrey P. Mass*, edited by Gordon M. Berger et al. (Los Angeles, Calif.: Figueroa Press, 2009), pp. 380–81.
175. Shinjō Tsunezō, *Chūsei suiunshi no kenkyū* (Hanawa Shobō, 1994), pp. 813–20; Morimoto Masa-hiro, "GoHōjō-shi no suisanbutsu jōnōsei no tenkai," *Nihonshi kenkyū* 359.7 (1992): 33.
176. EK doc. 2194, Tenshō 4 (1576) 11th month, auspicious day.

Shipwrecks did not always happen by chance. Evidence from the early modern period indicates that some coastal villages would actually cause shipwrecks; villagers deployed lights to fool crews into thinking that they were
traveling into a harbor and force them onto rocks.[177]

A band's ability to limit the authority of sea-lord captains may have extended to life aboard ship. In 1605, a ship full of English privateers "met
with a Juncke of the Japons, which had been pyrating along the coast of
China and Camboia."[178] Their gaze colored by the practices of their own
privateering vessels, where the crew held considerable power and treated the
captain as first among equals,[179] the English sailors were struck by a similar
lack of hierarchy on the Japanese ship: "They were ninetie men, and most
of them in too gallant a habit for Saylors, and such an equalitie of behavior
among them, that they seemed all fellows: yet one among them there was
that they called Capitaine, but gave him little respect."[180]

Gender in Sea-Lord Bands

Gender norms also influenced the actions of inhabitants in sea-lord domains
and such a perspective enables us to consider the history of late medieval
maritime women as well as men. Norms in sea-lord bands were subject to
several influences, including evolving gender expectations of Japanese society, land-based hierarchical structures of lordship, and the impact of dealing
with the maritime environment. This last may help account for similarities
between the actions of women in sea-lord bands and those in littoral communities in other parts of the world.

Imbued with land-centered biases, the mutable category of *kaizoku* signified both the perceived alterity of and potential criminality of groups of
sea people. From ancient times through the sixteenth century, Japanese accepted the possibility of female as well as male pirates. In 869, the Japanese

177. Kanaya, *Kaizokutachi no chūsei*, pp. 84–85.
178. "The Second Voyage of John Davis with Sir Edward Michelborne Knight, into the East-Indies, in the Tigre a ship of two hundred and fortie Tuns, with a Pinnasse called the Tigres Whelpe," in *The Voyages and Works of John Davis, the Navigator*, edited by Albert Hastings Markham (London: Printed for the Hakluyt Society, 1880), p. 178.
179. For Michelborne and Davis as privateers, see Markham, "Introduction," in *The Voyages and Works of John Davis, the Navigator*. For the relative equality among English privateers in this period, see Kenneth R. Andrews, *Elizabethan Privateering: English Privateering During the Span-ish War, 1585–1603* (Cambridge: Cambridge University Press, 1964), pp. 40–45; J. S. Bromley, "Outlaws at Sea, 1660–1720: Liberty, Equality and Fraternity among the Caribbean Freebooters," in *Bandits at Sea: A Pirates Reader*, edited by C. R. Pennell (New York: New York University Press, 2001), p. 180.
180. "The Second Voyage of John Davis with Sir Edward Michelborne Knight," p. 179.

court recorded the capture of four pirates, two women and two men.[181] The Kamakura bakufu's 1232 Jōei Formulary (*Goseibai shikimoku*) marked the family specifically as a locus of piratical activity and assumed that wives might both know of and participate in such activities. However, by limiting the wife's punishment to the confiscation of holdings, Kamakura lawmakers may have assumed that women participated in a lesser capacity than men.[182] Borrowing from ancient precedents, Kamakura law, and other sources, the Muromachi bakufu and sixteenth-century warlords condemned piracy as acts in which whole communities engaged or at least of which they possessed knowledge. It was thus a crime that obliged authorities to hold entire villages responsible.[183]

In the late medieval period, women participated in both the violent and nonviolent aspects of sea-lord bands. A glance around the world reveals that there was nothing anomalous about women pirates in this period.[184] In late medieval Japan, violence included the protection businesses at the heart of attempts by family-based bands attempting to assert maritime lordship. For example, in 1315, a "woman, Tokumame" was arrested for perpetrating an "evildoer toll barrier [*akutō sekisho*]"[185]—for intercepting ships trying to enter Hyōgo port and charging them protection money without the permission of the proprietor.

Evidence from land-based Japanese warfare suggests an ongoing, if decreasing, involvement of women in late medieval sea-lord mercenary bands in a military capacity. Through the fourteenth century, women actively participated in battles as "comrades" in equal status to, though in fewer numbers than, men.[186] Rates of female participation in warfare are thought to

181. Naganuma Kenkai, *Nihon no kaizoku* (Shibundō, 1955), p. 35.
182. *Chūsei hōsei shiryōshū*, vol. 1: *Kamakura bakufu-hō*, edited by Satō Shin'ichi et al. (Iwanami Shoten, 1955), pp. 8–9, no. 11; Tabata Yasuko, *Nihon chūsei no josei* (Yoshikawa Kōbunkan, 1987), p. 234.
183. Tabata, *Nihon chūsei no josei*, p. 250.
184. Marcus Rediker, "Liberty beneath the Jolly Roger: the Lives of Mary Read and Anne Bonney, Pirates," in *Bandits at Sea: A Pirates Reader*, edited by C. R. Pennell (New York: New York University Press, 2001), pp. 299–320; John C. Appleby, "Women and Piracy in Ireland: From Gráinne O'Malley to Anne Bonney," in *Bandits at Sea: A Pirates Reader* edited by C. R. Pennell (New York: New York University Press, 2001), pp. 283–98; Dian Murray, "Cheng I Sao in Fact and Fiction," in *Bandits at Sea: A Pirates Reader*, edited by C. R. Pennell (New York: New York University Press, 2001), pp. 253–82.
185. *Tōdaiji monjo—Settsu no kuni Hyōgo no seki*, doc. 34, Shōwa 4 (1315) 11th month; doc. 35, Shōwa 4 (1315) 11th month, in *Hyōgo-ken shi shiryō-hen chūsei*, vol. 5 (Kōbe-shi: Hyōgo-ken, 1990). This register of captives lists several other women, but their crimes were not specified: Inume, Himetsurume, and Wakakikume.
186. Thomas D. Conlan, *State of War: The Violent Order of Fourteenth-Century Japan*, Michigan Monograph Series in Japanese Studies, no. 46 (Ann Arbor: Center for Japanese Studies, The University of Michigan, 2003), pp. 111, 124, 128–29.

have decreased after the fourteenth century when changes in inheritance practices reduced women's autonomy.[187] However, in order to survive the endemic warfare of the fifteenth and sixteenth centuries, some women turned to fighting. They worked as infantry, accountants, quartermasters, and laborers and were conscripted as sex workers. Facing capture and enslavement, they might fight to the death in defense of their castles and homes.[188]

The social acceptance of women fighting at sea in late medieval Japan may have been encouraged by popular belief in Jingū, the empress who supposedly led conquests on the Korean Peninsula and gave birth to the god Hachiman. Medieval Japanese enshrined Jingū at sites throughout the Inland Sea world and believed her to be a deity protecting Japan.[189] In the summer of 1419, one court diarist reported several manifestations of Jingū in response to a Korean attack on Tsushima. The diarist recorded a report from the Kyushu Regional Governor (*Tandai*) in which Jingū led Japanese to victory in a battle: "At the most difficult time of the battle, something miraculous occurred. Four large ships with streaming brocade banners arrived unexpectedly out of nowhere. It seemed that their leader was a woman with immeasurable power. She boarded the enemy ships and, grappling with the enemy, threw three hundred of them into the sea to drown."[190]

Despite the biases inherent in land-based ethnographies of the sea, accounts of the practices of boat people in the late medieval littoral suggest that types of violence in the maritime world may have been gendered as a result of a division of labor in which women dove and men sailed ships.[191] A 1510 description of "pirates" (*kaizoku*) given by a Japanese informant to the Korean court describes how "they normally sail with women and children aboard their ships when making raids. . . . They are adept at archery and skilled at wielding swords. They dive deep into the ocean and drill holes in ships."[192] If the divers point to women, the archers and sword wielders may point to men.

187. Hitomi Tonomura, "Women and Inheritance in Japan's Early Warrior Society," *Comparative Studies in Society and History* 32.3 (July 1990): 592–623; Tabata Yasuko, "Chūsei no kassen to josei no chii," *Rekishi hyōron* 552 (1996.4): 12–23.

188. Fujiki Hisashi, *Kiga to sensō no sengoku o yuku* (Asahi Shinbunsha, 2001), ch. 6. Ebisawa Miki "Jūgoseiki Yamato no joseitachi," *Sōgō joseishi kenkyū* 12 (1995.5): 1–18.

189. Murai Shōsuke, *Ajia no naka no chūsei Nihon* (Azekura Shobō, 1988), p. 33.

190. Gosukōin, *Kanmon nikki* (Kunaichō Shōryōbu, 2002), Ōei 26 (1419) 8.13. In addition, a troop o' cavalry led by a woman was rumored to have charged out of Hirota Shrine, a center of Hachimar worship (*Kanmon nikki*, vol. 1, Ōei 26 (1419) 6.25).

191. Arne Kalland, *Fishing Villages in Tokugawa Japan* (Richmond, Surrey: Curzon Press, 1995) pp. 163–79.

192. CWS, *Chungjong sillok*, vol. 12, p. 12b, Chungjong 5 (1510) 8.24.

In medieval Japan, as well as other parts of the world, women also engaged in a wide range of nonviolent functions necessary to the survival of seafaring communities.[193] In Japan, women produced goods that were consumed locally, submitted to proprietors as dues, and sold in markets; women divers collected seaweed, shellfish, and other goods, and they participated in the manufacture of salt.[194] They connected centers of maritime production and distribution: women were a ubiquitous presence in medieval marketplaces in both the capital region and port cities as fishmongers, moneychangers, and in various artisanal capacities.[195]

As elite sea-lord families like the Noshima Murakami borrowed land-based warrior institutional structures and came to resemble land-based warrior families, gender roles followed suit. Because of the conceptual centrality of the "house" (*ie*) for both the Noshima Murakami, as the sea-lord family, and the individual families that constituted the band (*shū*) in the sixteenth century, women played important roles in sea-lord bands. All members of a family held status and owed obligations within warrior "houses," whether lord or retainer, male or female.[196] For example, both men and women bore responsibility for securing the peace in marriage alliances.[197] Such marriages occurred both among sea-lord families and between sea-lord families and patrons. Daimyo wives exercised considerable authority as administrators within the house; they could oversee retainers and grant tax exemptions to temples. When husbands were absent or incapacitated, the wife of a warlord could serve as castellan, which for some entailed even planning strategy and leading the defense of the castle.[198] Wives of sea lords also took control of castles at times and in that capacity engaged in some of the most important aspects of sea tenure: regulating maritime space, populations, and commerce through the receipt and administration

---

193. For example, among the seafarers of sixteenth-century Ireland, women sailed fishing boats, marketed fish and booty, and commonly ran the inns and taverns in ports that served as pawn-brokers, meeting and recruiting points, and centers of exchange of goods and information (Appleby, "Women and Piracy in Ireland," p. 284).
194. See chapter 1 and Kalland, *Fishing Villages in Tokugawa Japan*, p. 50.
195. Tabata Yasuko, "Women's Work and Status in the Changing Medieval Economy," translated by Hitomi Tonomura, in *Women and Class in Japanese History*, edited by Hitomi Tonomura et al., Michigan Monograph Series in Japanese Studies, no. 25 (Ann Arbor: Center for Japanese Studies, University of Michigan, 1999), p. 102. During the fourteenth century, a woman moneychanger named Ama Gozen dealt in bills of exchange at the port of Fukatsu in Bingo Province (Uozumi Sōgorō and Matsuoka Hisato, "Itsukushima sharyōzō *Hogourakyō* ni tsuite," *Shigaku zasshi* 61.3 [1952.3]: 57–58).
196. Tabata Yasuko, *Nihon chūsei josei shiron* (Hanawa Shobō, 1994), p. 109.
197. Tabata, *Nihon chūsei no josei*, pp. 153–55; Tabata, *Nihon chūsei josei shiron*, pp. 80–81; Nishio, *Sengoku-ki no kenryoku to kon'in*, p. 5.
198. Tabata, *Nihon chūsei josei shiron*, pp. 82–83.

of toll-barrier exemptions.[199] Thus, gender norms in the Japanese maritime world reflected the expectations of Japanese society, the influence of the discourses of lordship introduced by sea-lord families, and the impact of the maritime environment. Under such conditions, both women and men in sea-lord bands might face combat, engage in protection enterprises, and participate in productive and commercial occupations. Significant curtailment of women's roles in the Japanese maritime world only seems to have begun in the Tokugawa period.[200]

CONCLUSION

A chain reaction of patronage and domainal expansion fueled the rapid growth of the Noshima Murakami family's sea lordship in the sixteenth century, which enabled them to establish unitary dominion over increasingly integrated, far-reaching maritime networks in the Inland Sea. The Noshima and other sea lords consistently retained the upper hand in negotiating the terms of patronage. In return for providing protection, fighting proxy navy wars, and administering maritime holdings, the main line of the Noshima acquired resources to quash an attempt by a branch line to take over the house headship and received legitimization for their control over key nodes in Japan's maritime infrastructure. Of particular importance were the ports and barriers of Shiwaku and Kaminoseki. From these and other strongholds, the Noshima provided mercenary services, oversaw shipping organizations, transported travelers and cargo, and sold protection from both their own violence and the violence of others.

Patronage negotiations show how the Noshima Murakami and other sea lords appropriated the land-based rhetoric of lordship and received recognition as warrior lords. The Noshima also appropriated these methods for administering their domains, adapting tools of land-based lordship to the needs of their distinctly maritime power base. They engaged in sea tenure and administered a wide range of commercial maritime industries. Of particular importance for sea tenure was their transformation of protection businesses into a regulated institution, symbolized by the issuing of Noshima crest pennants at the request of travelers. Voyagers, warlords, and merchants across the archipelago actively sought out sea lords to ensure safety on the

---

199. *Mie-ken shi shiryō-hen kinsei*, vol. 1, p. 146, doc. 78, Tenshō 6 (1578) 8th month.
200. There is some evidence that changes in belief in defilement (*kegare*) caused some littoral communities to remove women from ships during the Edo period (Kalland, *Fishing Villages in Tokugawa Japan*, pp. 49–50).

seas. This ability to affect and protect the flow of commerce inspired perceptions that the Noshima were legitimate authorities among those external to their dominion. Internally, the Noshima worked to encourage perceptions of themselves as possessing transcendent, unitary authority over maritime networks by issuing law codes and adjudicating disputes. Ships and castles also formed an integral part of the sea-lord domain and extended Noshima authority both physically and symbolically over the sea lanes. They symbolized the strength of the institutional sinews of domains and were used as stages for panoply and the performance of lordship. As a result of this history of patronage, conquest, and lordship, the Noshima Murakami's domain became a recognized and accepted part of the late medieval political, economic, and cultural landscape. Such autonomous dominion had far reaching consequences and, as later chapters show in greater detail, impacted Japan's sixteenth-century military revolution, relations with other countries, and the unification of Japan at the end of the sixteenth century.

CHAPTER 4

Pirates, Guns, and Ironclads: Sea Lords and the Military Revolution in Sixteenth-Century Japan

There is but one way to fight a sea battle: big ships defeat small ships; big guns defeat small guns; many ships defeat few ships; many guns defeat few guns—and that's all![1]

The preponderance of sea-lord patronage records devoted to military services obscures the larger continuum of livelihoods engaged in by sea-lord bands and encourages a misperception that members of sea-lord bands led lives of unrelenting violence. Of course, as befit a population that wrote and ruled using warrior rhetoric, sea-lord families considered military services to be crucial parts of their band's livelihoods, and accomplishments in naval warfare helped define their reputations. They devoted considerable resources to developing military technology and tactics. In doing so, sea lords took advantage of their own dominance in the maritime world, as well as the relative inability of their patrons to operate in that space, and shaped technology and tactics for their own purposes: the interception of ships and the seizure and defense of the chokepoints that constituted the kernels of their domains. Their mercenary capacity to retain autonomy by shifting between patrons enhanced their ability to determine both the shape of technological innovation and when and how they would provide services. The scale of services sea-lord bands could offer increased as the extent of their dominion grew. As a result, sea-lord bands proved to be decisive factors in the outcomes of naval battles throughout late medieval Japan.

During the civil war from 1336–92, littoral magnates such as the Kusuna family won accolades for their commerce raiding, protective escort, amphibious assault, and other forms of naval combat.[2] In 1399, "pirates [kaizoku] from Shikoku and Awaji," who "closed in from the west in a hundred ships," helped shogun Ashikaga Yoshimitsu to suppress a rebellion.[3]

. Yu Dayou, *Zhengqi tangji* [1565], in *Siku weishou shujikan*, vol. 20 (Beijing: Beijing Chubanshe, 1998), ch. 5, p. 2b.
. EK doc. 730, Shōhyō 3 (1348) 4.2; Andrew Edmund Goble, *Kenmu: Go-Daigo's Revolution* (Cambridge, Mass.: Harvard University Press, 1996), pp. 131, 252.
. *Ōeiki*, in *Gunsho ruijū*, vol. 20: *Kassenbu* (Zoku Gunsho Ruijū Kanseikai, 1929), p. 308.

Successful prosecution of the Ōnin War of 1467–77 required commanders on both sides to arrange for the services of sea lords to carry and protect the armies traveling to the battlefields in Kyoto. In the sixth month of 1467, "pirates [*kaizoku*] in the vanguard" protected a fleet sponsored by daimyo from western Japan, including the Ōuchi, Kōno, and Ōtomo, that consisted of "perhaps six hundred great ships coming to the capital." Among those "pirates . . . in the vanguard" was the Kegoya band,[4] whose very name, which literally translates as "protection sellers," smacks of self-promotion as purveyors of military services. In the Sengoku period, sea lords found employment as naval mercenaries with powerful regional warlord (daimyo) houses across the archipelago. In east and central Japan, the Hōjō of Odawara, the Oda, and even the Takeda—rulers of a mostly land-locked, mountainous territory—sought the services of sea lords they sometimes labeled "pirates" (*kaizoku*) in order to gain advantages in commerce, ocean-going transportation, and naval warfare.[5] Equally exalted western daimyo depended on sea lords in times of war: Kōno, Hosokawa, Miyoshi, Ōuchi, Mōri, Ōtomo, Shimazu, and more.

In the sixteenth century, sea lords also shaped the naval dimensions of the military revolution sweeping across the archipelago. The military revolution model offers historians a way to comparatively explore intersecting transformations that accompanied manifestations of early modernity across the world in politics, society, and warfare (especially those related to guns, infantry, conscription, castle construction, shipbuilding, and institutions).[6] In Japan, the decentralized century and a half between about 1440 and 1600 witnessed dramatic military changes. Armies deployed gunpowder weapons extensively and in sophisticated ways. These included harquebus-style matchlock muskets, grenades (*hōrokubiya*)—explosive clay shells filled with gunpowder, which were thrown by hand or propelled lacrosse-style with a netted pole[7]—and various sizes and configurations of cannon. Smaller cavalry-based armies gave way to the large-scale mobilization of soldiers wielding pikes, bows, and guns. Regional warlords erected gigantic, nigh-impregnable, stonewalled bastions with soaring keeps. Specialized, heavily

4. Kyōgaku, *Kyōgaku shiyōsho*, Ōnin 1 (1467) 6.9 and 7.3, in YK, vol. 1, pp. 178–79.

5. *Mie-ken shi shiryō-hen, kinsei*, vol. 1 (Tsu-shi: Mie-ken, 1993), pp. 141–44, docs. 69–74; Udagawa Takehisa, *Setouchi suigun* (Kyōikusha, 1981), pp. 144–50.

6. Geoffrey Parker, *The Military Revolution: Military Innovation and the Rise of the West,* 2nd ed (Cambridge: Cambridge University Press, 1990); Kären Wigen, "Japanese Perspectives on the Time/Space of 'Early Modernity,'" *The XIX International Congress of Historical Sciences,* Oslo Norway (2000): 1–18, http://www.oslo2000.uio.no/program/papers/m1a/M1a-wigen.pdf, accessed 7.23.2009.

7. See illustrations traced from Edo-period sources in, H. A. C. Bonar, "On Maritime Enterprise in Japan," *Transactions of the Asiatic Society of Japan* 15 (1887): plates following p. 125.

armored—sometimes even ironclad—warships accoutered with matchlocks and cannon plied the seas. Warfare seems to have become more destructive and reliant on incendiary weapons.[8]

However, as traditionally rendered, military revolution narratives propound elitist, Eurocentric, and technologically deterministic arguments that ignore the contributions of lower-status service providers.[9] Partly as a result of what Morgan Pitelka calls "Momoyama mythohistory," "a narrative of great men, great art, and great conflicts,"[10] some scholars have attributed aspects of the military revolution to the genius of certain daimyo such as Oda Nobunaga and Toyotomi Hideyoshi. Others have credited the arrival of European guns as the key causal agent.[11]

Scholars have revised the application of the thesis to the case of Japan to take into account the importance of regional interaction and the development of institutions as much or more than technology itself. Chinese firearms began to be imported and used in warfare in Japan as early as the fifteenth century.[12] In the 1540s, Iberian traders began the large-scale dissemination of European harquebus-style matchlock firearms in Japan. In the 1520s and 1530s, they had entered into preexisting trade networks connecting ports in Kyushu, Tanegashima, Ryūkyū, the south China coast, and Southeast Asia that dealt in, among other goods, guns, black powder, and sulfur. By

8. Thomas Conlan, "Instruments of Change: Organizational Technology and the Consolidation of Regional Power in Japan, 1330–1600," in *War and State Building in Medieval Japan*, edited by John A. Ferejohn and Frances McCall Rosenbluth (Stanford, Calif.: Stanford University Press, 2010), pp. 124–58; Paul Varley, "Oda Nobunaga, Guns, and Early Modern Warfare in Japan," in *Writing Histories in Japan: Texts and their Transformations from Ancient Times Through the Meiji Era*, edited by James C. Baxter et al. (Kyoto: International Research Center for Japanese Studies, 2007), pp. 105–25; Parker, *The Military Revolution*, pp. 140–43; Kubota Masashi, *Nippon no gunji kakumei: Military Revolution in Japan* (Kinseisha, 2008).
9. Peter Lorge, *The Asian Military Revolution: From Gunpowder to the Bomb* (Cambridge: Cambridge University Press, 2008), pp. 7–10. For a helpful introduction to debates over various aspects of the military revolution, see Clifford J. Rogers, ed., *The Military Revolution Debate: Readings on the Military Transformation of Early Modern Europe* (Boulder, Colo.: Westview Press, 1995).
10. Morgan Pitelka, *Handmade Culture: Raku Potters, Patrons, and Tea Practitioners in Japan* (Honolulu: University of Hawai'i Press, 2005), p. 16.
11. Asao Naohiro, "The Sixteenth-Century Unification," translated by Bernard Susser, in *The Cambridge History of Japan*, vol. 4: *Early Modern Japan*, edited by John W. Hall et al. (Cambridge: Cambridge University Press, 1992), p. 54; Delmer M. Brown, "The Impact of Firearms on Japanese Warfare, 1543–1598," *Far Eastern Quarterly* 7.3 (1948): 236–53.
12. Conlan, "Instruments of Change," pp. 145–47; Varley, "Oda Nobunaga, Guns, and Early Modern Warfare in Japan," p. 106. The Ming Dynasty (1368–1644) was from its earliest days a major innovator, producer, user, and exporter of firearms (Sun Laichen, "Military Technology Transfers from Ming China and the Emergence of Northern Mainland Southeast Asia (c.1390–1527)," *Journal of Southeast Asian Studies* 34.3 (2003): 495–517). Japanese pirates also encountered firearms when Koreans deployed guns against them in the 1370s (Ki-Baik Lee, *A New History of Korea*, translated by Edward W. Wagner, with Edward J. Shultz [Seoul: Ichokak, 1984], p. 171).

the 1540s, many of these networks had come under the control of Wang Zhi and other Chinese commanders of bands of Japanese pirates. They found ready buyers among the warlords of sixteenth century like the Tanegashima, Shimazu, and Ōtomo, who then sponsored merchants and artisans to craft firearms on the imported models.[13] However, in order to acquire and exploit new weapon systems and technologies, the regional warlords had to invest considerable human, financial, and material resources, which required that they devise new institutions, new ways of organizing their domains and military forces.[14]

Examining the military revolution from the waterline underscores the degree to which the authority of the Oda and other daimyo attenuated at the coast. They depended on sea lords and other entrepreneurial specialists for naval services. As a result, understanding naval transformations requires consideration of the ambitions and interests of the bands of mercenary sea lords who actually innovated and employed the naval technologies and tactics. From this perspective, the case of Japan's military revolution resembles that of Ming China and certain countries in Europe, where well-trained, well-equipped, professional mercenary armies developed many of the tactics, military technologies, and institutions responsible for the military revolution.[15]

Of particular utility for a study of the contributions of sea lords to the military revolution, as well as the mythology of land-based daimyo that obscures the history of naval service specialists, are a series of battles that occurred in 1576 and 1578 in the Kizu River estuary and Osaka Bay (figure 15). A bounty of patronage correspondence, orders, battle reports, diary entries, and chronicles make possible such an exploration.

13. Murai Shōsuke, *Nihon chūsei kyōkai shiron* (Iwanami Shoten, 2013), pp. 260–314; Ōta Kōki, *Wakō: shōgyō, gunjishiteki kenkyū* (Yokohama: Shunpūsha, 2002), ch. 4. Udagawa Takehisa, *Teppō denrai: heiki ga kataru kinsei no tanjō* (Chūō Kōronsha, 1990), ch. 1; Olof G. Lidin, *Tanegashima: The Arrival of Europeans in Japan* (Copenhagen: NIAS Press, 2002); Anne Walthall, "Do Guns Have Gender: Technology and Status in Early Modern Japan," in *Recreating Japanese Men*, edited by Sabine Frühstück et al. (Berkeley: University of California Press, 2011), pp. 27–29.
14. Thomas Conlan, "Instruments of Change"; Stephen Morillo, "Guns and Government: A Comparative Study of Europe and Japan," *Journal of World History* 6, no. 1 (1995): 75–106.
15. One of the most technically advanced armies of the early modern world, that of the Swedish general and king Gustavus Adolphus (1594–1632), was a transnational force with a large number of mercenaries (Janice Thomson, *Mercenaries, Pirates, and Sovereigns: State-Building and Extraterritorial Violence in Early Modern Europe* [Princeton, N.J.: Princeton University Press, 1994], p. 30; Jeremy Black, *Military Change and European Society, 1550–1800* [London: Macmillan Education, 1991], p. 10). For the effectiveness of mercenary armies in China, see Kenneth Swope, *A Dragon's Head and a Serpent's Tail: Ming China and the First Great East Asian War, 1592–1598* (Norman: Oklahoma University Press, 2009), pp. 19–22.

TABLE 3
Dramatis personae for the battles of the Kizu River

Patrons	Background
Oda Nobunaga (1534–82)	Regional warlord seeking hegemony in central Japan by eliminating the Ikkō Ikki as a threat
Ōtomo Sōrin (1530–87)	Daimyo in Kyushu allied to Nobunaga
Ashikaga Yoshiaki (1537–97)	Last Ashikaga shogun, one leader of anti-Nobunaga coalition
Kennyo Kōsa (1543–92)	Patriarch of the Ikkō Ikki
Mōri Terumoto (1553–1625)	Powerful regional warlord in western Honshu, frequent patron of the Noshima Murakami, and one leader of anti-Nobunaga coalition
Kobayakawa Takakage (1533–97)	Uncle of Mōri Terumoto, intermediary between Mōri and sea lords
Kōno Michinao (d. 1587)	Warrior provincial governor in Iyo

Sea Lords	Background
Noshima Murakami Takeyoshi (1533–1604)	Leader of the Noshima Murakami band
Noshima Murakami Motoyoshi (1553–1600)	Son of Takeyoshi, leader of 1576 fleet
Innoshima Murakami Sukeyasu (d. 1608)	Leader of the Innoshima Murakami band, master of Tomo and several other ports
Kurushima Murakami Yoshitsugu	Member of the the Kurushima Murakami sea-lord band
Nomi Munekatsu (1527–92)	Sea lord affiliated with Kobayakawa Takakage
Saika Band	Band of semiautonomous villagers and mercenaries on land and sea from Kii Province
Kuki Yoshitaka (1542–1600)	Sea lord and leader of Nobunaga's naval forces, from Shima and Ise
Manabe Shime no hyōe (d. 1576)	Sea lord from Izumi who fought for Oda Nobunaga
Atagi	Sea-lord family based in Iwaya

The battles of the Kizu River occurred as part of Oda Nobunaga's decade-long conflict with the Ikkō Ikki Pure Land Buddhist sectarians, which lasted from 1570–80. During these campaigns, Nobunaga besieged the Ikkō Ikki's headquarters, the Ishiyama Honganji. In 1573, Nobunaga deposed Ashikaga Yoshiaki (1537–97), the final Ashikaga shogun, who then sought

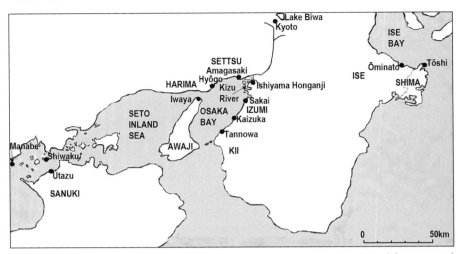

Figure 15. Map of the battles of the Kizu River, 1576–78. This map is adapted from several sources: *Hyōgo Kitazeki irifune nōchō*, edited by Hayashiya Tatsusaburō (Chūō Kōron Bijutsu Shuppan, 1981), pp. 260–61; Suzuki Masaya, *Sengoku teppō, yoheitai* (Heibonsha, 2004) pp. 6, 107; Usami Takayuki, *Nihon chūsei no ryūtsū to shōgyō* (Yoshikawa Kōbunkan, 1999), p. 86; Conrad Totman, *A History of Japan*, 2nd ed. (Malden, Mass.: Blackwell Publishing, 2000), p. xxviii.

refuge with a powerful warlord of western Japan, Mōri Terumoto. Kennyo Kōsa (1543–92), patriarch of the Ikkō sect, Ashikaga Yoshiaki, and Mōri Terumoto joined with other warlord houses such as the Takeda, Uesugi, and the Hōjō and forged an alliance to oppose Nobunaga.[16] Kōsa called on his allies to lift the siege of Osaka and deliver supplies and soldiers to the citadel. Attempts to do just that led to a series of naval engagements between 1576 and 1578.

These battles have been well studied as key steps along the way to the unification of Japan and as part of Japan's military revolution. As traditionally recounted, Nobunaga defeated the anti-Nobunaga coalitions by ingeniously devising ironclad ships and employing guns in new, effective ways. As a result of these battles, he was eventually able to force one of his most implacable foes, the Ikkō Ikki, to surrender their chief stronghold, the Ishiyama citadel. Their defeat heralds the subordination of religious institutions to the warrior rule of the Tokugawa period. The Ikkō Ikki citadel stood on

---

16. The 1576 coalition is actually known to some historians as the second anti-Nobunaga coalition. The first consisted of daimyo houses such as the Miyoshi, Rokkaku, Asakura, Azai, and Takeda as well as the Ikkō sectarians and lasted from around 1570 to 1573 (Jeroen Lamers, *Japonius Tyrannus: The Japanese Warlord Oda Nobunaga Reconsidered* [Leiden: Hotei Publishing, 2000], p. 165).

the southern bank of the Kizu River near Osaka Bay, and it was eventually turned into Osaka Castle by Toyotomi Hideyoshi, who based his regime in this port city. This campaign also represented Nobunaga's first large-scale military encounter with western daimyo, which would lead inexorably to Hideyoshi's eventual unification of Japan in 1590.[17]

However, by the time of the Kizu River estuary battles, the Noshima Murakami and other sea-lord houses had established domains that stretched across swathes of the Inland Sea and other maritime regions. Both sides in the conflict thus required the assistance of sea lords, who significantly impacted the duration, scale, shape, and outcome of the conflict. In 1576, the Noshima Murakami formed a coalition with other sea lords from the Inland Sea and seafarers from other regions and led a fleet that managed to break Oda Nobunaga's blockade and reprovision the citadel. In 1578, a powerful sea lord under the patronage of Nobunaga named Kuki Yoshitaka led a restrengthened fleet of ships, which included a flotilla of ironclad dreadnoughts (*atakebune*) that he himself designed, and destroyed a second fleet sponsored by the anti-Nobunaga alliance.

Sea lords did not fight for the same reasons, did not act according to the same logic, and did not experience warfare in the same ways that their patrons did. Sea-lord cultures of war, military tactics, and technologies evolved out of a synthesis of Japanese cultural practices with the dictates of their maritime environment. This means that sea-lord military techniques both included Japanese traits and reflected wider possibilities found in global naval processes. Such cultural border straddling enabled sea lords to position themselves as recognizable (and so hirable) by land-based sponsors, but also as exotic enough to remain untrustworthy—alien enough to retain autonomy. For example, in the late fifteenth century, Muromachi shogunal administrators and other authorities feared that the "warships" that they hired as naval proxies would capture valuable overseas trade ships.[18] In the sixteenth century, such mistrust can be seen in descriptions of pirates as "irregulars."[19]

A waterline perspective sheds considerable light on three interlocking dimensions of the battles of the Kizu River and the sixteenth-century military revolution: geography, naval organization and institutions, and tactics

17. Carol Tsang, *War and Faith: Ikkō Ikki in Late Muromachi Japan* (Cambridge, Mass.: Harvard University Press, 2007), ch. 6; Neil McMullin, *Buddhism and the State in Sixteenth-Century Japan* (Princeton, N.J.: Princeton University Press, 1984), ch. 3; Lamers, *Japonius Tyrannus*, pp. 102–5, chs. 7–8.

18. Kikei Shinzui and Kisen Shusho, *Inryōken nichiroku*, edited by Tamamura Takeji et al. (Kyoto: Shiseki Kankōkai, 1953), vol. 2, p. 795, Bunmei 17 (1483) 12.24.

9. Fujiki Hisashi, *Zōhyōtachi no senjō: chūsei no yōhei to doreigari* (Asahi Shinbunsha, 1995).

and technology. Exploration of these three dimensions reveals significant continuity from earlier periods as well as dramatic changes. As in other parts of the world, naval warfare in late medieval Japan occurred almost exclusively in and over chokepoints.[20] Sea lords dedicated themselves to developing tactics and technologies for attacking and defending chokepoints in order to expand and control the networks that comprised their domains over the course of the fifteenth and sixteenth centuries. They maintained their autonomy through the use of mercenarism, shifting between potential sponsors to remain independent. Such mercenarism hindered fast resolution of conflicts by making it difficult for a particular side or a single patron to build stable, enduring coalitions or to preserve overwhelming numerical superiority for any length of time. By maintaining dominance in the chokepoints and maritime networks where most naval conflicts occurred, by controlling the timing and methods by which services for patrons would be accomplished, and by focusing domainal institutions on building ships and managing seafarers, sea-lord bands helped direct the course of evolution for naval technology and tactics in the sixteenth-century military revolution. In order to meet changing needs of patrons, especially calls for extensive blockades, sea lords developed new technologies and tactics that augmented traditional commerce raiding tactics with maritime siege warfare elements and employed incendiaries and cannons to destroy ships as well as capture them.

GEOGRAPHY: THE CHOKEPOINT

A focus on controlling maritime chokepoints remained a constant, defining element of naval warfare both before and after the military revolution in Japan. In the late medieval period, most naval warfare followed the shipping lanes and occurred in littoral, not pelagic regions. Sea lords directed their energies to controlling these sinuous channels that slithered between the coasts of Honshu, Shikoku, and countless tiny mountainous islands. Land-based warlord patrons sought secure sea lanes for goods, soldiers, and materiel. Offloading such cargoes and personnel required that seafaring bands develop expertise in amphibious operations.

The sea-lord bands involved in the Osaka campaign based themselves in chokepoints, transformed many of these arterial channels and ports into domainal hubs of production, distribution, exchange, and protection networks, and had extensive experience attacking and defending their home channels

---

20. For the case of Europe, see Jan Glete, *Warfare at Sea, 1500–1650: Maritime Conflicts and the Transformation of Europe* (Cambridge: Cambridge University Press, 2002), p. 1.

as well as other passages. Earlier chapters detailed the expansion of families like the Noshima Murakami and the Kurushima Murakami, who fought for the Mōri during the Osaka campaigns. In addition, the anti-Nobunaga coalition counted on the Saika bands, a loosely knit, semiautonomous assemblage of both coastal and inland villages, who were a major commercial, piratical, and military presence in the Kii Peninsula south of Osaka.[21] The Noshima Murakami maintained commercial as well as military connections with the Saika; they granted the Saika a crest pennant in 1581.[22] Sea lords sponsored by the Oda had similar backgrounds. Kuki Yoshitaka came from Shima, a peninsula on the southern edge of Ise Bay; he and his shipmasters navigated, traded, and fought in the craggy inlets and passages around Ōminato and other ports in the region. His band participated in Ise Shrine's lucrative—and often toll-exempt—carrying trade, sailed as far as the Kantō region, and operated protection businesses. He had established a reputation as a puissant sea warrior and had proven himself effective in fighting the Ikkō sectarians at sea for Nobunaga in 1574.[23] The Manabe family came from Manabe Island, part of the Shiwaku Island chain, before they moved to Izumi Province; the Atagi controlled some of the shipping lanes attached to the port of Iwaya on Awaji.[24]

Patrons and other elite observers frequently employed variants on the term "traffic lanes" (*tsūro*) in order to identify the chokepoints that became maritime battlefields, partly out of recognition of the contributions of sea lords, who developed and protected commercial shipping networks and fought the battles that occurred in those spaces. In the 1560s, the Mōri used the term to emphasize the valuable services that the Noshima Murakami provided during battles for the straits of Shimonoseki, a set of chokepoints that contained important ports like Akamagaseki and Mojinoseki and that controlled access between Honshu and Kyushu.[25] Nobunaga called on sea lords to seize the "traffic lanes" when laying siege to the Honganji citadel.[26]

---

21. Suzuki Masaya, *Sengoku teppō, yoheitai: Tenkabito ni sakaratta Kishū Saikashū* (Heibonsha, 2004).
22. Takahashi Osamu, "Shinshutsu no 'Murakami Takeyoshi kashoki' ni tsuite," jō, *Wakayama Kenritsu Hakubutsukan kenkyū kiyō* 3.4 (1999): 41–52; "Shinshutsu no 'Murakami Takeyoshi kashoki' ni tsuite," ge, *Wakayama Kenritsu Hakubutsukan kenkyū kiyō* 3.5 (2000): 32–41.
23. *Mie-ken shi shiryō-hen chūsei*, vol. 2 (Tsu-shi: Mie-ken, 2005), pp. 566–67, doc. 9, Tenshō 1? (1573) 10.19; *Mie-ken shi shiryō-hen chūsei*, vol. 1, ge (Tsu-shi: Mie-ken, 1999) p.101, doc. 205, Tenshō 1? (1573) 10.30; Usami Takayuki, *Nihon chūsei no ryūtsū to shōgyō* (Yoshikawa Kōbunkan, 1999), pp. 81–90; Inamoto Noriaki, "Kuki-shi ni tsuite," *Mie-ken shi kenkyū* 1 (1985): 29–50; Tsang, *War and Faith*, pp. 224–27.
24. For the Manabe, see Fujita Tatsuo, *Nihon kinsei kokka seiritsushi no kenkyū* (Azekura Shobō, 2001), pp. 297–98. For the Atagi, see *Zōtei Oda Nobunaga monjo no kenkyū*, edited by Okuno Takahiro (Yoshikawa Kōbunkan, 1988), doc. 642, Tenshō 4? (1576) 5.23.
25. EK doc. 1834, Eiroku 4? (1561) 10.18; EK doc. 2070, Eiroku 12? (1569) 6.12.
26. *Zōtei Oda Nobunaga monjo no kenkyū*, doc. 644, Tenshō 4? (1576) 6.4.

The Osaka battles exemplify both the importance of chokepoints for land-based patrons and the reliance of those patrons on sea lords for control of "traffic lanes." Osaka Bay contains several major chokepoints, including ports and smaller harbors connected by riverine and road networks to the capital. The Ishiyama Honganji citadel lay just upstream from important estuarial toll barriers and major medieval entrepôt such as Watanabe, Tennōji, and Sakai. Ships weighing anchor from these places connected the capital region with several interlocking networks: other ports within Osaka Bay such as Amagasaki and Hyōgo, the wider Inland Sea, and shipping lanes that departed the archipelago for China, Korea, Ryūkyū, and Southeast Asia.[27] After he chronicled the surrender of the Ikkō citadel in his biography of Oda Nobunaga, Ōta Gyūichi (1527–1610) reflected on Osaka's location at the center of a web of networks: "Osaka is the most important place in Japan. In particular, it is close to Nara, Kyoto, and Sakai; from Yodo and Toba, ships sail straight to Osaka Castle's gates. . . . Endlessly interconnected rivers and streams surround it. . . . As billowing seas float ever away to the west, oceangoing ships from Europe, Korea, and China, and—it goes without saying—from various parts of Japan sail to and from here. It is a gathering place for merchants from the seven circuits and five home provinces in Japan who come to make their fortunes in trade."[28] The citadel of Osaka thus represented a nerve center that commanded terrestrial, riverine, and maritime trade networks as well as a vital access point for the capital region. According to historian Fujimoto Masayuki, the Mōri followed standard sixteenth-century military practice and perceived the Ishiyama citadel as a "fortified bridgehead." The Oda needed to parry the Mōri's lunge.[29]

In the spring of 1576, sea lords on both sides began to receive instructions to seize both the chokepoints around the Kizu River and the access points to Osaka Bay. Between the fourth and sixth months of 1576, the services of sea lords enabled Nobunaga to tighten the noose around the Osaka citadel on sea as well as on land. Nobunaga issued instructions that "the traffic lanes

27. Wakita Haruko, "Ports, Markets, and Medieval Urbanism in the Osaka Region," in *Osaka: The Merchant's Capital of Early Modern Japan*, edited by James L. McClain et al. (Ithaca, N.Y.: Cornell University Press, 1999), pp. 22–43; V. Dixon Morris, "Sakai: from Shōen to Port City," in *Japan in the Muromachi Age*, edited by John W. Hall et al. (Berkeley: University of California Press, 1977), pp. 145–58; V. Dixon Morris, "The City of Sakai and Urban Autonomy," in *Warlords, Artists, and Commoners: Japan in the Sixteenth Century*, edited by George Elison et al. (Honolulu: University of Hawai'i Press, 1981), pp. 23–54.

28. Ōta Gyūichi, *Shinchō-Kō ki* (Kadokawa Shoten, 1969), pp. 327–28; Ōta Gyūichi, *The Chronicle of Lord Nobunaga*, translated and edited by J. S. A. Elisonas and J. P. Lamers (Leiden: Brill, 2011), pp. 372–73.

29. Fujimoto Masayuki, *Nobunaga no Sensō: Shinchō-kō ki ni miru Sengoku gunjigaku* (Kōdansha, 2003), p. 275.

of Osaka, riverine and terrestrial, are to be most stringently blockaded."[30] He dispatched forces to defend the maritime approaches from the port of Amagasaki;[31] ordered the port of Kizu taken, "as that would completely cut off . . . the passageways" that the coalition had been using to resupply the citadel "from the sea";[32] and instructed the Manabe and other sea lords to patrol the seas offshore from his fortresses at Sumiyoshi.[33]

In order to relieve this siege, Mōri, Honganji, and shogunal officials requested that sea lords conduct a two-pronged, amphibious campaign. Noshima Murakami Motoyoshi and Nomi Munekatsu would lead a fleet of sea lords to retake the chokepoints in the Kizu River delta. Meanwhile, land forces would disembark at the port of Amagasaki to fight their way overland toward the Ikkō citadel.[34] Additionally, in order to thwart attempts by the Ōtomo or other Oda allies from striking at the bases of Mōri agents from behind, some Noshima Murakami forces sailed west in order to defend the narrow channels around Itsukushima and Hiroshima Bay.[35]

The strategies of both sides also required that sea lords hold the chokepoints to the north and south of Awaji Island, which dominated the approaches to Osaka Bay. By late 1575, the head of the Ikkō sectarians, Kennyo Kōsa, was urging that the Mōri safeguard the chokepoint between Awaji Island and Honshu by arranging for protection (i.e., sea-lord) forces around the port of Iwaya, located at the northern tip of Awaji.[36] Until the surrender of the Osaka citadel in 1580, sea lords in the anti-Nobunaga coalition repeatedly found themselves inundated by requests from Kennyo, the Mōri, and other patrons to sail to Iwaya.[37] The Kodama and Reizen families accepted appointments to take up the defense of Iwaya in 1577 and 1578.[38] In addition to Shiwaku, the Noshima port of Kasaoka proved an important staging point for sailing to Iwaya. Noshima Murakami Kagehiro sailed from there to secure the chokepoint between Awaji and Harima in early 1578.[39] The anti-Nobunaga

30. *Zōtei Oda Nobunaga monjo no kenkyū*, doc. 644, Tenshō 4? (1576) 6.4; ibid., see also docs. 636 and 638.
31. Ōta, *Shinchō-Kō ki*, p. 208.
32. Ibid., p. 209.
33. Ibid., p. 211; Ōta, *The Chronicle of Lord Nobunaga*, pp. 250–52.
34. EK doc. 2177, Tenshō 4? (1576) 4.4; EK doc. 2176, Tenshō 4? (1576) 3.2.
35. EK doc. 2181, Tenshō 4? (1576) 6.20.
36. DNK 9, *Kikkawa-ke monjo*, vol. 1, p. 56, doc. 84, Tenshō 3? (1575) 11.20.
37. *Wakayama-ken shi chūsei shiryō*, vol. 2 (Wakayama-shi: Wakayama-ken, 1983), p. 422, doc. 3, Tenshō 6? (1578) 3.8; ibid., pp. 422–23, doc. 5 Tenshō 6? (1578) 3.24; ibid., p. 423, doc. 6, Tenshō 6? (1578) 3.25.
38. YK, vol. 2, p. 970, doc. 106, Tenshō 5? (1577) 3.20; *Hagi-han batsuetsuroku*, edited by Nagata Masazumi (Yamaguchi-shi: Yamaguchi-ken Monjokan, 1967), vol. 3, pp. 182–85, doc. 44, doc. 57.
39. EK doc. 2218, Tenshō 5? (1577) 11.5; EK doc. 2219, Tenshō 5? (1577) 12.3; *Kasaoka-shi shi shiryō-hen*, vol. 2 (Kasaoka-shi, Okayama-ken: Kasaoka-shi, 2001), doc. 148, Tenshō 8 (1580) 1.17.

coalition could circumvent Nobunaga's control of the land as a result of these efforts by sea lords.[40] For his part, Nobunaga commissioned a sea-lord family based on Awaji, the Atagi, to "launch barrier ships," the smaller, faster ships in sea-lord fleets, in order to "drive away the maritime forces approaching from the Chūgoku region to deliver provisions to Osaka."[41]

NAVAL INSTITUTIONS AND SEA LORDS

The naval dimensions of the military revolution in Japan entailed institutional as well as technological developments. Naval institutions were needed to organize personnel into effective fighting units and to centralize the acquisition of resources necessary for assembling fleets of warships. Historians focused on the land have tended to assume that the major patrons in the Kizu River estuary battles possessed such institutional machinery, and they have argued that the sea battles were between "the Mōri navy" and "the Oda navy," respectively.[42] They did so partly because of shorthand usage common in the sources. The various leaders of the two sides used names of daimyo (like "Mōri"), provinces (like "Aki"), or even regions (such as "Chūgoku") to identify both the patrons and the service-providing clients in the military forces on each side.

However, an examination of the naval coalitions and shipbuilding related to the Osaka battles in 1576 and 1578 reveal the degree to which sea lords and other maritime service providers operated independently and possessed sophisticated naval institutions of their own, as well as the degree to which land-based warlords had only limited naval institutions and instead relied on sea-lord bands and other naval specialists. Sengoku warlords never owned enough ships to operate navies on their own. Sea lords met this demand and offered their expertise as commerce raiders, guards, and shippers to multiple warlord patrons. Naval forces remained informal, ad hoc, mercenary assemblages until after Hideyoshi's unification. The mercenarism of sea lords prolonged the campaigns and made decisive battles difficult because it destabilized large-scale coalitions.[43]

40. Hashizume Shigeru, *Setonaikai chiiki shakai to Oda kenryoku* (Kyoto: Shibunkaku Shuppan 2007), p. 238.

41. *Zōtei Oda Nobunaga monjo no kenkyū*, doc. 642, Tenshō 4? (1576) 5.23.

42. McMullin, *Buddhism and the State in Sixteenth-Century Japan*, p. 129.

43. Thomson, *Mercenaries, Pirates, and Sovereigns*, chs. 2–3. In this manner, they impacted warfare in ways similar to autonomous *tozama* war bands on land (Thomas D. Conlan, *State of War: The Violent Order of Fourteenth-Century Japan*, Michigan Monograph Series in Japanese Studies, no. 46 [Ann Arbor: Center for Japanese Studies, University of Michigan, 2003], p. 147).

tury, these shipyards were already producing vessels of over 400 and 700 *koku* lading, respectively. By the time of the Osaka battles, the Innoshima Murakami controlled the ports of Innoshima, Tajima, and Tomo, the shipwrights of which crafted ships of between 600 and 1,000 *koku* for the 1465 tally trade mission to China.[83]

Sea lords had thus developed institutional foundations necessary for constructing specialized, large-scale warships. *Atakebune* ancestors tended to be multipurpose craft: the same ship could be used for fishing, shipping, transport, or fighting. As chapter 3 showed, dreadnoughts represented the unprecedented capabilities of the sixteenth-century sea lords to exploit domainal holdings and markets in order to gather together significant amounts of naval stores and artisans, shipwrights, and sailors for specialized functions: sea tenure and the panoply of sea lordship, occupation of chokepoints, and war. As a result, historical records show that although some regional warlords did order and possess their own *atakebune*,[84] it was sea lords who designed, constructed, and owned many of these vessels.[85] They did so for their own purposes and their own environments.

What daimyo patrons could offer were pretexts and resources for the construction of additional dreadnoughts. In order to reassemble his blockade of the Osaka Honganji citadel in 1578, Oda Nobunaga employed Kuki Yoshitaka "to construct six great ships."[86] Eager to see these ships completed, Nobunaga instructed that "Kuki not lack for anything." Nobunaga required his deputy in Sakai, Matsui Yūkan, among others, to send supplies to Yoshitaka twice a month. Sakai was a center of both iron and gun production, so that may have been a source of the iron plates, guns, and ordnance that Yoshitaka installed on the ships.[87] In addition to the six new dreadnoughts, Yoshitaka worked with one of Nobunaga's retainers, Takigawa Kazumasu (1525–86) in fitting out one along the lines of a Chinese junk.[88] Kazumasu administered a delta region of Ise Province that once belonged to the Ikkō sect[89] and so would have been useful to Yoshitaka as a source of naval stores and labor.

83. *Hyōgo Kitazeki irifune nōchō*, edited by Hayashiya Tatsusaburō (Chūō Kōron Bijutsusha, 1981); Tenyo Seikei, *Boshi nyūminki*, in NMKBS, pp. 212–14.
84. Ōta, *Shinchō-Kō ki*, p. 149; EK doc. 2239, Tenshō 7? (1579) 6.3.
85. EK doc. 2382, Tenshō 11? (1583) 5.10; EK doc. 2378, Tenshō 11? (1583) 4.21; EK doc. 2241, Tenshō 7? (1579) 12.7; and see below.
86. Ōta, *Shinchō-Kō ki*, p. 248.
87. *Zōtei Oda Nobunaga monjo no kenkyū*, doc. 771, no year.6.10. For Sakai as a center of iron and firearms production, see Lidin, *Tanegashima*, ch. 9.
88. Ōta, *Shinchō-Kō ki*, p. 248.
89. Lamers, *Japonius Tyrannus*, pp. 139, 193.

TACTICS AND TECHNOLOGY

Because sea lords shaped battle tactics to fit chokepoints, when possible, they applied commerce raiding methods—the interception and taking of ships—to warfare. Sea-lord bands utilized distance weapons, hand-to-hand weapons, and the element of surprise in an integrated fashion in order to eliminate or capture enemy personnel and to seize and loot their ships. They did not initially aim to destroy ships. The battles of the Kizu estuary mark a turning point in tactics as sea lords found commerce raiding inadequate for defeating blockades composed of dreadnoughts. In order to defeat these floating castles, sea lords applied tools and methods for maritime siege warfare to destroy enemy ships. Such tactics included the use of incendiaries such as fire arrows, cannons, and grenades.

Commerce Raiding Tactics

At sea, as on land, throughout the late medieval period, the preference seems to have been to keep the enemy at a distance before closing with, boarding, and taking the enemy ship. In medieval Europe, fleets relied on boarding when the presence of several heterogeneous bodies of ships and warriors rendered impractical more complex tactics other than gradually closing and grappling with the enemy.[90] However, descriptions in seventeenth-century Japanese chronicles and Ming Chinese ethnographies of Japanese pirates suggest that sea-lord bands coordinated sophisticated maneuvers and formations by blowing conch shells, ringing bells, beating drums, and lighting flares.[91]

Distance weapons included bow and arrows and muskets. Wound reports and other records of sea battles document the prevalent use of bows and arrows at sea.[92] The introduction and proliferation of firearms in Japan did not drastically change the ways in which distance weapons were used.[93] Early

90. Glete, *Warfare at Sea 1500-1650*, pp. 36–37.
91. *"Bukebandaiki: Santō kaizoku-ke ikusa nikki*, ni no maki," *Suminoe* 228 (Spring 1998): 46; Zheng Ruozeng, *Chouhai tubian* (Beijing: Zhonghua Shuju, 2007), p. 204.
92. EK doc. 1713, Tenbun 10 (1541) 7.28; EK doc. 1832, Eiroku 4? (1561) 8.5; YK, vol. 2, p. 943, doc. 3; Daiei 7 (1527) 7.18; *Wakabayashi-ke monjo*, doc. 44, Eiroku 12 (1569) 8.9 in *Ōtomo suigun: Umi kara mita chūsei Bungo* (Ōita: Ōita Kenritsu Sentetsu Shiryōkan, 2003), p. 61. For deriving tactics from wound reports and the importance of bows and arrows in late medieval Japan, see Conlan *State of War*, ch. 2.
93. Suzuki Masaya, *Teppō to Nihonjin: "teppō shinwa" ga kakushitekita koto* (Chikuma Shobō, 2000), pp. 209–14; Varley, "Oda Nobunaga, Guns, and Early Modern Warfare in Japan," pp. 108–9; Conlan, "Instruments of Change," pp. 130, 146–47.

guns appear in records of sea battles as early as 1527.[94] These took a variety of shapes and configurations, such as the poetically named "Chinese fire spitter," a type of "fire lance" developed in China that could discharge lead pellets, flames, and sometimes arrows, though the early projectiles tended in Japan to be known as "stones."[95] Firearms were deployed to a much greater extent after the introduction of the European harquebus. These guns were around a meter long, of 10-20 mm caliber, and effective up to around 200 meters. One fired a harquebus by inserting a match (variously made of bark, bamboo, or cotton) into a lock on the gun; this match entered the firing pan and lit the black powder after one pulled the trigger.[96] Sea lords such as the Noshima Murakami appreciated the physical and psychological damage a fusillade of harquebus bullets could inflict, using them as early as 1550 to repel enemy seafarers.[97] However, they also recognized the limitations of using firearms when heavy seas or rain might render them inoperable.[98] And like other elites across late medieval Japan on land and sea, they treated guns as valuable gifts as much as tools for killing.[99] In 1578, when the Noshima came to an accord with Nobunaga, Noshima Murakami Takeyoshi also dispatched a messenger with a firearm as a present for Ōtomo Sōrin to let Sōrin know that the Noshima would be receptive to providing more services for him, an offer Sōrin was happy to accept.[100]

After unleashing hails of arrows and bullets, sea-lord bands closed on one another and used pole arms to either stab the enemy or knock them overboard.[101] Despite the caricatures of half-naked, hairy barbarians, a contemporaneous Chinese picture scroll of "Japanese pirates" gives further credence to the use of spears in naval warfare (figure 16). Sea-lord captains then

---

94. YK, vol. 2, p. 943, doc. 3 Daiei 7 (1527) 7.18. The battle was for Niho Island in Hiroshima Bay.

95. The tally trade expedition returning from China in 1469 brought back the "fire spitter" (*Daijōin jisha zōjiki*, Bunmei 1 (1469) 12.1, 12.6, NMKBS, p. 181). For "fire lances," see Joseph Needham, with the collaboration of Ho Ping-yü et al., *Science and Civilisation in China*, vol. 5: *Chemistry and Chemical Technology*, part 7: *Military Technology; The Gunpowder Epic* (Cambridge: Cambridge University Press, 1986), pp. 220–52. For other examples of early guns in Japan, their use in combat, and the term "stones," see Conlan, "Instruments of Change," pp. 145–47; Suzuki, *Teppō to Nihonjin*, pp. 28–35.

96. Udagawa Takehisa, "Teppō to ishibiya," *Nihon no bijutsu* 390 (1998): 17–30; Kenneth Chase, *Firearms: A Global History to 1700* (Cambridge: Cambridge University Press, 2003), pp. 24–25.

97. Bairin Shuryū, *Bairin Shuryū Suō gekō nikki*, in YK, vol. 1, p. 467, Tenbun 19 (1550) 9.19.

98. "*Bukebandaiki: Santō kaizoku-ke ikusa nikki*, ni no maki," p. 46.

99. Udagawa, *Teppō denrai*, pp. 21–22.

100. EK doc. 2224, Tenshō 6? (1578) 7.24.

101. *Shirai monjo*, p. 93, doc. 11, Tenbun 10 (1541) 6.12 in *Buke monjo no kenkyū to mokuroku*, edited by Akutagawa Tatsuo (Ishikawa Bunka Jigyō Zaidan, Ochanomizu Toshokan, 1988); EK doc. 1844, Eiroku 4 (1561) 12.2.

Figure 16. Sea battle featuring Japanese pirates employing spears. Detail from *The Scroll of the Japanese Pirates* (*Wokou tujuan* [*Wakō zukan*]). Photo courtesy of the Historiographical Institute, University of Tokyo (Tokyo Daigaku Shiryōhensanjo), and used with their permission.

typically directed crews to board opposing ships. Crews might employ "bear claws" and other grapples to pull ships together,[102] after which both sides entered into hand-to-hand combat with swords and other weapons.[103]

Sea lords devised these methods in order to take loot, prisoners, and, if possible, the entire ship. In battles, sea lords received from patrons de facto sanction to enrich themselves and, by doing so, to weaken the patron's enemy. After a battle for the straits of Shimonoseki in the eleventh month of 1561, the Mōri praised the Noshima Murakami for "seizing ten enemy ships."[104] Other sea-lord bands in the same battle captured "eight ships and thirteen prisoners alive," as well as several horses.[105] Fujiki Hisashi argues that "pirates" sold captives taken in battle as slaves for profit.[106]

When possible, sea lords preferred to take enemy ships by surprise. The Noshima Murakami received commendation for effectively conducting "sneak attacks" in battles for the Shimonoseki "traffic lanes" in 1561.[107] A description of what such actions might have entailed can be found in a late medieval genealogy of the Kōno family, for generations the warrior provincial governors of Iyo in Shikoku. This history contains a colorful depiction of a sneak attack carried out by one heroic ancestor, Kōno Michiari, against part of the 1281 Mongol invasion fleet. This literary description of thirteenth-century action is probably reasonably accurate for the fifteenth

102. *"Bukebandaiki: Santō kaizoku-ke ikusa nikki*, ni no maki," p. 46.
103. *Hagi-han batsuetsuroku*, vol. 4, p. 174, doc. 10, Meiō 8 (1499) 9.8; EK doc. 1842, Eiroku 4? (1561) 11.16.
104. EK doc. 1838, Eiroku 4? (1561) 11.9.
105. *Hagi-han batsuetsuroku*, vol. 3, pp. 176–77, docs. 22–23, Eiroku 4 (1561) 10.10.
106. Fujiki, *Zōhyōtachi no senjō*, 16–32, 134.
107. EK doc. 1834, Eiroku 4? (1561) 10.18.

and sixteenth centuries, when the account was likely written. Members of the Kōno possessed considerable knowledge of the maritime world. They evinced pride in an ancient seafaring heritage,[108] sponsored and sought to control many sea-lord bands, and repeatedly entered into marriage with the Kurushima Murakami sea-lord family.[109] The genealogical account shows several techniques that sea lords could employ in sneak attacks, including grappling, disguising themselves and their ship, and evading pursuit by changing directions and doubling back on their path.

> [Kōno Michiari and his uncle] boarded a small ship with some mariners and impersonated a fishing vessel. They rowed out to the enemy fleet and did nothing to arouse suspicion. . . . Then they attached hooks to one turreted vessel, and the two climbed onto the enemy ship. They took the enemy commander and lifted him down into their ship. This immediately roused a commotion on the Mongol ship—drums boomed and bells rang. In this chaos, his uncle took two or three heads and Michiari scattered large numbers of them. Then they rowed out, and in the night they sailed east and west until none followed them, and they returned safely.[110]

Sea lords developed such commerce raiding tactics by applying methods developed for protection enterprises. A favorite tactic for sneak attacks by sea lords of the Inland Sea seems to have been to hide in the shadow of islands, where atop promontories they erected observation posts from which to search for passing ships. Describing part of the sea off of Aki Province, the 1420 Korean ambassador Song Hŭigyŏng writes: "In the middle of the sea astride our path are stone islets resembling birds' heads. . . . As our ship gradually approached one island, a small ship emerged from it and raced toward us with the speed of an arrow."[111]

Song also confirmed the practice of sea lords disguising their boats as fishing and commercial craft in order to achieve the element of surprise. His account shows how difficult it was for even experienced travelers to determine the identity of an unknown ship. Despite the presence of seasoned Japanese escorts who were well versed in pirate methodology,[112]

108. *Yoshōki Jōzōinbon*, in *Yoshōki, Suiri gengi, Kōno bungenroku, kaiteiban*, edited by Yamauchi Yuzuru et al. (Matsuyama-shi: Iyo Shidankai, 1995), pp. 1–3. For background on the various versions of *Yoshōki*, see Yamauchi Yuzuru, "Kaidai," in *Yoshōki*, pp. 196–212.
109. Nishio Kazumi, *Sengokuki no kenryoku to kon'in* (Seibundō, 2005), pp. 19–25.
110. *Yoshōki Jōzōinbon*, p. 24.
111. Song Hŭigyŏng, *Nosongdang Ilbon haegnok* (*Rōshōdō Nihon kōroku: Chōsen shisetsu no mita chūsei Nihon*), edited by Murai Shōsuke (Iwanami Shoten, 1987), no. 85.
112. Song, nos. 47, 163.

Song's crew panicked at the approach of an unfamiliar craft: "Then, as the sun was setting, the ship approached. The crew all thought that they were pirates. . . . When it drew closer, we inquired as to their purpose. They answered, 'We are a fishing vessel.' When we looked again, many were sitting, hiding . . . my crew all grew suspicious and our faces lost all color."[113] Awareness of the maritime environment enabled the pirates in Song's account to take advantage of the glare and shadow from the setting sun to obscure themselves. In addition, until the sixteenth century, sea lords lacked specialized warships; they converted fishing and commercial craft for war by adding shields, armor, and temporary turrets.[114] Figure 17 shows how a large-scale fifteenth-century commercial vessel might be adapted for war by the addition of fore and aft castles where fighters could stand and fire arrows.[115] To achieve the element of surprise, sea lords could leave off such accouterments and borrow fishing tools from domainal inhabitants. Boat people especially seem to have been expert in using the same ship for fishing and piracy. In Song's words, "From catching fish to catching ships, one little boat does it all."[116]

Figure 17. Muromachi-period ship outfitted for battle. Detail of *Jingū Kōgō engi*, 1st scroll (jōkan). Photo courtesy of Konda Hachimangū, Osaka, Japan, and used with their permission.

113. Song, no. 154.
114. "*Bukebandaiki: Santō kaizoku-ke ikusa nikki,* ichi no maki," p. 44; Yamauchi, *Setouchi no kaizoku,* p. 144.
115. Ishii Kenji, *Zusetsu wasen shiwa* (Shiseidō, 1983), pp. 43, 50.
116. Song, no. 36.

In the sixteenth century, sea lords designed "barrier ships" (*sekibune*)[117] to meet their strategic needs for fast vessels that could achieve the element of surprise and that could be used to escort larger vessels. On such missions, barrier ships scouted ahead, sent up flares in warning, guided others ships into harbors and through dangerous channels, raced back to surround the protected vessels in times of danger, and patrolled harbors and inlets.[118]

Maritime Siege Warfare and the Battles of the Kizu River

The battles in the Kizu River estuary witnessed a significant shift in tactics. Sea lords, not their land-based warlord sponsors, devised tactical innovations in action at sea. They augmented traditional commerce raiding with the application of maritime siege warfare tactics in order to make effective use of and to defend against dreadnoughts. Victory for both sides in the two major battles in the chokepoints of Osaka Bay in 1576 and 1578 depended on acquiring sufficient dreadnoughts and on securing the services of sea lords who could adapt the siege warfare tactics necessary for using *atakebune* in order to achieve victory.

Atakebune have been seen as militarily ineffective because of Japan's naval defeats during the Korean War of 1592–98. They sometimes overturned in the rough seas between Japan and Korea, did not carry broadsides of cannon, and fared poorly against the ironclad Korean turtle ships and Ming vessels, which did employ broadsides.[119] However, whatever their failings in Korea, these ships originated in the domains of sea lords who invested resources and designed these ships for their own purposes. Sea lords wrought dreadnoughts for their own maritime environments, places like Ise Bay and the Seto Inland Sea: shallow, if fast-moving channels with seas calmer than those of the China Sea or the straits of Tsushima. Sea lords employed dreadnoughts militarily for commerce raiding, ship-to-ship combat, and maritime siege warfare. Sides of the ships could fold down in order to become boarding platforms, which facilitated grappling and the capture of opponents' ships, loot, and prisoners.[120] In commerce raiding operations,

---

117. *Zōtei Oda Nobunaga monjo no kenkyū*, doc. 642, Tenshō 4? (1576) 5.23.

118. "*Bukebandaiki: Santō kaizoku-ke ikusa nikki*, hoi no maki," p. 49.

119. Brown, "The Impact of Firearms on Japanese Warfare, 1543-1598," pp. 251–52; A. L. Sadler, "The Naval Campaign in the Korean War of Hideyoshi (1592-1598)," *Transactions of the Asiatic Society of Japan* 2nd ser. 14 (1937): 177–208; Swope, *A Dragon's Head and a Serpent's Tail*, pp. 116–21, 144, 274–76. For a discussion of the broadside and teleological assumptions about military technology, see N. A. M. Rodger, "The Development of Broadside Gunnery, 1450–1650," *Mariner's Mirror* 82.3 (1996.8): 301–24.

120. Ishii Kenji, *Wasen II* (Hōsei Daigaku Shuppankyoku, 1995), p. 123.

sea lords used *atakebune* to cut supply lines by intercepting and capturing enemy warships, resupply vessels, and commercial craft.[121]

The *atakebune* design also combined the idea of fortifications with the mobility of the sea. Historian Fujimoto Masayuki argued convincingly that they were maritime analogues of the "ancillary fortifications" (*tsukejiro*) used often on land to defend and besiege larger strongholds, to fortify thrusts into enemy territory, and to expand hold over territory and populations.[122] Dreadnoughts enabled sea lords to supplement sea castles with mobile fortifications, attack those strongholds with techniques of siege warfare, and securely connect home castles to supply bases and subsidiary fortifications. Thus, both *atakebune* and ancillary fortifications offered sea lords local, defensible bases of operations, watchtowers, and havens for the mooring and refitting of ships. Dreadnoughts also augmented and connected the ancillary fortifications constructed or captured on neighboring shores.[12] Dreadnoughts were slow moving but imposing vessels. They carried stores of grenades and harquebuses and brandished cannon, which transformed ships into floating gun and ordnance platforms, an important dimension in many discussions of the naval aspects of the military revolution.[124]

Such weapons increased the capabilities of sea lords for conducting sea-based sieges and applying those tactics to ship-to-ship battles, as well eliminating enemy soldiers in commerce raiding operations. These tactics included cannon barrages, sinking ships, and incendiary warfare using grenades and fire arrows. Before and after the proliferation of firearms, sea lords launched sneak attacks to commit arson and shot fire arrows with the purpose of burning enemy docks, shipyards, fortifications, and settlements.[12]

However, Japanese cannon in the sixteenth century lacked any standardization of size and design, which bespeaks an ad hoc approach to ordnance, not institutionalization. An array of terminology for cannons peppers the sources of the period, including: "stone fire-arrow" (*ishibiya*), "great barreled" (*ōzutsu*), and "great gun" (*ōdeppō*) cannons. Even these categories contain considerable variety. For example, *ishibiya* generally referred to cannon from abroad or cannon cast domestically based on foreign models. The term was often applied to Portuguese, Chinese, and Southeast Asian ver-

---

121. EK doc. 2399, Tenshō 11? 7.14; EK doc. 2402, Tenshō 11? (1583) 7.24.
122. Fujimoto, *Nobunaga no Sensō*, pp. 81–82, 275–76.
123. Yamauchi Yuzuru, *Kaizoku to umijiro: Setouchi no sengokushi* (Heibonsha, 1997), pp. 56–57; Fujimoto, *Nobunaga no Sensō*, pp. 81–82; EK doc. 2377, Tenshō 11? (1583) 4.14; EK doc. 2394, Tenshō 11? (1583) 7.1.
124. Parker, *The Military Revolution*, ch. 3.
125. *Hagi-han batsuetsuroku*, vol. 4, pp. 300–301, doc. 7, Daiei 7 (1527) 2.10; EK doc. 1711, Tenbun 10 1541 (Tenbun 10) 6.1; EK doc. 2378, Tenshō 11? (1583) 4.21.

sions of "Frankish Cannon" (Jp. *furanki*, Ch. *folangji*), breech-loaded cannon, which were anywhere from one to three meters long and of a range of calibers, from three to nine centimeters. They might be made of iron or bronze. The term "great barreled cannon" generally referred to simple pieces ignited with fuse cords without lock mechanisms.[126] It is likely that sea lords mounted such cannon in the armored turrets of *atakebune*, which were perforated with arrow slits and gun ports.[127] Japanese on land and sea applied the different sizes of cannon to different purposes. Smaller cannon could be installed as swivel guns on turrets and used as anti-personnel weapons, which would have made them useful to sea lords in commerce raiding. Larger cannons tended to be inaccurate, slow to load, and unwieldy, but they could be used against other ships and in sieges, making them useful as shipboard weapons, provided that timbers were reinforced to support the heavier weight and that they were placed carefully so as not to unbalance the ship.[128]

The acquisition of cannon seems to have been one item for which sea lords depended heavily on patrons. There is some evidence that southern Chinese merchants from Fujian imported Chinese cannon to Japan, and it is possible that the Chinese leaders of Japanese pirate bands, like Wang Zhi, could have transferred such weapons to those sea lords who agreed to join their bands.[129] One seventeenth-century chronicle of former sea-lord families even claims that European (*nanban*) gunners sailed in their fleets in the late sixteenth century.[130] However, the most likely sources for cannon were daimyo patrons. Among sea-lord sponsors, the Mōri, Ōtomo, and Oda assiduously sought cannon. The Mōri competed with the Ōtomo to secure cannon as the two warlord houses and sea-lord proxies contested the straits of Shimonoseki in the 1560s and 1570s. The Mōri also deployed *ishibiya* cannon in a 1568 campaign in Shikoku that involved the Kurushima Murakami and Noshima Murakami; at least one of these may have been of Southeast Asian manufacture.[131] Ōtomo Sōrin negotiated several times with Portuguese merchants and Jesuits for cannon and had other cannon cast on these models, which he variously used in battle and as gifts.[132] Oda Nobunaga requisitioned

126. Chase, *Firearms,* pp. 142–45; Arima Seiho, *Kahō no kigen to sono denryū* (Yoshikawa Kōbunkan, 1962), pp. 537–59; Udagawa, "Teppō to ishibiya," pp. 62–64.
127. Ishii, *Wasen II,* p. 123.
128. Chase, *Firearms,* pp. 23–26, 71; Parker, *The Military Revolution,* pp. 84–86.
129. For Fujianese merchants, see Kenneth M. Swope's discussion of the *Ming Dynastic History* in *A Dragon's Head and A Serpent's Tail,* p. 322, n. 24. Chinese acquired *folangji* in the 1520s and cast their own by the 1530s (Arima, *Kahō no kigen to sono denryū,* p. 556), but also had a long history of their own ordnance (Needham, *The Gunpowder Epic,* pp. 276–392).
130. "*Bukebandaiki: Santō kaizoku-ke ikusa nikki,*" ni no maki," p. 46.
131. EK doc. 2058, Eiroku 11 (1568), middle of 12th month; Udagawa, "Teppō to ishibiya," pp. 55–62.
132. Arima, *Kahō no kigen to sono denryū,* pp. 537–40; Udagawa, "Teppō to ishibiya," pp. 55–56.

temple bells, hired a Chinese man to cast cannon for him, and patronized the gunsmiths of Kunitomo (in today's Shiga Prefecture) and Sakai.[133]

From one or more of these sponsors, the Noshima Murakami acquired "great barreled" (ōzutsu) cannon to mount on their dreadnoughts.[134] Kuki Yoshitaka took advantage of Oda Nobunaga's resources to install cannon of at least two sizes[135] on all six of his 1578 dreadnoughts. Each of Yoshitaka's new ships carried three cannon that a Jesuit eyewitness described as "heavy ordnance"; he added that "I have no idea where these could have come from," suggesting that these may have been cast domestically.[136]

In the Osaka campaign, sea lords operated dreadnoughts largely in sea-castle mode. These atakebune complemented efforts on land, as both the Oda and anti-Nobunaga coalition maneuvered for position by erecting siege works and counter siege works.[137] In the summer of 1576, the Manabe and other pro-Oda sea lords followed Nobunaga's orders to blockade the approaches to the Ishiyama Honganji citadel by transforming their dreadnoughts into a fortification set across the river mouth.[138]

In response, the Noshima, Nomi and other members of the anti-Nobunaga sea-lord flotilla marshaled a superior number of fighters and ships, though numbers in this period should be understood as impressionist rather than exact accountings.[139] The first battle of the Kizu River estuary began in the middle of the sixth month of 1576 when the Noshima and others in the western alliance assembled at the port of Iwaya.[140] On the twelfth of the seventh month, they "set sail from Iwaya and . . . joined forces with the Saika gangs. The next day, [they] sailed . . . to the mouth of the Kizu River where [they] engaged the enemy."[141]

The dreadnought fortifications of the Manabe and other pro-Oda sea lords initially stymied their attempts to relieve the siege. As the Noshima Murakami and other anti-Nobunaga sea lords reported: "The enemy had many soldiers as well as great ships built with turrets extending up from the sides of each ship. They had two hundred escort vessels sailing on either

133. Kubota, Nippon no gunji kakumei, p. 69; Lidin, Tanegashima, ch. 9; Udagawa, "Teppō to ishibiya," pp. 47–49.

134. EK doc. 2382, Tenshō 11? (1583) 5.10).

135. The Sonkeikaku Bunko version of Nobunaga's biography claims that the larger guns required 1 catties (kin) of gunpowder, and the smaller, 10 (Fujimoto, Nobunaga no Sensō, p. 267).

136. Letter by Organtino Gnecchi-Soldo S.J. (1530–1609), quoted in Lamers, Japonius Tyrannus, p. 155; Kubota, Nippon no gunji kakumei, p. 67.

137. Ishiyama kassen hennen shiryō, pp. 186, 279; Fujimoto, Nobunaga no Sensō, pp. 81–82, 264–76.

138. Ōta, Shinchō-Kō ki, p. 212.

139. Fujimoto, Nobunaga no Sensō, pp. 262–65.

140. Zōtei Oda Nobunaga monjo no kenkyū, doc. 646, Tenshō 4? (1576) 6.16.

141. EK doc. 2183, Tenshō 4? (1576) 7.15.

side of the great ships, and they turned their rudders to take them into the mouth of the river. Then their land forces extended bridges to create an impregnable barrier. If we could not force a decision here in this battle, it did not seem that we would be able to get the provisions to the citadel."[142] To solve this dilemma, the Noshima and other Mōri-sponsored sea lords did not request aid from land-based patrons. They made the necessary tactical changes at sea themselves. They "consulted with the Saika"[143] and decided to change tacks from a commerce raiding strategy to a besieging strategy, which enabled the Noshima Murakami, Nomi, and Saika to inflict a devastating defeat on the pro-Oda forces.

They "attacked, going straight at them in turn."[144] While doing so, the Noshima and others "wielded objects such as those known as grenades [*hōrokubiya*], which. . . they hurled in and . . . burned all of their [the pro-Oda] great ships until not a single one remained."[145] The pro-Oda forces suffered devastating casualties because, "in a constant stream [the Oda] land forces had all boarded the turreted ships."[146] With those ships on fire, people stampeded to disembark; chaos ensued, and countless died; many of the Oda-sponsored sea-lord commanders went down with their ships.[147] The sea lord and Saika coalition claimed to have "destroyed several hundred enemy ships."[148] With victory in hand, the fleet led by the Noshima Murakami, Nomi, and the Saika delivered the provisions to Osaka.[149]

In preparing his fleet in 1578, Kuki Yoshitaka also recognized that commerce raiding tactics no longer sufficed; fighters at sea now had to have the power to destroy as well as to capture vessels. He designed his new *atakebune* accordingly. Reputedly, each ship measured around 33 meters in length and 11 meters in breadth,[150] carried both large and small cannon, and was armored in "iron plates to make them impervious to firearms."[151]

---

142. Ibid.

143. Ibid.

144. Ibid.

145. Ōta, *Shinchō-Kō ki*, p. 212; *The Chronicle of Lord Nobunaga*, p. 253.

146. EK doc. 2183, Tenshō 4? (1576) 7.15.

147. Ōta, *Shinchō-Kō ki*, p. 212; DNK 12, *Uesugi-ke monjo*, vol. 2, pp. 62–63, doc. 646, Tenshō 4? (1576) 7.27.

148. EK doc. 2183, Tenshō 4? (1576) 7.15.

149. Ibid.; Ōta, *Shinchō-Kō ki*, p. 212. See also EK docs. 2184–91.

150. Eighteen *ken* by 6 *ken*: these figures are drawn from the Sonkeikaku Bunko version of *Shinchō-Kō ki* (Fujimoto, *Nobunaga no Sensō*, p. 267). *Tamon'in nikki* also gives dimensions (12–13 *ken* long by 7 *ken*), but as Ishii Kenji notes, these dimensions do not match the usual ratio of the beam being one-third of the length on *atakebune* and probably would not be seaworthy (Ishii, *Wasen* II, p. 124).

151. *Tamon'in nikki*, edited by Tsuji Zennosuke et al. (Rinsen Shoten, 1978), vol. 3, pp. 21–22, Tenshō 6 (1578) 7.20.

The existence and configuration of these iron plates have been the subject of much debate. Suzuki Masaya, for example, dismisses the presence of the iron as myth; he argues that wooden armored plates sufficed to stop bullets and that the diarist who reported the iron plates simply conveyed hearsay.[152] However Yoshitaka's innovation in 1578 is well within the realm of possibility. Toyotomi Hideyoshi ordered Kuki and other admirals to provide him ironclad warships for his war in Korea from 1592–98.[153] Fujimoto Masayuki's discussion of *atakebune* as a type of ancillary fortification presents a convincing rationale for the armor. He argues that this iron armor did not cover the entire superstructure, as that would have made the ship too expensive to construct and impossibly top heavy. Instead, limited iron plating protected key personnel (such as those in charge of the cannon and other large guns), though such plating would have offered scant protection against the grenades hurled into ships. The added weight of the armor slowed the ships considerably. One Honganji official wrote of Kuki Yoshitaka's iron-plated flotilla in 1578, "it is said that these ships cannot move freely at sea."[154] But that did not matter because the Oda had a large fleet of escort vessels, and the dreadnoughts were designed to blockade a river mouth as floating fortresses.[155]

The Kuki completed the flotilla by the end of the sixth month in Ise and set sail around the horn of the Kii Peninsula, headed for Osaka. Rumors of the threat represented by these craft spread soon after the ships' departure. The Honganji sent an urgent missive to "every harbor and anchorage" in the Saika federation, ordering them to not let Yoshitaka's ships go "free on the seas, for if they come up [to Osaka] it will be catastrophic."[156] Seeking to "stop the great ships,"[157] Saika bands set sail from their several small harbor communities and rendezvoused off the coast of Tannowa, south of Osaka, where they engaged Kuki Yoshitaka's fleet. Yoshitaka's new fleet of dreadnoughts and escort craft lured the Saika in close, where their small, maneuverable vessels would be less of an asset, and made short work of them: "countless small Saika and Tannowa vessels approached and unleashed hails of arrows and bullets, attacking from all four sides." Once in close range, Yoshitaka's "seven great ships and escort vessels . . . fired their cannons all at once, destroying many of the smaller ships."[158]

152. Suzuki, *Teppō to Nihonjin*, pp. 130–31.
153. Iwao Seiichi, *Shinpen shuinsen bōeki shi no kenkyū* (Yoshikawa Kōbunkan, 1985), p. 25; Fujimoto *Nobunaga no Sensō*, p. 270.
154. *Manpukuji monjo*, quoted in Fujimoto, *Nobunaga no Sensō*, p. 272.
155. Fujimoto, *Nobunaga no Sensō*, pp. 270–73.
156. *Mie-ken shi shiryō-hen, kinsei*, vol. 1, p. 208, doc. 192 Tenshō 6? (1578) 7.8.
157. Ōta, *Shinchō-Kō ki*, p. 248.
158. Ibid.; *Chronicle of Lord Nobunaga*, p. 290.

On 7.17, Yoshitaka reached Sakai, and the next day he sailed for Osaka, where he employed dreadnoughts as floating fortresses in the river mouth, stationing them so as to "engage in protection [*keigo*] and block off the maritime approaches."[159] Observers and opponents appraised Kuki Yoshitaka's fleet as a serious threat. The Jesuit Organtino Gnecchi-Soldo predicted that because these vessels were "to seal off Vozâca [Osaka] Bay and to prevent ships with reinforcements or supplies from reaching the bastion, ... it really seems that with this the citadel of Vozáca will soon surrender."[160] Honganji officials warned Saika forces that it would be criminal to send less than five hundred gunners, and that they should do so before Yoshitaka's "great ships ... sailed into the river mouth and blocked the traffic lanes."[161] By the middle of the ninth month, Honganji was sending urgent messages to its branch temples and other members of the anti-Nobunaga coalition warning that "in the seventh month, the enemy ships sailed into the Kizu River and rendered the sea lanes completely impassable. If these ships are not defeated soon, this temple's fall is certain."[162]

Kuki guessed that the sea lords from western Japan together with the Saika forces would attempt to replicate the siege warfare of the 1576 battle, and that he needed to revise his strategy accordingly. Just as he did with the Saika off of Tannowa, he used his ships as floating fortresses, lured his enemies in close (but perhaps out of hand-tossed grenade range), and, mounting his many cannon of various dimensions, out-gunned and defeated his opponents. Ōta Gyūichi, Nobunaga's biographer, gives a detailed account of this battle: "On 11.6, some six hundred ships from western Japan sailed to the Kizu River estuary. Kuki and his great ships sailed forth to meet them, whereupon they were surrounded. ... The six great ships had many cannon on them. They would draw the enemy vessels in, select those that seemed to be flagships, and use the cannon to destroy them. As a result, the enemy feared to close with Yoshitaka's ships. [Kuki] chased several hundred enemy ships up the Kizu River. Onlookers could not but feel that Kuki had accomplished great deeds."[163] In the limited space of Osaka Bay and the Kizu River estuary, Yoshitaka's dreadnoughts would not have needed to move quickly. They could just use their imposing size and firepower to defeat the outnumbered fleet coming to resupply the citadel. Yoshitaka also probably outnumbered the

159. Ibid., p. 249; *The Chronicle of Lord Nobunaga*, pp. 290–91.
160. Letter by Organtino Gnecchi-Soldo S. J. (1530–1609), quoted in Lamers, *Japonius Tyrannus*, p. 155.
61. *Wakayama-ken shi chūsei shiryō*, vol. 2, pp. 426–27, doc. 12, Tenshō 6? (1578) 7.17. Also see *Tamon'in nikki*, vol. 3, pp. 21–22, Tenshō 6 (1578) 7.20.
62. *Ishiyama kassen hennen shiryō*, p. 278; *Honganji monjo*, doc. 38, Tenshō 6? (1578) 9.26.
63. Ōta, *Shinchō-Kō ki*, p. 255; *The Chronicle of Lord Nobunaga*, p. 297.

anti-Nobunaga coalition fleet. Defeats in 1577 and 1578 weakened the Saika to the point that they could only send a reduced force to fight against Kuki's fleet in Osaka Bay. In addition, it is likely that sea-lord mercenarism weakened the coalition in 1578, which helped ensure that Yoshitaka won the day. Bands like the Noshima Murakami evinced considerable willingness to consider serving the Oda, and it is not recorded if the Noshima fought in the 1578 battle.

ENDINGS

Based on panegyric accounts like that of Ōta Gyūichi quoted above, there is a tendency to end the history of the Osaka campaigns with this battle. However, it is important to keep in mind that the Ishiyama Honganji held on until 1580. They could do so because seafarers continued to find passages through the blockades due to the weaknesses in late sixteenth-century coalitions. Despite Yoshitaka's cinematic victory, later in the very same month, one of Oda Nobunaga's staunchest bulwarks in his blockade of the Honganji citadel, Araki Murashige (1536–85), switched to the anti-Nobunaga coalition. This defection created a gap in the interlocking ring of fortresses, which allowed some sea-lord "protection forces" sponsored by the Mōri to "land at Kizu Harbor" and unload provisions.[164]

Indeed, sea lords continued to find their services in demand to contest possession of chokepoints and to establish, run, and attack blockades as the Oda began to push into western Japan after 1578. Kuki Yoshitaka provided maritime support for these and other offensives.[165] This advance, coupled with the defection of the warlord Ukita Naoie to the Oda, forestalled further Mōri advances toward the capital.[166] The failure of land-based warfare pushed Mōri Terumoto to rely instead on sea lords. He requested that the Noshima Murakami, Kurushima Murakami, Innoshima Murakami, and other sea lords block off much of the Inland Sea against pro-Oda shipping, which gave sea lords license to seize merchant vessels as well as military vessels traveling to and from the capital. The scale of the blockade can be seen in this letter by the Mōri: "In previous years, we sent the Yashiro band [Kurushima Murakami] to Yanai and Ōbatake to intercept ships. . . . Now it has been ordered that [Noshima Murakami] Takemitsu should intercept ships at Kaminoseki. . . . In addition, the ships of Kawai Genzaemonnojō of

164. Lamers, *Japonius Tyrannus*, pp. 156–57. DNK 8, *Mōri-ke monjo*, vol. 3, pp. 42–43, doc. 832 Tenshō 6? (1578) 11.8; Suzuki, *Teppō to Nihonjin*, p. 136.
165. *Mie-ken shi shiryō-hen, kinsei*, vol. 1, p. 212, doc. 200 Tenshō 8? (1580) 7.6.
166. Lamers, *Japonius Tyrannus*, p. 161.

Tomo [Innoshima Murakami] have been instructed to take up a position in the seas off of Iyo, where they are to seize ships between Shiwaku and Tomo."[167] Nobunaga and Hideyoshi ordered Kuki Yoshitaka and various maritime forces from Awaji and other harbors to counter this threat. Much of this combat by sea-lord proxies continued to occur over and around the chokepoint of Iwaya.[168] Yet as we saw in chapter three, sea lords were willing to smuggle and run their own blockades, rendering such cordons permeable.

CONCLUSION

Maritime service professionals like sea lords and the Saika possessed specialized skills in naval warfare that enabled them to help shape Japan's sixteenth-century military revolution. The battles for the Ishiyama Honganji citadel in 1576 and 1578 are usually interpreted as a centerpiece of the unification of Japan and the eradication of autonomous religious power. However, from the perspective of the sea, these battles also demonstrate the continued weakness of land-based powers over the maritime world and their continued reliance on autonomous sea-lord clients. Sponsorship of sea lords gave patrons access to the sea that they might not have been able to acquire otherwise: the Mōri could expand eastward toward the capital, and Oda Nobunaga could defeat the Ikkō Ikki.

Naval warfare, like that of the Kizu River battles, was centered on chokepoints, places where sea lords established the nerve centers of their domains. Sea lords devoted considerable resources to attacking and defending those narrow channels. In addition, sea lords specialized in the construction of fleets and management of seafarers. They developed institutions and administrative capacity toward those ends. Land-based lords relied on oaths and linchpin figures to hold naval coalitions together. The weak bonds holding such assemblages together enhanced sea lords' autonomy. They could dictate how military services for patrons were to be discharged. Naval technological and tactical developments such as the *atakebune* and the innovations of Kuki Yoshitaka reflected sea-lord logics and ambitions, as well as those of their sponsors.

---

167. *Hagi-han batsuetsuroku*, vol. 3, p. 842, doc. 30 (Tenshō 7? (1579) 2.25); Kishida, *Daimyo ryōgoku no keizai kōzō*, pp. 52–53.

168. Hashizume, *Setonaikai chiiki shakai to Oda kenryoku*, pp. 297–300.

CHAPTER 5
Putting the Japanese in "Japanese Pirates"

Like the waters flowing through their domains, sea lords of the Seto Inland Sea such as the Noshima Murakami did not stay confined to the Japanese archipelago. Even though they established lordship over discrete domains and largely recognized the boundaries of other sea lords, the transborder communications made possible by their maritime environment and the reputations sea lords acquired enabled them to extend their influence well beyond domainal borders to the courts of foreign countries. Their domains encompassed major transportation arteries that linked Japan to the rest of East Asia. Sea lords interacted with foreign travelers on the shipping corridors of the archipelago and at the courts of warrior provincial governors and warlords. They also forayed beyond the straits of Shimonoseki to the coasts of China and Korea and participated in diplomatic, raiding, trading, and protection ventures overseas. As a result of these interactions, sea lords' reputations rippled across the sea lanes of East Asia and entered into the policy discussions of officials in Chosŏn Korea and Ming China. Sea lords both exploited and fell victim to these tides of information. They helped to give shape to and caused Korean and Chinese officials and other scholars to include them in the mutable, ambiguous category of "Japanese pirates" (Kn. waegu, Ch. wokou).[1] This exploration of the ways in which Inland Sea mariners engaged with the wider maritime world thus also reveals how the concept of "Japanese pirates" evolved as a result of transborder, maritime interactions involving individuals from China, Korea, and Japan. It is helpful to think of such interactions as having occurred multidimensionally,[2] as "stereophonic, bilingual, or bifocal" regional processes.[3]

Until recently, historians have tended to study cultural phenomena as the products of individual states, the heritage of particular nations, which limited the possibilities for understanding both those who roamed the

---

1. Tanaka Takeo pointed out the importance of seeing Japanese pirates as the sum of their representations in *Higashi Ajia tsūkōken to kokusai ninshiki* (Yoshikawa Kōbunkan, 1997), pp. 1–2.
2. Murai Shōsuke, *Ajia no naka no chūsei Nihon* (Azekura Shobō, 1988), pp. 20–21, 74–75; Paul Gilroy, *The Black Atlantic: Modernity and Double Consciousness* (Cambridge, Mass.: Harvard University Press, 1993), p. 4.
3. Gilroy, *The Black Atlantic*, pp. 2–3.

maritime world and the construction of images, ideas, and identities across borders.[4] The history of Japanese pirates has tended to be similarly one-dimensional. Murai Shōsuke has critiqued trends among scholars to define "Japanese pirates" by lands of origin. He argues that we should understand Japanese pirates as transborder, "multiethnic" (*taminzoku*), littoral inhabitants who belonged to a maritime "region" (*chiiki*) and who mixed elements of different countries, and followed largely maritime occupations: they fished, produced and sold salt, traded, and raided along the coasts of and on the seas between Korea, China, and Japan.[5] The undue focus on lands of origin has caused studies of Japanese pirates to bifurcate. Historians of the Inland Sea focused on issues like the relations between pirates, estate proprietors, and warlords in the Inland Sea region. Historians of overseas relations focused on the impact of Japanese pirates from places like Kyushu and Tsushima on Japan's relations with China and Korea.[6] As a result, the traditional image of Inland Sea *kaizoku* is one of domestic pirates who seldom strayed or had much influence beyond the confines of the archipelago.[7]

Yet Korean and Chinese scholar-officials clearly came to view the Seto Inland Sea as part of the wider piratical region of the East Asian maritime world. They did so because sea lords interacted with inhabitants from Korea and China and shaped the concept of "Japanese pirate." These encounters occurred as a result of sea lords seeking out patronage opportunities to engage in protection services. One reason that the overseas histories of late medieval Inland Sea seafarers have not been deeply explored is because the names of such mariners often do not survive. However, in many cases, the same sea-lord patronage networks that shaped domestic commerce, politics, and war also affected overseas piracy, trade, and diplomacy. By triangulating sources depicting sea-lord sponsorship mechanisms for "protection" both inside and outside the archipelago, it is possible to extrapolate the names of Inland Sea bands involved in overseas relations.

In East Asia in the fifteenth and sixteenth centuries, considerable differences of opinion existed regarding the proper execution of protection services and the place of violence in the maritime world. Nevertheless, all governments in East Asia recognized the necessity of providing protection for diplomatic and trade expeditions. The blanket euphemism in Japan for a wide variety of sea-lord services, "protection" (*keigo*), was matched in Chosŏn Korea and Ming China by the equally expansive term, "escort"

4. Ibid., ch. 1.
5. Murai Shōsuke, *Nihon chūsei kyōkai shiron* (Iwanami Shoten, 2013), pp. 123–25, 149–50.
6. Saeki Kōji, "Kaizoku-ron," in *Ajia no naka no Nihonshi III: Kaijō no michi*, edited by Arano Yasunori et al. (Tokyo Daigaku Shuppankai, 1992), p. 35.
7. See works by Udagawa Takehisa and Yamauchi Yuzuru in the bibliography.

(Kn. *hosong,* Ch. *husong*).[8] From the perspective of sea-lord bands and their Japanese patrons, diplomatic exchanges and trade all entailed some degree of autonomous, seaborne violence. Flotillas engaged in diplomacy and trade presented potentially alluring targets to pirates; neither central nor provincial authorities could secure Japan's coastlines without the protection that local sea-lord bands could provide. In contrast, the Chosŏn and Ming courts channeled relations with Japan into highly regulated systems of tribute trade and attempted to partition the use of force from ideally nonviolent systems of diplomacy and exchange. Chosŏn Korean and Ming Chinese policies granted a much smaller legitimate role to autonomous military organizations[9] in overseas exchange than the Muromachi bakufu, regional warlords, and other Japanese authorities permitted, with their considerable reliance on sea lords and other mercenaries. Korean and Chinese officials expected that the "King of Japan," the Ashikaga shogun, would arrange for "escorts" to protect and police diplomatic and trade embassies. Although well versed in Chinese practices of hiring barbarians to subdue barbarians, Korean and Chinese literati were not comforted that in Japan autonomous seafaring mercenaries—pirates—were hired to subdue other pirates because they found reason to doubt that "escorts" ever truly abandoned their piratical heritage.

In their encounters, sea lords and Korean and Chinese travelers and officials each represented themselves to the other in specific ways in order to achieve certain objectives.[10] Sea lords of the Seto Inland Sea presented themselves as purveyors of "protection" and represented themselves in ways that would enhance their reputation, expand their maritime dominion, and widen their trade networks. Such performances led to their incorporation in the geographies and categories of "Japanese pirates." In contrast, Korean and Chinese travelers and officials portrayed themselves as state agents out to eliminate a threat from the nonstate maritime world. Once back home, emissaries, as well as officials and other scholars, performed acts of artistic creation; they crafted travelogues, encyclopedias, and other accounts.

8. Hashimoto Yū, *Chūka gensō: Karamono to gaikō no Muromachi jidaishi* (Bensei Shuppan, 2011), pp. 221–22.
9. For private military forces in Ming China, see David Robinson, *Bandits, Eunuchs, and the Son of Heaven: Rebellion and the Economy of Violence in Mid-Ming China* (Honolulu: University of Hawai'i Press, 2001); Kenneth M. Swope, *A Dragon's Head and a Serpent's Tail: Ming China and the First Great East Asian War, 1592–1598* (Norman: University of Oklahoma Press, 2009), pp. 21–22.
10. Greg Dening, "The Theatricality of Observing and Being Observed: Eighteenth-Century Europe 'Discovers' the ? Century 'Pacific,'" in *Implicit Understandings: Observing, Reporting, and Reflecting on the Encounters between European and Other Peoples in the Early Modern Era*, edited by Stuart B. Schwartz (Cambridge: Cambridge University Press, 1994), pp. 451–83.

Previously constructed images of Japanese pirates, policy objectives, and genre conventions all affected such ethnographic analyses. These works engendered worldviews that defined the human and physical geographies of maritime regions by the Japanese pirates present there. Conceptualizations of regions are cultural constructions often shaped by the needs of political authorities or economic factors.[11] Chapter one showed that Japanese seascapes were influenced by the degree of control central authorities felt that they could exercise over the sea and were tempered by the strength of pirates on the waves. Similarly, the Korean and Chinese writers who discussed the maritime world ground teeth and ink stones in efforts to understand and eliminate what they saw as a "Japanese pirate" menace. In doing so, they discursively created fluctuating images of the East Asian maritime world as a space of *waegu* and *wokou*, the haunt of pirates from their own coasts, Europe, Southeast Asia, and Japan. Encounters with Inland Sea mariners and other Japanese stimulated Korean and Chinese writers to devise sophisticated geographical imaginings of Japan based on perceived distributions of pirate bases. By charting when and how the Seto Inland Sea entered Korean and Chinese regional representations as piratical space, it becomes possible to show how sea lords caused Korean and Chinese writers to revise the concept of "Japanese pirates" and to redefine their physical and cultural geographical understandings of Japan and the wider maritime world. Such an exploration reveals processes by which the concept of "Japanese pirate" evolved, uncovering some of the historically contingent processes that shaped this ambiguous concept.

CATEGORIES OF JAPANESE PIRATES

To understand the term "Japanese pirates" requires taking into account broad usages that demonized entire populations as well as narrow definitions tied to specific people, places, and events. The term "Japanese pirate" mixes a character for the epithet for Japanese often rendered "dwarf" (Kn. *wae* / Ch. *wo*) with one meaning "bandit" (*gu / ko*). Although records of Japanese identified as *wae* and *wo* attacking the continent exist from the fifth century C.E. onwards, usage of the term *waegu/wokou* as a noun only dates from the fourteenth century or so.[12] Korean and Chinese officials imbued the concept of "Japanese pirates" with several biases. Similar to the negative bias

---

11. Philip Steinberg, *The Social Construction of the Ocean* (Cambridge: Cambridge University Press, 2001).

12. Tanaka Takeo, *Wakō: Umi no rekishi* (Kyōikusha, 1982), pp. 12–15.

that Japanese elites attached to the Japanese category of "sea people" (*ama*), Chosŏn and Ming literati accepted the superiority of nations bounded by agricentric civilization, represented themselves as agents of that civilization, and correspondingly denigrated sea-based regions as uncivilized peripheries. They even used the term *wae/wo* to condemn the low-status, littoral inhabitants of their own coasts, who pursued migratory occupations, joined with foreign bands of merchants and pirates, and, from the perspective of political centers, often defied the laws of the land.[13] These shared prejudices were compounded by the sharing of intelligence on pirates between Korean and Chinese officials during diplomatic and tributary missions, which led to the evolution of tropes in representations of Japanese pirates. For example, both described *waegu* and *wokou* as bestial and barbaric: as half-naked, barefoot "water demons" who possessed uncanny skills in diving, swimming, fighting, and subsisting at sea. The prevalence of such imagery and descriptions of Japanese pirate attacks, which appeared in songs and stories, as well as in official discourse, caused the dominant Chinese perception of Japanese to shift from tributaries and Buddhist monks to bloodthirsty and cunning pirates.[14]

Such expansive stereotypes competed with usages applied to specific historical events, people, and places. Subsistence crises in the thirteenth century drove Japanese residing along the Kyushu littoral, Tsushima, and other islands to begin raiding the Korean Peninsula.[15] In the fourteenth century, political divisions in the archipelago coupled with instability in Korea and China weakened governments' control over coastlines, which allowed raids to intensify. By the late fourteenth century, Korean officials were employing the phrase "Japanese Pirates of the Three Islands" to characterize the region encompassing Tsushima, Iki, and northwest Kyushu as particularly piratical, with a maritime culture distinct from other parts of Japan.[16] In the fifteenth century, these and other pirates expanded the scope of their raiding and trading to encompass the northeastern and eventually the southeastern

13. Murai, *Nihon chūsei kyōkai shiron*, pp. 153–74; John E. Wills, Jr., "Maritime China from Wang Chih to Shih Lang: Themes in Peripheral History," in *From Ming to Ch'ing: Conquest, Region, and Continuity in Seventeenth-Century China*, edited by Jonathan D. Spence et al. (New Haven, Conn.: Yale University Press, 1979), pp. 204–10.
14. Wang Yong, "Realistic and Fantastic Images of 'Dwarf Pirates': The Evolution of Ming Dynasty Perceptions of the Japanese," translated by Laura E. Hess, in *Sagacious Monks and Bloodthirsty Warriors: Chinese Views of Japan in the Ming-Qing Period*, edited by Joshua A. Fogel (Norwalk, Conn.: Eastbridge Press, 2002), pp. 17–41. Tanaka, *Wakō: Umi no rekishi*, pp. 178–80.
15. Benjamin H. Hazard, "The Formative Years of the Wakō, 1223-1263," *Monumenta Nipponica* 22.3 (1967): 260–77.
16. Nakamura Hidetaka, *Nihon to Chōsen* (Shibundō, 1966), p. 80; Tanaka, *Wakō: Umi no rekishi*, p. 41; Murai, *Nihon chūsei kyōkai shiron*, pp. 128–30.

coasts of China. Some bands of raiders and traders in this period were composed of a "multiethnic" mixture of littoral inhabitants from Korea and Japan who blended aspects of both cultures, spoke a distinctive dialect, and
wore distinctive clothes.[17]

Piracy ebbed in the early fifteenth century as a result of the growth of
political stability in all three countries. In Japan, victory of the Ashikaga in
the civil war between the Northern and Southern Courts, the maturation
of powerful warrior provincial-governor houses, and the incorporation of
those houses within the Muromachi bakufu all coincided with the establishment of the Ming (1368–1644) and Chosŏn (1392–1910) dynasties. China
and Korea both launched punitive expeditions against pirates and instituted
systems of tributary trade. They condemned as pirates any who failed to follow the rules of these systems of diplomacy and exchange.

Piracy revived in the late fifteenth century as political disorder swept
across Japan. In the early sixteenth century, Chinese sea merchants and local gentry families, who had traditionally ignored official bans on private
overseas travel, joined with the fisher folk and salt makers on their own
coasts as well as Japanese, Southeast Asian, and European pirates and merchants. Japanese became a minority in this "multiethnic" population, which
continued to be known as "Japanese pirates."[18] At the same time, Chinese
officials grew increasingly frustrated with Japanese tributary missions that
seemed to be edging more and more into piracy themselves and becoming
more and more violent, such that the Ming emperor abrogated the tribute
trade in 1549. The multiethnic Japanese pirate bands sought markets for the
silks and other products resulting from the commercial boom occurring
along China's southeast coast, dispatched regular trade expeditions to ports
in Japan and Southeast Asia, and based themselves on islands off the coast
of southeast China as well as in the harbors of western Japan, where they
recruited heavily for raiding and trading campaigns. At the heights of their
influence, Chinese leaders of these bands, such as Wang Zhi (d. 1557) and
Xu Hai (d. 1556), controlled many of the shipping networks connecting Japan to China and Southeast Asia and forged alliances with Japanese regional
warlords such as the Tanegashima, Shimazu, Ōtomo, Matsura, and Ōuchi.
A sustained, combined effort of removing bans on maritime trade, suppressing pirates militarily, and co-opting the "pirate" leaders reduced this latter
wave of piracy by the 1570s.[19]

17. Murai, *Nihon chūsei kyōkai shiron*, pp. 156–67; Murai Shōsuke, *Chūsei Wajinden* (Iwanami Shoten, 1993).
18. Murai, *Nihon chūsei kyōkai shiron*, pp. 167–74.
19. Jurgis Elisonas, "The Inseparable Trinity: Japan's Relations with China and Korea," in *The Cambridge History of Japan*, vol. 4: *Early Modern Japan*, edited by John W. Hall et al. (Cambridge:

Sea-lord bands of the Seto Inland Sea entered into these waves of piracy through the auspices of sponsors desirous of their protection services. Sea-lord bands first came to the attention of the Chosŏn court as the agents responsible for both perpetrating attacks on and providing escorts for the flotillas of several ambassadors who traveled to Japan in the first half of the fifteenth century. Negotiations over the terms of protection with both envoys and Japanese patrons afforded sea lords opportunities to secure recognition of their domains and to expand protection and other commercial enterprises. Sea lords sometimes manipulated how others saw them, playing on Korean assumptions about pirates. Their reputations remained firmly entrenched in the minds of Korean officials through the sixteenth century. Japanese officials and merchants invoked the specter of Inland Sea pirates in order to secure better trading privileges with Korea; sea-lord bands themselves participated in tributary trade and unlicensed commercial and raiding expeditions across East Asia.

In the fifteenth and sixteenth centuries, Chinese officials added Inland Sea mariners to rosters of Japanese pirates because of the ways in which sea-lord bands contributed to tribute trade missions. In the mid-sixteenth century, sea lords took advantage of patronage relations with daimyo like the Ōuchi and Ōtomo in order to join the pirate companies of expatriate Chinese merchants like Wang Zhi and Xu Hai. They participated in attempts by daimyo to revive the defunct tributary trade, efforts which the Ming court viewed as nothing more than an intensification of the Japanese pirate menace. Ties with both expatriate Chinese merchants and Japanese daimyo enabled sea lords to meet, interact with, and protect envoys authorized by the Ming emperor in 1555 to travel to Japan in hopes of ending the Japanese pirate threat.

ENVOYS, ESCORTS, AND THE SHAPING OF KOREAN PERCEPTIONS OF JAPANESE PIRATES

Sea lords of the Inland Sea region encountered Korean envoys most in the period from 1375 to 1443. These emissaries arrived on a variety of missions: to request that Japanese authorities suppress pirates; to collect intelligence on Japanese pirates and other aspects of Japan's political landscape;

Cambridge University Press, 1991), pp. 235–65; Tanaka Takeo, *Wakō: Umi no rekishi*; James Chin, "Merchants, Smugglers, and Pirates: Multinational Clandestine Trade on the South China Coast, 1520–50," in *Elusive Pirates, Pervasive Smugglers: Violence and Clandestine Trade in the Greater China Seas*, edited by Robert Antony (Hong Kong: Hong Kong University Press, 2010), pp. 43–57.

to reciprocate for a Japanese embassy having traveled to Korea; or to honor the accession or death of a shogun. Ambassadors and members of their retinues also made records of their journeys and reported on their travels to the Chosŏn Court in Seoul. In doing so, they became one of the Chosŏn government's best sources of information on Japan.[20] In order to impress upon central and provincial Japanese authorities their high level of civilization and demonstrate the beneficence of their king in his neighborly (*kyorin*) diplomacy with Japan, the Korean court often selected high-ranking scholar-officials when selecting ambassadors. It was hoped that such figures could convince Japanese authorities to eliminate pirates.[21] These envoys were well schooled in the allusions, rhymes, and other devices of Chinese poetry, which functioned as a lingua franca in East Asia in this period. They could turn stanzas that reached sublime levels of artistry and conveyed incontrovertible truths of policy, and, in so doing, could persuade their poetic interlocutors of the truth and merit of their perspectives. Thus, poetic lenses and the genre requirements of the poetic travelogue as well as the experiences of previous ambassadors prefigured the gaze of many envoys before they reached Japan.[22]

The visits of Korean envoys to Japan presented to sea lords of the Seto Inland Sea opportunities to devise different kinds of protection enterprises, which enhanced their maritime dominion and expanded the scope of the commercial networks under their control. The earliest and simplest form of protection business consisted of ambushing ambassadors in chokepoints, extorting protection, and seizing their cargoes. Korean envoys carried large quantities of valuable gifts for the Ashikaga shogun, whom they recognized as the king of Japan, equal in status to their own king because both were tributaries of the Ming emperor. Sea lords and other "pirates" would have

20. Nakamura, *Nihon to Chōsen*, pp. 70–110. Seki Shūichi, "Chōsen Ōchō kanjin no Nihon kansatsu," *Rekishi hyōron* 592.8 (1999): 16–20; Suda Makiko, "Chūsei kōki ni okeru Akamagaseki no kinō to Ōuchi-shi," *Hisutoria* 129 (2004): 76–87.
21. Kenneth R. Robinson, "Centering the King of Chosŏn: Aspects of Korean Maritime Diplomacy, 1392–1592," *Journal of Asian Studies* 59.1 (2000): 109–25; Etsuko Hae-Jin Kang, *Diplomacy and Ideology in Japanese-Korean Relations: From the Fifteenth to the Eighteenth Century* (Houndmills, Basingstoke, Hampshire: Macmillan Press, 1997), ch. 2.
22. Murai Shōsuke, *Higashi Ajia ōkan: kanshi to gaikō* (Asahi Shinbunsha, 1995), ch. 4; Murai Shōsuke, "Poetry in Chinese as a Diplomatic Art in Premodern East Asia," translated by Haruko Wakabayashi and Andrew E. Goble, in *Tools of Culture: Japan's Cultural, Intellectual, Medical, and Technological Contacts in East Asia, 1000s–1500s*, edited by Andrew E. Goble et al. (Ann Arbor, Mich.: Association for Asian Studies, 2009), pp. 49–69; For the potential power of a Chinese poem, see Ivo Smits, "Song as Cultural History, Reading *Wakan Rōeishū* (Interpretations)," *Monumenta Nipponica* 55.3 (2000): 405.

considered these gifts valuable prizes. One of the earliest examples of such an ambush occurs in the accounts of Yang Su, an ambassador who traveled to Japan in 1410 in order to convey Korea's condolences for the death of retired shogun Yoshimitsu (1358–1408). Yang carried gifts including bolts of cloth, tiger skins, and ginseng.[23] He reported that in the Inland Sea, "ferocious pirates stole everything, leaving us in a very precarious situation. . . . They conceal themselves on remote islands. They often sail out, threaten, and rob trading ships."[24]

Foreknowledge that such interceptions would probably occur colored the expectations of later ambassadors and became essential traits in Korean taxonomies of Japanese pirates. Yang's experiences particularly affected the next ambassador to reach Japan, Song Hŭigyŏng, in 1420. Song directly alluded to Yang Su's misadventures in his travelogue and claimed that he encountered pirates in the same place that Yang had. In the seas off Takasaki, in Aki Province, he recorded that pirates darted at them from behind an island.[25] As a result, Song and other subsequent ambassadors strove to ensure that the Muromachi shogunate and other authorities provided sufficient escorts for them.

To become involved in the protection business for Korean envoys, sea lords accepted sponsorship offers from shogunal administrators (*bugyō*), warrior provincial governors, and estate proprietors. Eager to avoid international incidents and to help Koreans unfamiliar with Japanese waterways and anchorages, the Muromachi bakufu instituted a system for ensuring the protection of Korean envoys. Once ships entered international gateways such as Hakata or Akamagaseki, officials like the Kyushu regional governor (*Kyushu tandai*) or members of the Ōuchi family, who were provincial governors and powerful regional lords based in western Honshu and northern Kyushu, sent a messenger to Kyoto. The bakufu authorized the envoy to advance to the capital and issued communiqués (*migyōsho*) instructing warrior provincial governors and the Kyushu regional governor to assemble and dispatch protection (*keigo*) forces. Warrior provincial governors relayed shogunal communiqués to deputy governors, who then forwarded instructions to local magnates and estates. With central and regional authorities as their sponsors, sea-lord bands thus participated in both peaceful and violent capacities: they arranged protective escort, navigational assistance, and

23. CWS, *T'aejong sillok*, vol. 19, pp. 10a-b, T'aejong 10 (1410) 2.4.
24. CWS, *T'aejong sillok*, vol. 21, p. 8a, T'aejong 11 (1411) 1.26.
25. Song Hŭigyŏng, *Nosongdang Ilbon haegnok (Rōshōdō Nihon kōroku: Chōsen shisetsu no mita chūsei Nihon)*, edited by Murai Shōsuke (Iwanami Shoten, 1987), no. 85.

corvée for transporting luggage, gifts, and horses until the envoy's procession reached Kyoto.[26]

Sea lords of the Inland Sea often relied on patronage connections with the Ōuchi in order to secure work as escorts for Korean envoys. The Ōuchi pursued close relations with and sought trading privileges from Korea, going so far as to herald an ancestral link to an ancient Korean dynasty.[27] The Ōuchi continuously sought to augment the number of sea lords in their employ in order to protect the Korean envoys so as to further their own overseas ambitions. For example, Song Hŭigyŏng recorded that upon arrival in Akamagaseki, "many escorts" became available once the Ōuchi received proper authorization.[28] In 1443, the Ōuchi dispatched sea lords in four ships to provide protection for a Korean envoy as far as the port of Onomichi.[29]

The Chosŏn court also equipped its emissaries with letters giving them the authority to independently court local lords in the archipelago for protective escort.[30] In the Inland Sea region, Korean envoys relied heavily on the Ōuchi for this purpose. The 1429 envoy, Pak Sosaeng, explained that "Lord Ōuchi" bore "responsibility for the pirates of Shika [Hakata], Kamado [Kaminoseki], and Shajima [Yashirojima]."[31] The 1432 reciprocal ambassador to Japan carried a letter for the Ōuchi lord, requesting him to "please select some ships for escort."[32]

Sea lords could exploit these protection systems in several ways. Some sea lords took advantage of the great need of the Ōuchi for their services by raiding Korean envoys and relying on their patrons to shield them from prosecution. In 1433, after "pirates" in the Inland Sea stole documents and goods from a Korean reciprocal ambassador, the ambassador ordered his interpreter to complain to the king of Japan (shogun), who reportedly grew incensed and ordered an investigation and the return of the stolen property. Exploiting his links to sea lords, the Ōuchi lord arranged for the return of

---

26. Hashimoto, *Chūka gensō*, pp. 221–40; Suda, "Chūsei kōki ni okeru Akamagaseki no kinō to Ōuchi-shi," pp. 77–80; DNK 10, *Tōji hyakugō monjo*, vol. 11, doc. 69.6, Eiwa 1 (1375) 12.9; Song, no. 74; Song, no. 154.

27. Kenneth R. Robinson, "Treated as Treasures: The Circulation of Sutras in Maritime Northeast Asia from 1388 to the Mid-Sixteenth Century," *East Asian History* 21 (2001.6): 50–51; Suda Makiko, "Muromachiki ni okeru Ōuchi-shi no taichō kankei to senzokan no keisei," *Rekishigaku kenkyū* 761.4 (2002): 1–18.

28. Song, no. 81.

29. CWS, *Sejong sillok*, vol. 102, p. 6b, Sejong 25 (1443) 10.13; Suda, "Chūsei kōki ni okeru Akamagaseki no kinō to Ōuchi-shi," p. 77.

30. Suda, "Chūsei kōki ni okeru Akamagaseki no kinō to Ōuchi-shi," pp. 81–84.

31. CWS, *Sejong sillok*, vol. 46, p. 14a, Sejong 11 (1429) 12.3; Suda, "Chūsei kōki ni okeru Akamagaseki no kinō to Ōuchi-shi," pp. 82–83.

32. CWS, *Sejong sillok*, vol. 57, pp. 7b-8a, Sejong 14 (1432) 7.26.

the property but "apologized [to the Korean envoy] because the island pirates had escaped and he had not been able to catch them."[33] Given their links to sea lords and the maritime world, it is possible that the Ōuchi were complicit in or at least aware of this raid, and that sea lords convinced their patrons to let them go.[34]

Sea lords also capitalized on the fact that the protection blanket offered by the shogunal communiqué system sometimes left swathes of the sea uncovered. When such orders failed to arrive, some local elites felt reticent to engage in protection without authorization, a situation encountered by the 1443 Korean envoy.[35] In certain maritime districts, these shogunal edicts had no effect because of the strength of sea lords. In these cases, sea lords made private arrangements with the envoys and members of their retinues. Such negotiations ensued when the 1420 reciprocal ambassador, Song Hŭigyŏng, arrived in the Kamagari region of Aki Province, and he learned from companions that two branches of the Tagaya sea-lord family had divided control over this region, and Song needed to make provisions for protection privately.[36] Among these companions who provided local expertise and intelligence to Song were the Hakata monk-merchant Sō Kin and Hirakata Yoshihisa, who was the grandson of a Chinese émigré and scion of a wealthy merchant family.[37] They informed Song that although the shogun issued communiqués to the various warrior provincial governors and local magnates along Song's return route, these orders failed to mobilize any local elites.[38] So, to ensure a safe passage, Sō Kin negotiated with the Tagaya, hiring one member of their band to physically accompany them to ensure their safety. Song recounted: "The writ of the king [of Japan] does not extend here. As he does not have control over this area, there are also no escort vessels forthcoming. . . . If a ship coming from the east has an eastern pirate on board, then the western pirate will not harm it. If a ship coming from the west has a western pirate on board, then the eastern pirate will not harm it. So, Sō Kin paid seven thousand in coin to hire an eastern pirate to come sail aboard our ship."[39] Making protection deals such as these won sea lords more than short-term monetary gain. Successful completion of a

33. CWS, *Sejong sillok*, vol. 62, p. 1b, Sejong 15 (1433) 10.6.
34. Suda, "Chūsei kōki ni okeru Akamagaseki no kinō to Ōuchi-shi," p. 87.
35. CWS, *Sejong sillok*, vol. 102, pp. 6b-7a, Sejong 25 (1443) 10.13.
36. Kawai Masaharu, "Tagaya-shi no rekishi," in *Tagaya suigun to Maruyajō ato*, edited by Maruyajō Ato Chōsadan (Shimokamagari-chō, Hiroshima-ken: Shimokamagari-chō, 1981), pp. 7–8.
37. For Sō Kin, see Song nos. 70, 85, 162; for Hirakata Yoshihisa, see Song, no. 52.
38. Song, no. 148; Suda, "Chūsei kōki ni okeru Akamagaseki no kinō to Ōuchi-shi," p. 78.
39. Song, no. 162.

protection commission here helped win them access to the overseas trade networks centered in Hakata. By the 1470s the Tagaya were well known to both Hakata merchants and the Ōuchi as an elite force, one of "the three islander protection forces."[40] An opportunity to tie themselves to such significant backers of and participants in overseas trade like Sō Kin[41] would have been very valuable for Tagaya shipping concerns, already a major player in domestic shipping networks. Fourteen ships claimed Kamagari as port of registry in the 1445–46 Hyōgo log, all but one over one hundred *koku* in lading.[42]

Sea lords treated negotiations over protection as key moments of encounter with both foreign and domestic travelers in which they could manipulate images of themselves in order to enhance their protection business. The 1443 Korean ambassador's report to his king included a description of a stopover on the island of Shikoku during his return voyage. It demonstrates that sea-lord escorts seem to have been fully cognizant of Korean stereotypes of them as "wicked and coarse"[43] and so played on those reputations in order to gain more protection money: "We had reached Iyo Province when our seafarer escorts, in a horde, screamed and charged at us, brandishing sticks, as if to steal all of the gifts and leave. I told them, 'These are gifts from your king [shogun] and deputy shogun. Why would you commit such an affront?' Three times I asked them, but they only screamed more and more. With no other recourse, I paid them silver and they desisted."[44] A first glance reveals this to be a simple Korean evocation of Japanese pirate barbarism, but it is also possible to read this as a record of a performance. No doubt possessing more serious weapons than sticks, it is entirely possible that the escorts felt that they had been underpaid, and so they staged a little bit of theater, playing the role of barbarian in order to extort more protection money. By doing so, the escorts confirmed the Korean officials' worst expectations about Japanese seafarers and reinforced for Korean officials the idea that in Japan, "pirates" were called on to police "pirates," with disastrous results.

It is also possible that the 1443 Korean ambassador expected that Japanese escorts would understand him and discuss matters rationally because of the experiences of some of his predecessors. For example, in his travelogue, Song Hŭigyŏng included passages in which he registered surprise at

---

40. Sagara Shōjin, *Shōjinki*, Bunmei 10 (1478) 10.26, in YK, vol. 1, p. 356.
41. Saeki Kōji, "Muromachiki no Hakata shōnin Sō Kin to Higashi Ajia," *Shien* 136 (1999): 101–21.
42. Mutō Tadashi, "Chūsei no Hyōgo no tsu to Setonaikai suiun," in *Hyōgo Kitazeki irifune nōchō*, edited by Hayashiya Tatsusaburō (Chūō Kōron Bijutsu Shuppan, 1981), pp. 268–69.
43. Song, no. 162.
44. CWS, *Sejong sillok*, vol. 102, p. 7b, Sejong 25 (1443) 10.13. Suda, "Chūsei kōki ni okeru Akamagaseki no kinō to Ōuchi-shi," p. 81.

the degree to which some "escorts" could connect with him on a personal level by engaging in civilized behavior, especially hospitality and conversation. Some sea lords exploited moments of encounter in order to rehabilitate their piratical images, make a positive impression, and, perhaps, secure additional patronage by acting with civility and culture. Song recorded that off the coast of Bizen Province, "the escort Tō Sukemoto sought to come aboard and see me. I permitted it. When Sukemoto arrived, I had some wine decanted, and we drank. Sukemoto also brought wine from his ship for me."[45] To have such an encounter with a pirate startles Song enough both to equate all Japanese with pirates and to admit to meeting a civilized Japanese pirate. In order to convey the complicated mixture of suspicion toward Japanese pirates, surprise at Sukemoto, and the hope that this was a significant, promising precedent, Song crafted a Chinese poem structured as a micronarrative of juxtapositions:

> As the bright dawn lifts curtains cloudy and hazy,
>
> My ship threads the narrow channels with turrets soaring and holds heavy.
>
> My escort comes aboard and offers me wine!
>
> Even in Japan, it seems there are those of true sensitivity.[46]

That "escort" and "Japan" contrasts with "offers me wine" and "sensitivity" is suggested by the imagery in the first two lines.

Later, during the same the voyage, members of the Tagaya sea-lord band of Kamagari interacted closely with Song Hŭigyŏng in such a way that they ensured a positive protection experience for the Koreans. By so doing, they hoped to expand the business relationship from protection to physically hosting these (and perhaps future) ambassadorial retinues in lodgings, a business engaged in by other port-managing sea lords. The Tagaya endeavored to allay Song's fears through conversation and tea:

> A Japanese pirate reached here in a launch, and, coming over to me, he said, "Please, be at ease!" . . . "I have explained [your situation] to these people. They say, 'come close to their house and take lodgings here.' Please your honor, you can stay this one time!" The men and women, young and old, boarded small ships and hurried to come

---

45. Song, no. 153; Hashizume Shigeru, *Setonaikai chiiki shakai to Oda kenryoku* (Kyoto: Shibunkaku Shuppan, 2007), p. 175.

46. Song, no. 153. Hashimoto Yū argues that the presentation of wine from Song to Tō is indicative of recompense made in gifts of wine and food (*shukōryō*) for protection in fifteenth-century Japan (Hashimoto, *Chūka gensō*, pp. 224–25).

over here, asking if they could come aboard and see me. I permitted it. . . . In the middle of all this, their chieftain, a peculiar monk, came over to talk. We exchanged words, and there were no differences between the two of us. He and I talked quite happily, exchanging answers. [He] pointed out my route for the morrow and then invited me to disembark and come to his house in order to enjoy some tea.[47]

In a poem about this encounter, Song contrasts the cold, desolate seascape with a fond remembrance of the surprisingly warm hospitality afforded him by the escorts who provided protection and navigational assistance:

> I circulate among seas and islands where cliffs soar high
>   and steep;
>
> Clapboard shacks and brushwood gates open out on the sea
>
> Aboard ship, I sought only protection and a guide,
>
> But then comes the invitation—come inside my house and
>   drink tea![48]

However, such positive experiences remained in Korean eyes anomalous, and the images of Japanese pirates as fearsome, powerful, threatening sea lords retained their hold on the Chosŏn imagination. As a result of the encounters between Korean envoys and Japanese sea-lord escorts, Korean officials demarcated Japanese maritime regions based on the locations of Japanese pirate territories. These assessments reflected the strength of sea lords in particular chokepoints. The 1429 Korean ambassador to Japan, Pak Sosaeng, described how the chokepoint of Akamagaseki separated the maritime systems of the Seto Inland Sea from those joining Kyushu, Tsushima, Iki, and Korea: "Tsushima, Iki, inner and outer Ōshima [Azuchi Ōshima and Munakata Ōshima], Shika [Hakata], Hirado, and other places all constitute domains of pirates west of Akamagaseki. North of Shikoku, Kamado [Kaminoseki], Shajima [Yashirojima], and other places all constitute domains of pirates east of Akamagaseki. Their myriad warriors must number ten thousand strong, with no fewer than one thousand ships."[49] Notable in this description is the presence of islands associated with Inland Sea sea-lord bands and protection businesses. As early as 1340, Kaminoseki was known among Japanese littoral magnates as far away as the Kumano region as an effective chokepoint at which to operate protection businesses.[50] It became

---

47. Song, no. 162.
48. Ibid.
49. CWS, *Sejong sillok*, vol. 46, p. 13b, Sejong 11 (1429) 12.3.
50. *Mera monjo*, doc. 1048, Ryaku'ō 3 (1340) 3.14, in *Kumano Nachi Taisha monjo*, vol. 3 (Zoku Gunsho Ruijū Kanseikai, 1974), p. 194.

an important commercial shipping and shipbuilding center in the fifteenth century.[51] By 1532, the presence of a "Murakami Lord" in Kaminoseki suggests that either the Noshima Murakami or the Kurushima Murakami had established themselves as powers there.[52] Yashirojima was a holding of the Kurushima Murakami for much of the sixteenth century.[53]

Interactions with Japanese sea lords in the Inland Sea caused the Korean court to deem the maritime boundaries of the archipelago porous. Chosŏn officials found it conceivable that the strength of Japanese pirate gangs in the Seto Inland Sea region would embolden them enough to join with pirates in other regions and to spill out onto the sea-lanes in an attack of Korea: "If pirates of the eastern and western regions ever came together as one and mobilized their forces, it would be difficult to defend against them. The pirates of the western sea lanes make their headquarters on Tsushima. Pirates of Shikoku enter and leave by the gates of Akamagaseki."[54] The very real threat posed if such an alliance were to materialize led the court to make arrangements with specific Japanese warrior provincial governors in order to contain this threat. Pak explained, "If these pirates seem to be headed west, then Sō Sadamori is supposed to issue orders to the people not to allow the pirates to replenish their water supplies, and Lord Ōuchi is to issue commands closing travel to the west. These actions would prevent pirates from coming or going."[55]

However, other Korean officials found the sponsorship of pirates by the Ōuchi and other warrior provincial governors cause for alarm. In 1430, after getting word that the Ashikaga had confirmed the Ōuchi in their conquest of Hakata and other parts of Kyushu, a Korean military official expressed concern about the power of the Ōuchi, fearing that they would lead pirates from the Inland Sea to attack Iki and Tsushima. Without Tsushima as a reliable bulwark, "Japanese of Shikoku, who always gather to commit piracy with several thousand ships," would come to Chosŏn, after which "the control of our country's sea lanes, near and far, would belong to dangerous barbarians."[56]

Korean observers also identified distinctive cultural commonalities among inhabitants of the Japanese littoral that crossed the domainal and

---

51. *Hyōgo Kitazeki irifune nōchō*; Tenyo Seikei, *Boshi nyūminki*, NMKBS, pp. 200–203.
52. *Chūgoku Kyushu oharae kubarichō*, in YK, vol. 1, p. 544.
53. EK doc. 1818, Eiroku 1 (1558) 7.27; EK doc. 1969, Eiroku 9 (1566) 10.3.
54. CWS, *Sejong sillok*, vol. 46, pp. 13b–14a, Sejong 11 (1429) 12.3.
55. Ibid., p. 14a, Sejong 11 (1429) 12.3.
56. CWS, *Sejong sillok*, vol. 48, pp. 20b–21a, Sejong 12 (1430), 5.19; Hirase Naoki, "Shugo daimyo Ōuchi-shi to kaihen no busō seiryōku: kaizoku, keigoshū, wakō," *Yamaguchi-ken chihōshi kenkyū* 71 (1994.6): 29.

operational borders of pirate bands. Song Hŭigyŏng initially found the Tagaya sea-lord band of Kamagari to be depraved, expressing a Confucian distaste for the nonagricultural Japanese maritime world extending from the far western littoral through the Inland Sea.[57] Pak's description traced a similar vein, "Generally, these pirates (haejŏk) know no ceremony and have little righteousness. They do not compromise and do not reflect upon themselves."[58] Such ethnographic generalizations operated as geographical discourse and incorporated the Inland Sea region into the wider East Asian maritime world in the minds of Korean officials.

Chosŏn officials' understanding of Japanese pirates was also shaped by the importation of Chinese legal definitions, including the ancient Chinese juridical tradition equating piracy with rebellion and lawlessness.[59] As a result of this Sinitic influence, Chosŏn officials were well disposed to believe a Japanese informant's report on the state of the Japan during the internecine strife from 1467–77 known as the Ōnin War. The informant, Saburōtarō, portrayed Japan as a realm where the loss of political order left the Seto Inland Sea region a wilderness. The presence of sea-lord mercenaries on the various sides of the conflict meant that there was no possibility of protection and that pirates roamed the seas as voracious sea wolves. Saburōtarō advised a prospective Chosŏn ambassador to avoid the "southern [Inland Sea] route because the two sides are still divided by deep gulches and wooden palisades . . . pirates would surely take his ship there."[60] Instead, Saburōtarō suggested that, like merchants from Hakata and his home of Iki, the Chosŏn ship should take the northern sea route to Wakasa Province, thence by ship over Lake Biwa to the capital.[61]

Some Japanese merchants and authorities reinforced images of the Inland Sea as piratical when they exploited the growing reputations of actual sea-lord bands in order to extract trading concessions from Korea in the fifteenth and sixteenth centuries. Japanese trade with Chosŏn Korea occurred as a form of tributary exchange, for which purpose the Chosŏn court authorized a series of licenses over the course of the fifteenth century. The Korean court bestowed on emissaries copper seals (tosŏ) that granted them permission to trade and gave letters of introduction (sŏgye) and passports (munin) to Japanese authorities in Kyushu and Tsushima for the purpose of identifying those seeking to trade with Korea. After 1438, the Sō, warrior provincial governors on Tsushima, requested and received from the Korean court sole

---

57. Song, 162.
58. CWS, Sejong sillok, vol. 46, 14a, Sejong 11 (1429) 12.3.
59. See ch. 1.
60. CWS, Sŏngjong sillok, vol. 69, pp. 21a-b, Sŏngjong 7 (1476) 7.26.
61. Ibid.

authority over distributing passports. Chosŏn officials condemned those who arrived without such credentials as pirates.[62] Using this system, several authorities with access to the Inland Sea corridor and Inland Sea seafarers, including the Muromachi shogunate, the Ōuchi, and Hakata merchants like Sō Kin dispatched embassies for trade and to request copies of the Buddhist canon printed in Korea. Although Inland Sea seafarers made up part of these crews,[63] the names of Inland Sea sea lords exerted considerable influence on Korean official memory when they appeared in the documents of what historians have called "imposter embassies."[64]

In the Korean system of licensed, tribute trade, the higher the status accorded by the Chosŏn court, the higher the value of gifts and the greater the privileges awarded by the court to the embassy. Endeavoring to exploit this system, wealthy monk-merchants based in Hakata colluded with members of the Sō family on Tsushima, who had access to the passports necessary for conducting trade with the Korean government. These cabals dispatched embassies that they endowed with falsified documents in attempts to claim a higher status than would ordinarily be deserved, and in so doing, to receive more valuable goods in return for presenting gifts to the Chosŏn king. Many of these imposter embassies occurred in the 1460s and 1470s, when civil war distracted Japan's central authorities and the Chosŏn government was revising its diplomatic policies. To be successful, imposter embassies had to be convincing to Korean officials as having come from a legitimate source. For example, some employed names and titles that enabled them to pose as prominent bakufu officials or representatives of kings of Ryūkyū and other countries.[65]

In 1471, a former participant in the 1443 reciprocal embassy submitted to the Chosŏn court a diplomatic handbook on Japan and Ryūkyū entitled *Record of Lands in the Eastern Seas* (*Haedong chegukki*). This handbook contains a long list of contacts, some of which represent imposter embassies. Many entries contain the names of powerful bakufu officials,

62. Kenneth R. Robinson, "From Raiders to Traders: Border Security and Border Control in Early Chosŏn, 1392–1450," *Journal of Korean Studies* 16 (1992): 106–7.

63. Kenneth R. Robinson, "A Japanese Trade Mission to Chosŏn Korea, 1537–1540," in *Tools of Culture: Japan's Cultural, Intellectual, Medical, and Technological Contacts in East Asia, 1000s–1500s*, edited by Andrew E. Goble et al. (Ann Arbor, Mich.: Association for Asian Studies, 2009), pp. 77–82.

64. Kenneth R. Robinson, "Centering the King of Chosŏn: Aspects of Korean Maritime Diplomacy, 1392–1592," *Journal of Asian Studies* 59.1 (2000): 116–17.

65. Ibid., pp. 110–12; 116–22; Kenneth R. Robinson, "The Jiubian and Ezogachishima Embassies to Chosŏn, 1478-1482," *Chōsenshi kenkyūkai ronbunshū* 35 (1997.10): 56–86; idem., "The Imposter Branch of the Hatakeyama Family and Japanese-Chosŏn Korea Court Relations, 1455–1580s," *Ajia bunka kenkyū* 25 (1999.3): 67–87; Hashimoto Yū, *Chūsei Nihon no kokusai kankei: Higashi Ajia tsūkōken to gishi mondai* (Yoshikawa Kōbunkan, 2005), pp. 9–13, 21–73.

warrior provincial governors, and major ports like Akamagaseki and Kaminoseki.[66] However, imposter embassy masterminds also dipped deeper into the Inland Sea and drew on the reputations that sea lords had established in Korea—they exploited Korean assumptions that Japanese pirates ruled parts of the Inland Sea. These cabals concocted embassies that they felt the Chosŏn court would accept as legitimate by devising the imaginary but convincing title of "pirate admiral," which they tied to the names of people and places with connections to sea lords, protection enterprises, and chokepoints. To add an extra patina of legitimacy, these pirate admirals were given Japanese imperial lineage names like Fujiwara or Minamoto. Table 4 lists a selection of "pirate admirals" particularly illustrative of sea-lord power in the Inland Sea.

TABLE 4

A selection of imaginary "pirate admirals" from *Haedong chegukki*[67]

1	Pirate Admiral Fujiwara no Ason Murakami Bitchū no kami Kunishige of Aki Province
2	Pirate Admiral and Governor of Ōbatake in Suō Province, Minamoto no Ason Yoshihide
3	Pirate Admiral Minamoto Sadayoshi of Kamadanoseki in Iyo Province
4	Pirate Admiral Tamanoi Fujiwara no Ason Kuniyoshi of Minoshima in Buzen Province

The "Murakami of Aki" signifies the Innoshima Murakami family based on the island of Innoshima, near the maritime boundary between Bingo and Aki Provinces, which Song Hŭigyŏng identified as a warren of pirates.[68] The Innoshima Murakami circulated widely among powerful sponsors of foreign trade, variously serving the Yamana and Ōuchi families, among others.[69] By 1434, the Innoshima Murakami family had become sufficiently important maritime powers that shogunal officials and other patrons bandied their names about as possible protectors for overseas trading vessels.[70] The port of Ōbatake also possessed a reputation linked to sea lordship and foreign trade. A letter from a participant in a 1486 Japanese trade

66. Sin Sukchu, *Haedong chegukki (Kaitō shokokki: Chōsenjin no mita chūsei no Nihon to Ryūkyū)*, edited by Tanaka Takeo (Iwanami Shoten, 1991), pp. 152–54, 338–39.
67. Ibid., pp. 149, 152, 156, 174, 338–41, 347.
68. Song no. 85.
69. EK doc. 1221, Shōchō 1 (1428) 10.20; EK doc. 1564, Meiō 8? (1499) 6.8; EK doc. 1563, Meiō 8? (1499) 3.24
70. Mansai, *Mansai jugō nikki*, edited by Hanawa Hokinoichi and Ōta Toshirō, *Zoku gunsho ruijū ho* 1 (Zoku Gunsho Ruijū Kanseikai, 1928), vol. 2, p. 547, Eikyō 6 (1434), 1.20.

mission to China described Ōbatake: "It is said that many pirates course the seas here."[71] Ōbatake was also the location of Kōjiro-ho, the home of the Kōjiro family of sea lords, who often sailed under Ōuchi patronage. They provided "protection" for Ōuchi-sponsored trade missions to Ming China and, in 1542, participated in a proxy war sponsored by Ōuchi Yoshitaka against the Noshima Murakami and other sea lords from Iyo.[72] The third toponym is located on the island estate of Yugeshima,[73] which, as chapter two detailed, was the home of successive waves of sea-lord bands, some of whom engaged in the protection business for overseas and domestic travelers. The use of the name Kamadanoseki highlights the pairing of barriers and pirates, which was a common trope in Japan in this period. The fourth place-name, Minoshima, occupies a chokepoint in the Inland Sea along the coast of Kyushu and became part of the Noshima Murakami domain in the 1560s.

The use of the names of sea lords from the Inland Sea region for imposter embassies reflects the degree to which knowledge of sea lords' reputations as rulers of maritime regions extended outside the Inland Sea as far as Tsushima and Korea. The appearance of "pirate admiral" imposter embassies shows how sea lords indirectly affected interactions between Japan and Chosŏn Korea through sheer force of reputation. However, the rule of such "pirate admirals" over parcels of maritime space also confirmed Korean stereotypes and conflated Japanese authorities and *waegu* in Korean eyes.

The choice of some Inland Sea sea-lord bands to join with expatriate Chinese merchants resulted in their continuing to indirectly influence affairs with Chosŏn and to occupy a prominent position in Korean perceptions of "Japanese pirates" well into the sixteenth century. Between the 1540s and 1570s, the Sō, daimyo of Tsushima, sought to enhance their trading privileges with Korea by offering their services as an essential source of accurate intelligence on Japanese pirates. They hired commercial agents in the major ports of western Japan to feed them information on the movements of pirates, which they then passed on to Korea. The Chosŏn court came to regard this intelligence highly.[74] For example, in Akamagaseki, the Sō hired the Itō family of merchants to send them "periodic reports" on the "insurrections of pirate ships" that departed the Inland Sea for the coasts

71. Kikei Shinzui and Kisen Shūshō, *Inryōken nichiroku*, edited by Tamamura Takeji et al. (Kyoto: Shiseki Kankōkai, 1953), vol. 2, pp. 872–73, Bunmei 18 (1486), 7.3.
72. *Ōbatake-chō shi* (Ōbatake-chō, Yamaguchi-ken: Ōbatake-chō, 1992), pp. 80–81; EK doc. 1720, Tenbun 11 (1542) 4.6.
73. See Tanaka Takeo's note on Kamadanoseki in Sin, *Haedong chegukki*, p. 156.
74. Saeki Kōji, "Jūroku seiki ni okeru kōki Wakō no katsudō to Tsushima Sō-shi," in *Sakoku to kokusai kankei*, edited by Nakamura Tadashi (Yoshikawa Kōbunkan, 1997), pp. 32–37.

of China and Korea.[75] In 1556, the Sō dispatched an envoy named Chōkyū to Korea to convey recently acquired intelligence on the piracy situation in Japan. Korean officials interviewed Chōkyū. He avowed that he had traveled to and met with informers from the major ports in western Japan. His informers told him that sea lords from the Shikoku region of the Seto Inland Sea served the Chinese sea merchant Wang Zhi: "We asked about his sources for this information, and he answered, 'In the first month of this year, while traveling to Hakata, I had people from Akamagaseki, Satsuma, and other places tell me that there is a Chinese man named Wufeng [Wang Zhi] who leads the Japanese pirates who raid Great Ming.' . . . When we asked, 'From what lands do his pirates come?' He answered, '[seafarers from] the four provinces of Awa, Iyo, Sanuki, Tosa in Shikoku [among other places].'"[76] Given the reputation for veracity that the Sō and their informants had acquired and congruencies with other contemporaneous accounts explored below, it is safe to take this as a relatively accurate assessment of participation by Inland Sea sea-lord bands in overseas raiding and trading ventures. However, residents of Tsushima also participated in the raids of the 1550s,[77] and it is possible that the Sō played on Korean assumptions about the Japanese maritime world. The Korean court even suspected that the Sō might have used the reputations of Wang Zhi and sea lords of Shikoku to hide their own piratical complicity. One Chosŏn official questioned Chōkyū, "about similar stories in previous years in which there were also Tsushima islanders among the raiders."[78] Nevertheless, the reports of the Sō both depended on and reinforced the strength of the reputations of Inland Sea sea lords in Korean official memory. Korean authorities considered the Inland Sea and its inhabitants part of a larger trans-East Asian population of "Japanese pirates" through the sixteenth century.

TRIBUTARIES AND THE TORRENTS OF PIRATES: THE IMPACT OF SEA LORDS ON CHINESE CONSTRUCTIONS OF JAPANESE PIRATES

Sea lords of the Seto Inland Sea were able to make their abilities known to figures like Wang Zhi, to influence Chinese definitions of Japanese pirates and to contribute to changing Chinese representations of Japan's geography as a result of their participation in successful and failed tribute trade

75. Ibid, p. 44–45; YK, vol. 4, p. 590, doc. 4, no year.8.21.
76. CWS, *Myŏngjong Taewang sillok*, vol. 20, pp. 28a-b, Myŏngjong 11 (1556) 4.1.
77. Saeki, "Jūroku seiki ni okeru kōki Wakō no katsudō to Tsushima Sō-shi," pp. 33–34.
78. CWS, *Myŏngjong Taewang sillok*, vol. 20, pp. 28a-b, Myŏngjong 11 (1556) 4.1.

embassies in the fifteenth and sixteenth centuries. After Zhu Yuanzhang (1328–98) founded the Ming Empire in 1368, he and his successors implemented the tribute trade as a tool for conducting relations with Japan, Korea, Ryūkyū, and several other Asian polities. In this system, the Chinese emperor granted gifts to ambassadors who accepted the suzerainty of China on behalf of their ruler by kowtowing and presenting tribute at an audience with the emperor. The Ming court also bestowed official seals and calendars on the tributary country and formally invested the ruler of that country as a vassal "king." Typically, the Ming court's Ministry of Rites, which took charge of the reception of foreigners, issued one hundred new paper tallies every time a new Ming emperor ascended the throne, which then necessitated a new reign-era name. Each embassy would demonstrate its bona fides by matching half of a paper tally with its mate kept in China and by presenting documents stamped with the seal of the "king of Japan," hence the name "tally trade" (*kangō bōeki*) applied by Japanese historians to this system. Each mission proceeded first to a designated port (Ningbo in the case of Japan) and then traveled up to the capital, which was Nanjing until 1421 and then Beijing for the rest of the dynasty. There each embassy presented itself in audience before the emperor. Appreciative of the expense faced by the Japanese in fitting out these expeditions, the Ming court agreed to purchase a certain amount of goods in official trade and permitted a certain degree of private trading by embassy members while in China.[79]

Although tributary missions were supposed to be peaceful, rhetoric related to piracy and violent incidents that Chinese officials labeled piratical suffuse the sources documenting Japan's tribute trade with the Ming Dynasty in the fifteenth and sixteenth centuries. Such piracy carried different meanings to authorities in Japan and China, meanings that were often mutually incompatible and that eventually led Chinese officials to consider the entire Japanese tributary apparatus, if not the entire Japanese population, piratical.

For Ming emperors and scholar-officials, the category of "Japanese pirates" represented the opposite of well-regulated tribute trade. It epitomized unrestricted maritime intercourse and signified the antithesis of the idealized vision of the Ming dynastic founder, Zhu Yuanzhang, for a sedentary,

---

79. Wang Yi-T'ung, *Official Relations between China and Japan, 1368–1549* (Cambridge, Mass.: Harvard University Press, 1953); Charlotte von Verschuer, *Across the Perilous Sea: Japanese Trade with China and Korea from the Seventh to the Sixteenth Centuries,* translated by Kristen Lee Hunter (Ithaca, N.Y.: East Asia Program, Cornell University, 2006), ch. 5. Tanaka Takeo, "Japan's Relations with Overseas Countries," with Robert Sakai, in *Japan in the Muromachi Age,* edited by John W. Hall et al. (Berkeley: University of California Press, 1977), pp. 164–67.

agricentric, self-sufficient realm.[80] In official dynastic memory, this piracy signified active rebellion against the Ming Chinese political order. Zhu Yuanzhang originally issued injunctions against Chinese engaging in private overseas trade in 1371 in order to hinder the activities of coastal Chinese who challenged Zhu Yuanzhang's hegemony, engaged in foreign trade, and, as a result, received the epithet *wo* from the Chinese court. Unregulated interaction with Japan by such *wo* people led to incidents such as one in which Japanese supposedly conspired with a traitorous official named Hu Weiyong to overthrow the Ming founder.[81] The maritime bans became dynastic policy as later emperors repeatedly issued further injunctions, even though many merchants and gentry families on the southeast coast ignored the bans, and members of bureaucratic factions occasionally questioned them. The latter saw more lenient trade policies as an antidote to instability and piracy along the southeast coast.[82]

As conditions for permitting Japan to enter into a tributary relationship, the Ming court thus required that Japan eliminate piracy. Some officials in the Ministry of Rites even insisted that Japan desist from exporting weapons, though that prohibition did not become policy until later in the dynasty.[83] In 1401, the retired shogun, Ashikaga Yoshimitsu (1358–1408) agreed to fulfill the conditions for Japan's participation in the tribute trade in exchange for a gold seal for the "king of Japan" and tallies. He tacitly accepted the separation of pirates from trade and repeatedly dispatched prisoners to China whom he identified as captured pirates in order to secure trading privileges and recognition as the legitimate king of Japan.[84] Then, in 1434, as part of the agreement by which the Chinese allowed Japan to restart regular tributary relations, which had been severed by the previous shogun, Ashikaga Yoshimochi (1386–1428), a Chinese reciprocation ambassador reiterated requests that the Japanese interdict piracy and repatriate Chinese captured by pirates.[85]

In contrast, Japanese authorities in the fifteenth and sixteenth centuries all accepted the interdependence of commerce and violence in Japan. They

80. Timothy Brook, *Confusions of Pleasure: Commerce and Culture in Ming China* (Berkeley: University of California Press, 1998), pp. 18–19.
81. Murai, *Nihon chūsei kyōkai shiron*, pp. 151–53; Murai, *Ajia no naka no chūsei Nihon*, p. 84; Wang, "Realistic and Fantastic Images of 'Dwarf Pirates,'" pp. 27, 40 n. 32.
82. Kwan-wai So, *Japanese Piracy in Ming China during the Sixteenth Century* (East Lansing: Michigan State University Press, 1975).
83. Verschuer, *Across the Perilous Sea*, pp. 114, 145–46; Sakuma Shigeo, *Nichimin kankeishi no kenkyū* (Yoshikawa Kōbunkan, 1992), pp. 153–54.
84. Wang, *Official Relations between China and Japan, 1368-1549*, pp. 21, 43–44; Tanaka, "Japan's Relations with Overseas Countries," pp. 164–66.
85. *Mansai jugō nikki*, vol. 2, p. 588, Eikyō 6 (1434) 6.17.

understood the rhetoric of piracy as a tool for the delegitimization of opponents and a signifier for the autonomous, naval service specialists that they needed to employ in order to engage in both domestic and overseas trade. For their part, sea lords of the Setonaikai understood and entrepreneurially exploited the intersections of commerce, diplomacy, and violence related to the tribute trade with China. Their participation helped provoke Chinese officials to equate Japanese tributary trade participants with "Japanese pirates." Sea lords entered into patron-client relationships with the religious, aristocratic, and warrior authorities that sponsored and fitted out tributary embassies. Sea-lord bands participated in peaceful and violent capacities; they helped supply, construct, outfit, sail, and protect the ships of the tributary embassies. Competition among tributary sponsors led to violence that further elevated the prominence of sea-lord participants. Such practices disturbed those Chinese officials, who—like Korean emissaries—became aware that in Japan "pirates" were hired to guard against other "pirates." In 1434, one shogunal advisor, the Shingon Buddhist monk Mansai (1378–1435), recorded in his diary concerns passed on by a Chinese ambassador: "The Chinese court was horribly worried and their people deeply anxious about the protection [*keigo*] forces unfailingly stationed as a prophylactic against piracy."[86]

Illustrative of the wide range of activities indicated by the term "protection," sea lords participated in both the preparations for tributary embassies as well as the voyages of embassies. The dispatch of tributary missions required the ingathering of considerable goods and resources. For example, the 1465 mission carried large amounts of sulfur (some forty thousand *hiki*) from Kyushu, copper from western Honshu, swords, fans, horses, and other trade goods, as well as the fodder, food, water, and other necessities for the animals, crew, and passengers. All of these goods had to be carried to ports such as Hyōgo, Sakai, and Hakata to be loaded onto the designated tributary vessels. Conveying these cargoes required the services of laborers, commercial agents (*toi*), sailors, and pilots to direct ships in and out of harbors. Sea lords would have been among the "pirates [*kaizoku*] of various provinces" ordered by the shogunate to arrange "protection" for these cargo shipments.[87] In addition, shogunal administrators ordered estate proprietors within their patronage networks to dispatch labor forces to transport goods and passengers. Sea-lord estates, including Innoshima and Yugeshima, provided logistical and protection services for the China trade. Not just cogs in a system that linked centers of production and consumption, by participating in the

86. Ibid.
87. Tenyo Seikei, *Boshi nyūminki*, NMKBS, p. 203.

tribute trade, estate residents cast ripples into the wider maritime world and carried the overseas world home.

Shipwrights based in sea-lord domains constructed some of the behemoth vessels used in the China trade, which were some of the largest ships ever assembled in late medieval Japan. For example, the 1465 crossing included vessels from yards in Innoshima, Tajima, Onomichi, Tomo, and Kaminoseki of 600, 1,000, 700, 1,000, and 500 *koku* lading, respectively.[88] By 1465, Innoshima and Tajima belonged to the Innoshima Murakami family, while Tomo became an Innoshima holding in the 1540s, in time for the final crossing in 1547. The Noshima Murakami occupied Kaminoseki as early as 1532.

Such giant vessels required expertise to sail. Sailors as well as guards and escorts were assembled via patron-client networks. For missions administered by the Ōuchi family, captains and officers came from ports such as Hakata, Mojinoseki, or Akamagaseki. Other sponsors relied on the ports of Hyōgo and Sakai.[89] In order to ensure sufficient numbers of sailors, which meant everyone not an officer, more extensive patronage networks were required. By 1547, sailors from thirty-nine provinces, as well as Kyoto and Sakai, reportedly sought the chance to serve in the flotillas.[90] Some groups sent both sailors and protection specialists,[91] and it is likely that sea-lord bands participated in similarly multifaceted ways.

Heavily laden with trade goods, such vessels would have been valuable prizes. The tribute trade system became an important revenue source for Japanese authorities in the fifteenth and sixteenth centuries. The profits for Japanese officials and merchants were potentially enormous. Tally trade expeditions enabled Chinese coinage to circulate as currency in Japan; profits from the silk and precious metals ran potentially into the hundreds of thousands of cash strings (each string containing one thousand copper coins).[92] Over the course of the fifteenth century, the scale of the trade increased dramatically. By the 1450s, Japanese tributary embassies to China consistently brought more ships, people, and goods for trade than the Ming court had originally anticipated or felt it could economically recompense with "gifts." Charlotte von Verschuer estimates that Japanese tally trade vessels carried fifteen times more goods in 1453 than they had in 1433, and the value of

88. Ibid., pp. 212–14.
89. Ibid., pp. 212–19; Yanai Kurōdo Akinao, *Dai Min fu*, in Makita Tairyō, *Sakugen nyūminki no kenkyū* (Kyoto: Bukkyō Bunka Kenkyūjo, 1955), p. 294; Tanaka, "Japan's Relations with Overseas Countries," p. 166.
90. Yanai, *Dai Min fu*, p. 294.
91. *Ishiyama Honganji nikki*, Tenbun 7 (1538) 1.17, 2.5, in NMKBS, p. 427.
92. Verschuer, *Across the Perilous Sea*, pp. 150–63.

those goods in 1453 was nine times what they were in 1433.[93] This tendency of Japanese to test Chinese limits for tribute trade, to bend, if not break, the rules of the trade pushed the Japanese toward piracy in the eyes of Ming officials.[94]

In order to secure satisfactory terms for their growing amounts of trade goods in the official trade granted by the Chinese court, Japanese ambassadors were not above playing on Chinese conceptual linkages between Japanese and pirates. During the tributary mission of 1511–13, the ambassador, Ryōan Keigo (1425–1514), threatened the Ming court with a revival of piracy if the Chinese did not proffer a favorable rate of exchange for the swords and other products carried by the Japanese embassy: "If your country spurns the fortune our embassy carries, then you will throw away the benefits of our small country's generations-long effort to interdict piracy. Your intent to refuse us and change the established precedents risks squandering the good will of our country's king. He will abandon his tributary obligations. Some time after, pirates will hear of it and again gather. And who will be responsible for their crimes?"[95] From the perspective of Chinese officials, Ryōan Keigo's threat confirmed fears of links between tributary embassies and pirates.

The Muromachi shogunate's practice of hiring sea lords to safeguard these expensive expeditions contributed to perceptions among members of the Ming court that tributary embassies were descending into piracy and, eventually, that the Inland Sea ports from which the flotillas set sail occupied piratical geography. Initially, protection for the tally trade employed the same institutional and patronage mechanisms as with Korean envoys. The shogun, deputy shogun, and bakufu administrators issued communiqués to warrior provincial governors, who relayed orders to other regional elites, including merchants in ports like Hyōgo, Sakai, and Hakata, and sea lords.[96] The patronage connections of Inland Sea sea-lord bands to Japanese tributary embassies extend back to the inaugural missions. In the early 1400s, sea lords known to us only as "barrier masters" (*sekikata*), who controlled parts of the island estate of Yugeshima, exploited their histories of sponsorship by

93. Ibid., p. 127.

94. Sakuma, *Nichimin kankeishi no kenkyū*, pp. 149–54; Verschuer, *Across the Perilous Sea*, pp. 126–33; Wang, *Official Relations between China and Japan, 1368–1549*, ch. 4.

95. Ryōan Keigo, *Jinshin nyūminki*, in *Dai Nihon shiryō* (Tokyo Teikoku Daigaku, 1901–), ser. 9, vol. 4, p. 111; Wang, *Official Relations between China and Japan, 1368–1549*, p. 76.

96. Igawa Kenji, *Daikōkai jidai no Higashi Ajia: Nichi-Ō tsūkō no rekishiteki zentei* (Yoshikawa Kōbunkan, 2007), pp. 17–49; Saeki Kōji, "Muromachi jidai no kenminsen keigo ni tsuite," in *Kodai chūseishi ronshū*, edited by Kyushu Daigaku Kokushigaku Kenkyūshitsu (Yoshikawa Kōbunkan, 1990), p. 466.

the Tōji temple complex and the Kōno family of provincial governors in Iyo in order to secure positions providing protection for the tally trade.[97]

Records related to the return of an embassy in 1434 contain one of the best-documented episodes of Inland Sea sea-lord bands providing protection for the tribute trade. Sea lords took advantage of strife in the archipelago and accepted patronage offers with officials in the Muromachi shogunate in order to insinuate themselves into the China trade. The Ashikaga shogun, Yoshinori (1394–1441), and his administrators worried that ongoing warfare over the port of Hakata in Kyushu among the Shōni, Ōuchi, and Ōtomo warrior provincial governor houses would spill over and endanger the China trade flotilla. In particular, they worried that "pirates" from Tsushima and Iki affiliated with these factions would assault the China trade ships.[98] To help fill any holes in the web of protection for the China trade ships, the shogunate offered patronage to Inland Sea sea lords. The Buddhist monk Mansai recorded in his diary that "pirates [kaizoku] from the region around Suō and Iyo had been instructed to calculate the time of probable return and then to sail out and station themselves off of the island of Azukijima so as to inform the returning trading ships of the situation in Kyushu."[99] Azukijima here refers to Azuchi Ōshima, a small island that occupies a strategic point overlooking the sea lanes linking Hakata, Tsushima, Iki, the Gotō Islands, and the continent.[100] In addition to its position as a bone of contention caught between warring daimyo, Hakata was typically the first port of call for most returning ships. The Inland Sea region named in Mansai's entry contained island chains that housed several prominent sea-lord families such as the Noshima Murakami and the Kurushima Murakami. The shogun later expanded the scope of his protection communiqué to include "Shikoku pirates together with Bingo pirates and others."[101] Among the bands who accepted offers to sail out to Azukijima were "pirates [kaizoku] known as the [Innoshima] Murakami of Bingo."[102] As late as the 1420s, the Innoshima Murakami had accepted the patronage of the Ashikaga as well as the Yamana. A powerful warrior provincial governor family and allies of the Ashikaga, the Yamana served as shogunal officials.

97. NET p. 367, doc. 263, Ōan 4 (1371) 3.6; NET pp. 383–84, doc. 276, no year.8.13; NET pp. 384–85 doc. 278, no year.8.18.
98. *Mansai jugō nikki*, vol. 2., p. 405, Eikyō 4 (1432) 7.12; ibid., pp. 549–550, Eikyō 6 (1434) 1.26; Saeki "Muromachi jidai no kenminsen keigo ni tsuite," pp. 465–66.
99. *Mansai jugō nikki*, vol. 2, p. 546, Eikyō 6 (1434) 1.19.
100. Saeki, "Muromachi jidai no kenminsen keigo ni tsuite," p. 466.
101. *Mansai jugō nikki*, p. 553, Eikyō 6 (1434) 1.30.
102. Ibid., p. 547, Eikyō 6 (1434) 1.20.

They had actually paid to fit out one of the China trade ships returning in 1434.[103] The protection efforts succeeded; all of the trade ships plus the reciprocal embassy from China arrived in Japan safely.[104]

Sea lord protection services proved invaluable to tally trade sponsors because the level of violence in the trade escalated in the mid-fifteenth century along with the numbers of ships, participants, and trade goods.[105] This increase in the frequency of incidents of violence on the tally trade caused more Chinese officials to begin equating the Japanese tributaries with pirates.[106] In 1453, Chinese officials complained of Japanese embassy members stealing and beating lodge employees, as well as local functionaries, to death.[107] In the eleventh month of 1468, an inebriated follower of the Japanese ambassador killed a Chinese merchant with his sword.[108] In 1477, Japanese embassy members tussled with lodge guards and fought with members of another tributary delegation.[109] During the 1485–86 mission, a Chinese merchant hired to help provision the return voyage embezzled funds and absconded to the south, whereupon the Japanese hired a Sakai merchant living in Beijing to hunt down the merchant. This Sakai merchant cut down the Chinese merchant.[110] During the embassy of 1496, Japanese were accused of murdering Chinese in Shandong, causing the emperor to restrict to fifty the numbers of Japanese who could advance from the port of Ningbo to the capital.[111]

In an attempt to preserve trading privileges and allay Ming officials' anxiety, and in apparent disregard of the concerns relayed by the Chinese ambassador in 1434, the Muromachi shogunate turned to sea lords to prevent further incidents. In 1499, the shogunate ordered an increased naval mercenary presence on tally trade ships: "[The sponsor of] each ship will arrange its own protection forces (*keigo*) to sail aboard it in case a merchant or

103. EK doc. 1220, Ōei 34 (1427) 12.11; EK doc. 1221, Shōchō 1 (1428) 10.20; Saeki, "Muromachi jidai no kenminsen keigo ni tsuite," p. 465.

104. Saeki, "Muromachi jidai no kenminsen keigo ni tsuite," p. 467.

105. Sakuma, *Nichimin kankeishi no kenkyū*, pp. 149–56.

106. Wang, "Realistic and Fantastic Images of 'Dwarf Pirates,'" pp. 20–21; *Xianzong shilu*, Chenghua 5 (1469) 5.18, CCNSMJ, vol. 1, p. 248.

107. *Yingzong shilu*, Jingtai 4 (1453) 10.3, CCNSMJ, vol. 1, p. 218; Wang, *Official Relations between China and Japan, 1368–1549*, p. 66.

108. *Xianzong shilu*, Chenghua 4 (1468) 11.26, CCNSMJ, vol. 1, p. 245; Wang, *Official Relations between China and Japan, 1368–1549*, p. 70.

109. *Xianzong shilu*, Chenghua 13 (1477) 11.17, CCNSMJ, vol. 1, pp. 262–63; Wang, *Official Relations between China and Japan, 1368–1549*, p. 72.

110. *Rokuon nichiroku*, Meiō 8 (1499) 8.6, in YK, vol. 1, p. 379; Igawa, *Daikōkai jidai no Higashi Ajia*, pp. 171–72.

111. *Xiaozong shilu*, Hongzhi 9 (1496) 8.6, CCNSMJ, vol. 1, p. 287; Wang, *Official Relations between China and Japan, 1368–1549*, p. 74.

anyone else becomes violent."[112] Also known as "riding along" (*uwanori, na-kanori*), this form of protection entailed hiring sea lords to travel on board the actual tally trade ships so as to have them close at hand when embassy officers required military action or navigational assistance. Among the Inland Sea bands that specialized in this form of protection in this period were the Kurushima Murakami and the Noshima Murakami.[113] This form of protection practice also presented sea lords avenues for redress. For example, having been ordered by the Muromachi bakufu to dispatch extra protection forces for tally trade ships for the 1512 embassy, the Ōtomo instructed "ride-along bands" (*nakanori*) to travel on and protect the China trade ships. On the return trip, these "ride-along bands" hijacked a ship after quarreling with the captain and sailed it to Tonoura port in Hyūga Province. In order to recapture the tally trade ship, the Ōtomo called on the services of additional sea-lord bands.[114]

As the bakufu weakened in the latter half of the fifteenth century, the Ashikaga lost their monopoly of the tribute trade to two warrior provincial governor houses, the Ōuchi and the Hosokawa, as well as Sakai merchants and religious centers, who bought participation in the trade by sponsoring the outfitting of ships. Ultimately, participation in the tribute trade depended on access to the tallies, the shogun's seal as king of Japan, and the Zen monks who scribed the documents used in the trade. The Hosokawa and the Ōuchi competed to be the ones to dictate this access as well as to control the bakufu. The rivalry between members of these two houses generated many of the opportunities for sea-lord violence in the tally trade that proved crucial for inspiring Ming officials to equate tributary embassies with pirates and for shaping Chinese perceptions of Japanese pirates.

In 1508 Ōuchi Yoshioki (1477–1528) helped Hosokawa Takakuni (1484–1531) to engineer the accession of Ashikaga Yoshitane (1466–1523) as shogun. In 1511, the Ōuchi dispatched a tributary embassy using Hongzhi-period tallies. In China, this embassy received new Zhengde reign-era (1506–21) tallies, which the Ōuchi seized. Shogun Yoshitane awarded the Ōuchi the exclusive use of the Zhengde tallies to dispatch embassies and the responsibility to arrange protection. However, in 1521, Ashikaga Yoshitane broke with Hosokawa Takakuni and drove Takakuni from the capital. In response, Takakuni overthrew Yoshitane and enthroned Ashikaga Yoshiharu (1511–50) as shogun. Takakuni and Yoshiharu abrogated Yoshioki's tributary privileges, but Yoshioki refused to hand over the Zhengde tallies.

112. *Rokuon nichiroku*, Meiō 8 (1499) 8.6, in YK, vol. 1, pp. 379–80.
113. EK doc. 1979, no year.6.15; EK doc. 1709, Tenbun 9? (1540) 9.26.
114. Hashimoto, *Chūsei Nihon no kokusai kankei*, pp. 253–56; Udagawa, *Nihon no kaizoku* (Seibundō 1983), pp. 136–37.

In 1523, both the Ōuchi and the Hosokawa sent tributary embassies to China that claimed to be legitimate representatives of the "king of Japan" (table 5). The Ōuchi expedition carried the active Zhengde (1506–21) reign-era allies under the ambassadorship of the Zen monk Kendō Sōsetsu. Takakuni dispatched an embassy headed by a Zen monk named Rankō Zuisa and a Chinese merchant named Song Suqing. They carried the defunct Hongzhi 1488–1505) reign-era tallies and sought to explain to the Ming court that he Ōuchi had stolen the Zhengde tallies. Violence erupted between the two embassies in what is known as the Ningbo Incident.[115]

TABLE 5
The 1523 Ningbo Incident

Sponsor	Ōuchi Yoshioki	Hosokawa Takakuni
Shogun	Ashikaga Yoshitane	Ashikaga Yoshiharu
Tally	Zhengde	Hongzhi
Chief envoy(s)	Kendō Sōsetsu	Rankō Zuisa and Song Suqing

The naval warfare, arson, raiding, and other forms of violence that occurred during the Ningbo Incident are characteristic of both sea-lord band military services and Chinese representations of "Japanese pirates." Though the Ōuchi-sponsored fleet arrived first, Song Suqing bribed the Maritime Trade supervisor of Ningbo so as to have their cargo unloaded first and to then have the Hosokawa ambassador, Rankō Zuisa, ranked above the Ōuchi-sponsored ambassador, Kendō Sōsetsu. Incensed, Kendō's company took up arms, killed Rankō, burned Song Suqing's ship to the waterline, and pursued Song Suqing inland, burning and looting as they went. Song escaped them, was subsequently arrested by Ming forces, and died in prison. Kendō and company returned to Ningbo pillaging along the way. They kidnapped the battalion commander of Ningbo, stole a ship, and sank the ships of those guards who pursued them.[116]

After the Ningbo Incident, the strife between the Ōuchi and the Hosokawa continued in two forms that, for Chinese officials, involved piracy. Violence between the two persisted at sea as sea-lord bands fought proxy wars and operated protection businesses for their patrons. We have seen how the Noshima Murakami in this period took the opportunity to shop

---

115. Hashimoto, *Chūsei Nihon no kokusai kankei*, pp. 210–20.
116. Tanaka Takeo, *Wakō to kangō bōeki* (Shibundō, 1953), pp. 105–6; Elisonas, "The Inseparable Trinity," p. 238; *Shizong shilu*, Jiajing 2 (1523) 6.15, CCNSMJ, vol. 2, pp. 322–23; Zheng Ruozeng, *Chouhai tubian* (Beijing: Zhonghua Shuju, 2007), p. 172.

their services between both sides in this conflict for maximum gain. For example, in 1541, the Noshima Murakami and another sea-lord family, the Imaoka, accepted Ōuchi sponsorship to intercept, inspect, assess a toll on, and provide protection for China trade ships.[117] Their actions impeded the ultimately futile attempts of the Hosokawa and Sakai merchants to outfit another trading fleet to China.[118] But in the 1520s and 1530s, the Noshima also accepted the sponsorship of various members of the Hosokawa family.[119]

At the same time, in order to repair Japan's reputation in China, both sides dispatched embassies to China and requested that the kings of Ryūkyū and Korea act as intermediaries and deliver messages to China for them. The Ōuchi and Hosokawa both understood that they could use language related to piracy as potent rhetoric in overseas diplomacy, but they and their continental interlocutors interpreted such language differently. For example, in 1525, the Ōuchi dispatched an imposter embassy to Chosŏn pretending to be from Shogun Ashikaga Yoshiharu, claiming that the Ningbo Incident had occurred because the Ōuchi—who bore the legitimate tallies—pursued "pirates" (kanzoku) who had stolen defunct tallies in order perpetrate a fraudulent attempt to engage in tribute trade.[120] In contrast, in a 1527 letter to the Ming court, the Hosokawa-controlled bakufu described its version of what happened at Ningbo and condemned "Kōjiro Gentarō, a retainer of Ōuchi . . . Yoshioki, as the leader of the evildoers."[121] The Kōjiro were sea-lords based around the small port of Ōbatake who often provided naval expertise for their Ōuchi patrons.

The Japanese employed the rhetoric of piracy in order to delegitimize the actions of their opponents, but for Ming officials, such communications seem to have had the effect of reifying images of all Japanese, or at least all Japanese seafarers, as pirates. The 1523 Ningbo Incident marked a key shift in Chinese perceptions of Japanese pirates. After Ningbo, the Ming court began strictly enforcing rules for Japanese tributary embassies: "three ships, one hundred people, and once every ten years." The court designated as pirates those that did not follow these rules.[122] In addition, Ming officials in

---

117. EK doc. 1730, Tenbun 11? (1542) 5.21; EK doc. 1770, Tenbun 20? (1551) 4.20; Hashimoto, *Chūsei Nihon no kokusai kankei*, pp. 228–29.

118. Hashimoto, *Chūsei Nihon no kokusai kankei*, pp. 201–5; Igawa, *Daikōkai jidai no Higashi Ajia*, pp. 163–64.

119. See ch. 3.

120. Quoted in Hashimoto, *Chūsei Nihon no kokusai kankei*, pp. 221–22.

121. Gesshū Jukei, *Gen'un bunshū*, Jiajing 6 (1527) 8th month, in *Zoku zenrin kokuhōki*, doc. 2, *Shintei zenrin kokuhōki, shintei zoku zenrin kokuhōki*, edited by Tanaka Takeo (Shūeisha, 1995); Hirase, "Shugo daimyō Ōuchi-shi to kaihen no busō seiryoku," pp. 27–28; Hashimoto, *Chūsei Nihon no kokusai kankei*, pp. 223–25.

122. Sakuma, *Nichimin kankeishi no kenkyū*, pp. 162–65.

creasingly identified and condemned congruencies between the actions of tributary embassies and Japanese pirates. Almost heedless of the issue of legitimacy that so concerned the Hosokawa and the Ōuchi, records of court deliberations instead evince alarm over the possibility of Japanese joining with Chinese expatriates such as Song Suqing, whom Ming officials perceived as having incited Japanese to break the rules of the tribute system and to commit crimes in China.[123] Chinese officials worried about the long-term implications of the Ningbo Incident because the violence that the Kōjiro and other Inland Sea sea-lord proxies unleashed in China resembled other recent cases of piracy involving Japanese. As early as 1524, Chinese and Portuguese sea merchants had begun defying Ming maritime bans, recruiting merchants and sailors from Ryūkyū, Japan, and Southeast Asia, and gathering at islands along the chokepoints and shipping lanes of China's southeast coast such as Shuangyu in the Zhoushan Islands. They used these havens as bases for conducting unlicensed trade and raiding up and down the coast, earning them the pejorative "Japanese pirates" from Chinese officials.[124]

Futhermore, despite the victory of the Ōuchi in achieving dominance over the tribute trade after the Ningbo Incident, members of Japanese tribute embassies continued to perpetrate incidents resembling those made notorious by "Japanese pirates": kidnapping, attacking ships, and breaking restrictions on frequency and numbers of ships and crew. Because the Ōuchi based themselves along the Inland Sea and had established deep client networks among Inland Sea sea lords, it is likely that members of those sea-lord bands participated in these missions as guards and, as such, may have engaged in incidents of violence. For example, in 1538, one Ōuchi-sponsored crew kidnapped Chinese coastal residents. The Japanese Zen monk Sakugen Shūryō (1501–79) recorded that when the 1538 embassy reached the coast of China, "in the middle of night, sailors poled a longboat . . . to an island where several fishing boats had been moored by the shore. Our sailors attacked the fishing smacks and seized three fishermen as captives." The ship's officers subsequently interrogated the prisoners in order to ascertain their location and to acquire directions to Ningbo.[125]

Official reception of the final tributary expedition in 1547 required extensive negotiations because members of the Chinese court perceived several characteristics of it as "piratical." The embassy contravened the rules limiting Japanese arrivals to once a decade and exceeded permissible numbers of ships and crew. In deliberations, the Minister of Rites employed the

123. *Shizong shilu*, Jiajing 4 (1525) 4.14, CCNSMJ, vol. 2, pp. 326–27.
124. Chin, "Merchants, Smugglers, and Pirates," pp. 44–48.
125. *Sakugen Washō shotoshū* jō, Tenbun 8 (1539) 5.2 in NMKBS, p. 481.

precedents of the Ningbo Incident and Song Suqing to warn of the dangers of appeasing such Japanese missions.[126] The ambassador, Sakugen Shūryō, justified the large number of ships by claiming that one was an "escort vessel" needed to defend against pirates.[127] Indeed, the travelogue of another officer on the embassy claimed that they fought off an assault by pirates in twenty-eight ships, who killed nine sailors, injured three more, and stole a longboat.[128] In addition, the provincial governor over coastal Zhejiang and Fujian, Zhu Wan, implicated members of the 1547 embassy in a supposed conspiracy by local officials to assassinate him in response to his suppression of Chinese maritime commerce and violence.[129] For this accusation to withstand scrutiny, Zhu assumed that his brother officials would accept the reputation of Japanese tribute missions for pugnacity. The Ming court perceived sufficient correlations between piracy and this tribute mission to essentially end Japan's tributary privileges in 1549 by endowing Sakugen Shūryō with only a single tally.[130]

As the case of the final tribute embassy shows, Japanese seafarers caused Chinese officials to label tributary embassies as piratical by arriving in expeditions that sought tribute trade privileges without proper credentials or in expeditions that failed to meet restrictions on the number of ships, number of embassy members, armaments, and timing. Warlords in western Japan sponsored and dispatched several such expeditions between 1544 and 1558 that the Chinese court rejected and turned away. Once refused, some of these rejected embassies raided littoral villages in retaliation or traded with coastal communities illegally before returning.[131] Just as with the formal embassies received by the Chinese government, these missions too would have included protection forces, sailors, and other crew recruited via patron client relations from among Inland Sea sea-lord families. For example, in 1546, Ōtomo Yoshiaki (1502–50) used an invalid, older tally (probably obtained from the Hosokawa) and was turned away for coming at the wrong time.[132] The Ōtomo did have access to a large number of retainers who specialized in the sea and whom the Ōtomo called on for "protection" endeav

126. *Shizong shilu,* Jiajing 27 (1548) 6.5, CCNSMJ, vol. 2, p. 355.
127. *Shizong shilu,* Jiajing 28 (1549) 6.16, CCNSMJ, vol. 2, p. 358–59.
128. Yanai, *Dai Min fu,* p. 294.
129. So, *Japanese Piracy in Ming China during the Sixteenth Century,* p. 53; *Shizong shilu,* Jiajing 2 (1549) 3.2, CCNSMJ, vol. 2, pp. 357.
130. Verschuer, *Across the Perilous Sea,* p. 143.
131. Igawa, *Daikōkai jidai no Higashi Ajia,* pp. 146–81.
132. Zheng Shun'gong, *Riben yijian* (Beijing: Gushu Shiwen Diange, 1939), "Qionghe huahai," ch. 2, p. 5b; Kage Toshio, *Sengoku daimyo no gaikō to toshi ryūtsū: Bungo Ōtomo-shi to Higashi Ajia Sekai* (Shibunkaku, 2006), p. 258.

ors domestically and overseas.[133] But the Ōtomo also sponsored sea lords; the Noshima Murakami provided "naval services" for Ōtomo Yoshiaki on at least one occasion.[134]

These failed tributary embassies sought to enhance their commercial prospects by acquiring the guidance and support of expatriate Chinese merchants and smugglers in Japan also labeled "Japanese pirates" by the Ming court. Such efforts increased Ming perceptions of Japanese tribute trade embassies and their associated seafarers as piratical. One chief of these expatriate merchants was Wang Zhi. In the 1540s, Wang actively sailed back and forth between Japan and his base on Shuangyu. In 1544, Wang arrived in Japan on a ship that the Ming court had refused to recognize as a tributary embassy and that had spent time engaging in illicit commerce along the Chinese coast.[135] By the 1550s, Wang had become one of the most powerful Chinese merchant leaders of "Japanese pirates" and an attractive sponsor for sea lords. Although he spent most of his time at his bases in the Gotō Islands and the port city of Hirado, Wang Zhi attracted Inland Sea sea lords to his service through the auspices of patrons such as Ōuchi Yoshitaka (1507–51) and Ōtomo Sōrin (1530–87).

While in Japan, Wang Zhi did not portray himself as a "pirate." Instead, he endowed himself with titles and symbols that would gain him access to people of influence and attract both warlord patrons and sea-lord clients in Japan. Under the name Wufeng, Wang developed a reputation as a captain and a Confucian scholar.[136] He drew on rhetorics of lordship, calling himself "the king of Hui."[137] The 1556 Tsushima envoy, Chōkyū, presented eyewitness testimony of Wang's pretensions to lordship in his interview with the Chosŏn court: "We asked him, 'Have you seen Wufeng?' He replied, 'I saw him in Hirado. He led around three hundred people and sailed in one great ship. Normally, he wears clothes of high quality. All in all, there are about two thousand people who follow him.'"[138]

Wang's associations with Inland Sea seafarers likely began around 1550, when he involved himself in Japan's tribute trade with China and linked himself and his band to the Ōuchi. Wang had learned that the leader of the 1547 embassy, Sakugen Shūryō, had sought and failed to acquire, by

133. Kage, *Sengoku daimyo no gaikō to toshi ryūtsū*, pp. 271–72, n. 58.
134. EK doc. 1665, Tenbun 1? (1532) 7.20.
135. Igawa, *Daikōkai jidai no Higashi Ajia*, pp. 148, 176.
136. Tsuji Zennosuke, *Zōtei kaigai kōtsū shiwa* (Naigai Shoseki Kabushikigaisha, 1930), pp. 260–61; and Nanpo Bunshi, *Teppōki*, quoted in Igawa, *Daikōkai jidai no Higashi Ajia*, p. 149.
137. Zheng, *Chouhai tubian*, p. 619.
138. CWS, *Myŏngjong Taewang sillok*, vol. 20, pp. 28a-b, Myŏngjong 11 (1556) 4.1.

"trading Japanese goods," a "painting of wild pear with land and sea" drawn by a Zen master that he saw in a Chinese temple. Wang acquired the piece and brought it to the court of Ōuchi Yoshitaka,[139] forging bonds that he could exploit for purposes of maritime trade. In order to learn of and present the painting in Yamaguchi, Wang had to cultivate an extensive network of contacts in both China and Japan among the monks, officials, sponsors, and seafarers responsible for managing and carrying out the tribute trade. While in Ōuchi ports as well as the Ōuchi capital of Yamaguchi, Wang Zhi likely secured the connections with Inland Sea sea lords that led Chinese and Korean officials to include Inland Sea seafarers within the category of Japanese pirates. As Chōkyū, Tsushima's 1556 envoy to Korea, reported: "Wufeng . . . led people from Awa, Iyo, Sanuki, and Tosa in Shikoku . . . to make bands and to come and raid."[140]

Wang also connected himself, his Japanese warlord patrons, and their sea-lord clients to Chinese officials who might be inclined to back a renewal of Japan's rescinded tributary status. Two embassies received permission from the Ming emperor to travel to Japan in 1555 in order to help to bring an end to the pirate menace. In contrast to the case of the Korean court in the fifteenth century, which sent its best poets to serve as diplomats, in this period Ming Chinese officials balanced two contradictory imperatives when selecting envoys. They could not dispatch high-ranking officials— that would give too much honor to a land of pirates. But they still needed to send men who could represent the reigning Jiajing emperor and convey the "civilizing" missive that would convince Japanese authorities to more actively quash pirates.[141] A self-confessed "plain clothed" man of no rank or position named Zheng Shun'gong received permission to lead a mission on behalf of his patron, Yang Yi, a commander-in-chief in charge of pirate suppression in several southeastern coastal provinces. Two licentiate students, Jiang Zhou and Chen Keyuan, led the second embassy to Japan. Their sponsor, the politically powerful Hu Zhongxian (1511–65), replaced Yang Yi as commander-in-chief in 1556.[142] Sponsored by competing commanders-in-chief, the two sets of emissaries represented competing factions in the

---

139. Quoted in Tsuji, *Zōtei kaigai kōtsū shiwa*, pp. 260–61; Tanaka, *Wakō: Umi no rekishi*, pp. 135–36.
140. CWS, *Myŏngjong Taewang sillok*, vol. 20, pp. 28a-b, Myŏngjong 11 (1556) 4.1.
141. For issues of status and envoys, see Ronald P. Toby, *State and Diplomacy in Early Modern Japan: Asia in the Development of the Tokugawa Bakufu* (Princeton, N.J.: Princeton University Press, 1984), p. 197.
142. *Shizong shilu*, Jiajing 36 (1557) 8.24, CCNSMJ, pp. 477–78; So, *Japanese Piracy in Ming China during the Sixteenth Century*, pp. 70–71, ch. 4; Kanbe Teruo, "Tei Shunkō to Shō Shū: Ōtomo Sōrin to atta futari no Minjin," *Ōita Daigaku kyōiku fukushi kagakubu kenkyū kiyō* 21.2 (1999): 109–24.

Ming court and sought to win positions through deeds accomplished in eliminating the pirate threat.[143]

During their travels to try and convince Japanese warlords and other authorities to eradicate piracy, these envoys and their followers gathered considerable amounts of intelligence on pirates, the sea-lanes in and around Japan, and Japanese society. En route to Japan, Zheng Shun'gong entered into conversations with mariners from the Japanese island of Yakushima, located south of Kyushu, who gave him considerable information about navigating to and around the archipelago.[144] He spent perhaps six months at the court of Ōtomo Sōrin, where he interacted closely with Zen monks, met Wang Zhi, and secured promises from Sōrin to quell pirates.[145] In addition, Zheng dispatched two of his followers to Kyoto in order to secure the support of Emperor Go-Nara.[146]

Jiang Zhou and Chen Keyuan focused on enticing Wang Zhi and other *wokou* captains to return to China with promises of pardons and a liberalization of trade policies with Japan. Wang persuaded Jiang and Chen that seeking out the powerless rulers of Japan was futile. Instead, while Chen returned to China to report, Wang agreed to travel with and introduce Jiang Zhou to figures capable of realizing their ambitions of suppressing pirates and encouraging peaceful trade. Together they traced parts of Wang's vast network of ports and patrons; they visited Hirado and Hakata and focused on Ōtomo Sōrin as a key agent in the elimination of pirates. Jiang also used these connections to dispatch messengers to the Sō of Tsushima and Ōuchi Yoshinaga (1532–57) in Yamaguchi; those messengers carried offers that promised trading privileges in return for aid in eliminating pirates.[147]

Both embassies thus relied on two powerful Inland Sea-based warlords and sponsors of sea-lord bands: the brothers Ōtomo Sōrin and Ōuchi Yoshinaga. Through them, the Ming envoys could have met, interacted with, and recruited Inland Sea sea lords to their various causes. The presence of European Jesuits and merchant-adventurers, Chinese merchants, and Japanese sea lords made Sōrin's domain a vibrant center of intercultural and

---

143. Zheng, *Riben yijian*, "Qionghe huahai," ch. 6, pp. 10a, 11b; ch. 7, pp. 6a; ch. 9, p. 6b; Kanbe, "Tei Shunkō to Shō Shū," pp. 111–16; Nakajima Takashi, "Tei Shunkō no rainichi ni tsuite," *Tōyō Daigaku Bungakubu kiyō, Shigakka-hen* 19 (1993): 65.

144. Zheng, *Riben yijian*, "Fuhai tujing," ch. 1, p. 4b.

145. Zheng, *Riben yijian*, "Qionghe huahai," ch. 7, p. 6a; "Fuhai tujing," ch. 1, pp. 2a, 8b.

146. Zheng, *Riben yijian*, "Qionghe huahai," ch. 7, p. 6a.

147. *Shizong shilu*, Jiajing 35 (1556) 4.6, CCNSMJ, vol. 2, pp. 454–55; *Shizong shilu*, Jiajing 36 (1557) 11.6, CCNSMJ, vol. 2, pp. 480–81; Jiang Zhou, "Minjin Shō Shū shibun," *Zoku zenrin kokuhōki*, doc. 27; Tanaka Takeo, *Chūsei taigai kankeishi* (Tokyo Daigaku Shuppankai, 1975), p. 320.

commercial exchange, his court a clearinghouse for information on the circum-China Sea world, and his coasts a hotbed of intersections between pirates and protection. Zheng Shun'gong found ports under Ōtomo control to be full of pirates,[148] but he also learned firsthand about the importance of sea-lord protection enterprises in Japanese waters. When his followers returned from Kyoto, Zheng noted that they required safe-passage flags. Although Zheng claims that the Japanese emperor and Ōtomo Sōrin supplied these flags to his followers,[149] it is likely that the imperial court and the Ōtomo bought those flags (i.e. "crest pennants" [monmaku]) from sea-lord bands such as the Noshima Murakami. In this period, neither the imperial court nor individual daimyo had much sway over the seas.

Sōrin's brother, Yoshinaga, had been adopted by Ōuchi Yoshitaka and sought to lay claim to the Ōuchi domain after Sue Harukata assassinated Yoshitaka in 1551. With Yoshitaka's death, one of the chief sponsors channeling sea-lord activity into the tribute trade disappeared, and Zheng Shun'gong claimed that expatriate Chinese merchants such as Wang Zhi filled that void. He remarked that the Ōuchi capital had become a "gathering place for fugitives"[150] like Wang, who presumably sponsored sea lords who once served the Ōuchi. Mōri Motonari's crippling defeat of Sue Harukata in 1555 did not deter Ōuchi Yoshinaga from continuing to attempt to recreate Ōuchi influence in the maritime world. He had retained possession of the Ōuchi family's tribute trade credentials and frequently sponsored the Shira and other sea-lord families to engage in "protection."[151] On at least one occasion he attempted to recruit the Noshima Murakami.[152]

Sea-lord bands also joined in the return voyages of the envoys to China. Wang Zhi accompanied the flotilla. He had agreed to help suppress pirates in return for trade privileges, and to help representatives of Ōtomo Sōrin and Ōuchi Yoshinaga, who sought to restart tributary trade in return for having consented to eliminate pirates. Sōrin dispatched one mission to return Zheng Shun'gong[153] and outfitted another with the help of his brother Ōuchi Yoshinaga. The latter mission included a "giant ship" that carried Chinese captured by pirates for repatriation as a gesture of good faith.[15] Zen monks led these expeditions. Sōrin had provided his monk-diploma with a defunct tally and a request for Chinese books in order to demonstrate

148. Zheng, Riben yijian, "Qionghe huahai," ch. 9, p. 7a.
149. Ibid., pp. 7a–7b; Kanbe, "Tei Shunkō to Shō Shū," pp. 115–16.
150. Zheng, Riben yijian, "Qionghe huahai," ch. 4, p. 22a.
151. Shirai monjo, in Buke monjo no kenkyū to mokuroku, edited by Akutagawa Tatsuo (Ishikaw Bunka Jigyō Zaidan, Ochanomizu Toshokan, 1988), pp. 213–21.
152. EK doc. 1769, no year.4.20.
153. Zheng, Riben yijian, "Qionghe huahai," ch. 7, p. 6a; ch.9, p. 7b.
154. Shizong shilu, Jiajing 36 (1557) 11.6, CCNSMJ, vol. 2, pp. 480–81.

his sincerity in his desire to be "civilized," whereas Yoshinaga had endowed his ambassador with a letter stamped with the seal of the king of Japan. Naval "escorts" provided protection for the flotilla.[155] Both daimyo assumed that the Ming court would accept their embassies as evidence of good faith, and therefore as legitimate.[156] However, Ming officials found the credentials and performances of Yoshinaga's and Sōrin's embassies wanting as potential tributaries; some officials were disturbed at the ties these embassies had to Wang Zhi.

So the Ming court treated these envoys and their followers from the Inland Sea region as "pirates" (*zei*) and dispatched military forces, who set the Japanese ships afire. The survivors retreated into the mountains of the Zhoushan Islands, collected naval stores including paulownia oil and iron nails, and built a second group of ships. The Ming navy sank one of these as the surviving "Japanese" escaped out to sea and embarked on a series of raids along the coast before returning to Japan.[157] The presence of escorts, incidences of combat, and construction of ships suggests that naval experts like sea lords participated in these failed tribute embassies. These embassies were followed by one in 1558 dispatched by Mōri Motonari, who seems to have employed the tributary credentials his forces seized from Ōuchi Yoshinaga.[158] As earlier chapters have shown, Motonari sought to succeed the Ōuchi as the paramount power in western Honshu and was a frequent sponsor of the Noshima Murakami and other sea-lord bands.

Having returned to China, Zheng Shun'gong and Jiang Zhou contributed to ongoing scholarly efforts to understand and define Japan and Japanese pirates by compiling accounts of their journeys.[159] His patron Yang Yi having fallen from favor, Zheng Shun'gong was incarcerated upon returning to China in 1557. While in prison, he composed *Mirror on Japan* (*Riben yijian*), which he completed in 1565. In the three volumes of *Mirror on Japan*, Zheng offers a detailed account of the history of Chinese interaction with Japan and the rise of what he calls "fugitives" (*liubu*), Chinese expatriate sea merchants like Wang Zhi. In treatises on Japanese language,

---

155. *Shizong shilu*, Jiajing 36 (1557) 8.24, CCNSMJ, vol. 2, p. 477.

156. Ibid.; Zheng, *Riben yijian*, "Qionghe huahai," ch. 7, p. 6a; ch. 6, pp. 12a–12b; Kage, *Sengoku daimyo no gaikō to toshi ryūtsū*, pp. 258–61; So, *Japanese Piracy in Ming China during the Sixteenth Century*, pp. 105–10.

157. *Shizong shilu*, Jiajing 37 (1558) 7.11, CCNSMJ, vol. 2, p. 490; ibid., Jiajing 37 (1558) 11.13, CCNSMJ, vol. 2, p. 493; ibid., Jiajing 38 (1559) 7.19, CCNSMJ, vol. 2, p. 503; Kage, *Sengoku daimyo no gaikō to toshi ryūtsū*, pp. 262–63.

158. Zheng, *Riben yijian*, "Qionghe huahai," ch. 6, p. 12b; Itō Kōji, *Chūsei Nihon no gaikō to Zenshū* (Yoshikawa Kōbunkan, 2002), pp. 200, 294.

159. Accounts of Japan and Japanese pirates were so prevalent as to constitute a genre in sixteenth-century China (Wang, "Realistic and Fantastic Images of 'Dwarf Pirates'"; Tanaka, *Wakō: Umi no rekishi*, ch. 6).

culture, geography, cartography, history, and society, Zheng examined what made the Japanese environment so conducive to piracy and what gave Japanese people such a penchant for piracy.[160] The accounts of Jiang Zhou and Chen Keyuan were collected by a protégé of Hu Zhongxian named Zheng Ruozeng and published in several forms.[161]

Although the two Zhengs and other sixteenth-century Chinese writers did not necessarily hold high office, their perspectives reflect the positions of patrons and factions that extended to the pinnacles of Ming governance. They reached conclusions similar to their Korean counterparts and used the concept of "Japanese pirate" to characterize maritime space in and around the Japanese archipelago. Like Pak Sosaeng, Zheng Shun'gong identified chokepoints and barriers as the geographical boundaries between various littoral regions where different sea lords ruled. He wrote, "there are many toll barriers established on islands, in ports, and in chokepoints [aikou]."[162] Zheng noted that barriers were particularly numerous in the Inland Sea space between Akamagaseki and the capital, and he explained that those barriers offered facilities for travelers to moor and to take lodgings for the night.[163] Although Zheng of course appreciated the prominence of key nodes like Akamagaseki and Hyōgo,[164] his discussions of other barriers in the Inland Sea point to a recognition of the domains of sea lords. He identified the barrier of Isonoseki attached to Nojima in Awaji as a particularly significant base, possibly because of its strategic position overlooking the narrow straits between Awaji and Honshu. His attention to Nojima confirmed the testimony of a band of Japanese pirates captured in 1556, who confessed that they had sailed from their home of Nojima at the behest of Chinese sea merchants.[165]

Zheng also acknowledged the strength of the Noshima Murakami in his assessment of Shiwaku. Although he mistakenly conflated Shiwaku with the nearby port of Tsurajima, Shun'gong did identify Shiwaku as an important chokepoint, boundary, and way station: a "cluster of seven islands that serves as a port for those going to the Southern Sea and Sanuki regions as well as those entering the Sanyō and Bitchū regions."[166] As we have seen, the Noshima Murakami took advantage of Shiwaku's dominant geographical position in a chain of islands linking Honshu and Shikoku to bound their

160. For background on Zheng Shun'gong, see So, *Japanese Piracy in Ming China during the Sixteenth Century*, pp. 22, 70–71; Tanaka, *Wakō: Umi no rekishi*, pp. 197–98; Ōtomo Shin'ichi, *Nihon Ikkan (Riben yijian): honbun to sakuin* (Kasama Shoin, 1974), pp. 477–94; Kanbe, "Tei Shunkō to Shō Shū."
161. Tanaka, *Wakō: Umi no rekishi*, pp. 195–96; Kanbe, "Tei Shunkō to Shō Shū," pp. 118–20.
162. Zheng, *Riben yijian*, "Juedao xinbian," ch. 1, p. 25a.
163. Zheng, *Riben yijian*, "Fuhai tujing," ch. 3, p. 4b.
164. Ibid., pp. 7a–8b; Zheng, *Riben yijian*, "Qionghe huahai," ch. 2, p. 2a.
165. *Shizong shilu*, Jiajing 35 (1556) 3.17, CCNSM, vol. 2, p. 453.
166. Zheng, *Riben yijian*, "Fuhai tujing," ch. 3, p. 8b.

maritime domain, operate an extensive protection enterprise, regulate ship traffic, manage commercial shipping enterprises, and oversee lucrative port and lodging establishments. Thus the strength of sea lords in these choke-points both shaped Chinese perceptions of Japanese geography and added nuance to their interpretation of "Japanese pirates."

Zheng Shun'gong and other Chinese writers also echoed the conclusions of Japan hands in Chosŏn that Japanese—wherever their origin—lacked morality. According to Zheng, Japanese failed to follow the precepts of the five Confucian relationships. There was more than a tinge of agricentrism in these remarks: Zheng Shun'gong accused Japanese fisher folk of possessing their own ethical system, not the more proper morality of the farmer. Such ethical deficiencies made them particularly susceptible to the tantalizing lures of profit from illicit trade and raiding dangled by Chinese fugitives.[167] Zheng considered such alliances particularly dangerous because of the risk that Japanese seafarers would disseminate their wicked ways by marrying their daughters to Chinese fugitives, which would, in Zheng's eyes, breed dangerous, transborder, maritime families.[168]

Zheng employed the term "Japanese pirate" as a tool of regionality: he explicitly extended the meaning of "Japanese pirates" from the residents of Kyushu to the population of the entire western Japanese littoral. He charac-terized their practices as piracy perpetrated both at the invitation of expatri-ate merchants and under the guise of trade, by which he meant the seafarers who contravened tributary regulations: "Fugitives hide on barbarian islands and invite barbarians to raid us. These barbarians come from the Eastern Sea province of Kii, the southern and western sea circuits, the Sanyō and San'in regions, even as far as Wakasa. How can these western barbarians not be lured into raiding? Although they call themselves merchants, in truth they have become robbers and pirates."[169] Zheng raised specific examples from the Inland Sea region. He described tactics such as ambushing ships in chokepoints, which were indicative of Inland Sea sea lords. He also tied Japanese pirates to the tribute trade by singling out the Inland Sea province of Izumi, the location of the port of Sakai, which was the chief port for the Hosokawa tributary missions: "The inhabitants of Izumi made a living by accumulating treasures. In the past, there were those who . . . formed vio-lent gangs, sailed small ships in the seas between the provinces of Tosa and Bungo, hid in harbors such as Nojima, sought out merchants ships, and stole from them. In the Elder Fire Dragon Year of the Jiajing reign [1556], the

167. Zheng, *Riben yijian*, "Qionghe huahai," ch. 3, p. 9a; ch. 4, p. 19a.
168. Ibid., ch. 3, pp. 7b-8a.
169. Ibid., ch. 4, p. 19b; Elisonas, "The Inseparable Trinity," pp. 254–55.

Hosoya [of Izumi] followed [the Chinese fugitive smuggler lord] Xu Hai and raided in China."[170] In Zheng's eyes, such practices rendered large swathe of the Inland Sea region and its inhabitants particularly piratical: "Among the barbarians of the central southern sea [today's Seto Inland Sea] there are places known as criminals' islands, meaning a region of pirates."[171]

Zheng Shun'gong's *Mirror on Japan* shows that mid-sixteenth-century Chinese had at their disposal ethnographic analyses of Japanese sea-lore practices with which they could link the Inland Sea, its seafarers, and tribu tary trade embassies to the category of Japanese pirates and a wider piratical maritime world. Contemporaries like Zheng Ruozeng echoed this associa tion of tribute trade with raiding by compiling lists of bases of "Japanese pirates" that corresponded quite closely to locations where the sponsors participants in, and aspirants to the tribute trade resided. Included in these lists were Inland Sea provinces like Nagato and Bungo that housed both sea lord bands and patrons.[172]

The experiences of fifteenth- and sixteenth-century Chinese official with Japanese sea lords, tribute trade embassies, and other "Japanese pirates" indelibly marked Chinese official memory. Japanese pirates were branded as evildoers who shifted back and forth between raiding and trading. The "Chapter on Japan" in the *Ming Dynastic History* (*Ming shi*, completed 1739) conveys the frustration that Ming officials felt toward such figures with ret rospective vitriol: "Japanese are of a cunning nature. Sometimes they laded their ships with local products and weapons when they sailed to our coast When they had the opportunity, they readied their weapons and attacked and plundered us without restraint. If such attacks seemed impossible, they presented their wares and claimed to present tribute. Hence, the southeas coast suffered."[173]

CONCLUSION

In exploring the history of Japan's overseas relations from the waterline from the perspectives of "sea lords," we have seen that the Inland Sea focu to their lordship and patronage did not limit their ability to travel and en gage in raiding and trading ventures overseas. Instead, it is likely that th reputations they amassed as a result of their domestic patronage and lord

170. Zheng, *Riben yijian,* "Qionghe huahai," ch. 4, p. 20b.
171. Ibid.
172. Igawa, *Daikōkai jidai no Higashi Ajia,* p. 175.
173. "Riben zhuan," *Ming shi,* ch. 322, CCNSS, vol. 1, p. 289; See also Kwan-wai So's translation of "The Story of Japan," in *Japanese Piracy in Ming China during the Sixteenth Century,* p. 170.

ship inspired Japanese authorities and expatriate Chinese merchants to hire them for missions overseas. As they did so, sea lords of the Setonaikai impacted the wider East Asian maritime world and became incorporated into the mutable category of "Japanese pirates," conceptions of which spread and evolved as a result of maritime encounters. Japanese seafarers interacted with Chinese and Korean travelers, who conveyed representations of those encounters to the scholar-officials who translated and grafted images of "Japanese pirates" onto human and physical geographies. The concept of "Japanese pirate" thus became an evolving marker of regionality for the East Asian maritime world that was created, transformed, and shared through intercultural exchange. Sea-lord bands caused their own incorporation into the concept of "Japanese pirates" through encounters with Korean ambassadors and contributions to both accepted and rejected tribute trade embassies with China. In Korea and China, reports, chronicles, travelogues, and other writings inscribed sea lords as Japanese pirates and their home waters between Akamagaseki and Kyoto as a piratical space.

Sea lords capitalized on the need by the Muromachi bakufu, provincial governors, and the Korean ambassadors for protection and manipulated patronage networks in order to enhance their own protection enterprises. Sea lords interacted with the envoys themselves and secured commercial connections with Hakata merchants and others involved in trade with Chosŏn. These contacts enabled sea lords to exert indirect influence over the shape of Japanese-Korean relations. The various sponsors of imposter embassies, the Sō family, and others kept memories of the threat from Inland Sea-based Japanese pirates alive in Chosŏn official memory for their own ends.

Sea lords participated in tributary embassy sent to Ming China in myriad ways both violent and peaceful. Sea lords helped construct, outfit, and sail the ships. They also engaged in "protection" for the missions. Sea lords and other participants on many of these embassies perpetrated acts of violence. These varied contributions contributed to a tendency among Chinese officials to conflate members of Japan's embassies with pirates. Tally-trade patronage also afforded sea-lord bands opportunities to make contacts with Chinese expatriate merchants like Wang Zhi, who sought mercenaries for their raiding and trading expeditions in China. Mid-sixteenth-century envoys to Japan who sought to reduce the threat from "Japanese pirates" by winning the support of daimyo and promising an amelioration of trade restrictions brought back firsthand accounts of the strength of "pirates" in the waterways of the Inland Sea.

For Inland Sea sea-lord bands, participation in this wider maritime world brought the outside world into the estates, islands, ports, lodges, and shipyards of their domains, binding common as well as elite mariners to the rest of East Asia. Interaction did take the forms of violence, protection from that violence, and language of violence, but sea-lord bands also showed that they had some mastery of nonviolent forms of intercultural exchange: especially trade and hospitality. Through an exploration of these interactions it becomes possible to see how Inland Sea-based seafarers could affect and even at times manipulate how others saw them in order to expand their own influence. In doing so, they helped shape the concept of "Japanese pirate" that Chinese and Korean officials used to define the peoples and spaces of the East Asian maritime world.

CHAPTER 6

Taming Leviathan: The Transformations of Sea Lords in Early Modern Japan

Early modern states are often credited with achieving unprecedented degrees of "political integration," "administrative centralization," and "regulation of . . . daily life."[1] However, the powers of these states tended to weaken when their agents took to the seas, which rendered the suppression of pirates a difficult process. In many regions around the world, the strength of pirates' autonomy enabled them to insist that states accommodate their interests and grant them concessions before they would submit. It took offers of blanket pardons and privateering commissions as much as threats of nooses and cannonballs to convince Caribbean buccaneers and Atlantic pirates to accede to English law. In order to subdue the successive "waves of pirates" that came to dominate China's southeast coast, emperors in the Ming and Qing dynasties eased trade restrictions and hired pirates as naval forces. Even upon receipt of a letter of marque or other form of commission, privateers and other hired naval experts retained considerable latitude to act as they saw fit.[2]

The elimination of pirates in early modern Japanese waters necessitated that similar accommodations be made to seafarers. Like much else in early modern Japan (ca. 1590–1800), the disappearance of pirates needs to be located along the continuum between powers aspired to or claimed by the early modern Japanese hegemons and the extent to which those powers were actually exercised in local reaches of the archipelago.[3] It is common to enumerate

---

1. Victor Lieberman, "Transcending East-West Dichotomies: State and Culture Formation in Six Ostensibly Disparate Areas," *Modern Asian Studies* 31.3 (1997): 473, 474, 480.
2. Janice Thomson, *Pirates, Mercenaries, and Sovereigns: State Building and Extraterritorial Violence in Early Modern Europe* (Princeton, N.J.: Princeton University Press, 1994), chs. 2–3. This pattern repeated itself several times across the Ming and Qing Dynasties, beginning with figures like Wang Zhi seen in chapter five, continuing with sea lords like Zheng Zhilong and Zheng Chenggong, and culminating with the surrender of the woman pirate known to us as Zheng Yi Sao in 1810. For a comparative synthesis of these successive "waves of piracy," see Robert J. Antony, *Like Froth Floating on the Sea: The World of Pirates and Seafarers in Late Imperial South China* (Berkeley: University of California, Berkeley Institute of East Asian Studies, 2003), ch. 2.
3. This continuum has been well explored in English-language scholarship: Philip C. Brown, *Central Authority and Local Autonomy in the Formation of Early Modern Japan: The Case of Kaga Domain* (Stanford, Calif.: Stanford University Press, 1993); Mark Ravina, *Land and Lordship in Early Modern Japan* (Stanford, Calif: Stanford University Press, 1999); Luke Roberts, *Mercantilism in*

the eradication of pirates as one of the achievements of Japan's early modern unifiers, the warlords Toyotomi Hideyoshi (1537–98) and Tokugawa Ieyasu (1543–1616). After the death of Hideyoshi, Ieyasu and his heirs established an enduring shogunal regime that ruled Japan for more than two centuries. Other historians have credited the ability of coastal domainal lords to channel retainers' piratical tendencies into more salubrious activities like smuggling, trade, intercultural mediation, and coastal defense.[5]

This chapter intertwines the histories of two powerful sea-lord bands of the Seto Inland Sea, the Noshima Murakami and the Kurushima Murakami in the late sixteenth and early seventeenth centuries in order to explore the unification of Japan from the waterline. It demonstrates that the oft-noted absence of pirates in the seas of early modern Japan owed less to military suppression or particular edicts by the unifiers and more to dialogue, negotiation, and compromise with sea lords; transformations in linguistic, legal, and symbolic realms, including redefinitions of piracy; and, during the seventeenth and eighteenth centuries, considerable historical invention.

Compromise was necessary because sea lords and the various land-based daimyo vying for hegemony held mutually incompatible views regarding the degree to which seafarers could legitimately territorialize the sea and deploy naval violence.[6] Sea lords like Noshima Murakami Takeyoshi (1533–1604) and Kurushima Murakami Michifusa (1561–97) inherited from two centuries of sea-lord ancestors a vision of the sea as a space consisting of maritime networks of production, distribution, exchange, transportation, and protection all under their autonomous dominion. Their worldview was one in which oceangoing commerce and other sea travel required protection and in which protection and other forms of violence could be mar-

a Japanese Domain: The Merchant Origins of Economic Nationalism in 18th-Century Tosa (Cambridge: Cambridge University Press, 1998); Luke S. Roberts, Performing the Great Peace: Political Space and Open Secrets in Tokugawa Japan (Honolulu: University of Hawai'i Press, 2012); Ronald P. Toby, "Review Article: Rescuing the Nation from History: The State of the State in Early Modern Japan," Monumenta Nipponica 56.2 (2001): 197–237.

4. Although Mary Elizabeth Berry argues that accommodation and compromise proved essential for Hideyoshi's unification on land, she and other English-language historians have tended to explain the elimination of pirates as an abrupt, top-down process (Mary Elizabeth Berry, Hideyoshi (Cambridge, Mass.: Harvard University Press, 1982), pp. 133–34, ch. 6; Jurgis Elisonas, "The Inseparable Trinity: Japan's Relations with China and Korea," in The Cambridge History of Japan vol. 4: Early Modern Japan, edited by John W. Hall et al. (Cambridge: Cambridge University Press, 1991), pp. 262–65).

5. Robert Hellyer, "Poor but Not Pirates: The Tsushima Domain and Foreign Relations in Early Modern Japan," in Elusive Pirates, Pervasive Smugglers: Violence and Clandestine Trade in the Greater China Seas, edited by Robert J. Antony (Hong Kong: Hong Kong University Press, 2010), pp. 115–26.

6. Kishida Hiroshi, Daimyo ryōgoku no keizai kōzō (Iwanami Shoten, 2001), pp. 366, 383.

keted as commercial services. As they negotiated terms of sponsorship with Hideyoshi and other daimyo, the Noshima and Kurushima imparted this interpretation of maritime lordship. In return for providing naval expertise, sea lords sought to continue to independently engage in mercenarism, exercise violence, conquer and consolidate domains, and establish and operate protection businesses and other enterprises. They tempered their demands by presenting themselves in ways patrons found familiar and comforting— as land-based warrior lords, not alien sea people. Sea lords bolstered their claims to lordship by code switching and using land-based titles, symbols, and deeds of confirmation. Proficiency in cultural forms valued in land-based elite society, such as linked-verse poetry, the tea ceremony, and even kickball (*kemari*), aided such endeavors.[7]

For their part, the unifiers embraced worldviews dating back to the seventh-century Ritsuryō period that viewed the sea as an appendage subordinate to the head of state on land. Although this worldview ostensibly treated sea-lord autonomy as anathema, until unification was achieved, Hideyoshi and other warlords relied on sea lords to carry and protect trade and to fight sea battles. By necessity they acknowledged the maritime dominion of sea lords and accepted their enterprising combinations of commerce and violence. In fact, by continuing to engage in warfare, mercenarism, and protection businesses through the 1580s, right up to the eve of unification, the Noshima Murakami and Kurushima Murakami safeguarded their late medieval reputations as powerful warriors and naval experts and ensured that their demands remained on the busy policy agendas of land-based hegemons.

Sea lords tended not to oppose integration into the unified land-based realm because Hideyoshi's conquests in western Japan in the late 1580s rendered protection enterprises, mercenarism, and other such ventures unprofitable. Instead, after Hideyoshi militarily imposed his will on Shikoku and Kyushu, sea lords like the Noshima and Kurushima exploited their skills in code switching as land-based warrior lords and their naval expertise to convince Hideyoshi and other warlords, notably Mōri Terumoto (1553–1625), to accept them as integral parts of the confraternity of warrior lords and retainers that would rule and administer unified Japan. The histories of the Noshima and the Kurushima in the late sixteenth and early seventeenth centuries illustrate two different courses that sea lords might sail into the early modern period. The Noshima Murakami became powerful warrior retainers of a domainal lord (daimyo), the Mōri, whereas the Kurushima Murakami won acceptance as minor domainal lords under first the Toyotomi and later the Tokugawa.

---

7. See chapter 3.

In exchange for being treated as land-based warrior lords and retainers, former sea lords were compelled to take on the land-centered, warrior aspects their titles and status implied. They were called on to tether the sea and seafarers to the territories of the domains and the wider realm of Japan. Only after major "pirate" bands like the Noshima and Kurushima accepted their positions as lords and retainers did Hideyoshi issue edicts that redefined pirates and that used the suppression of those pirates to extend sovereignty to the seas near and far. Former sea-lord houses initially found their naval prowess in demand for controlling the littoral population, subduing the newly redefined pirates, and leading naval forces for the unifiers as well as domainal lords.

But former sea-lord families lost their late medieval maritime domains and the capabilities that derived from that autonomous dominion. Sea lords could no longer entrepreneurially develop commercial maritime enterprises—violent or peaceful—deploy naval violence at will, move mercenary-like between patrons, control the shape and direction of naval technology, or participate freely in the cosmopolitan overseas world as raiders and traders. In addition, the Toyotomi and Tokugawa adopted Chinese visions of diplomacy and trade that required former sea-lord houses and other mariners to help separate out acts of and threats of violence from commercial ventures.

The integration of the formerly autonomous, nonstate maritime world into the terrestrial territory of the domain and the wider realm was a prolonged process that extended into the early decades of Tokugawa rule. Integration eventually caused changes in the ways in which Japanese perceived and remembered pirates, and by extension the late medieval maritime environment, as terracentric and agricentric attitudes revived in early modern Japan. Complicit in this process, former sea-lord houses bolstered and legitimized their early modern presence as warrior lords and domainal retainers by inventing pasts as pirates and loyal vassals as well as by transferring emblems of nautical authority over to the unifiers and other daimyo.

SEA LORDS AMONG THE UNIFIERS: 1578-88

For the Noshima Murakami and the Kurushima Murakami the coalescing of daimyo power blocs in the 1570s and 1580s did not signify imminent unification as hindsight might suggest. Instead, the emergence of powerful warlords like Mōri Terumoto, Oda Nobunaga (1534–82), Hashiba (later Toyotomi) Hideyoshi and alliances like the anti-Nobunaga coalition meant that sea lords could ask for more in recompense by playing one side against another. Although the number of potential sponsors decreased, those sponsors needed sea-lord naval services more than ever as the scale of war increased. Patrons were willing to pay handsomely for services such as fighting naval battles, blockading the Inland Sea or delivering provisions to besieged citadels.

Contacts between sea lords of the Inland Sea and the Oda extended back to 1569 or so,[8] but significant interactions did not occur until the Kizu River estuary campaigns between 1576 and 1578.[9] In addition, in 1578, Hideyoshi began leading Oda forces westward from the capital in order to reduce the capabilities of the Mōri and other western daimyo to resupply the Honganji citadel.[10] To support their invasion of Mōri territory, Oda forces gradually brought the islands of Shōdoshima and Awajishima under their control. Nobunaga sponsored the maritime forces there, along with sea lords like Kuki Yoshitaka (1542–1600), to attack sea lords sponsored by the Mōri.[11] By the spring of 1582, Hideyoshi had advanced into Mōri territories in Bitchū Province. While the forces of Mōri Terumoto and his allies worked to blunt this strike on land, the Noshima Murakami, Kurushima Murakami, and other sea-lord houses provided naval auxiliaries and blockades.

However, sea-lord bands also perceived the conflict between the Mōri bloc and the Oda bloc as an excellent opportunity to enhance their autonomous dominion by considering offers from both sides. While defying pro-Oda forces at sea in the spring of 1582, the Noshima Murakami, Kurushima Murakami, and other sea-lord bands entertained a flurry of offers from Hideyoshi to accept Oda patronage. Concurrent with his westward push, Hideyoshi initiated an epistolary campaign with those sea lords that defeated the Oda forces in 1576 at the Kizu River estuary, particularly the Noshima Murakami, Kurushima Murakami, and Nomi.[12] The Noshima and the Kurushima houses exchanged correspondence with the Oda to the point that Mōri leaders warned their subordinates of the great danger posed by the possibility of the Noshima Murakami or Kurushima Murakami houses switching sides: "Do not be careless about the coastal forces."[13]

Initially, the high commands of the Kurushima Murakami and the Noshima Murakami did not agree completely on which side to support. The

8. *Zōtei Oda Nobunaga monjo no kenkyū*, vol. 2, edited by Okuno Takahiro (Yoshikawa Kōbunkan, 1988), hoi doc. 21, Eiroku 12? (1569) 10.26.
9. For details, see chapter four.
10. *Wakayama-ken shi chūsei shiryō*, vol. 2 (Wakayama-shi: Wakayama-ken, 1983), p. 422, doc. 3, Tenshō 6? (1578) 3.8.
11. Hashizume Shigeru, *Setonaikai chiiki shakai to Oda kenryoku* (Shibunkaku, 2007), pp. 301–4.
12. Yamauchi Yuzuru, *Setouchi no kaizoku: Murakami Takeyoshi no tatakai* (Kōdansha, 2005), pp. 111, 118–20.
13. EK doc. 2277, Tenshō 10? (1582) 4.5.

practice of a house dividing among opposing factions had become a prac tice of long standing by the sixteenth century.[14] The head of the Kurushim Murakami band, Michifusa, favored accepting the Oda offers. Michifus also counted on the marriage between his sister and Noshima Murakam Takeyoshi to sway the Noshima. Takeyoshi's heir, Motoyoshi, does seem t have indicated a desire follow his mother's family, which may have height ened tensions within the Noshima house.[15]

In addition, the leaders of the Noshima and Kurushima exploited th differences within their houses as a prod to extract concessions from th Mōri. The Mōri interpreted mercenary inclinations among the Noshima an Kurushima houses as the result of "not resolving differences with the tw islands [Noshima and Kurushima],"[16] as a "failure to take sufficient care."[1] So, when Terumoto "received word of angry exchanges between Noshim Murakami Motoyoshi and members [of the Noshima] house," Terumot ordered the immediate dispatch of an express messenger with gifts and folded-paper edict.[18] Patrons often used such forms of edicts to bestow to exemptions and other privileges. In addition, Terumoto's uncle, Kobaya kawa Takakage, who usually took charge of negotiating with sea lords fo the Mōri, dispatched representatives from other sea-lord bands in the Mōr patronage web to try and convince the Noshima and Kurushima lords of th benefits that would ensue if they remained with the Mōri.[19]

Rejecting the rewards offered by the Mōri, early in the fourth month o 1582, the head of the Kurushima Murakami, Michifusa, agreed to join th Oda.[20] This decision splintered the Kurushima Murakami house and frac tured the Mōri's maritime defensive perimeter. Not all of the Kurushim followed Michifusa. Close retainers of Michifusa, Murakami Yoshitsug and Murakami Yoshisato, led some members of the Kurushima band t serve the Mōri.[21] Although documentation of the negotiations with Hideyo shi does not survive, later events suggest that Michifusa bound Hideyosh to a promise to confirm and enforce the Kurushima Murakami's status as

14. For the fourteenth century, see Thomas D. Conlan, *State of War: The Violent Order of Fourteenth Century Japan*, Michigan Monograph Series in Japanese Studies, no. 46 (Ann Arbor: Center fo Japanese Studies, The University of Michigan, 2003), p. 35.

15. Nishio Kazumi, *Sengokuki no kenryoku to kon'in* (Seibundō, 2005), pp. 196–203; Yamauchi, *Setou chi no kaizoku*, pp. 115–16.

16. EK doc. 2278, Tenshō 10? (1582) 4.7.

17. See the letter from Mōri Terumoto to Ninomiya Naritatsu quoted in Yamauchi, *Setouchi n kaizoku*, pp. 115–16.

18. Ibid.

19. EK doc. 2278, Tenshō 10? (1582) 4.7.

20. EK doc. 2299, Tenshō 10? (1582) 4.20.

21. Yamauchi, *Setouchi no kaizoku*, p. 117.

major maritime power in the waters off of Iyo. The Kurushima Murakami also anticipated reaping the benefits of commerce raiding and other violence that would eventuate, gaining license from the Oda to attack Noshima and Mōri shipping. Soon after switching to the Oda, the Kurushima prepared to assault strategic littoral points of the Mōri domain, including Itsukushima, which contained both important centers of worship as well as a port and marketplace key to the region's economy.[22] Kurushima Michifusa's decision to switch patrons weakened the Mōri's ability to withstand Oda advances. A cousin and close retainer of Mōri Terumoto remarked bitterly, "this expedition of Hashiba's [Hideyoshi's] depended entirely on gaining the aid of that offshore house [i.e., the Kurushima Murakami]."[23]

Noshima Murakami Takeyoshi exploited the sense of crisis driven into the Mōri by Kurushima Murakami Michifusa's decision to change sponsors. Takeyoshi kept the lines of communication open with both the Mōri and with the Oda and delayed a final decision so as to secure the best deal that would ensure his band's autonomy on the seas. Ten days or so after Kurushima's switch, Noshima Murakami Takeyoshi and Motoyoshi received multiple letters from Hideyoshi. In an attempt to weaken Noshima connections with the Mōri, Hideyoshi predicted the imminent defeat of the Mōri, describing the ease with which he had begun to push back the Mōri's eastern flank. He also enjoined the Noshima lords to "devote yourself to the public authority [Nobunaga], heedless of any private concerns."[24]

By positioning themselves between the Mōri and the Oda, the Noshima and Kurushima received rewards and retained autonomy. At the same time, by agreeing to negotiate, these sea lords also made possible acts of what historian Yamauchi Yuzuru has called "information warfare" by Hideyoshi.[25] In a series of letters to other powerful regional lords in western and central Japan, Hideyoshi presented himself as master of the seas and exaggerated the degree to which he had incorporated the famous sea lords Noshima and Kurushima. For example, in a letter to the Uehara, a warlord in Bitchū Province and ally of the Mōri, Hideyoshi bragged that "Shiwaku, Noshima, and Kurushima have been ordered to send hostages and at once surrender their castles."[26] Such propaganda may have contributed to the Uehara

---

22. EK doc. 2299, Tenshō 10? (1582) 4.20.
23. EK doc. 2301, Tenshō 10? (1582) 4.24.
24. EK doc. 2296, Tenshō 10? (1582) 4.19; Yamauchi, *Setouchi no kaizoku*, pp. 112–13.
25. Yamauchi, *Setouchi no kaizoku*, p. 120.
26. *Shinpen Marugame-shi shi*, vol. 4: *Shiryō-hen* (Marugame-shi, Kagawa-ken: *Marugame-shi Shi Hensan Iinkai*, 1994), doc. 156, Tenshō 10? (1582) 4.24. Hideyoshi sent a letter with similar boasts to the Mizoe of Ōmi (Hashizume, *Setonaikai chiiki shakai to Oda kenryoku*, p. 308; Yamauchi, *Setouchi no kaizoku*, p. 120).

decision to join Hideyoshi a month after receiving the letter.[27] Such propa
ganda likely drew on Hideyoshi's ambitions to eliminate sea-lord domain
and claim lordship over the seas for the Oda. By having sea lords surrende
their castles, Hideyoshi would have eliminated the hold of the Noshima anc
Kurushima over chokepoints from which they administered protection en
terprises, shipping concerns, and other maritime networks. However, it i
likely that in 1582 Hideyoshi's ambitions were tempered by an awarenes
that he desperately needed sea-lord services.

At this point, if they knew of Hideyoshi's propaganda, the sea lords ig
nored it as bluster. They were cognizant of the advantage that they possessec
in negotiations. By drawing out the negotiations before choosing to remai
in service to the Mōri, the Noshima Murakami succeeded in extracting sig
nificant rewards. In contrast to Hideyoshi's boasts about taking hostages
the threat of facing both the Noshima Murakami and the Kurushima Mura
kami in league with the Oda convinced the Mōri to return hostages sent b
the Noshima to Mōri Terumoto in the 1570s.[28] The Noshima Murakami no
only preserved control of chokepoints and castles but also secured legiti
mate title to an increased sphere of maritime control. Although it is not clea
how much the Mōri knew of competing offers from Hideyoshi, Kobayakaw.
Takakage sent a counteroffer to the Noshima the day after Hideyoshi sen
his letters. In his epistle, Kobayakawa Takakage endorsed the requests fo
confirmation of additional littoral holdings submitted by the Noshima lords
Takeyoshi and Motoyoshi: "Your single-hearted loyalty is without compare
Thus, regarding the list of 'lands' that you requested . . . Terumoto is makin
the arrangements now."[29] It took generous rewards such as these from th
Mōri, as well as gifts from the Kōno, warrior provincial governors of Iyo anc
a part of the Mōri bloc, to enable Takeyoshi to convince his son Motoyosh
and the other Noshima Murakami to remain with the Mōri.[30]

This "list of lands" awarded to the Noshima included Kurushima Mura
kami territories. The move by the Kurushima Murakami presented th
Noshima Murakami and other Mōri-sponsored sea-lord bands a whol
new array of targets for legitimate raiding: Kurushima shipping and Kuru
shima holdings. After an initial naval setback against the Kurushima,[31] th

27. Yamauchi, *Setouchi no kaizoku,* p. 121.
28. *Miyakubo-chō shi* (Miyakubo-chō, Ehime-ken: Miyakubo-chō, 1994), p. 1125, doc. 159, Tensh
    11? (1583) 3.1; ibid., p. 1126, doc. 164, Tenshō 11? (1583) 6.28; EK doc. 2390, Tenshō 11? (1583) 6.:
29. EK doc. 2300, Tenshō 10? (1582) 4.20; as chapter three explained, the Mōri used the term "lands
    to refer to both littoral and inland holdings.
30. Nishio, *Sengokuki no kenryoku to kon'in,* pp. 198–99.
31. EK doc. 2301, Tenshō 10? (1582) 4.24.

Noshima Murakami led an assault on the island fortress of Kurushima it-self, which they put to the torch in the sixth month of 1582.[32] From Kuru-shima, a combined fleet composed of the Noshima and other Mōri-affiliated sea lords sailed to defeat the Kurushima fleet in a battle off the coast of the large nearby island of Iyo Ōshima.[33] Eager for control over more islands and sea routes, the Noshima Murakami reveled in the conquest and consolida-tion of former Kurushima littoral holdings such as the Kutsuna Islands.[34] In turn, the Kurushima launched counterattacks, thus sparking a feud that lasted from the spring of 1582 until the return of the Kurushima Murakami to central Inland Sea waters under the aegis of Hideyoshi in 1585.

The success of the Noshima Murakami's strategy of prolonging negotia-tions is also evident in the apparently unsolicited and unreciprocated receipt by the Noshima of oaths (*kishōmon*) in which Mōri commanders expressed their relief and gratitude by swearing to support Noshima interests. The use of an oath in this way contravened precedents for the ways in which *kishōmon* were usually employed in interactions between sea lords and sponsors. *Kishōmon* were employed in diverse ways in late medieval Japan, from cementing the bonds between members of leagues of common cause, to swearing oaths of fealty, to providing testimony to a shogunal court.[35] The Noshima Murakami and the Mōri occasionally exchanged oaths as a way to record mutual obligations.[36] But in the spring of 1582, high-ranking retain-ers of a higher status house and patron (the Mōri) swore to represent the in-terests of the heads of a house of clients of lower status (Noshima Murakami Takeyoshi and Motoyoshi). For example, just two or three days after the Kurushima switch, writing on behalf of Kobayakawa Takakage and Mōri Terumoto, Nomi Munekatsu sent a signed oath that thanked Takeyoshi and Motoyoshi for not abandoning the Mōri, while at the same time recognizing and tacitly accepting the Noshima strategy of delay by highlighting sympa-thy that the Noshima may have had for the Kurushima.[37] Munekatsu prom-ised that Takakage would represent them whenever necessary to ensure that every possible concern of the Noshima Murakami would be addressed. The oath left unspecified any discussion of reward, leaving that for the Noshima to decide.

32. EK doc. 2309, Tenshō 10? (1582) 5.9.
33. EK doc. 2310, Tenshō 10 (1582) 5.19; EK doc. 2440:3, Tenshō 10 (1582) 5.19; EK doc. 2440:4, Tenshō 10 (1582) 6.30.
34. EK doc. 2302, Tenshō 10 (1582) 4.25.
35. Satō Shin'ichi, *Shinpen komonjogaku nyūmon* (Hōsei Daigaku Shuppankyoku, 1997), pp. 220–36.
36. See chapter 3.
37. Yamauchi, *Setouchi no kaizoku*, p. 113.

- In regards to this past incident, although you feel sympathy for the Kuru-shima, Takeyoshi's decision to continue providing loyal, single-hearted service for Terumoto and Takakage fulfills our most fervent hopes.
- From now on, when Takakage acts as intermediary, he will not shrink from standing for you in return for your providing services for us.
- Whenever your house has a concern, it will not be ignored.

If we are dishonest in even the slightest degree about any of the above, it will be clearly witnessed by Hachiman Daibosatsu, Itsukushima Daimyōjin of this province, and Mishima Daimyōjin of your province.[38]

In continuity with the case of the earlier oaths, these *kishōmon* also appeal to great sea gods of the Inland Sea region, which may have signified the value that both patron and sea lord placed in the Noshima's maritime expertise and dominion. The Noshima highlighted their control of this stage of the patronage relationship by not responding in kind.

Instead, possession of these eloquent pledges enabled the Noshima Murakami to exert considerable pressure on Mōri leaders, especially after the assassination of Oda Nobunaga by Akechi Mitsuhide on 1582.6.1, which impelled Hideyoshi to invite Terumoto to sign a truce a scant three days later. Only in hindsight does this cease-fire become a significant harbinger of unification.[39] Nevertheless, both Terumoto and Hideyoshi worked to strengthen their fragile peace against the potential riptides unleashed by the feud of the Noshima Murakami and Kurushima Murakami, who each pushed their respective patrons to legitimize raids and counterraids. Sea lords felt little obligation to abide by the agreements of their patrons in this period, when aspiring hegemons found it difficult to limit even close retainers' self-redress of injury.[40]

A few days after signing the truce with Hideyoshi, Terumoto wrote to Noshima Murakami Takeyoshi in order to inform him of the assassination and cease-fire and to request that the Noshima refrain from attacking Oda shipping.[41] The truce thus abrogated the blockade of Oda ships that had been in place since 1579. To offset the loss in plunder, the Noshima Murakami and other sea lords forced Terumoto to sanction their conquest of additional Kurushima holdings on nearby islands such as Yashirojima, Nōmijima,

---

38. EK doc. 2282, Tenshō 10? (1582) 4.11.
39. Berry credits the "remarkable cordiality of" the relationship between Kobayakawa Takakage and Hideyoshi as a key ingredient for the success of the peace accord (Berry, *Hideyoshi*, p. 73).
40. Katsumata Shizuo, "The Development of Sengoku Law," with Martin Collcutt, in *Japan Before Tokugawa: Political Consolidation and Economic Growth, 1500 to 1650*, edited by John W. Hall et al. (Princeton, N.J.: Princeton University Press, 1981), pp. 105–9.
41. EK doc. 2313, Tenshō 10? (1582) 6.8.

Iwagijima, and Yugeshima.[42] The last was well known as a salt-producing center and shipping port as well as a former estate and territory that the Noshima had coveted since the fifteenth century.

In turn, the Kurushima forces raided Noshima settlements and ships as retaliation for Noshima occupation of Kurushima holdings throughout 1583 and into 1584.[43] The Kurushima also required the restitution of their domain in Iyo as a condition for continuing to provide services for Hideyoshi. Although Fujita Tatsuo argues that Hideyoshi saw in the fulfillment of the Kurushima's terms an opportunity to further extend sovereignty over the seas,[44] Hideyoshi's actions also suggest that he felt the need to placate his sea-lord clients.

The degree to which patrons felt it necessary to placate their sea-lord clients caused the Noshima-Kurushima feud to ratchet up tensions between Terumoto and Hideyoshi, just when the two patrons were beginning to normalize relations beyond a cease-fire. For example, in the sixth month of 1584, as the Mōri dispatched hostages to Hideyoshi as a guarantee of good faith in preparation for a more permanent peace,[45] the Mōri called on the Noshima to restrain themselves from striking back against the Kurushima. Kobayakawa Takakage wrote to Noshima Murakami Takeyoshi and Motoyoshi: "Members of the Kurushima gang have been making raids against your islands since last year. You have forborn with admirable patience, and we must ask that you not stop being patient at this time."[46] By the tenth month of 1584, the Kurushima had pressured Hideyoshi sufficiently that he sent messengers to a high-ranking retainer of Mōri Terumoto named Ankokuji Ekei (1539–1600) to orchestrate the return of the Kurushima to Iyo.[47] Once he received Hideyoshi's instructions, Mōri Terumoto had to demonstrate to Hideyoshi that he was sincerely making a good faith effort to do so in order for Hideyoshi to support Mōri claims to western Honshu and Shikoku.[48] However, despite promises to Hideyoshi, in order to ensure continued services by the Noshima, Mōri Terumoto dissembled and promised the opposite: "Given the pacification of capital and countryside, doubtless you have heard rumors that the Kurushima will be returning to Iyo. Please

42. EK doc. 2314, Tenshō 10? (1582) 6.19; EK doc. 2365, Tenshō 10? (1582) 12.18; EK doc. 2366, Tenshō 10? (1582) 12.18; EK doc. 2333, Tenshō 10? (1582) 9.1; YK, vol. 2, pp.116–17, doc. 3, Tenshō 12 (1584) 10.6.
43. EK doc. 2415, Tenshō 12? (1584) 6.20.
44. Fujita Tatsuo, *Nihon kinsei kokka seiritsushi no kenkyū* (Azekura Shobō, 2001), p. 53.
45. DNS, ser. 11, vol. 7, p. 512; DNS, ser. 11, vol. 9, p. 15; Berry, *Hideyoshi*, pp. 81–82.
46. EK doc. 2415, Tenshō 12? (1584) 6.20.
47. EK doc. 1434, Tenshō 12? (1584) 10.18.
48. Fujita, *Nihon kinsei kokka seiritsushi no kenkyū*, pp. 30–31.

rest assured that there is no way we would permit that to occur."[49] As if to help make Terumoto's pretense a reality, in the eleventh month of 1584, the Kurushima struck Noshima holdings in the Kutsuna Islands, inviting further Noshima retaliation.[50]

In early 1585, the Noshima captains exerted further pressure on the Mōri to allow them to expand militarily and to keep their new littoral holdings because Hideyoshi, working through the Mōri, required the Noshima to relinquish control over a keystone of their domain, the island of Shiwaku. As a result of Noshima administration, Shiwaku had become an important port, dockyard, hostelry, and barrier, a central hub in the transportation infrastructure of the archipelago. Hideyoshi sought to remove it from the Noshima's domainal networks in order to harness its shipping for the conquest of Shikoku and Kyushu. He assigned it to a trusted vassal, Konishi Yukinaga (1555–1600).[51] In return, the Noshima added part of the Dōgo coast on the northwest peninsula of Iyo to their domain. This holding came with a commission to defend that peninsula against the invading forces of Chōsokabe Motochika, who sought to conquer Shikoku.[52] In early 1585 the Noshima Murakami took advantage of their expanding foothold on the Dōgo coast to seize further littoral territory from the Kurushima.[53]

However, in the second month of 1585, as Hideyoshi began to make plans for his summer invasion of Shikoku, he ordered the Mōri to make possible the Kurushima's return. To reassure the Noshima Murakami, Kobayakawa Takakage and Nomi Munekatsu resorted to sending the Noshima more unreciprocated oaths. They again invoked maritime deities, swore that they had no choice but to obey Hideyoshi's decisions, and promised to represent Noshima interests with Hideyoshi if only the Noshima would stop fighting with the Kurushima: "Hideyoshi has ordered that Kurushima Michimasa [Michifusa] return home. We had no recourse but to accept the order. Naturally, if Michimasa plans any sort of violence again, we will ac-

49. EK doc. 2441, Tenshō 12? (1584) 11.11.
50. Yamauchi Yuzuru, *Kaizoku to umijiro: Setouchi no sengokushi* (Heibonsha, 1997), p. 59.
51. The process by which Hideyoshi acquired Shiwaku is unclear. However, a letter by a Jesuit who visited Shiwaku in the summer of 1585 states that Shiwaku had been granted to Konishi in order to prepare for the invasion of Shikoku (Yamauchi Yuzuru, *Chūsei Setonaikai chiikishi no kenkyū* (Hōsei Daigaku Shuppankyoku, 1997), p. 185; Yamauchi, *Kaizoku to umijiro*, p. 163). Shiwaku continued to be a major shipping center in the Edo period (*Shiwaku ninmyō kyōyū monjo*, in *Shinpen Kagawa sōsho shiryō-hen*, vol. 2 (Takamatsu-shi: Kagawa-ken Kyōikuiinkai, 1981), pp. 431–38.
52. EK doc. 2444, Tenshō 12 (1584) 12.21. This peninsula contained the political and economic center of Iyo and was the last part of Iyo remaining outside of Chōsokabe control (EK doc. 2460, Tenshō 13? [1585] 5.18 and 5.26).
53. EK doc. 2448, Tenshō 13? (1585) 2.9; EK doc. 2451, Tenshō 13? (1585) 2.17. The Noshima pushed from Higashinojō in Fuchū to the hamlet of Nakanogō (EK doc. 2444, Tenshō 12 [1584] 12.21).

according to the previous discussion. We hereby promise not to ignore you three, father and sons, and that we will stand with you."[54]

The strife between the Noshima Murakami and the Kurushima Murakami only ended after Hideyoshi secured the surrender of the Chōsokabe in the seventh month of 1585. This conquest of Shikoku brought much of the Inland Sea littoral within Hideyoshi's jurisdiction, and he included the Noshima and Kurushima sea-lord bands in his postinvasion redistribution of territories. The Noshima-Kurushima conflict—and the maritime autonomy that made it possible—contradicted the ambitions of Hideyoshi and Terumoto to pacify the seas and threatened the viability of the cease-fire. However, by continuing their feud until it became unprofitable to continue, the Kurushima Murakami and the Noshima Murakami gained the ability to negotiate from a position of strength and demand recognition as warrior lords. The ongoing need of both Hideyoshi and Terumoto for sea-lord services caused both to accept a certain degree of independent action by seafarers.

The strong positions of sea-lord bands like the Kurushima and the Noshima in the negotiations after the conquest of Shikoku are evident in the degree to which they convinced Hideyoshi and Terumoto to uphold their claims to maritime dominion. Hideyoshi nominally moved toward eliminating the threat posed by sea-lord independence by treating their chokepoint-based fastnesses like the fortifications of other warlords: he began to order them surrendered as part of a larger policy of pacification through castle demolition (*shirowari*).[55] Sea lords constructed sea castles as the nerve centers of their domains and as fortifications in chokepoints that enabled protection businesses and sea tenure. Hideyoshi explicitly identified such sea-castle and toll-barrier installations as a threat to his plans to assert jurisdiction over the seas. By the fall of 1585, Hideyoshi had granted much of the newly captured province of Iyo to Kobayakawa Takakage[56] and ordered him to arrange for various local elites to relinquish and destroy unnecessary castles.[57] In the fourth month of 1586, he ordered Mōri Terumoto to craft domainal laws that "reduced unnecessary castles" and "interdicted toll barriers on sea and land."[58] In spite of such efforts, remaining records from this process of castle demolition suggest that sea lords proved themselves too

54. EK doc. 2449, Tenshō 13 (1585) 2.10. See also EK doc. 2454, Tenshō 13 (1585) 2.23.
55. Fujita, *Nihon kinsei kokka seiritsushi no kenkyū*, p. 157. For more on *shirowari*, see Berry, *Hideyoshi*, pp. 132–33.
56. Berry, *Hideyoshi*, pp. 83–84.
57. EK doc. 2484, Tenshō 13? (1585) int. 8.14; EK doc. 2487, Tenshō 13? (1585) 9.29.
58. DNK 8, *Mōri-ke monjo*, vol. 3, pp. 227–28, doc. 949, Tenshō 14 (1586) 4.10; Fujiki Hisashi, *Toyotomi heiwarei to sengoku shakai* (Tokyo Daigaku Shuppankai, 1985), pp. 220–22; Fujita, *Nihon kinsei kokka seiritsushi no kenkyū*, pp. 156–57; Kishida, *Daimyo ryōgoku no keizai kōzō*, p. 366.

CHAPTER 6

important for Hideyoshi or the Mōri to completely dismantle Noshima and Kurushima power bases, leading to compromises.

Although obliged to Hideyoshi for returning them to prominent positions in Iyo, the Kurushima Murakami's ability to represent themselves as warrior lords with special expertise in naval matters—to code switch—convinced Hideyoshi that they were worthy of preservation. Although he denied their autonomous maritime lordship, Hideyoshi did not deny that these pirates, these sea lords, had a right to domains. By forcing sea lords to live up to their self-portrayals as land-based lords, Hideyoshi found a way to turn sea wolves into sea dogs: to retain their valuable naval services and keep them under control.

Instead of appreciating definitions of wealth tied to the strategic value of chokepoints or the potential commercial value of ports, Hideyoshi defined the value and status of sea lords (and other warriors) in terms of agricentric production: bushels of rice (*koku*).[59] In the resulting compromise, the Kurushima Murakami abandoned claims to their home island and castle of Kurushima and several other island fortresses,[60] but they also accepted littoral holdings in nearby Nii County in Iyo and other places worth some fourteen thousand *koku* that enabled them to remain powerful sea lords. The Kurushima held this territory throughout the Toyotomi period.[61]

In contrast, the Noshima Murakami and other sea lords not so beholden to Hideyoshi continued to operate relatively autonomously as sea lords for more than another year, until after Hideyoshi's conquest of Kyushu in 1587. In addition to Shiwaku, which they gave up before Hideyoshi's conquest of Shikoku, the Noshima forsook only two small, subsidiary strongholds located off the Iyo coast, Mushijima and Nakatoshima. These lie near Kurushima and no doubt had been especially useful in prolonging the feud against the Kurushima, to the dismay of their patrons. In return, the Noshima retained control of their other expansive networks of islands and ports, including their headquarters and stronghold on the islet of Noshima. They also received sanction for their occupation of a considerable amount of littoral territory: "former Kurushima holdings on Yashirojima, the island

59. Wakita Osamu, "The Kokudaka System: A Device for Unification," *Journal of Japanese Studies* 1. (1975): 310–11; Berry, *Hideyoshi*, pp. 121–31.
60. EK doc. 2491, Tenshō 14? (1586) 3.5.
61. *Ehime-ken shi shiryō-hen kinsei*, jō, edited by *Ehime-ken shi* Hensan Iinkai (Matsuyama-shi: Ehime-ken, 1984), doc. 4 *Yoyō Kōno kafu*; doc. 14, Tenshō 14 (1586) 3.20; Yamauchi, *Kaizoku to umijiro*, p. 205. One *koku* (180 liters of rice) was considered enough to feed one man for a year. Totman characterizes daimyo with incomes of between 10,000 and 20,000 *koku* as minor lords (Conrad Totman, *Early Modern Japan* [Berkeley: University of California Press, 1993], p. 120).

of Nōmijima and Etajima, as well as the holdings of the Imaoka [another sea-lord family]."[62] Although unfamiliar to the Noshima, these territories possessed chokepoint geographies conducive to protection businesses and sea tenure. In addition, Kobayakawa Takakage presented the Noshima with another unreciprocated oath in which he swore to continue representing their interests before Terumoto and Hideyoshi.[63]

The case of the Noshima Murakami also suggests that, regardless of whatever edicts Hideyoshi and Terumoto might issue or even the loss of key holdings like Shiwaku, sea lords often succeeded in maintaining their protection business, and thus the recognition necessary to legitimize their dominion, because travelers' perceptions took time to change. Many travelers, even those under Hideyoshi's protection, preferred to have the real assurance of pirates like the Noshima when voyaging by ship across the Inland Sea. In the summer of 1586, despite being "favored by the Kanpaku, lord of the realm," the Jesuits still feared to travel at sea without the protection of the Noshima Murakami. So Takeyoshi "fulfilled the brother's request, commanding that he be bestowed with a banner of silk with his [Noshima Murakami Takeyoshi's] sigil so that they could display the pennant in case they encountered a suspicious ship."[64]

Sea lords of the Inland Sea only faced the termination of large-scale protection businesses and other aspects of their maritime autonomy after Hideyoshi conquered Kyushu and forced the Shimazu, powerful warlords in southern Kyushu, to capitulate in the fifth month of 1587. Control of Kyushu did enable Hideyoshi to ensure that trusted lords and vassals controlled coastal territories;[65] among these were former sea-lord bands. However, more important for sea-lord bands was that Hideyoshi's pacification of western Honshu, Shikoku, and Kyushu rendered many of their livelihoods obsolete. Once the Noshima and Kurushima perceived that it had simply become unprofitable for them to continue to operate as they had in the past, they chose to accept integration into Hideyoshi's polity. No more embattled, competing power blocs existed for sea lords to play one against the other; sea lords no longer received requests to conduct proxy naval operations that they could exploit as pretexts to convince travelers to pay for protective escort.

62. EK doc. 2489, Tenshō 13 (1585) 11.1; Yamauchi, *Chūsei Setonaikai chiikishi no kenkyū*, p. 185; Yamauchi, *Kaizoku to umijiro*, p. 164.
63. EK doc. 2489, Tenshō 13 (1585) 11.1; Yamauchi, *Chūsei Setonaikai chiikishi no kenkyū*, p. 185; Yamauchi, *Kaizoku to umijiro*, p. 164.
64. Luis Frois, *Historia de Japam*, edited by José Wicki, S.J. (Lisbon: Ministério da Cultura e Coordenação Científica Secretaria de Estado da Cultura, Biblioteca Nacional, 1984), vol. 4, pp. 248–49.
65. Berry, *Hideyoshi*, p. 134.

Furthermore, by agreeing to participate in Hideyoshi's naval campaigns in Kyushu, and later the Kantō and Korea, sea lords more and more were perceived to be part of Hideyoshi's realm. Once such perceptions gripped the imaginations of authorities and travelers, they stopped seeking out sea lords for protection, and sea lords thus found it difficult to pretend that travelers required their protection from violence on the seas.

The Noshima Murakami and the Kurushima Murakami both participated in the Kyushu campaigns. For example, Hideyoshi assigned the Noshima special responsibilities in "fitting out ships" and granted them pride of place along with Kuki Yoshitaka, Konishi Yukinaga, and others as the leaders of naval forces providing "protection" (keigo).[66] Naval operations included sea-lord specialties such as a blockade of the Shimazu capital of Kagoshima.[67]

However, it was an investigation into charges of piracy shortly after the cessation of hostilities that conveyed to the Noshima, and perhaps other sea-lord bands, the degree to which they could no longer operate as autonomously and mercenarily as they had before Hideyoshi's conquests. In agreeing to provide "protection" for his pacification of Kyushu, sea lords received license from Hideyoshi to seize Shimazu shipping. In the past, sea lords had interpreted such instructions liberally, engaging in commerce raiding and selling protection from that violence as they saw fit. But in 1587, Hideyoshi perceived the participation of sea-lord bands in the campaign as a sign that they accepted his authority to determine the legitimacy of nautical violence. In Hideyoshi's eyes, that license ended when he said it did. A month or so after their surrender to Hideyoshi, the Shimazu complained to Hideyoshi's magistrates in Shikoku and Kyushu that a member of the Noshima Murakami band named Sei Uemon had "committed piracy [zokusen]," possibly intercepting a Shimazu ship carrying gifts and necessities for the journey of the Shimazu lord, Yoshihisa, as well as his daughter, to Kyoto as required by the terms of surrender. This "piracy" probably occurred in a chokepoint off the coast of Itsukijima, a tiny island located on the sea lanes between Iyo and Aki Provinces.[68]

The Sei Uemon incident came to light as historians combed archives in a quest for Hideyoshi's actual first antipiracy edict that preceded and is

---

66. Yamauchi, Setonaikai chiikishi no kenkyū, p. 186; Miyakubo-chō shi, p. 1074, doc. 16, Tenshō 15? (1587) 4.8.

67. George Sansom, A History of Japan, 1333–1615 (Stanford, Calif.: Stanford University Press, 1961), p. 322. For more on the Kyushu campaign, see Berry, Hideyoshi, pp. 88–90.

68. YK, vol. 3, p. 568, doc. 161, Tenshō 15? (1587) 7.8; DNK 11, Kobayakawa-ke monjo, vol. 1, pp. 478–79, doc. 502, Tenshō 16 (1588) 7.8. Kishida, Daimyo no ryōgoku to keizai kōzō, pp. 379–81; Yamauchi Setouchi no kaizoku, pp. 168–69.

mentioned in his more famous edict from the summer of 1588. For Hideyo-shi, Sei Uemon's piracy defied his ambitions to pacify Japan and to claim lordship over the seas.[69] But for sea lords, the significance of the Sei Uemon incident lay in the resolution. In the end, Hideyoshi turned not to mili-tary suppression or the confiscation of holdings as he would later, but to a compromise that enabled the Noshima and other sea-lord bands to secure privileged positions and thrive in unified Japan. This incident enabled the Noshima to communicate to Hideyoshi their reputation for naval prow-ess, convincing him of his need for their services. In particular, Hideyoshi sought to institute legal processes that would eliminate piracy and, through those procedures, extend his sovereignty to the maritime world. However, both Hideyoshi and the Noshima recognized that Hideyoshi still needed sea lords to help him to exercise that jurisdiction.

After receiving the Shimazu complaint, Hideyoshi's magistrates con-ducted an investigation and sent messengers with questions for the Noshima Murakami lords. The Noshima pled ignorance. Noshima Murakami Moto-yoshi, for example, replied to the magistrates that no Sei Uemon belonged to their band. Magistrates wrote to the Noshima again advising Motoyoshi to settle the matter with them to avoid having the incident brought before Hideyoshi.[70] Motoyoshi continued to deny any knowledge of the affair, at-testing that "there is no evidence."[71] Motoyoshi may even have disregarded the magistrates' threats, confident that the investigators lacked expertise in the maritime world, that Hideyoshi dearly needed their services, and that the Mōri would back them. The magistrates' response fortified Motoyoshi's confidence. They threatened that if sufficient evidence came to light, "pun-ishment would not end with those who carried out the attack, but would extend to Your Person [Motoyoshi] as well." But, in the same letter, they reminded Motoyoshi of the need Hideyoshi had for Noshima services, ex-horting Motoyoshi to continue to help in the "pacification of the seas."[72] Motoyoshi persisted in ignoring whatever threats Hideyoshi's magistrates employed, so in the middle of the eighth month of 1587, the magistrates forwarded the case to Hideyoshi.[73]

Hideyoshi perceived sea-lord services as sufficiently valuable that he forestalled a rush to judgment. Like his magistrates, Hideyoshi equivo-cated. In a vermilion-seal edict that he dispatched to the Noshima's trusted

69. Fujita, *Nihon kinsei kokka seiritsushi no kenkyū*, pp. 153–55, 160–67; Kishida, *Daimyo no ryōgoku to keizai kōzō*, pp. 365–91.
70. YK, vol. 3, p. 568, doc. 161, Tenshō 15? (1587) 7.8.
71. YK, vol. 3, p. 568, doc. 163, Tenshō 15? (1587) 7.27.
72. Ibid.
73. YK, vol. 3, p. 569, doc. 165, Tenshō 15? (1587) 8.22.

intermediary with land-based authorities, Kobayakawa Takakage, Hideyo-shi condemned the attack and ordered punishment, but he also acknowl-edged the possibility for error in dealing with the alien conditions of the maritime world. Although he wanted to bring the maritime world within his grasp, he recognized that he needed experts like the Noshima to actually accomplish that: "Regarding Noshima, word has reached us that members of this band have engaged in piratical acts. This is outrageous and unspeakable. As such, they must be punished. Although I so order, if you know of any ex-tenuating circumstances, they should be reported immediately. In any case, Murakami Motoyoshi should come up to Osaka immediately to explain his side."[74] The extant evidence does not permit firm conclusions about Sei Ue-mon's existence or Noshima Murakami complicity. After all, in the 1570s, local seafarers in Kyushu had impersonated the Noshima and Kurushima Murakami,[75] possibly to inspire greater fear in potential victims.

In the end, the Noshima were not punished severely (if at all) for Sei Uemon's piracy. Instead, Hideyoshi treated them as he did the Kurushima Murakami and other potentially difficult lords: he recognized them as war-rior lords, converted their value into bushels of rice, and moved them to dif-ferent domains. In the spring of 1588, Hideyoshi recognized the Noshima's worth as eighteen thousand *koku*, placed them under the administration of Kobayakawa Takakage and Mōri Terumoto, and dispersed them to small holdings in Chikuzen Province in northern Kyushu, Ōtsu County in Nagato Province along the Sea of Japan, and parts of Suō Province along the Inland Sea.[76] The Noshima Murakami initially protested the shift of domains, but Takakage wrote to Noshima Murakami Takeyoshi and Motoyoshi of their fate: "Regarding the latest [missive] from the Master of the Realm (Tenka—i.e., Hideyoshi), You two, Father and Son, are to move to Chikuzen. We need you to understand that there is nothing that can be done."[77] Although they lost their autonomous maritime domains, far from being suppressed as pi-rates, the Kurushima Murakami and the Noshima Murakami had cloaked their maritime dominion and authority in language and symbols that Hideyoshi esteemed as worthy; hence, he recognized and appointed them as minor lords and important vassals, respectively.

74. *Kobayakawa-ke monjo*, vol.1, p. 265, doc. 286, no year.9.8; Kishida, *Daimyo ryōgoku no keizai kōzō* pp. 366–67.
75. EK doc. 2091, Eiroku 13? (1570) 7.24.
76. Yamauchi, *Setouchi no kaizoku*, pp. 171–78; Yamauchi, *Chūsei Setonaikai chiikishi no kenkyū* pp. 190–94; Kishida Hiroshi, "*Hakkakoku onjidai bungenchō* ni miru Mōri-shi no Chōsen e no dōin taisei," in *Chūgoku chiiki to taigai kankei*, edited by Kishida Hiroshi (Yamakawa Shuppan sha, 2003), pp. 135, 137.
77. *Miyakubo-chō shi*, pp. 1075–76, doc. 19, Tenshō 16? (1588) 3.27. See also *Miyakubo-chō shi*, p. 1094 doc. 73, Tenshō 16? (1588) 4.17.

SEA LORDS AND THE SUPPRESSION OF PIRACY IN EARLY MODERN JAPAN

Having agreed to positions as vassals or minor lords within first Toyotomi, and then Tokugawa Japan, the Noshima, Kurushima, and other former sea lords had to make their rhetoric of land-based lordship a reality. They gradually metamorphosed into members of the early modern land-based warrior class and began to help bind and integrate the maritime world into the land-based territories of the domains and wider realm of Japan, a lengthy process that took half a century. Their naval expertise enabled them to play important roles in eliminating "piracy" in Japan and changing the meaning of the term *kaizoku* to fit the needs of the early modern hegemons, Toyotomi Hideyoshi and the Tokugawa, as well as domainal lords.

Hideyoshi articulated his strategy for dealing with sea lords and pirates most clearly in a famous edict he issued on the eighth of the seventh month of 1588. However, it is only by understanding the decade-long interactions between Hideyoshi and sea lords such as the Noshima and Kurushima that this decree makes sense; the edict's own language reveals that it was issued as part of a longer process.[78] Hideyoshi could implement his antipiracy policies only after securing the services of "pirates" like the Noshima Murakami and the Kurushima Murakami, as well as those of longer standing within his administration, like Kuki Yoshitaka. Pragmatically, Hideyoshi made sure he had sufficient resources in place before he implemented his new policy and gave former sea lords the task of registering and integrating the maritime world into his realm. The Noshima Murakami and Kurushima Murakami transferred the seats of their power and received confirmation of their new territories in Shikoku, Kyushu, and western Honshu before Hideyoshi issued his famous edict of 1588.

When read in conjunction with other antipiracy decisions by Hideyoshi, the 1588 decree illuminates Hideyoshi's ambitious plans for the maritime world. In order to outlaw piracy, he actually defined piracy in new ways, setting firm definitions that replaced late medieval ambiguity. He restricted the activities and delineated the roles of the former sea-lord houses tasked with carrying out the terms of the diktat. Finally, this and other decrees provided a means by which Hideyoshi could assert maritime sovereignty, bringing the sea into territories under his jurisdiction.

---

78. Fujiki, *Toyotomi heiwarei to sengoku shakai*, p. 219. Fujita, *Nihon kinsei kokka seiritsushi no kenkyū*, ch. 5. We should also heed Philip Brown's cautionary note that Hideyoshi's edicts were not carried out consistently or in the same ways across the archipelago (Brown, *Central Authority and Local Autonomy*).

- While pirate ships on the seas of the various provinces have been strictly forbidden, lately it has come to our attention that gangs of pirates are operating around Itsukijima between Iyo and Bingo Provinces. Such acts have been judged illegal.
- Regarding all those who handle ships in the various provinces and bays, from captains to fishermen: the retainer administrating each locale shall immediately investigate [the aforementioned] and order them to jointly swear oaths proclaiming that hereafter they shall never, to the slightest degree, engage in piracy. The lords of each province will collect the oaths and forward them here.
- If retainers [*kyūnin*] or local lords [*ryōshu*] are careless and pirate gangs operate, they [the pirates] are to be prosecuted. Those responsible for the territories where the guilty are based are to have their domains and other holdings confiscated in perpetuity.

The above are to be strictly enforced. If there are any who violate these statutes, they are to be punished immediately.[79]

Hideyoshi targeted several types of piracy with this edict. The first article redefines pirates by drawing on the ancient conception of piracy as rebellion.[80] Although the land-centeredness that originated with the Ritsuryō reforms had weakened during the late medieval period, Hideyoshi and other early modern Japanese authorities shaped their governance by revitalizing agricentric, terracentric ideologies. In this antipiracy decree, Hideyoshi articulated a vision of maritime sovereignty couched in the ancient, Ritsuryō conception of the seas as territories inseparable from the lands of the domains and provinces under the control of a political center. By piratical rebellion Hideyoshi meant the act of exploiting potentially ambiguous maritime spaces on the borders between provinces, which defied Hideyoshi's and domainal lords' reterritorialization of the sea.

Having redefined piracy to fit his needs, Hideyoshi used this pronouncement to target several incidences of piracy simultaneously. Among those was one referenced by the place-name, Itsukijima, perhaps the Sei Uemon affair. As naval retainers under the aegis of the Kobayakawa, whose collection of documents houses a copy of the famous 1588 edict, the Noshima would have

79. *Kobayakawa-ke monjo,* vol. 1, pp. 478–79, doc. 502, Tenshō 16 (1588) 7.8. An original copy of the *kaizoku chōjirei* exists in the Kobayakawa family document collection, as well as in the collections of several other coastal daimyo: the Shimazu of Satsuma, Ōtomo of Bungo, Katō of Higo, Tachibana of Chikugo, and Katō of Awaji. With the exception of slight discrepancies in *kana* usage, the copies are identical (Fujiki, *Toyotomi heiwarei to sengoku shakai,* p. 218).
80. See chapter 1.

been made aware of this edict's contents. As minor lords in Shikoku, the Kurushima would have been similarly informed. This decree put them, and other former sea lords, on alert that the era of autonomous maritime domains and protection enterprises was over.

In contrast, the phrase "pirate ships on the seas of the various provinces have been strictly forbidden" encompasses an unknown number of earlier piratical events and antipiracy edicts, most likely making reference to Hideyoshi's earlier efforts to remove sea-lord bands from their sea castles and to end their protection businesses. The incorporations of the Noshima and Kurushima as vassal and minor lord, respectively, were contingent on their abandonment of specific chokepoint-based strongholds that housed protection businesses.[81] Similarly, after his conquest of Kyushu, Hideyoshi bade his magistrates to destroy castles and mansions in the provinces of Chikuzen, Chikugo, and Hizen and added that "although it has been ordered that pirates and robbers be eliminated in the various provinces, the Fukabori of Hizen . . . located at the edge of the sea, interfere with the shipping not only of China [Daitō], but also of the 'Southern Barbarians' [Iberians] and other merchants."[82] An Edo-period chronicle of territories once ruled by the Fukabori specifies that the Fukabori forced "passing commercial ships from Kyoto, Osaka, Sakai, Hakata, and Shimonoseki to pay tribute [protection money] to pass."[83]

Consideration of these castle-reduction and antipiracy edicts as a unified corpus of laws suggests that Hideyoshi sought to forever sunder any connection between private protection businesses and trade, both foreign and domestic. Fujiki argues that Hideyoshi proscribed piracy partly in order to revive regular trade relations with the continent, including that conducted as tribute trade with China.[84] The Ming court treated pirates as the opposite of regulated tribute trade. Hideyoshi followed the examples of the Ashikaga shogunate and daimyo like Ōtomo Sōrin, who, by showing the Chinese authorities that they had eliminated pirates from the sea-lanes connecting China and Japan, sought to demonstrate sincerity in desiring normalized diplomatic relations with China.[85]

The second and third clauses conveyed to sea lords that, instead of being autonomous maritime powers, they were henceforth to become "retainers" and "lords" with specific responsibilities for registering and policing

81. Fujita, *Nihon kinsei kokka seiritsushi no kenkyū*, p. 157.
82. "Toyotomi Hideyoshi shuinjō," quoted in Fujiki, *Toyotomi heiwarei to sengoku shakai*, pp. 219–20, as well as Fujiki's discussion of the document.
83. "Nabeshima Naoshige fukōho," quoted in Fujiki, *Toyotomi heiwarei to sengoku shakai*, p. 221.
84. Fujiki, *Toyotomi heiwarei to sengoku shakai*, pp. 229–48.
85. See chapter 5.

the littoral population. Those who failed to properly suppress piracy would have their holdings confiscated and thus be expelled from the political order. Hideyoshi's rehabilitation of land-centered, agricentric ideologies can also be seen in his condemnation of the entire littoral population of the archipelago as potentially piratical, suggesting that Hideyoshi and other land-based authorities continued to perceive an experiential divide between the land and the sea. They saw the sea as a space so dangerous that all who dealt with the maritime environment could be pirates, requiring the assistance of former sea-lord houses to pacify—setting (former) pirates to catch pirates. By requiring an oath, Hideyoshi co-opted a flexible mechanism used for centuries in the maritime world by sea-lord bands and patrons to set conditions for each other, by estate residents to cement communal bonds, and by extended families to establish guidelines across the lineage.

The registration of the littoral population also presaged military campaigns in eastern Japan (1590) and on the continent (1592–98), for which Hideyoshi sought to establish the institution of a navy. Hideyoshi set ratios for the number of mariners, ships, and soldiers that a daimyo had to supply for the invasions based on Hideyoshi's assessment of that lord's territory calculated in bushels of rice. Daimyo without naval expertise tasked former sea-lord houses in their service with the maritime requisitions.[86] The Noshima Murakami constructed, outfitted, and supplied ships as well as mariners for the Mōri during the Korean War.[87]

The antipiracy order has also been interpreted as one of a series of what historians have labeled "pacification edicts" (*heiwarei*). It is often seen as a corollary of a decree ordering the disarmament of nonsamurai, the so-called sword-hunt edict. It may be that Hideyoshi's agricentric focus in the sword-hunt edict required him to issue an additional one targeting the seas. The disarmament decree forbade "the possession of weapons by commoners [*hyakushō*]," whom Hideyoshi directed to instead "possess only farming implements and devote themselves to cultivation" with the goal that "the land of the realm be safe and the myriad people be contented."[88] Hideyoshi even issued the antipiracy edict and sword-hunt edicts on the same day. Fujiki Hisashi has argued that the clause requiring mariners to take oaths closely

86. Elisonas, "The Inseparable Trinity," pp. 264–65, 271–72; Miki Seiichirō, "Chōsen eki ni okeru gun'yaku taikei ni tsuite," *Shigaku zasshi* 75.2 (1966): 1–26.

87. Kishida, "*Hakkakoku onjidai bungenchō*," pp. 142, 157–58.

88. DNK 16, *Shimazu-ke monjo*, vol. 1, pp. 348–49, Tenshō 16 (1588), 7th month; Berry, *Hideyoshi*, pp. 102–6. The language of this edict supports Amino's argument that translating *hyakushō* as "farmer" perpetuates "agricultural fundamentalism" (Amino Yoshihiko, *Rethinking Japanese History*, translated and with an introduction by Alan S. Christy; preface and afterword by Hitomi Tonomura, Michigan Monograph Series in Japanese Studies, no. 74 [Ann Arbor: Center for Japanese Studies, University of Michigan, 2012], ch. 1, ch. 5).

resembles the role of pledges in the implementation of the sword hunt. In addition, officials sometimes forwarded the collection of oaths sworn by local mariners to the capital together with the weapons from the disarmament campaigns, leading Fujiki to postulate that the two orders may have had similar objectives—disarming and pacifying the country on land and sea. Hideyoshi sought to force those who claimed samurai status on land and on the waves to choose to be either disarmed commoners or warrior lords and retainers.[89]

Three years later, sea-lord families, as well as others with multi-occupational heritages, faced the stark choice of enwalling themselves in the status confines of either warrior or commoner as Hideyoshi pressed his vermilion seal to a decree freezing the status order. This 1591 directive also barred warriors from departing their master's service without leave,[90] starkly prohibiting the late medieval mercenary practices of sea lords.

Finally, by adjudicating the transborder nature of those he considered pirates, Hideyoshi demonstrated that his position as master of the realm gave him the prerogative to administer the maritime world.[91] Hideyoshi attempted to extend maritime sovereignty to and make territory of the deep-water reaches that extended beyond the coasts of individual domains by making them subject to antipiracy laws and naval campaigns. As early as 1589, Hideyoshi issued directives instructing daimyo recipients that: "I have ordered not only the provinces [inclusive of coastal waters] of Japan but even the high seas [*kaijō*] pacified."[92] For instance, Hideyoshi ordered the Matsura based in the northwest Kyushu port of Hirado to capture pirates led by a Chinese known to Japanese authorities as "Tekkai, who claimed to be a merchant captain, but who crossed to China and engaged in piracy [*bahan*]."[93] From their new anchorages in Chikuzen and Nagato, the Noshima would have been in an opportune location to aid the Mōri and the Toyotomi in such endeavors. Both holdings commanded some of the sea lanes connecting Japan to the continent.[94] In the eleventh month of 1588, Mōri Terumoto praised the services of the Noshima in "capturing pirates [*zokusen*] who scatter among the islands and bays."[95] Edicts extending sovereignty through pirate suppression continued to be issued after Hideyoshi's death into the early decades of rule by the Tokugawa shogunate. For

89. Fujiki, *Toyotomi heiwarei to sengoku shakai*, pp. 222–23; See also, Elisonas, "The Inseparable Trinity," pp. 263–64.

90. Berry, *Hideyoshi*, pp. 106–10.

91. Fujiki, *Toyotomi heiwarei to sengoku shakai*, p. 228.

92. Quoted in Iwao Seiichi, *Shinpen shuinsen bōekishi no kenkyū* (Yoshikawa Kōbunkan, 1985), p. 57.

93. Ibid.

94. Kishida, "Hakkakoku onjidai bungenchō," p. 157.

95. *Miyakubo-chō shi*, p. 1100, doc. 88, Tenshō 16? (1588) 11.11.

example, in 1621, the Tokugawa ordered the Matsura, daimyo of Hirado, to ensure that the "Dutch and English do not commit piracy [*bahan*] on the high seas near Japan [*Nihon chikaki kaijō*]."[96]

NAVAL MILITARY SERVICE IN EARLY MODERN JAPAN

As the leaders of warrior houses with seafaring skills, some former sea-lord families like the Noshima Murakami and Kurushima Murakami were called upon to participate in the foundational military campaigns of the early modern age. However, the Noshima and Kurushima found post-unification military service intrinsically different from that of earlier periods. There occurred a cultural shift in Japan that rendered the autonomous use of military force as part of commercial ventures, especially at sea, less and less an acceptable option for those of the warrior class. Separation of status meant that, as warriors, former sea-lords had to divest themselves of nonviolent and violent commercial maritime enterprises, from salt making to shipping to protection.[97] Violence could only be unleashed at a lord's command, not as an independently marketed service.

In addition, the opportunities available in this period to exercise their expertise in naval warfare did not present compelling, viable alternative sponsors. The mercenarism that so typified their families' late medieval military careers had been interdicted by Hideyoshi's 1591 directive forbidding change of status, and most campaigns occurred in regions remote from their power bases. Moreover, being forced to transfer into unfamiliar territories may have increased their reliance on their patrons and inspired a corresponding change in the ways in which they provided military services.

Instead, under Hideyoshi and the Tokugawa, the Kurushima and Noshima fought together within the institutional confines of a navy. Kurushima Michifusa and his brother Tokui Michiyuki helped lead the western wing of Hideyoshi's "naval forces" (*funade*) in the siege of Odawara in remote eastern Japan in 1590.[98] Both the Kurushima Murakami and the Noshima Murakami participated in Hideyoshi's 1592–98 war with Chosŏn Korea and Ming China. In the initial invasion order in 1592, the "Kurushima brothers," Michifusa and Michiyuki, led a force of seven hundred in the fifth division.[99] Both perished in sea battles at the hands of Yi Sunsin (1545–98) and

96. Quoted in Nagazumi Yōko, *Shuinsen* (Yoshikawa Kōbunkan, 2001), pp. 78–79. Also see DNK 16, *Shimazu-ke monjo*, doc. 1090, Keichō 4? (1599) 4.1.
97. Katsumata Shizuo, *Sengoku jidairon* (Iwanami Shoten, 1996), pp. 2–3, 286–87.
98. *Mōri-ke monjo*, vol. 4, pp. 484–88, doc. 1559, no date.
99. *Mōri-ke monjo*, vol. 3, pp. 143–48, doc. 885, Tenshō 20 (1592) 3.13.

his famous turtle ships: Michiyuki in 1593 at Tangpo; Michifusa in 1597 at Myŏngnyang.[100] The Noshima Murakami lords commanded a force of three thousand during the war and in 1598 helped defend Sŏsaengpo, a port taken during the second invasion.[101]

The warfare that ensued during the upheavals surrounding the supplanting of Toyotomi supremacy by the Tokugawa after the death of Hideyoshi led to similarly little side switching among sea lords. Tokugawa Ieyasu seized the hegemony by defeating a coalition of pro-Toyotomi daimyo at the battle of Sekigahara, which is usually seen as an acme of samurai side switching.[102] However, this climactic showdown witnessed little mercenarism by naval service providers. The Kurushima Murakami remained squarely in the pro-Toyotomi camp, and the Noshima Murakami followed the lead of Mōri Terumoto. After Kobayakawa Takakage's death in 1597 and Toyotomi Hideyoshi's death in 1598, the Mōri moved the Noshima Murakami back to the Inland Sea in holdings in Takehara and Ebashima in Aki.[103] Then, in the spring of 1599, the leading members of the Noshima Murakami all swore blood oaths to "provide loyal, single-hearted service" for Mōri Terumoto.[104] These oaths reversed the symbolic inversion of power relations represented by the aforementioned oaths of the 1580s. When warfare erupted in 1600, Terumoto ordered the Noshima to help seize the castle of a Tokugawa partisan, Katō Yoshiaki, in Shikoku. Noshima Murakami Motoyoshi was killed in this battle.[105]

After Sekigahara, the Kurushima Murakami submitted to the Tokugawa, who reassigned the Kurushima to the domain of Mori, an inland territory of Bungo Province, some 30 kilometers from the Kyushu coast. This transfer effectively severed Kurushima ties with the sea, though of course they were still responsible for meeting the "military levy" (*gun'yaku*) and other obligations domainal lords owed the Tokugawa.[106] In contrast, the Noshima Murakami house fractured. The main line remained retainers of the Mōri. Noshima Murakami Takeyoshi moved to a small, one thousand *koku* holding on Yashirojima, where he died in 1604. In 1618, Takeyoshi's grandson

---

100. Kenneth M. Swope, *A Dragon's Head and a Serpent's Tail: Ming China and the First Great East Asian War, 1592–1598* (Norman: University of Oklahoma Press, 2009), pp. 116–19, 251.

101. *Ehime-ken shi shiryō-hen kinsei* jō, doc. 67, no date; *Miyakubo-chō shi*, pp. 1057–58, doc. 24, Keichō 3 (1598) 4.20; Swope, *A Dragon's Head and a Serpent's Tail,* pp. 228–29.

102. Ieyasu's victory is usually attributed to his convincing Kobayakawa Hideaki (1577–1602) and other lords to switch sides at a key moment in the battle (Sansom, *A History of Japan, 1333–1615,* pp. 393–94).

103. Yamauchi, *Setouchi no kaizoku,* p. 179.

104. *Mōri-ke monjo,* vol. 3, pp. 527–30.

105. Yamauchi, *Setouchi no kaizoku,* pp.181–82.

106. Yamauchi, *Chūsei Setonaikai chiikishi no kenkyū,* pp. 213–14.

Mototake assumed the post of "domainal admiral" for Mōri Terumoto, based in the port of Mitajiri on the coast of Suō Province. His duties included investigating and suppressing piracy, escorting Mōri alternate attendance processions, and protecting the ships of foreign embassies. Other Noshima lords took positions with other daimyo. For example, Takeyoshi's cousin, Noshima Murakami Kagehiro (d. 1627), took service with Hosokawa Tadaoki, lord of Nakatsu domain in Buzen. Kagehiro helped lead the naval contingent of the Tokugawa forces in the 1614–15 siege of Osaka, during which Ieyasu destroyed the Toyotomi.[107]

For the first few decades of the Tokugawa period, extralegal prospects still existed for those who wished to autonomously engage in violence and commerce overseas. One key contact for seafarers of the Inland Sea would have been the Matsura of Hirado. The Noshima Murakami had established commercial and protection connections with the Matsura as early as the 1560s.[108] Adam Clulow has documented the degree to which Japanese flocked to the Matsura port of Hirado in the first part of the seventeenth century to join piratical expeditions outfitted by the Matsura as well as Chinese sea-lord organizations and English and Dutch trading companies.[109] For example, the Chinese sea lord Li Dan (d. 1625) based his band in Japan in Hirado. His organization was inherited and expanded by Zheng Zhilong (1604–61) and Zhilong's half-Japanese son, Zheng Chenggong, aka Koxinga (1624–62). The Zheng provided considerable opportunities for raiding, trading, protection businesses, and warfare along the coast of China as they brought much of the trade connecting Japan, China, and Southeast Asia under their control until the Qing conquest of Taiwan in 1683.[110] Other Japanese found work as mercenaries, who served local sovereigns and European trading companies in Southeast Asia.[111]

However, many of the vessels on which Japanese mariners would have voyaged overseas were those authorized and regulated by the Tokugawa with a system of vermilion-seal licenses (*goshuin*) for trade in China and

---

107. Yamauchi, *Setouchi no kaizoku*, pp. 182–87; Yamauchi, *Chūsei Setonaikai chiikishi no kenkyū*, p. 199; *Miyakubo-chō shi*, p. 1058, doc. 25, no year.8.13.
108. YK, vol. 3, p. 522, no year.9.26.
109. Adam Clulow, "From Global Entrepôt to Early Modern Domain: Hirado, 1609–1641," *Monumenta Nipponica* 65.1 (2010): 1–35; idem, "The Pirate and the Warlord," *Journal of Early Modern History* 16.6 (2012): 523–42.
110. Patricia Carioti, "The Zheng's Maritime Power in the International Context of the Seventeenth Century Far Eastern Seas," *Ming Qing yanjiu* 5 (1996): 29–67; Tonio Andrade, *Lost Colony: The Untold Story of China's First Great Victory over the West* (Princeton, N.J.: Princeton University Press, 2011).
111. Adam Clulow, "Unjust, Cruel and Barbarous Proceedings: Japanese Mercenaries and the Amboyna Incident of 1623," *Itinerario* 31.1 (2007): 15–34.

Southeast Asia. In developing and implementing this system of licensed trade, possibly with memories of sea lords and complaints of pirates from neighboring countries in mind, the Tokugawa adopted the Chinese and Korean interpretations of piracy as the opposite of properly run systems of diplomacy and trade. Like Hideyoshi, they explicitly prescribed a separation of maritime commerce from acts of violence. The Tokugawa forbade owners and commanders of vermilion-seal ships to perpetrate piracy and other acts of violence or to even export weapons. In return, as representatives of the Tokugawa polity, vermilion-seal vessels became inviolate. Anyone who attacked them risked incurring the wrath of the Tokugawa. These rules extended even to foreign recipients of vermilion-seal licenses at war with other foreign countries.[112] Tokugawa Ieyasu further decoupled violence from maritime commerce by abandoning those seafaring merchants who committed piracy and other forms of violence abroad to the justice of the local potentate; Ieyasu repudiated such merchants and denied them the blessings of Japanese sovereignty.[113] Although records do not document participation by former sea-lord families in the vermilion-seal trade, several merchants and daimyo from the western littoral did receive such licenses.[114]

The separation of piracy from commerce in the vermilion-seal trade system presaged the adoption of a wider diplomatic system based on Chinese models and centered on the land of Japan, which the Tokugawa implemented in full in the 1630s. The Tokugawa outlawed Christianity, eliminated private travel overseas, barred Japanese living abroad from returning home, and restricted the construction of large oceangoing ships. They reconstructed Japan's system of foreign relations around the Tokugawa shogunate and particular daimyo domains, channeling all intercourse with foreign countries into four gates: the domain of Tsushima for Korea; the port of Nagasaki for China, Southeast Asia, and the Dutch; the domain of Satsuma for Ryūkyū; and Matsumae domain for Ezo.[115] This reshaping of Japan's diplomatic posture coincided with the suppression of the Shimabara Rebellion of 1637–38,

---

112. Iwao, *Shinpen shuinsen bōekishi no kenkyū*, pp. 85–109; Nagazumi, *Shuinsen*, pp. 78–80. Robert Innes, "The Door Ajar: Japan's Foreign Trade in the Seventeenth Century" (Ph.D. Diss., University of Michigan, 1980), p. 112.

113. Adam Clulow, "Like Lambs in Japan and Devils outside Their Land: Diplomacy, Violence, and Japanese Merchants in Southeast Asia," *Journal of World History* 24.2 (2013): 335–58.

114. A list of known *shuin* recipients can be found in Iwao, *Shinpen shuinsen bōekishi no kenkyū*, table 7, an insert between pp. 220–21.

115. Ronald P. Toby, *State and Diplomacy in Early Modern Japan: Asia in the Development of the Tokugawa Bakufu* (Princeton, N.J.: Princeton University Press, 1984); Innes, "The Door Ajar"; Murai Shōsuke, *Umi kara mita Sengoku Nihon: rettōshi kara sekaishi e* (Chikuma Shobō, 1997), ch. 6; Tsuruta Kei, "The Establishment and Characteristics of the Tsushima Gate," *Acta Asiatica* 67 (1994): 30–48.

the last major war fought in the Edo period. Thus, after 1640, former sea-lord houses had little outlet for their naval expertise outside of domainal needs and—like other members of the warrior class Japan—had no more wars to fight. They became domainal lords and officials.

NEW PIRATES FOR A NEW AGE: COMMEMORATING PIRATES AS NAVAL VASSALS

As part of their transformation into land-based members of the warrior class and domainal officials and lords, members of former sea-lord houses, like many other early modern warrior families, crafted genealogies and participated in the creation of historical chronicles in the latter half of the seventeenth century. These accounts stripped out late medieval, maritime autonomy and nonwarrior livelihoods from the historical record and implanted a history of loyal military service. In doing so, these histories legitimized the positions of former sea-lord families by inventing pasts as faithful retainers and, in so doing, helped enhance the centrality and commemorate the supremacy of their domainal lords—the Mōri, in the case of the Noshima Murakami—or of the Tokugawa, in the case of the Kurushima Murakami. These accounts historiographically bound the maritime world to the realms of the domainal lord and the Tokugawa. Neo-Confucian historiographical ideals, which gained strength in samurai society during the seventeenth century, facilitated the rewriting of sea-lord history. Scholars schooled in its traditions required history to illuminate moral lessons such as the triumph of values like loyalty.[116]

Noshima Murakami genealogies retroactively cloak any contradictory, mercenary actions in their record with a mantle of imperial aegis. They claimed descent from Emperor Murakami (926–67) and Kitabatake Akiie (1318–38), an imperial loyalist who fought for the Southern Court in the fourteenth-century war of the Northern and Southern Courts. Ties to the imperial household were cemented by fictitious invitations to participation in poetry exchanges, which highlighted claims by the Noshima Murakami in the Edo period to high-status society through mastery of elite cultural forms. Patronage by the imperial house occurred simultaneously with

---

116. Kate Wildman Nakai, "Tokugawa Confucian Historiography: The Hayashi, Early Mitō School and Arai Hakuseki," in *Confucianism and Tokugawa Culture*, edited by Peter Nosco (Princeton, N.J.: Princeton University Press, 1984), pp. 64–65; Herman Ooms, *Tokugawa Ideology: Early Constructs, 1570–1680* (Princeton, N.J.: Princeton University Press, 1985).

the Noshima faithfully following a succession of warrior houses from the Ashikaga shogunate, to the Ōuchi, to the Mōri.[117] Imagined imperial sponsorship culminated in the receipt by Noshima Murakami Takeyoshi of an imperial edict naming him "Admiral of the Seas of Japan" (*kainai shōgun*), institutionally connecting the Noshima and the seas to the imperial realm. Noshima Murakami scholars went so far as to forge this edict and preserve it in the family archives.[118] Although it is not clear when the forgeries and genealogies were made, these Noshima family histories appear in narrative form in an early eighteenth-century Mōri collection of documents and family histories of those it considered its vassals.[119]

These genealogical projects provided fodder for Mōri domainal scholars hungry for evidence of historical exploits that vassals' ancestors carried out in devotion to the domainal lord's ancestors. These exploits could be used to celebrate the ascent of the Mōri as well as justify the positions of former sea-lord retainers in Mōri domainal administrations. One such work, *Annals of a Warrior House's Eternal Glory: A Chronicle of the Battles of the Pirate Houses of the Three Islands* (*Bukebandaiki: santō kaizoku-ke ikusa nikki*), did so by explicitly transposing the autonomy of sea lords so discordant to the early modern political order into a more harmonious tune of vassalage by "pirates." This work purports to be a history of former seafaring houses and the creation of Murakami Kihei Motoyoshi, a lord of the Innoshima Murakami house in the late sixteenth century. However, much of the chronicle narrates the exploits of Noshima Murakami Takeyoshi and the Noshima Murakami family, and the text is first mentioned as having circulated among Mōri domainal scholars in the mid-seventeenth century.[120] The title alone reveals a remarkable transformation: for the first time, seafarers treated the term "pirate" (*kaizoku*) as an expression of their identity. This means that members of former sea-lord houses and Mōri scholars together adopted the perspectives of their land-based lords, isolated the late medieval usage of *kaizoku* meaning "naval service provider," and used that definition to reconstruct the medieval histories of seafaring bands like the Noshima Murakami. This

---

117. *Miyakubo-chō shi*, pp. 1139–46.

118. *Miyakubo-chō shi*, p. 1102, doc. 96. Other forged documents include edicts from emperors and shoguns naming Murakami Takeyoshi and his son Motoyoshi to various honorary titles (*Miyakubo-chō shi*, pp. 1102–3).

119. *Hagi-han batsuetsuroku*, edited by Nagata Masazumi (Yamaguchi: Yamaguchi-ken Monjokan, 1967), vol. 1, pp. 593–95.

120. Katayama Kiyoshi, "*Bukebandaiki* kaidai," *Sumiyoshi* 226 (Fall 1997): 50–54; "*Bukebandaiki: Santō kaizoku-ke ikusa nikki*, san no maki," edited by Katayama Kiyoshi, *Sumiyoshi* 229 (Summer 1998): 47.

new usage of "pirate" transformed the sea from autonomous space to space tethered to the land and turned once independent sea lords into pirates who faithfully fulfilled their lords' commands.

For example, the 1555 Battle of Itsukushima became a Confucian parable of loyal service by pirate vassals instead of a story of mercenary fence sitting, which the late medieval documentary record indicates. In hindsight this battle represented a crucial turning point for the Mōri family, the ignition for Mōri Motonari's rocket-like ascent to regional preeminence. Former sea-lord families had to prove that their ancestors helped propel Motonari in order to justify their reaping of benefits in the Tokugawa period.

There is no evidence of the Noshima Murakami having actually participated in the battle. However, the *Annals of a Warrior House's Eternal Glory* inserts Noshima Murakami Takeyoshi as a prominent hero of the battle of Itsukushima. Takeyoshi leads the Noshima, Kurushima, and Innoshima—the pirate houses of the three islands—as "loyal subordinates" (*mikata*) of Motonari in Motonari's righteous war to avenge the betrayal by Sue Harukata (1521–55) of their liege, Ōuchi Yoshitaka (1507–51).[121] Official Mōri chronicles confirmed this rewriting of the history of the battle of Itsukushima; domainal scholars bolstered such accounts by forging letters of commendation and other documents.[122] The Noshima Murakami genealogy supports this interpretation of the battle of Itsukushima, noting that Takeyoshi became a *mikata* and came to Motonari's aid.[123]

The Kurushima Murakami underwent a similarly radical historiographical transformation, though in contrast to the Noshima, they downplayed their piratical, maritime heritage in order to help legitimize their metamorphosis into terrestrial lords. As lords of one of the smaller domains in the Tokugawa period, they warranted inclusion in the various encyclopedic Edo-centric tomes recounting genealogies and histories of daimyo and Tokugawa retainers. One of the most important of these was the 1643 *Genealogies of the Houses of the Kan'ei Period* (*Kan'ei shoka keizuden*), compiled by shogunal officials based on materials submitted by the various warrior families at the behest of the third Tokugawa shogun, Iemitsu (1604–51), who sought

121. "*Bukebandaiki: Santō kaizoku-ke ikusa nikki*, ichi no maki," edited by Katayama Kiyoshi, *Suminoe* 227 (Winter 1997): 46–50.
122. For an official Mōri domainal chronicle, see Kagawa Masanori and Kagawa Sen'a, *Intoku taiheiki*, edited by Yonehara Masayoshi (Tōyō Shōin, 1981), vol. 2, ch. 26, pp. 252–54. One such forged letter of commendation, dated Kōji 1 (1555) 11.1, is contained in *Hagi-han batsuetsuroku*, vol. 5, p. 133, doc. 2. These accounts also naturally elide Mōri Motonari's complicity in Ōuchi Yoshitaka's death.
123. *Miyakubo-chō shi*, p. 1148.

to categorize and rank the major warrior houses of Japan.[124] In their entry in the Kan'ei *Genealogies*, the Kurushima amputated their entire history as an autonomous sea-lord house and instead attached—prosthesis-like—the lineage of the Kōno family, who had been warrior provincial governors in Iyo. To do so, they took advantage of the intermarriage between Kurushima Murakami Michiyasu (1519–67) and the Kōno and the fact that the Kōno family died out in 1587. In the Kan'ei *Genealogies*, the entry for the Kurushima begins with several generations of the Kōno family and continues unbroken from the final Kōno daimyo, Michinao, to Kurushima Michiyasu. Michiyasu was "taken as a son-in-law," was granted the *michi* character to use in his name, and received the Kōno family crest, genealogy, and histories. He received such honors because the Kurushima had "become hereditary elders for the Kōno house and performed leal service several times," ever since Michiyasu's "ancestor, a Murakami from Shinano Province, became a masterless samurai and wandered down into Iyo."[125] The Kan'ei *Genealogies* recounted several of the Kurushima's great deeds, including providing assistance to Mōri Motonari at Itsukushima and participating in Hideyoshi's invasion of Korea, before finally submitting to the Tokugawa. The Kurushima commemorated their change in identity and domain with a change in name. Instead of using the Chinese characters usually employed to write the Inland Sea place-name "Kurushima," they identified with a series of characters that spelled "Kurushima" phonetically, severing any linguistic-geographical connection with their late medieval past.[126] The Kurushima's genealogical constructions were reinforced by notations in "military mirrors" (*bukan*), commercially printed rosters of daimyo as well as Tokugawa administrators that circulated widely and popularly in Edo society. These rosters categorized the Kurushima, and every other warrior family, by their wealth and status as measured in bales of rice[127] and listed them as part of the Kōno lineage, as well as the Ochi, the family that the Kōno claimed as progenitors.[128]

124. Mary Elizabeth Berry, *Japan in Print: Information and Nation in the Early Modern Period* (Berkeley: University of California Press, 2006), pp. 113–15.
125. Ōta Sukemune, comp., *Kan'ei shoka keizuden*, edited by Saiki Kazuma et al., vol. 13 (Zoku Gunsho Ruijū Kanseikai, 1990), p. 34.
126. Ibid., pp. 34–38. In the Tokugawa bakufu's revised genealogical collection, *Kansei chōshū shokafu* (completed in 1812), the Kurushima genealogy was separated from the Kōno main line but was still included as a descendent of the Ochi and a Kōno branch that began with Kurushima Michiyasu. Hayashi Jussai and Hotta Masaatsu, comps., *Shintei Kansei chōshū shokafu*, edited by Takayanagi Mitsutoshi et al., vol. 10 (Zoku Gunsho Ruijū Kanseikai, 1965), pp. 147–53, 163–67.
127. Berry, *Japan in Print*, p. 112.
128. *Kaitei zōho dai bukan*, 3 vols., edited by Hashimoto Hiroshi (Meicho Kankōkai, 1965), pp. 165, 252, 396, 833, 865, 1004.

Although these various commemorative fantasies of the Noshima and Kurushima were devised for specific audiences,[129] by the early eighteenth century, interdomainal networks of scholars spread stories of Inland Sea "pirates" as vassals across Japan, which inspired some writers to coin the neologism "navy" (*suigun*) in order to identify the families of former sea lords. Perhaps the earliest work to employ this term was the *History of the Southern Sea Region* (*Nankai tsūki*, ca. 1719) by Kasai Shigesuke (1632–?). In a chapter of this work entitled "A Record of How the Noshima of Iyo Led an Invasion of Ming China," Kasai transformed the Noshima Murakami, Kurushima Murakami, and other sea lords into loyal servants of Japanese expansion and daimyo overseas ambitions.

A native of Sanuki in Shikoku, Kasai studied the Takeda School of military arts and subsequently taught military studies for the Kuroda family, daimyo of Chikuzen Domain.[130] When writing *History of the Southern Sea Region*, Kasai drew on his learning in the Takeda School, whose foundational text, the early seventeenth-century *Kōyō gunkan*, was among the earliest works in Japan to employ the term *kaizoku* to refer to naval vassals.[131] He then fused those ideas with material drawn from Chinese, Korean, and Japanese sources. Kasai was particularly keen on studying domainal histories. According to a student, Kasai's reading ranged from "the Six National Histories to the various annals and chronicles created by each province."[132]

Kasai synthesized these materials in order to rewrite the history of "Japanese pirates" (*wakō*).[133] He removed any cosmopolitan ambiguity inherent in the term. As chapter five showed, historically Chinese and Koreans used the term "Japanese pirates" (Ch. *wokou*, Kn. *waegu*) to refer to an evolving mélange of seafarers from China, Korea, Europe, and other regions as well as various parts of the Japanese archipelago. Instead, Kasai defined the *wakō* as Japanese. He removed Chinese from the ranks of "Japanese pirates" by drawing on Ming sources and relegating the Chinese participants to being "fugitives." He then inserted the Noshima Murakami as the ringleaders of other pirate-naval vassals like the Kurushima Murakami and Innoshima Murakami. These "pirate houses of the three islands" served Japanese daimyo such as the Ōuchi and led assaults on China in the sixteenth cen-

---

129. Roberts, *Performing the Great Peace*, ch. 6.
130. See Kasai's 1719 dedicatory inscription and the enconium to Kasai, "*Nankai tsūki* jo," by Takeda Sadanao, a student of Kasai's, in Kasai Shigesuke, *Nankai tsūki, Shintei zōho shiseki shūran*, vol. 20, edited by Kondō Keizō (Rinsen Shoten, 1967), pp. 1–2.
131. DNS ser. 10, vol. 7, p. 107.
132. Takeda, "*Nankai tsūki* jo," in Kasai, *Nankai tsūki*, p. 2.
133. He was actually one of the first Japanese to refer to Japanese as *wakō*.

tury.[134] But in Kasai's eyes, of all the pirate houses, it was the Noshima Murakami who became naval vassals without peer:

> Proud of their martial heritage, in everyday life warriors equip themselves in order to meet the unexpected. This means that, regardless if they were [going abroad] as sailors or merchants, they [pirates] trained in military arts and enjoyed fighting. Because of this, pirates endlessly went out to foreign countries and decided to engage in battles. Incidents in which they took the victories could not be said to be few. In particular, the Noshima served as a navy [*suigun*] over several generations; they grew particularly brave and skilled in battle and strategy, with long practice of doing fell deeds. Therefore, as regards the way of using naval warfare, they were inferior to none in either China or Japan.[135]

With this chapter, Kasai transformed the late medieval period into a mythic age in which pirate-heroes did great deeds overseas as well as in Japan and loyally dedicated themselves to their lords. Unlike other pirate histories, Kasai accepted that pirates engaged in commercial as well as maritime livelihoods, but Kasai relegated such activities to the past. He historiographically bolstered the Tokugawa closure of avenues for autonomous overseas adventuring and the attempts by the unifiers to demarcate status and occupation. Although it is not clear who read Kasai, echoes of his work appear in the oeuvres of eighteenth- and nineteenth-century armchair military scholars, who perpetuated the myths of the Noshima and other sea lords as *suigun* in so-called secret military treatises of the pirate houses.[136] The popularity and prevalence of the term *suigun* in historiography today about Inland Sea seafarers is a testament to the potency of the narratives bequeathed us by these early modern genealogies, chronicles, and treatises.

In addition, by interpreting pirates as the vassals and agents of land-based lords, these genealogical and historical works helped perpetuate a perception that the sea and seafarers were not nonstate entities. Instead, pirate vassals helped integrate them into the territory of domains and the wider realm of Japan. These accounts thus need to be understood as part of a broader terracentric cultural shift in the Tokugawa period. Cartographers attempted to minimize the dangers from the uncontrollable, unknowable

---

134. Kasai, *Nankai tsūki,* p. 164.
135. Ibid., p. 167.
136. See for example the 1740 *Santōryū suigun ridanshō,* in *Kaiji shiryō sōsho,* vol. 12, edited by Sumita Masa'ichi (Genshōdō Shoten, 1930).

aspects of the sea by crafting maps that anchored the proximal seas to the land of Japan.[137] Elites continued to exoticize "sea people"—especially women divers—as other.[138] Early modern Japanese in general tended to treat commoners (*hyakushō*) tied to agriculture as having higher status than those without such connections.[139]

LEVIATHAN ON A LEASH

In order to help encourage perceptions that the sea and seafarers were fettered to the realm, the early modern unifiers also appropriated some of the material cultural elements that sea-lord families had imbued with political symbolism and pageantry. Perhaps most visibly, hegemons adopted the panoply and splendor of dreadnoughts (*atakebune*) that once marked the autonomy and strength of sea lords. For his invasion of Korea, Hideyoshi took the design and construction of dreadnoughts out of the hands of sea lords. He designated the *atakebune* as the flagships of his navy, made domainal lords responsible for the construction, upkeep, and deployment of these floating artillery fortresses, and institutionalized ways in which daimyo (inclusive of former sea-lord houses) provided dreadnoughts. This institutionalization extended to standardizing the dimensions of timbers employed in the construction of such "great ships."[140]

In contrast, the Tokugawa largely treated *atakebune* as floating castles. They equated the construction and fitting out of dreadnoughts—as castles on the sea—with the construction and repair of castles on land. Tokugawa Ieyasu had praised Kuki Yoshitaka's tactical innovations in dreadnought design and deployment that led to the 1578 victory over the anti-Nobunaga naval coalition.[141] Once he seized the hegemony after the battle of Sekigahara, Ieyasu recognized and moved to mitigate the potential danger in daimyo possessing such potent symbols and weapons. In 1609, as part of his preparations for destroying the Toyotomi in Osaka, Tokugawa Ieyasu ordered

---

137. Marcia Yonemoto, "Maps and Metaphors of the 'Small Eastern Sea' in Tokugawa Japan (1603-1868)," *Geographical Review* 89, no. 2 (1999): 176–78.

138. Ronald P. Toby, "Imagining and 'Imaging' Anthropos in Early Modern Japan," *Visual Anthropological Review* 14.1 (1998): 32–33.

139. Amino, *Rethinking Japanese History*, p. 14.

140. William Wayne Farris, "Shipbuilding in Japanese Maritime History: Origins to 1600," *Mariner's Mirror* 95.3 (August 2009): 277; Conrad Totman, *The Green Archipelago: Forestry in Pre Industrial Japan* (Berkeley: University of California Press, 1989), pp. 58–60; *Ehime-ken shi shiryō hen kinsei*, jō, pp. 60–61, doc. 69, Tenshō 20 (1592) 7.16.

141. *Mie-ken shi shiryō-hen, kinsei,* vol. 1 (Tsu-shi, Mie-ken: Mie-ken, 1993), p. 211, doc. 196 no.year.9.30.

that, "the great ships of the western lords moored in various places are to be confiscated because the western lords and others seem inclined to put their castles in repair and to construct ships. . . . All great ships of 500 *koku* or greater lading are to be delivered to Awaji to be confiscated and thence sailed to Sunpu and Edo."[142] By this logic, *atakebune* became entirely vestigial in 1615, when the Tokugawa limited daimyo to only a single, residential castle and ordered all others destroyed.[143]

The third shogun, Tokugawa Iemitsu exploited the connections between dreadnoughts, castles, and political symbolism in attempts to exalt and legitimize Tokugawa authority, while limiting the access other lords had to such symbols. As part of his 1635 revision of the *Laws Governing Military Houses* (*Buke shohatto*), Iemitsu strengthened Ieyasu's interdiction of dreadnoughts by outlawing the construction of ships above 500 *koku* in lading, and reinforced previous efforts to curtail autonomous maritime authority by forbidding the establishment of unsanctioned domainal toll barriers.[144] At the same time, as is well known, Iemitsu ordered a flurry of building projects that awed viewers with massive gilded spectacles suffused with iconography of dominion and legitimacy. These projects included the reconstructions and renovations of major castles, such as the Tokugawa's home castle of Edo and Nijō Castle (the Tokugawa residence in Kyoto), as well as the Tōshōgū Shrine at Nikkō dedicated to the deified Tokugawa Ieyasu.[145] However, what is less well known is that these projects had a maritime analogue.

Iemitsu symbolized the Tokugawa's mastery of the seas of Japan and the complete appropriation of sea-lord, ship-based power by taking the late medieval concept of dreadnought-sea castle to an early modern sublime. In 1632, Iemitsu commanded his admiral, Mukai Tadakatsu (1582–1641), to construct a behemoth vessel known as the *Atakemaru* (literally, *The Dreadnought*). In 1635, the same year as Iemitsu forbade the construction of great ships by other daimyo, Tokugawa shipwrights completed the *Atakemaru*. It was a third again as large as any dreadnought built previously, stretching some 61 meters in length and 22 meters in the beam. It displaced perhaps 1,700 tons. Two hundred oarsmen, at two men per oar, could row this ship at around 2 knots (perhaps as much as 5 for short distances) with the help of a small sail that measured some 24 *tan* (21.6 m) in width. Mukai sheathed

142. DNS, ser. 12, vol. 6, p. 647.

143. DNS, ser. 12, vol. 21, pp. 329–31.

144. *Gotōke reijō*, in *Kinsei hōsei shiryō sōsho*, vol. 2, edited by Ishii Ryōsuke (Sōbunsha, 1959), p. 4, doc. 5; Roberts, *Performing Great Peace*, p. 25.

145. Karen Gerhart, *The Eyes of Power: Art and Early Tokugawa Authority* (Honolulu: University of Hawai'i Press, 1999); William H. Coaldrake, *Architecture and Authority in Japan* (London: Routledge, 1996), pp. 129–92.

parts of the vessel in bronze plates.[146] He also outfitted the *Atakemaru* with a
dragon's head in the prow and a castle tower atop turrets that ran the length
of the ship. According to naval historian Ishii Kenji, the gilding, carvings,
and other decorations on the *Atakemaru* may have rivaled the reconstruction of Tōshōgū Shrine ordered by Iemitsu.[147] Supposedly the *Atakemaru's*
turrets elevated a person close to 20 meters above the waterline such that
all of Edo fell beneath one's gaze when standing atop this Tokugawa sea
castle.[148] This hulking splendor would have equally dominated the seascape
of Edo Bay and impressed upon observers the maritime as well as terrestrial
power of the Tokugawa. Such a massive ship could not move very effectively
even in calm seas (and not at all in the open ocean). Instead, Mukai Tadakatsu adapted sea-lord tactics from campaigns like the Kizu River battles of
1576 and 1578 and tethered the *Atakemaru* to the land as a floating fortress
overlooking Edo Bay.[149] Moreover, because sea lords made their reputations
and maintained maritime dominance by exploiting their advantage of mobility, it was symbolically in the interest of the Tokugawa to moor the ship.
Seeing the goliath *Atakemaru* tied to the shore may have represented the
leashing and immobilizing of the sea and sea lords, a celebration and com-
memoration of the taming of leviathan.

146. Ishii Kenji, *Wasen* II (Hōsei Daigaku Shuppankyoku, 1995), pp. 1–21.
147. Ibid., pp. 18–19.
148. Ibid., p. 20.
149. Ibid., p. 14.

Character List

agehama 揚浜
aikou 隘口
Aio Futajima 秋穂二島
Akamagaseki 赤間関
Akamatsu 赤松
Akechi Mitsuhide 明智光秀
akujū 悪従
akutō 悪党
ama 海民, 海人, 海士, 海部, 海女, 海夫, 蜑
Ama Gozen 尼御前
Ama no shō 海部の荘
Amagasaki 尼崎
Amako 尼子
Amako Haruhisa 尼子晴久
amiba 網場
aminiwa 網庭
Amino Yoshihiko 網野善彦
Ankokuji Ekei 安国寺恵瓊
Araki Murashige 荒木村重
Ariwara no Yukihira 有原行平
Ashikaga Takauji 足利尊氏
Ashikaga Yoshiaki 足利義昭
Ashikaga Yoshiharu 足利義晴
Ashikaga Yoshimitsu 足利義満
Ashikaga Yoshimochi 足利義持
Ashikaga Yoshinori 足利義教
Ashikaga Yoshitane 足利義植
Ashikaga Yoshiteru 足利義輝
Atagi 安宅
atakebune 安宅船
Atakemaru 安宅丸
Awaji 淡路
Awaji no Rokurō 淡路の六郎
Awaya Ukon no suke Motoyoshi 粟屋右近充元如
Azai 浅井

Azuchi Ōshima 小豆大島
azukari dokoro shiki 預所職
Azukijima 小豆島

bahan 八幡
Bairin Shuryū 梅霖守龍
Bairin Shuryū Suō gekō nikki 梅霖守龍周防下向日記
Baishōron 梅松論
Ben no Bō Shōyo 辨房承譽
bikuni 比丘尼
Bingo 備後
Bingo Ōta no shō nengu hikitsuke 備後太田庄年貢引付
bokujū 僕従
Bōnotsu 坊津
Bonten 梵天
bōsen 防戦
Boshi nyūminki 戊子入明記
bugyō 奉行
bukan 武鑑
Buke shohatto 武家諸法度
Bukebandaiki santō kaizoku-ke ikusa nikki 武家万代記三島海賊家戦日記
busen 夫銭

Chen Keyuan 陳可願
chiiki 地域
Chōkyū 調久
Chōsokabe Motochika 長宗我部元親
Chouhai tubian 籌海図編
chūgen 中間
Chūgoku Kyushu oharae kubarichō 中国九州御祓賦帳
Chūsho Iehisa-kō gojōkyō nikki 中書家久公御上京日記

dabetsu yakusen 駄別役銭
Dai Min fu 大明譜
Daiganji 大願寺
daiku 大工
Dainichi Nyōrai 大日如来
Daitō 大唐
Daitokuji 大徳寺
Date 伊達
Dōgo 道後
dokko 独鈷
Dōkō Genzaemon 道光源左衛門
Dōyū 道祐
Dōzen 道前
266

Ebashima 江場島
eboshi 烏帽子
ebune 家船
Eison Shōnin 永尊上人
Engi shiki 延喜式
Etajima 江田島

folangi 仏狼機
Fujiki Hisashi 藤木久志
Fujimoto Masayuki 藤本正行
Fujita Tatsuo 藤田達生
Fujiwara 藤原
Fujiwara no Ason Murakami Bitchū no kami Kunishige
　　藤原朝臣村上備中守国重
Fujiwara no Sumitomo 藤原純友
Fukabori 深堀
Fukatsu 深津
Fukuda Matajirō 福田又次郎
funabito 船人
funadama 船霊
funade 船手
Funai 府内
funako 船子
furanki 仏狼機
furyo no sainan 不慮之災難
Fusaaki oboegaki 房顕覚書
Futagami 二神
Futagami Taneyasu 二神種康
Futagamijima 二神島
Fuzhou 福州

Gandō 雁道
gekokujō 下剋上
genin 下人
Genji 源氏
Genpei jōsuiki 源平盛衰記
Gen'un bunshū 幻雲文集
Genzo 源三
Gesshū Jukei 月舟寿桂
Go-Daigo 後醍醐
gokenin 御家人
Go-Nara 後奈良
Goseibai shikimoku 御成敗式目
Go-Shirakawa 後白河
Goshuin 御朱印

Gotō rettō 五島列島
gun'yaku 軍役
gusainin 供祭人
Gyōbu no jō Shigehiro 刑部丞重弘
Gyōhen 行遍
Gyōkai 行快
Gyōki 行基

Habu 埴生
Hachiman Daibosatsu 八幡大菩薩
Hachiman gudōkun 八幡愚童訓
Haedong chegukki 海東諸国記
haejŏk 海賊
Hagi-han batsuetsuroku 萩藩閥閲録
hairen 海人
hakama 袴
Hakata 博多
Hashiba Hideyoshi 羽柴秀吉
hatsuo 初穂
Hayashiya Tatsusaburō 林屋辰三郎
Heian-kyō 平安京
Heike monogatari 平家物語
Heiwarei 平和令
Heyaji Kojima 邊屋路小島
Hibinoseki 日比関
Hiburishima 日振島
hiki 疋
Himetsurume 姫鶴女
hinōgyōmin 非農業民
hinoki 檜
Hirado 平戸
hirahira ひらひら
Hirakata Yoshihisa 平方吉久
Hirota Jinja 廣田神社
Hoida Motokiyo 穂田元清
Hōjō 北条
Hōjō Tokimune 北条時宗
Hoketsu Norinobu 法華津範延
hōkōshū 奉公衆
Hongzhi 弘治
hōraku renga 法楽連歌
hōrokubiya 焙烙火矢
Hōryūji 法隆寺
Hōsenji 宝泉寺
Hosokawa 細川

Hosokawa Harumoto 細川晴元
Hosokawa Sumimoto 細川澄元
Hosokawa Tadaoki 細川忠興
Hosokawa Takakuni 細川高国
hosong (Kn.) 護送
Hosoya 細屋
Hotate Michihisa 保立道久
husong (Ch.) 護送
Hu Weiyong 胡惟庸
Hu Zhongxian 胡宗憲
Hyakkanjima 百貫島
hyakushō 百姓
hyō 俵
Hyōetarō 兵衛太郎
Hyōgo 兵庫
Hyōgo Kitazeki irifune nōchō 兵庫北関入船納帳

ichimi shinsui 一味神水
ie 家
Iki 壱岐
ikki 一揆
Ikkō Ikki 一向一揆
Ikuchi 生口
Ikuchi Gyōbu no suke Kagemori 生口刑部丞景守
Ikuchijima 生口島
Imabari 今治
Imagawa Ryōshun 今川了俊
Imaoka 今岡
Imazu 今津
Innoshima 因島
Innoshima Murakami 因島村上
Innoshima Murakami Bitchū no kami Yoshisuke 因島村上備中守吉資
Innoshima Murakami Shinkurōdo Yoshimitsu 因島村上新蔵人吉充
Innoshima Murakami Sukeyasu 因島村上祐康
Inoue Mataemon no jō Harutada 井上又右衛門尉春忠
Inryōken nichroku 蔭涼軒日録
Inume 犬女
Irago 伊良湖
irihama 入浜
rui igyō 異類異形
Ishi Hyōe nyūdō 醫師兵衛入道
ishibiya 石火矢
Ishii Kenji 石井謙治
Ishiyama Honganji 石山本願寺
isonoseki 磯関

269

Itō 伊藤
Itsukijima 伊津喜島 (斎島)
Itsukushima Daimyōjin 厳島大明神
Itsukushima Jinja 厳島神社
itten 一点
Iwagijima 岩城島
Iwashimizu Hachimangū 石清水八幡宮
Iwaya 岩屋
Iyo Ōshima 伊予大島
Izanagi 伊弉諾

Jiajing 嘉靖
Jiang Zhou 蔣洲
jige keigo 地下警固
Jingū Kōgō 神功皇后
jinin 神人
Jinkaishū 塵芥集
Jinshin nyūminki 壬申入明記
jiriki kyūsai 自力救済
jitō shiki 地頭識
Jōzōinbon Yoshōki 上蔵院本予章記
jūhakku gusō 十八口供僧

kaburi kako 頭水夫
Kagawa Masanori 香川正矩
Kagawa Saemon no jō Hirokage 香川左衛門尉廣景
Kagawa Sen'a 香川宣阿
kaichū kōzoku 海中寇賊
kaijin 海人
kaijō 海上
Kainai Shōgun 海内将軍
kaisen 廻船
Kaisen shikimoku 廻船式目
kaizoku 海賊
kakitsuke 書付
kako 水夫
Kamadanoseki 鎌田関
Kamadonoseki 竈関
Kamagari 蒲刈
Kamakura 鎌倉
Kaminoseki 上関
Kamo Jinja 賀茂神社
Kamon no kami 掃部頭
Kan Saykō no suke 間左京亮

Kanazawa Bunko 金沢文庫
kandaka 貫高
kandori 梶取
kandori ken hyakushō 梶取兼百姓
kandori mishin 梶取未進
Kanehisa Shōyū gorō Kagekatsu 包久少輔五郎景勝
Kan'ei shoka keizuden 寛永諸家系図伝
Kaneyoshi Shinnō 懐良親王
Kangen 乾元
kangō bōeki 勘合貿易
kanmon 貫文
Kanmon nikki 看聞日記
Kannon 観音
kanrei 管領
kanzoku 奸賊
karani 唐荷
Karyaku 嘉暦
kasafuda 傘符
Kasai Shigesuke 香西成資
Kasaoka 笠岡
Kashima chiranki 鹿島治乱旗
kasho 過所
kassen 合戦
Katata 堅田
Katō 加藤
Katō Yoshiaki 加藤嘉明
Kawabuchi Kyūzaemon 川淵久左衛門
Kawai Genzaemonnojō 河井源左衛門尉
kegare 穢
Kegoya 警固屋
keigo 警固
keigomai 警固米
kemari 蹴鞠
Kendō Sōsetsu 謙道宗設
Kennyo Kōsa 顕如光佐
Ki no Tsurayuki 紀貫之
Kibe 木部
Kikei Shinzui 季瓊真蘂
Kikkawa 吉川
Kikō Daishuku 季弘大叔
kimoku 鬼目
Kinashi Matagorō Mototsune 木梨又五郎元恒
Kisen Shūshō 亀泉集証
kishōmon 起請文

Kitabatake Akiie 北畠顕家
Kitanoshō 北荘
Kizu 木津
Kobayakawa 小早川
Kobayakawa Ikuchi Inaba nyūdō 小早川生口因幡入道
Kobayakawa Takakage 小早川隆景
Kodama 児玉
Kodama Uchikura daibu Narihide 児玉内蔵大夫成英
Kodama Yajirō 児玉弥二郎
Kōfukuji 興福寺
kōgi 公儀
Koizumi Kobayakawa 小泉小早川
Kojiki 古事記
Kōjiro 神代
Kōjiro Gentarō 神代源太郎
Kōjiro-ho 神代保
Kokon chomonjū 古今著聞集
koku 石
kokudaka 石高
kokugaryō 国衙領
Komiya 小宮
Kongōbuji 金剛峰寺
Konikki 古日記
Konishi Yukinaga 小西行長
Konjaku monogatari 今昔物語
Kōno 河野
Kōno Michiari 河野通有
Kōno Michinao 河野通直
Kōno Norimichi 河野教通
Kōnoshima 神島
kosen 故戦
Kōya 高野
Kōyō gunkan 甲陽軍艦
kugonin 供御人
Kujira 鯨
Kuki Moritaka 九鬼守隆
Kuki Yoshitaka 九鬼嘉隆
Kumano 熊野
kumon 公文
Kure 呉
Kuroda 黒田
Kurushima Murakami 来島村上
Kurushima Murakami Jibunoshin 来島村上治部進
Kurushima Murakami Kawachi no kami Yoshitsugu 来島村上河内守吉継

272

Kurushima Murakami Michifusa 来島村上通総
Kurushima Murakami Michiyasu 来島村上通康
Kurushima Murakami Uemonnojō 村上右衛門尉
Kurushima Murakami Yoshisato 来島村上吉郷
Kurushima Murakami Zushonosuke 来島村上図書助
Kushi 串
kusunoki 楠
Kutsuna 忽那
Kuwahara 桑原
Kuwahara Uemon daibu Motokatsu 桑原右衛門大夫元勝
Kyōgaku 経覚
Kyōgaku shiyōsho 経覚私要鈔
kyorin 交隣
kyūnin 給人
Kyushu Tandai 九州探題

Lake Biwa 琵琶湖
Li Dan 李旦
liubu 流逋

Makura no sōshi 枕草子
Manabe 真鍋
Manabe Shime no hyōe 真鍋七五三兵衛
Mansai 満済
Mansai jugō nikki 満済准后日記
matsu 松
Matsui Yūkan 松井友閑
Matsura 松浦
Matsura Takanobu 松浦隆信
Mazu 媽祖
Michikajima 見近島
Michiyukiburi 道ゆきぶり
migyōsho 御教書
Mihara 三原
Mikajima-shū 三ヶ島衆
mikata 味方
Minabe 南部
Minamoto 源
Minamoto Michichika 源通親
Minamoto no Ason Yoshihide 源朝臣藝秀
Minamoto no Yoritomo 源頼朝
Minamoto Sadayoshi 源貞義
Mineaiki 峰相記
Ming shi 明史

Mingzhou 明州
Minoshima 蓑島
Mishima 三島
Mishima Daimyōjin 三島大明神
Mitajiri 三田尻
Miyakubo-chō 宮窪町
Miyoshi 三好
Mizoe 溝江
Mojinoseki 門司関
mon 文
monmaku 紋幕
Monomōshi 祝師
Mori 森
Mōri Uma no tō Motonari 毛利右馬頭元就
Mōri Shōyūtarō Terumoto 毛利少輔太郎輝元
Mōri Takamoto 毛利隆元
Motoyoshi-jō 元吉城
muen 無縁
Mukai Kyōemonnojō 向井強右衛門尉
Mukai Tadakatsu 向井忠勝
Mukaishima 向島
muku 椋
Munakata Ōshima 宗像大島
muni 無二
munin 文引
Murai Shōsuke 村井章介
Murakami suigun 村上水軍
Muro 室
Mushijima 務司島
Muzuki 睦月
myō 名
Myŏngjong Taewang sillok 明宗大王実録
Myŏngnyang 鳴梁
Myōsei 明誓
myōshu 名主

Nachi 那智
Nagai Sadashige 長井貞重
Nagoya-jō 名護屋城
naikai 内海
nakanori 中乗
Nakatoshima 中途島
Nakatsu 中津
Nan shi 南史

Nanban 南蛮
Naniwa 難波
Nankai tsūki 南海通記
Nankaidō 南海道
Nanpo Bunshi 南浦文之
Naoshima 直島
Nasu Gorō nyūdō [Rengan] 那須五郎入道 [連願]
Nichūreki 二中歴
nie 贄
Nihon chikaki kaijō 日本近海上
Nihon sandai jitsuroku 日本三代実録
Nii-gun 新居郡
Ningbo 寧波
Ninmyō 人名
Ninomiya Naritatsu 二宮就辰
niten 二点
Nojima 野島
Nomi 乃美
Nomi Hyōbu no suke Munekatsu 乃美兵部丞宗勝
Nōmijima 能美島
Norito 祝詞
Noshima 能島
Noshima Murakami 能島村上
Noshima Murakami Gyōbu shōyū Takemitsu 能島村上刑部少輔武満
Noshima Murakami Mototake 能島村上元武
Noshima Murakami Shōyū gorō Kagehiro 能島村上少輔五郎景廣
Noshima Murakami Shōyū tarō Motoyoshi 能島村上少輔太郎元吉
Noshima Murakami Takashige 能島村上隆重
Noshima Murakami Takeyoshi 能島村上武吉
Noshima Murakami Yoshikata 能島村上吉堅
Nosongdang Ilbon haegnok 老松堂日本行録
Nuwa 怒和
nyūkai 入海

Ōbatake 大畠
Ochi 越智
Oda Nobunaga 織田信長
Odawara 小田原
Ōdeppō 大鉄炮
Ōeiki 大永記
ofunade kumigashira 御船手組頭
Ogasawara 小笠原
Ōhama 大浜
Ōhama Hachiman Jinja 大浜八幡神社

275

okawashi 御交
Oki 隠岐
Oki-ke 沖家
Ōkushi 大串
Ōminato 大湊
Ōmishima 大三島
Onomichi 尾道
origami gechijō 折紙下知状
ōryō 押領
Ōta Gyūichi 太田牛一
Ōta no shō 太田荘
Ōta Sukemune 太田資宗
Ōtani 大谷
Oto Tachibana-hime 弟橘媛
Ōtomo 大友
Ōtomo Sōrin 大友宗麟
Ōtomo Yoshiaki 大友義鑑
Ōtsu-gun 大津郡
Ōuchi 大内
Ōuchi Yoshinaga 大内義長
Ōuchi Yoshioki 大内義興
Ōuchi Yoshitaka 大内義隆
Ōuchi-shi okitegaki 大内氏掟書
Oyama 小山／大山
Ōyamazaki 大山崎
Ōyamazumi Jinja 大山祇神社
Ōzutsu 大筒

Paipo 白波
Pak Sosaeng 朴瑞生

rakuichi-rakuza 楽市楽座
Rankō Zuisa 鸞岡瑞佐
Rasetsu 羅刹
reisen 礼銭
Reizen 冷泉
renga 連歌
ri (Ch. li) 里
Riben yijian 日本一艦
Riben zhuan 日本伝
Ritsuryō 律令
Rokkaku 六角
Rokuon nichiroku 鹿苑日録
Rokuon'in saigoku gekōki 鹿苑院西国下向記

Rokuon'indono Itsukushima mōdeki 鹿苑院殿厳島詣記
rōzeki 狼藉
Ruijū sandai kyaku 類聚三代格
Ruson oboegaki 呂宋覚書
ryō 領
Ryōan Keigo 了菴桂悟
ryōshu 領主
Ryūkyū 琉球

Saburōtarō 三郎太郎
Sadafusa Shinnō 貞成親王
Sagara Shōjin 相良正任
Saigyō 西行
Saika 雑賀
Saikaidō 西海道
Sakai 堺
Sakō Saemon no jō 佐甲左衛門尉
Sakō Tōtarō 佐甲藤太郎
Sakugen Shūryō 策彦周良
Sakugen Washō shotoshū 策彦和尚初渡集
Sankashū 山家集
santen 三点
Santōryū suigun ridanshō 三島流水軍理断抄
sanzoku 山賊
sao 竿
sappo 札浦
Sasuke 左助
satanin 沙汰人
satsumai 札米
Sei Shōnagon 清少納言
Sei Uemon 清右衛門
Sejong sillok 世宗実録
seki 関
sekibune 関船
sekidachi 関立
Sekigahara 関ヶ原
sekikata 関方
sekisho 関所
sendō 船頭
sengoku 戦国
Sen'yōmon'in 宣陽門院
Setoda 瀬戸田
Setonaikai 瀬戸内海
Shigi no shō 信貴庄

shiki 職
shima 島
Shimabara 島原
Shimashiri 島尻
Shimazu 島津
Shimazu Iehisa 島津家久
Shimazu Yoshihisa 島津義久
Shimonoseki 下関
Shimotsui 下津井
Shinagawa 品川
Shinchō-Kō ki 信長公記
Shinkaku Kō'ō taiyū 心覺高王大夫
shio 塩
shioana 塩穴
shiohama 塩浜
Shiozaki 塩崎
Shirai 白井
Shirai Fusatane 白井房胤
shirowari 城割
Shirōzaemon 四郎左衛門
shitaji chūbun 下地中分
shite シテ
Shitennō 四天王
Shiwaku 塩飽
Shizong shilu 世宗実録
Shōan 正安
Shōchū 正中
Shōdoshima 小豆島
shōen 荘園
Shōjinki 正任記
Shoken nichiroku 蔗軒日録
shokunin 職人
shomu shiki 所務職
Shōmyōji 称名寺
Shōni 少弐
shū 衆
Shuangyu 雙嶼
shugo 守護
shukōryō 酒肴料
Sin Sukchu 申叔舟
sō 僧
Sō 宗
Sō Kin 宗金
Sō Sadamori 宗貞盛

Sōchō 宗長
Sōgi 宗祇
sŏgye 書契
Song Hŭigyŏng 宋希璟
Song Suqing 宋素卿
Sŏngjong sillok 成宗実録
sōsendō 惣船頭
Sue Harukata 陶晴賢
sugi 杉
Sugi Jirōzaemonnojō 杉次郎左衛門尉
suigun 水軍
suishangren 水上人
Suma 須磨
Sumiyoshi 住吉
Sunpu 駿府
Susano'o 須佐之男
Suzuki Masaya 鈴木眞哉

Tachibana 橘
Tachibana Narisue 橘成季
T'aejong sillok 太宗実録
Tagarasunoura 田烏浦
Tagaya 多賀谷
Taiheiki 太平記
Taiji 泰地
Taira no Kiyomori 平清盛
Taisanji 太山寺
Taishakuten 帝釈天
Tajima 田島
Takai Tōemonnojō Mototaka 高井藤右衛門尉元任
Takakura 高倉
Takakura-in Itsukushima gokōki 高倉院厳島御幸記
Takasaki 高崎
Takeda 武田
Takeda Shingen 武田信玄
Takehara 竹原
Takigawa Kazumasu 滝川一益
taminzoku 多民族
Tamon'in nikki 多聞院日記
Tanamori Fusaaki 棚守房顕
tandai 探題
Tanegashima 種子島
Tangpo 唐浦
Tannowa 淡輪

tare shio 垂塩
Tarōemon 太郎衛門
Tarumi 垂水
Tekkai てっかわい
Tendai 天台
Tenka 天下
Tenman Daijizai Tenjin 天満大自在天神
Tenmoku 天目
Tennōji 天王寺
Tenyo Seikei 天与清啓
teppō 鉄砲
Teppō-ki 鉄砲記
Tō Sukemoto 騰資職
Toba 鳥羽
Tōdaiji 東大寺
Togawa Taira Uemon no jō Hideyasu 富川平右衛門尉秀安
toi 問
toimaru 問丸
Tōji 東寺
tokai 渡海
Tōkaidō 東海道
Tokubei Tenjiku monogatari 徳兵衛天竺物語
Tokugawa Iemitsu 徳川家光
Tokugawa Ieyasu 徳川家康
Tokui Michiyuki 得居通幸
Tokumame 得万女
tomari 泊
Tomoda Okifuji 友田興藤
Tomonoura 鞆浦
tone 刀禰
Tonoura 外浦
Tosa nikki 土佐日記
Tōshi 答志
Toshinari 俊成
Tōshōgū 東照宮
Tōshun no bō 藤春房
tosŏ 図書
Toyoashiwara 豊葦原
Toyo-Tama-Bime-no-Mikoto 豊玉姫命
Toyotomi Hideyoshi 豊臣秀吉
tozama 外様
tsu 津
Tsuharame 津原目
tsukejiro 付城

Tsukushi no michi no ki 筑紫道記
Tsurajima 連島
Tsurihama 釣浜
tsūro 通路
Tsuruga 敦賀
Tsushima 対馬
Tsuwaji 津和地

ue 上
Uehara 上原
Uesugi 上杉
Ugashima 宇賀島
Uji shūi monogatari 宇治拾遺物語
ukebumi 請文
ukimai 浮米
Ukita Naoie 宇喜多直家
umi *海*
umi no ryōshu *海の領主*
ura 浦
Urado 浦戸
urazeni 浦銭
Ushimado 牛窓
utamakura 歌枕
Utazu 宇多津
uwanori 上乗

waegu 倭寇
Wakakikume 若菊女
wakisendō 脇船頭
wakō 倭寇
Wamyō ruijushō 和名類聚抄
Wang Zhi 王直
Wangzhi 王制
Watanabe no tsu 渡辺津
watari 渡
watari aruku bushi 渡り歩く武士
wokou 倭寇
Wufeng 五峰
Wu Jing 呉兢

Xianzong shilu 憲宗実録
Xu Hai 徐海
Xunzi 荀子

yagura 櫓
Yakushima 屋久島
yama 山
Yamaji 山路
Yamana 山名
Yamato no kami 大和守
Yamato Takeru 大和武
Yamauchi Yuzuru 山内譲
Yanai 柳井
Yanai Kurōdo Akinao 柳井蔵人郷直
Yang Su 梁需
Yang Yi 楊宜
Yasaka Hōkanji 八坂法観寺
Yashirojima 屋代島
Yasutomi 保富
Yi Sunsin 李舜臣
Yingzong shilu 英宗実録
Yodo 淀
Yoshimura Magojirō Sukeyuki 吉村孫次郎助行
Yoyō Kōno kafu 予陽河野家譜
Yu Dayou 兪大猷
Yue 越
Yugeshima 弓削島

zasshō 雑掌
zei 賊
Zenrin kokuhōki 善隣国宝記
Zhang Bolu 張伯路
Zheng Chenggong 鄭成功
Zheng Ruozeng 鄭若曾
Zheng Shun'gong 鄭舜功
Zheng Zhilong 鄭芝龍
Zhengde 正徳
Zhengqi tangji 正気堂集
Zhen'guan zhengyao 貞観政要
Zhoushan 舟山
Zhu Wan 朱紈
Zhu Yuanzhang 朱元璋
zōhyō 雑兵
Zoku zenrin kokuhōki 続善隣国宝記
zokusen 賊船
Zuikei Shūhō 瑞渓周鳳

Bibliography

Unless otherwise specified, the place of publication for Japanese works is Tokyo.

PRIMARY SOURCES

Ama. In *Shinpen Nihon koten bungaku zenshū*. Vol. 59, *Yōkyokushū*. Vol. 2, edited by Koyama Hiroshi and Satō Ken'ichirō, 533–48. Shōgakukan, 1998.

Antony, Robert J., ed. *Pirates in the Age of Sail*. New York: Norton, 2007.

"Bukebandaiki: Santō kaizoku-ke ikusa nikki, hoi no maki." *Suminoe* 230 (Fall 1998): 42–66.

"Bukebandaiki: Santō kaizoku-ke ikusa nikki, ichi no maki." Edited by Katayama Kiyoshi. *Suminoe* 227 (Winter 1997): 43–64.

"Bukebandaiki: Santō kaizoku-ke ikusa nikki, ni no maki." Edited by Katayama Kiyoshi. *Suminoe* 228 (Spring 1998): 41–62.

"Bukebandaiki: Santō kaizoku-ke ikusa nikki, san no maki." Edited by Katayama Kiyoshi. *Suminoe* 229 (Summer 1998): 37–62.

Chosŏn wangjo sillok. Edited by Kuksa P'yŏnch'an Wiwŏnhoe. 49 vols. Seoul: Tamgudang, 1986.

Chūgoku Chōsen no shiseki ni okeru Nihon shiryō shūsei: Min jitsuroku no bu. 6 vols. Kokusho Kankōkai, 1975.

Chūgoku Chōsen no shiseki ni okeru Nihon shiryō shūsei: Ri-chō jitsuroku no bu. 11 vols. Kokusho Kankōkai, 1976.

Chūgoku Chōsen no shiseki ni okeru Nihon shiryō shūsei: Seishi no bu. 2 vols. Kokusho Kankōkai, 1975.

Chūsei hōsei shiryōshū. Edited by Satō Shin'ichi and Ikeuchi Yoshisuke. 5 vols. Iwanami Shoten, 1955–65.

Classical Japanese Prose: An Anthology. Compiled and Edited by Helen C. McCullough. Stanford, Calif.: Stanford University Press, 1990.

Coleridge, Samuel Taylor. *The Rime of the Ancient Mariner and Other Poems*. New York: Dover, 1992.

Collection of Tales from Uji: A Study and Translation of Uji Shūi Monogatari. Translated and Edited by D. E. Mills. Cambridge: Cambridge University Press, 1970.

Dai Nihon komonjo iewake 2, Asano-ke monjo. Compiled by Tokyo Teikoku Daigaku Shiryō Hensanjo. Tokyo Teikoku Daigaku Shuppankai, 1906.

Dai Nihon komonjo iewake 8, *Mōri-ke monjo.* Compiled by Tokyo Teikoku Daigaku Shiryō Hensanjo. 4 vols. Tokyo Teikoku Daigaku Shuppankai, 1920–24.

Dai Nihon komonjo iewake 9, *Kikkawa-ke monjo.* Compiled by Tokyo Teikoku Daigaku Shiryō Hensanjo. 3 vols. Tokyo Teikoku Daigaku Shuppankai 1925–32.

Dai Nihon komonjo iewake 10, *Tōji monjo.* Compiled by Tokyo Teikoku Daigaku Shiryō Hensanjo. 15 vols. Tokyo Daigaku Shuppankai, 1925–.

Dai Nihon komonjo iewake 11, *Kobayakawa-ke monjo.* Compiled by Tokyo Teikoku Daigaku Shiryō Hensanjo. 2 vols. Tokyo Teikoku Daigaku Shuppankai, 1927.

Dai Nihon komonjo iewake 12, *Uesugi-ke monjo.* Compiled by Tokyo Teikoku Daigaku Shiryō Hensanjo. 3 vols. Tokyo Teikoku Daigaku Shuppankai 1931–63.

Dai Nihon komonjo iewake 16, *Shimazu-ke monjo.* Compiled by Tokyo Teikoku Daigaku Shiryō Hensanjo. 4 vols. Tokyo Teikoku Daigaku Shuppankai, 1942-

Dai Nihon komonjo iewake 17, *Daitokuji monjo.* Compiled by Tokyo Teikoku Daigaku Shiryō Hensanjo. 16 vols. Tokyo Teikoku Daigaku Shuppankai, 1943-

Dai Nihon shiryō. Compiled by Tokyo Teikoku Daigaku Shiryō Hensanjo. Tokyo Teikoku Daigaku Shuppankai, 1901–.

Ehime-ken shi shiryō-hen kinsei. Jō. Edited by *Ehime-Ken Shi* Hensan Iinka Matsuyama-shi: Ehime-ken, 1984.

Ehime-ken shi shiryō-hen kodai chūsei. Edited by *Ehime-ken Shi* Hensan Iinka Matsuyama-shi: Ehime-ken, 1983.

The English Factory in Japan, 1613–1623. Compiled and Edited by Anthony Farrington. 2 vols. London: The British Library, 1991.

Ennin. *Diary: The Record of a Pilgrimage to China in Search of the Law.* Translate and Edited by Edwin O. Reischauer. New York: Ronald Press Co., 1955.

Four Japanese Travel Diaries of the Middle Ages. Edited and Translated by Herbert E. Plutschow and Hideichi Fukuda. Ithaca, N.Y.: China-Japan Program Cornell University, 1981.

Frois, Luis, S. J. *Historia de Japam.* Edited by José Wicki, S. J. 5 volumes. Lisboa Ministério da Cultura e Coordenação Cientifica Secretaria de Estado da Cultura, Biblioteca Nacional, 1984.

Fujiwara Seika. *Nankō nikki zankan.* In *Fujiwara Seika-shū.* Vol. 2, edited by Kokumin Seishin Bunka Kenkyūjo, 377–89. Kyoto: Shibunkaku Shuppan, 1941.

Genpei jōsuiki. Edited by Ichiko Teiji. 6 vols. Miyai Shoten, 1991.

Gilbert, W. S., and Arthur Sullivan. *Pirates of Penzance,* 1879.

Gosukōin. *Kanmon nikki.* 2 vols. Kunaichō Shoryōbu, 2002.

Gotōke reijō. In *Kinsei hōsei shiryō sōsho.* Vol. 2, edited by Ishii Ryōsuke, 1–295 Sōbunsha, 1959.

Hagi-han batsuetsuroku. Edited by Nagata Masazumi. 5 vols. Yamaguchi-shi Yamaguchi-ken Monjokan, 1967.

Hayashi Jussai and Hotta Masaatsu, comps. *Shintei Kansei chōshū shokafu.* Edited by Takayanagi Mitsutoshi, Okayama Taiji, and Saiki Kazuma. 26 vols. Zoku Gunsho Ruijū Kanseikai, 1964–67.

Heike monogatari. Edited by Takagi Ichinosuke, Ozawa Masao, Atsumi Kaoru, and Kinda'ichi Haruhiko. Vols. 32 and 33 of *Nihon koten bungaku taikei.* Iwanami Shoten, 1960.

Hiroshima-ken shi. Kodai chūsei shiryō-hen. 5 vols. Hiroshima-shi: Hiroshima-ken, 1978–84.

Honganji monjo. Edited by Chiba Jōryū and Kitanishi Hiromu. Kashiwa Shobō, 1986.

Hyōgo-ken shi shiryō-hen chūsei. Compiled by *Hyōgo-ken Shi* Henshū Senmon Iinkai. 9 vols. Kōbe-shi: Hyōgo-ken, 1990.

Hyōgo Kitazeki irifune nōchō. Edited by Hayashiya Tatsusaburō. Chūō Kōron Bijutsu Shuppan, 1981.

Imagawa Ryōshun. *Michiyukiburi.* Edited by Ineda Toshinori. In *Shinpen Nihon koten bungaku zenshū.* Vol. 48, *Chūsei nikki kikōshū: Kaidōki, Tōkan kikō, Ben no Naishi nikki, Izayoi nikki hoka*, edited by Nagasaki Ken, 392–426. Shōgakukan, 1994.

———. *Rokuon'indono Itsukushima mōdeki.* In *Gunsho ruijū.* Vol. 18, *Nikki-bu: kikō-bu*, 1099–1108. Zoku Gunsho Ruijū Kanseikai, 1899–.

Ishiyama kassen hennen shiryō. Vol. 12 of *Taikei Shinshū shiryō.* Edited by Shinshū Shiryō Kankōkai. Kyoto: Hōzōkan, 2010.

Kaempfer, Engelbert. *Kaempfer's Japan: Tokugawa Culture Observed.* Translated and Edited by Beatrice Bodart-Bailey. Honolulu: University of Hawai'i Press, 1999.

Kagawa Masanori and Kagawa Sen'a. *Intoku taiheiki.* Edited by Yonehara Masa-yoshi. 6 vols. Tōyō Shoin, 1980–84.

Kaiji shiryō sōsho. Edited by Sumida Masa'ichi. 20 vols. Genshōdō, 1965.

Kaitei zōho dai bukan. Edited by Hashimoto Hiroshi. 3 vols. Meicho Kankōkai, 1965.

Kasai Shigesuke. *Nankai tsūki.* Vol. 20 of *Shintei zōho shiseki shūran.* Edited by Kondō Keizō. Rinsen Shoten, 1967.

Kasaoka-shi shi shiryō-hen. Vol. 2. Kasaoka-shi, Okayama-ken: Kasaoka-shi, 2001.

Kashima chiranki. In *Gunsho ruijū.* Vol. 21, Kassenbu, 49–53. Zoku Gunsho Ruijū Kanseikai, 1930.

Katō, Eileen. "Pilgrimage to Dazaifu: Sogi's *Tsukushi no Michi no Ki.*" *Monumenta Nipponica* 34.3 (1979): 333–67.

Kawabuchi Kyūzaemon. *Ruson oboegaki.* In *Kaihyō sōsho.* Vol. 6, 1–15. Kōseikaku, 1928.

Kikei Shinzui and Kisen Shusho. *Inryōken Nichiroku.* Edited by Tamamura Takeji and Katsuno Ryūshin. 5 vols. Kyoto: Shiseki Kankōkai, 1953.

Ki no Tsurayuki. *Tosa nikki.* Edited by Suzuki Tomotarō. In *Nihon koten bungaku taikei.* Vol. 20, *Tosa, Kagerō, Izumi Shikibu, Sarashina*, 5–82. Iwanami Shoten, 1957.

Kitabatake Chikafusa. *A Chronicle of Gods and Sovereigns: Jinnō Shōtōki of Kitabatake Chikafusa.* Translated and Edited by H. Paul Varley. New York: Columbia University Press, 1980.

Kojiki. Vol. 1 of *Shinpen Nihon koten bungaku zenshū.* Edited by Yamaguch Yoshinori and Kōnoshi Takamitsu. Shōgakukan, 1997.

Kojiki. Translated and Edited by Donald Philippi. University of Tokyo Press, 1968.

Konjaku monogatarishū. Vols. 22–26 of *Nihon koten bungaku taikei.* Edited by Yamada Yoshio, Yamada Tadao, Yamada Hideo, and Yamada Toshio. Iwanam Shoten, 1959–63.

Kōyasan monjo. 7 Volumes. Kyōto: Kōyasan Monjo Kankōkai, 1936–41.

Linschoten, Jan Huygen van. *Iohn Huighen van Linschoten. His discours of voyage into ye Easte & West Indies.* Translated by John Wolfe. London: 1598. Reprint Amsterdam: Theatrum Orbis Terrarum, Ltd. and Norwood, N.J.: Walter J Johnson Inc., 1974.

Mansai. *Mansai jugō nikki.* Edited by Hanawa Hokinoichi and Ōta Toshirō. *Zoku Gunsho ruijū, hoi* 1. 2 vols. Zoku Gunsho Ruijū Kanseikai, 1928.

Mera Monjo. Vol. 3 of *Kumano Nachi Taisha monjo.* Zoku Gunsho Ruijū Kanseikai 1974.

Mie-ken shi shiryō-hen chūsei. 3 Vols. and Supplements. Tsu-shi, Mie-ken: Mie-ken 1997–2005.

Mie-ken shi shiryō-hen kinsei, vol. 1. Tsu-shi, Mie-ken: Mie-ken, 1993.

Minamoto Michichika. *Takakura'in Itsukushima gokōki.* Edited by Ōsone Shōsuke In *Shin Nihon koten bungaku taikei.* Vol. 51, *Chūsei nikki kikōshū,* edited b Fukuda Hideichi, 1–23. Iwanami Shoten, 1990.

Minamoto Shitagō. *Wamyō ruijushō.* Edited by Masamune Atsuo. Kazama Shobō 1962.

Miyakubo-chō shi. Edited by *Miyakubo-chō Shi* Henshū Iinkai. Miyakubo-chō Ehime-ken: Miyakubo-chō, 1994.

Murasaki Shikibu. *The Tale of Genji.* Translated and Edited by Royall Tyler. Lon don: Penguin, 2001.

———. *Genji monogatari.* Edited by Abe Akio, Akiyama Ken, Imai Gen'e, and Su zuki Hideo. Vols. 20–25 of *Shinpen Nihon koten bungaku zenshū.* Shōgakukan 1995.

Nakajima-chō shi shiryōshū. Edited by Nakajima-machi Kyōikuiinkai. Nakajima machi, Ehime-ken: Nakajima-machi Kyōikuiinkai, 1975.

Nichimin kangō bōeki shiryō. Compiled by Yutani Minoru. Kokusho Kankōkai 1983.

Nichūreki. In *Kaitei shiseki shūran.* Vol. 23, edited by Kondō Heijō, 1–252. Kondō Shuppanbu, 1903.

Nihon engyō taikei shiryō-hen kodai chūsei. Vol. 1. Edited by Nihon Engyō Taike Henshū Iinkai. Nihon Engyō Kenkyūkai, 1982.

Nihon engyō taikei shiryō-hen kodai chūsei hoi. Vol. 1. Edited by Nihon Engyō Taikei Henshū Iinkai. Nihon Engyō Kenkyūkai, 1982.

Norito: A Translation of the Ancient Japanese Ritual Prayers. Translated and Ed ited by Donald Philippi. The Institute for Japanese Culture and Classics Kokugakuin University, 1959.

Ōeiki. In *Gunsho ruijū.* Vol. 20, *Kassenbu,* 302–17. Zoku Gunsho Ruijū Kanseika 1929.

Ōta Gyūichi. *The Chronicle of Lord Nobunaga.* Translated and Edited by J. S. A. Elisonas and J. P. Lamers. Leiden: Brill, 2010.

———. *Shinchō-Kō ki.* Edited by Okuno Takahiro and Iwasawa Yoshihiko. Kadokawa Shoten, 1969.

Ōta Sukemune, comp. *Kan'ei shoka keizuden.* Edited by Saiki Kazuma, Hayashi Ryōshō, and Hashimoto Masanobu. 15 vols. Zoku Gunsho Ruijū Kanseikai, 1980–97.

Ōtomo suigun: Umi kara mita chūsei Bungo. Ōita-shi: Ōita Kenritsu Sentetsu Shiryōkan, 2003.

Rodrigues, João. *João Rodrigues's Account of Sixteenth-Century Japan.* Translated and Edited by Michael Cooper. London: Hakluyt Society, 2001.

Roku'onin saigoku gekōki. In *Shintō taikei Bungaku-hen.* Vol. 5, *Sankeiki,* edited by Shinjō Tsunezō, 151–73. Shintō Taikei Hensankai, 1984.

Ruijū sandaikyaku. In *Kokushi taikei.* Vol. 25, *Ruijū sandaikyaku, Kōnin kyakushō.* Edited by Kuroita Katsumi. Yoshikawa Kōbunkan, 1965.

Scripture of the Lotus Blossom of the Fine Dharma. Translated and Edited by Leon Hurvitz. New York: Columbia University Press, 1976.

"The Second Voyage of John Davis with Sir Edward Michelborne, Knight, into the East-Indies, in the *Tigre,* a ship of two hundred and fortie Tuns, with a Pinasse called the *Tigres Whelpe....*" In *The Voyages and Works of John Davis, the Navigator,* edited, with an introduction and notes by Albert Hastings Markham, 157–84. London: Printed for the Hakluyt Society, 1880.

Sei Shōnagon. *The Pillow Book.* Translated and Edited by Meredith McKinney. New York: Penguin, 2006.

Setoda-chō shi shiryō-hen. Edited by Setoda-chō Kyōikuiinkai Chō-shi Hensanshitsu. Setoda-chō, Hiroshima-ken: Setoda-chō Kyōikuiinkai, 1997.

Shimazu Iehisa. *Chūsho Iehisa-kō gojōkyō nikki.* In *Shintō taikei bungaku-hen.* Vol. 5, *Sankeiki,* edited by Shinjō Tsunezō, 299–320. Shintō Taikei Hensankai, 1984.

Shinpen Kagawa sōsho. 3 vols. Takamatsu-shi: Kagawa-ken Kyōikuiinkai, 1981.

Shinpen Marugame-shi shi. Vol. 4, *Shiryō-hen.* Marugame-shi, Kagawa-ken: *Marugame-shi Shi* Hensan Iinkai, 1994.

Shintei zenrin kokuhōki, shintei zoku zenrin kokuhōki. Edited by Tanaka Takeo. Shūeisha, 1995.

Shirai monjo. In *Buke monjo no kenkyū to mokuroku,* edited by Akutagawa Tatsuo, 185–234. Ishikawa Bunka Jigyō Zaidan, Ochanomizu Toshokan, 1988.

Shiwaku ninmyō kyōyū monjo. In *Shinpen Kagawa sōsho shiryō-hen.* Vol. 2, 431–38. Takamatsu-shi: Kagawa-ken Kyōikuiinkai, 1981.

Sin Sukchu. *Haedong chegukki [Kaitō shokokuki]: Chōsenjin no mita chūsei no Nihon to Ryūkyū.* Edited by Tanaka Takeo. Iwanami Shoten, 1991.

Sōgi. *Tsukushi no michi no ki.* Edited by Kawazoe Shōji. In *Shin Nihon koten bungaku taikei.* Vol. 51, *Chūsei nikki kikōshū,* edited by Fukuda Hideichi, 405–32. Iwanami Shoten, 1990.

Song Hŭigyŏng. *Nosongdang Ilbon haegnok [Rōshōdō Nihon kōroku]: Chōsen shisetsu no mita chūsei Nihon.* Edited by Murai Shōsuke. Iwanami Shoten, 1987.

Sōshin. *Tokubei Tenjiku monogatari*. In *Edo hyōryūki sōshū*. Vol. 1, edited by Yamashita Tsuneo, 488–504. Hyōronsha, 1992.

Tachibana Narisue. *Kokon chomonjū*. Edited by Nishio Kōichi and Kobayashi Yasuharu. 2 vols. Shinchōsha, 1983.

Taiheiki. Edited by Gotō Tanji, Kamada Kisaburō, and Okami Masao. Vols. 34–36 of *Nihon koten bungaku taikei*. Iwanami Shoten, 1960–62.

The Tale of the Heike. Translated and Edited by Helen C. McCullough. Stanford. Calif.: Stanford University Press, 1988.

Tamon'in nikki. Edited by Tsuji Zennosuke. 5 vols. Kadokawa Shoten, 1968.

Tyler, Royall, trans. *Japanese Nō Dramas*. London: Penguin, 1992.

――――. *Japanese Tales*. New York: Pantheon Books, 1987.

Uji shūi monogatari. Edited by Kobayashi Yasuharu and Masuko Kazuko. Vol. 50 of *Shinpen Nihon koten bungaku zenshū*. Shōgakukan, 1996.

Vocabvlario da lingoa de Iapam. Edited by Doi Tadao. Iwanami Shoten, 1960.

Wakasa gyoson shiryō. Edited by Fukui Kenritsu Toshokan and Fukui-ken Gōdoshi Kondankai. Fukui-shi: Fukui-ken Gōdoshi Kondankai, 1963.

Wakayama-ken shi chūsei shiryō. 2 Vols. Edited by *Wakayama-ken Shi* Hensan Iinkai. Wakayama-shi: Wakayama-ken, 1983.

Wu Jing. *Zhen'guan zhengyao* [Jōgan Seiyo]. Translated and Edited by Harada Taneshige. In *Shinyaku Kanbun taikei*. Vols. 95–96. Meiji Shoin, 1978.

Xunzi. *The Works of Hsüntze*. Translated and Edited by Homer H. Dubs. 2 vols. Taipei: Confucius Publishing Co., 1973.

Yamaguchi-ken shi shiryō-hen chūsei. 4 vols. Yamaguchi-shi: Yamaguchi-ken, 1996–2008.

Yi Sunsin, *Nanjung ilgi* [*Ranchū nikki*]: *Jinshin waran no kiroku*. Edited by Kitajima Manji. 3 vols. Heibonsha, 2000–2001.

――――. *Nanjung ilgi: War Diary of Admiral Yi Sun-sin*. Edited by Sohn Pow-key Translated by Ha Tae-hung. Seoul: Yonsei University Press, 1977.

Yoshōki, Suiri gengi, Kōno bungenroku, kaiteiban. Edited by Yamauchi Yuzuru and Kageura Tsutomu. Matsuyama: Iyo Shidankai, 1995.

Yu Dayou. *Zhengqi tangji*. 1565. In *Siku weishou shujikan*. Vol. 20, 47–568. Beijing Beijing Chubanshe, 1998.

Zheng Ruozeng. *Chouhai tubian*. Beijing: Zhonghua Shuju, 2007.

Zheng Shun'gong. *Riben yijian*. Beijing: Gushu Shiwen Diange, 1939.

Zōtei Oda Nobunaga monjo no kenkyū. Edited by Okuno Takahiro. 3 Vols. Yoshi kawa Kōbunkan, 1988.

SECONDARY SOURCES

Adolphson, Mikael S. *The Gates of Power: Monks, Courtiers, and Warriors in Pre modern Japan*. Honolulu: University of Hawai'i Press, 2000.

Aida Nirō. *Chūsei no sekisho*. Yoshikawa Kōbunkan, 1983. Originally Published 1943 by Unebi Shobō.

Akasaka Norio, Nakamura Ikuo, Harada Nobuo, and Miura Sukeyuki, eds. *Hito to mono to michi to*. Iwanami Shoten, 2003.

Akimichi Tomoya. "Setouchi no Seitaigaku: Setouchi no gyorō to seien." In *Umi to rettō Bunka*. Vol. 9, *Setouchi no ama bunka*, edited by Amino Yoshihiko and Ōbayashi Taryō, 51–82. Shōgakukan, 1991.

Amino Yoshihiko. *Rethinking Japanese History*. Translated and with an Introduction by Alan S. Christy, Preface and Afterword by Hitomi Tonomura. Michigan Monograph Series in Japanese Studies, Number 74. Ann Arbor: Center for Japanese Studies, The University of Michigan, 2012.

———. *Kaimin to Nihon shakai: These are What Japan Has Raised in Its History*. Shin Jinbutsu Ōraisha, 1998.

———. *Nihon chūsei shiryōgaku no kadai: keizu, gimonjo, monjo*. Kōbundō, 1996.

———. "Emperor, Rice, and Commoners." In *Multicultural Japan: Paleolithic to Postmodern*, edited by Donald Denoon, Mark Hudson, Gavan McCormack, and Tessa Morris-Suzuki, 235–44. Cambridge: Cambridge University Press, 1996.

———. *Akutō to kaizoku: Nihon chūsei no shakai to seiji*. Hōsei Daigaku Shuppankyoku, 1995.

———. *Chūsei no hinin to yūjo*. Akashi Shoten, 1994.

———. *Igyō no ōken*. Heibonsha, 1986.

———. "Chūsei no seien to shio no ryūtsū." In *Kōza Nihon gijutsu no shakaishi*. Vol. 2, *Engyō, gyogyō*, edited by Amino Yoshihiko and Nagahara Keiji, 43–92. Nihon Hyōronsha, 1985.

———. "Kodai, chūsei, kinsei shoki no gyorō to kaisanbutsu no ryūtsū." In *Kōza Nihon gijutsu no shakaishi*. Vol. 2, *Engyō gyogyō*, edited by Amino Yoshihiko and Nagahara Keiji, 197–272. Nihon Hyōronsha, 1985.

———. *Nihon chūsei no hinōgyōmin to tennō*. Iwanami Shoten, 1984.

———. "Mishin to minoshiro." In *Chūsei no tsumi to batsu*, edited by Amino Yoshihiko, Sasamatsu Hiroshi, and Ishii Susumu, 133–52. Tokyo Daigaku Shuppankai, 1983.

———. *Chūsei Tōji to Tōjiryō shōen*. Tokyo Daigaku Shuppankai, 1978.

———. *Muen kugai raku: Nihon chūsei no jiyū to heiwa*. Heibonsha, 1978.

Amino Yoshihiko and Nagahara Keiji, eds. *Kōza Nihon gijutsu no shakaishi*. Vol. 2, *Engyō, gyogyō*. Nihon Hyōronsha, 1985.

Amino Yoshihiko and Ōbayashi Taryō, eds. *Umi to rettō bunka*. Vol. 9, *Setouchi no ama bunka*. Shōgakukan, 1991.

Amino Yoshihiko, Sasamatsu Hiroshi, and Ishii Susumu, eds. *Chūsei no tsumi to batsu*. Tokyo Daigaku Shuppankai, 1983.

Anderson, John L. "Piracy and World History: An Economic Perspective on Maritime Predation." In *Bandits at Sea: A Pirates Reader*, edited by C. R. Pennell, 82–106. New York: New York University Press, 2001.

Andrade, Tonio. *Lost Colony: The Untold Story of China's First Great Victory over the West*. Princeton, N.J.: Princeton University Press, 2011.

Andrews, Kenneth R. *Elizabethan Privateering: English Privateering During the Spanish War, 1585–1603.* Cambridge: Cambridge University Press, 1964.

Antony, Robert J. *Like Froth Floating on the Sea: The World of Pirates and Seafarers in Late Imperial South China.* Berkeley: Institute of East Asian Studies, University of California Berkeley, 2003.

Antony, Robert J., ed. *Elusive Pirates, Pervasive Smugglers: Violence and Clandestine Trade in the Greater China Seas.* Hong Kong: Hong Kong University Press, 2010.

Appleby, John C. "Women and Piracy in Ireland: From Gráinne O'Malley to Anne Bonney." In *Bandits at Sea: A Pirates Reader*, edited by C. R. Pennell, 283–98. New York: New York University Press, 2001.

Arai Takashige. *Akutō no seiki.* Yoshikawa Kōbunkan, 1997.

Arano Yasunori, Ishii Masatoshi, and Murai Shōsuke. "Jiki kubunron." In *Ajia no naka no Nihonshi.* Vol. 1, *Ajia to Nihon*, edited by Arano Yasunori, Ishii Masatoshi, and Murai Shōsuke, 1–57. Tokyo Daigaku Shuppankai, 1992.

Arano Yasunori, Ishii Masatoshi, and Murai Shōsuke, eds. *Ajia no naka no Nihonshi*, 6 vols. Tokyo Daigaku Shuppankai, 1992.

Arima Kaori. "Muromachi bakufu bugyōnin hakkyū kasho ni tsuite no ichi kōsatsu." *Komonjo kenkyū* 48 (1998.10): 55–66.

Arima Seiho. *Kahō no kigen to sono denryū.* Yoshikawa Kōbunkan, 1962.

Arnesen, Peter J. *The Medieval Japanese Daimyo: The Ōuchi Family's Rule of Suō and Nagato.* New Haven: Yale University Press, 1979.

Asao Naohiro. "The Sixteenth-Century Unification." Translated by Bernard Susser. In *The Cambridge History of Japan.* Vol. 4, *Early Modern Japan*, edited by John W. Hall and James L. McClain, 40–95. Cambridge: Cambridge University Press, 1991.

———. "Shogun and Tennō." With Marius B. Jansen. In *Japan Before Tokugawa: Political Consolidation and Economic Growth, 1500 to 1650*, edited by John W. Hall, Nagahara Keiji, and Kozo Yamamura, 248–70. Princeton, N.J.: Princeton University Press, 1981.

Asao Naohiro, Ishii Susumu, Hayakawa Shōhachi, Amino Yoshihiko, Kano Masaoka, and Yasumaro Yoshio eds. *Iwanami kōza Nihon tsūshi.* Vol. 10, *chūsei 4.* Iwanami Shoten, 1994.

Bakhtin, Mikhail. "Discourse in the Novel." In *The Dialogic Imagination: Four Essays*, edited by Michael Holquist, translated by Caryl Emerson and Michael Holquist, 259–422. Austin: University of Texas Press, 1981.

Batten, Bruce L. *Gateway to Japan: Hakata in War and Peace, 500–1300.* Honolulu: University of Hawai'i Press, 2006.

———. *To The Ends of Japan: Premodern Frontiers, Boundaries, and Interactions.* Honolulu: University of Hawai'i Press, 2003.

Baxter, James C. and Joshua A. Fogel, eds. *Writing Histories in Japan: Texts and Their Transformations from Ancient Times through the Meiji Era.* Kyoto: International Research Center for Japanese Studies, 2007.

Bentley, Jerry H., Renate Bridenthal, and Kären Wigen, eds. *Seascapes: Maritime Histories, Littoral Cultures, and Transoceanic Exchanges.* Honolulu: University of Hawai'i Press, 2007.

Benton, Lauren. "Legal Spaces of Empire: Piracy and the Origins of Ocean Regionalism." *Comparative Studies in Society and History* 47.4 (2005): 700–724.

Berger, Gordon M., Andrew E. Goble, Lorraine F. Harrington, and G. Cameron Hurst, eds. *Currents in Medieval Japanese History: Essays in Honor of Jeffrey P. Mass.* Los Angeles: Figueroa Press, 2009.

Berry, Mary Elizabeth. *Japan in Print: Information and Nation in the Early Modern Period.* Berkeley: University of California Press, 2006.

———. *The Culture of Civil War in Kyoto.* Berkeley: University of California Press, 1994.

———. *Hideyoshi.* Cambridge, Mass.: Harvard University Press, 1982.

Birt, Michael P. "Samurai in Passage: The Transformation of the Sixteenth-Century Kanto." *Journal of Japanese Studies* 11.2 (1985): 369–99.

Bitō Masahide. "Thought and Religion: 1550–1700." In *The Cambridge History of Japan.* Vol. 4, *Early Modern Japan*, edited by John W. Hall and James L. McClain, 373–424. Cambridge: Cambridge University Press, 1991.

Black, Jeremy. *European Warfare, 1494–1660.* London and New York: Routledge, 2003.

———. *A Military Revolution? Military Change and European Society, 1550–1800.* London: Macmillan Education, 1991.

Blok, Anton. "The Peasant and the Brigand: Social Banditry Reconsidered." *Comparative Studies in Society and History* 14.4 (September 1972): 494–503.

Bonar, H. A. C. "On Maritime Enterprise in Japan." *Transactions of the Asiatic Society of Japan* 15 (1887): 103–25.

Boxer, Charles R. *The Christian Century in Japan, 1549–1650.* Berkeley: University of California Press, 1951.

Braudel, Fernand. *The Mediterranean and the Mediterranean World in the Age of Philip II.* Translated by Siân Reynolds. 2nd ed. 2 vols. Berkeley: University of California Press, 1995.

Breuker, Remco E., ed. *Korea in the Middle: Korean Studies and Area Studies: Essays in Honour of Boudewijn Walraven.* Leiden: CNWS Publications, 2007.

Bromley, J. S. "Outlaws at Sea, 1660–1720: Liberty, Equality and Fraternity among the Caribbean Freebooters." In *Bandits at Sea: A Pirates Reader*, edited by C. R. Pennell, 169–94. New York: New York University Press, 2001.

Brook, Timothy. *Confusions of Pleasure: Commerce and Culture in Ming China.* Berkeley: University of California Press, 1998.

Brown, Delmer M. "The Impact of Firearms on Japanese Warfare, 1543–98." *Far Eastern Quarterly* 7.3 (1948): 236–53.

Brown, Philip C. *Central Authority and Local Autonomy in the Formation of Early Modern Japan: The Case of Kaga Domain.* Stanford, Calif.: Stanford University Press, 1993.

Butler, Lee. *Emperor and Aristocracy in Japan, 1467–1680: Resilience and Renewal.* Cambridge, Mass.: Harvard University Asia Center, 2002.

Carioti, Patrizia. "The Zheng's Maritime Power in the International Context of the 17th c. Far Eastern Seas." *Ming Qing yanjiu* 5 (1996): 29–67.

Chase, Kenneth. *Firearms: A Global History to 1700.* Cambridge: Cambridge University Press, 2002.

Chin, James. "Merchants, Smugglers, and Pirates: Multinational Clandestine Trade on the South China Coast, 1520–50." In *Elusive Pirates, Pervasive Smugglers: Violence and Clandestine Trade in the Greater China Seas*, edited by Robert Antony, 43–58. Hong Kong: Hong Kong University Press, 2010.

Clulow, Adam. "Like Lambs in Japan and Devils outside Their Land: Diplomacy Violence, and Japanese Merchants in Southeast Asia." *Journal of World History* 24.2 (2013): 335–58.

———. "The Pirate and the Warlord." *Journal of Early Modern History* 16.6 (2012) 523–42.

———. "From Global Entrepôt to Early Modern Domain: Hirado, 1609–1641." *Monumenta Nipponica* 65.1 (2010): 1–35.

———. "Unjust, Cruel and Barbarous Proceedings: Japanese Mercenaries and the Amboyna Incident of 1623." *Itinerario* 31.1 (2007): 15–34.

Coaldrake, William. *Architecture and Authority in Japan.* London: Routledge, 1996

Conlan, Thomas D. "Instruments of Change: Organizational Technology and the Consolidation of Regional Power in Japan." In *War and State Building in Medieval Japan*, edited by John A. Ferejohn and Frances McCall Rosenbluth 124–58. Stanford, Calif.: Stanford University Press, 2010.

———. *State of War: The Violent Order of Fourteenth-Century Japan.* Michigan Monograph Series in Japanese Studies, Number 46. Ann Arbor: Center for Japanese Studies, The University of Michigan, 2003.

Cooper, Michael. *Rodrigues the Interpreter: An Early Jesuit in Japan and China* New York: Weatherhill, 1974.

Corbin, Alain. *The Lure of the Sea: The Discovery of the Seaside in the Western World, 1750–1840.* Translated by Jocelyn Phelps. Oxford: Polity Press, 1994.

Cronon, William. *Changes in the Land: Indians, Colonists, and the Ecology of New England.* New York: Hill and Wang, 1983.

Cronon, William, ed. *Uncommon Ground: Rethinking the Human Place in Nature* New York: Norton and Co., 1995.

Cuevas, Bryan J., and Jacqueline I. Stone, eds. *The Buddhist Dead: Practices, Discourses, Representations.* Honolulu: University of Hawai'i Press, 2007.

Dening, Greg. "The Theatricality of Observing and Being Observed: Eighteenth Century Europe 'Discovers' the ? Century 'Pacific.'" In *Implicit Understandings: Observing, Reporting, and Reflecting on the Encounters between European and other Peoples in the Early Modern Era*, edited by Stuart B. Schwartz, 451–83. Cambridge: Cambridge University Press, 1994.

———. *Mr. Bligh's Bad Language: Passion, Power and Theatre on the Bounty.* Cambridge: Cambridge University Press, 1992.

————. *Islands and Beaches: Discourse on a Silent Land: Marquesas, 1774–1880.* Melbourne: Melbourne University Press, 1980.

Denoon, Donald, Mark Hudson, Gavan McCormack, and Tessa Morris-Suzuki, eds. *Multicultural Japan: Paleolithic to Postmodern.* Cambridge: Cambridge University Press, 1996.

Dolce, Lucia. "Mapping the 'Divine Country': Sacred Geography and International Concerns in Mediaeval Japan." In *Korea in the Middle: Korean Studies and Area Studies: Essays in Honour of Boudewijn Walraven,* edited by Remco E. Breuker, 288–312. Leiden: CNWS Publications, 2007.

Ebisawa Miki. "Jūgoseiki Yamato no joseitachi." *Sōgō joseishi kenkyū* 12 (1995): 1–18.

Elison, George, and Bardwell L. Smith, eds. *Warlords, Artists, and Commoners: Japan in the Sixteenth Century.* Honolulu: University of Hawai'i Press, 1981.

Elisonas, Jurgis. "Christianity and the Daimyo." In *The Cambridge History of Japan.* Vol. 4, *Early Modern Japan,* edited by John W. Hall and James L. McClain, 301–72. Cambridge: Cambridge University Press, 1991.

————. "The Inseparable Trinity: Japan's Relations with China and Korea." In *The Cambridge History of Japan.* Vol. 4, *Early Modern Japan,* edited by John W. Hall and James L. McClain, 235–300. Cambridge: Cambridge University Press, 1991.

Farris, William Wayne. "Shipbuilding and Nautical Technology in Japanese Maritime History: Origins to 1600." *Mariner's Mirror* 95.3 (2009): 260–83.

————. *Japan's Medieval Population: Famine, Fertility, and Warfare in a Transformative Age.* Honolulu: University of Hawai'i Press, 2006.

————. *Heavenly Warriors: The Evolution of Japan's Military, 500–1300.* Cambridge, Mass.: Council on East Asian Studies, Harvard University, 1992.

————. *Population, Disease, and Land in Early Japan, 645–900.* Cambridge, Mass.: Council on East Asian Studies, Harvard University, and the Harvard Yenching Institute, 1985.

Ferejohn, John A., and Frances McCall Rosenbluth, eds. *War and State Building in Medieval Japan.* Stanford, Calif.: Stanford University Press, 2010.

Fogel, Joshua A., ed. *Sagacious Monks and Bloodthirsty Warriors: Chinese Views of Japan in the Ming-Qing Period.* Norwalk, Conn.: Eastbridge, 2002.

Friday, Karl. *The First Samurai: The Life and Legend of the Warrior Rebel, Taira Masakado.* Hoboken, N.J.: John Wiley & Sons, 2008.

Fujiki Hisashi. *Kiga to sensō no sengoku o yuku.* Asahi Shinbunsha, 2001.

————. *Zōhyōtachi no senjō: chūsei no yōhei to doreigari.* Asahi Shinbunsha, 1995.

————. *Toyotomi heiwarei to sengoku shakai.* Tokyo Daigaku Shuppankai, 1985.

Fujiki Hisashi, ed. *Mōri-shi no kenkyū.* Yoshikawa Kōbunkan, 1984.

Fujimoto Masayuki. *Nobunaga no sensō: Shinchō-Kō ki ni miru sengoku gunjigaku.* Kōdansha, 2003.

Fujimoto Yorihito. "Chūsei zenki no kandori to chiikikan no kōryū." *Nihon rekishi* 678 (2004.11): 19–36.

Fujita Tatsuo. *Nihon kinsei kokka seiritsushi no kenkyū.* Azekura Shobō, 2001.

Gay, Suzanne. "The Lamp-oil Merchants of Iwashimizu Shrine: Transregiona Commerce in Medieval Japan." *Monumenta Nipponica* 64.1 (2009): 1–51.

_____. *The Moneylenders of Late Medieval Kyoto*. Honolulu: University of Hawai' Press, 2001.

Gerhart, Karen. *The Eyes of Power: Art and Early Tokugawa Authority*. Honolulu University of Hawai'i Press, 1999.

Gilroy, Paul. *The Black Atlantic: Modernity and Double Consciousness*. Cambridge Mass.: Harvard University Press, 1993.

Glete, Jan. *Warfare at Sea, 1500–1650: Maritime Conflicts and the Transformation of Europe*. London and New York: Routledge, 2000.

Goble, Andrew E. *Kenmu: Go-Daigo's Revolution*. Cambridge, Mass.: Council or East Asian Studies, Harvard University, 1996.

Goble, Andrew E., Kenneth R. Robinson, and Haruko Wakabayashi, eds. *Tools o Culture: Japan's Cultural, Intellectual, Medical, and Technological Contacts ir East Asia, 1000s–1500s*. Ann Arbor: Association for Asian Studies, 2009.

Goodwin, Janet. *Selling Songs and Smiles: The Sex Trade in Heian and Kamakur Japan*. Honolulu: University of Hawai'i Press, 2007.

Grossberg, Kenneth. *Japan's Renaissance: The Politics of the Muromachi Bakufu* Cambridge, Mass.: Council on East Asian Studies, Harvard University, 1981.

Hall, John W. *Government and Local Power in Japan 500–1700: A Study Based or Bizen Province*. Princeton, N.J.: Princeton University Press, 1966.

Hall, John W., and James L. McClain, eds. *The Cambridge History of Japan*. Vol. 4 *Early Modern Japan*. Cambridge: Cambridge University Press, 1991.

Hall, John W., and Jeffrey P. Mass, eds. *Medieval Japan: Essays in Institutional His tory*. Stanford, Calif.: Stanford University Press, 1974

Hall, John W., Nagahara Keiji, and Kozo Yamamura, eds. *Japan Before Tokugawa Political Consolidation and Economic Growth, 1500 to 1650*. Princeton, N.J Princeton University Press, 1981.

Hall, John W., and Toyoda Takeshi, eds. *Japan in the Muromachi Age*. Stanford Calif.: Stanford University Press, 1977.

Harley, J. B., and David Woodward, eds. *History of Cartography*. Vol. 2, bk. 2, *Car tography in the Traditional East and Southeast Asian Societies*. Chicago: Uni versity of Chicago Press, 1987.

Harootunian, H. D. "Disciplining Native Knowledge and Producing Place: Yanagit Kunio, Origuchi Shinobu, Takata Yasuma." In *Culture and Identity: Japanes Intellectuals During the Interwar Years,* edited by J. Thomas Rimer, 99–12. Princeton, N.J.: Princeton University Press, 1990.

Harrington, Lorraine F. "Social Control and the Significance of *Akutō*." In *Cour and Bakufu in Japan: Essays in Kamakura History,* edited by Jeffrey P. Mass 221–50. New Haven, Conn.: Yale University Press, 1982.

Hashimoto, Mitsuru. "*Chihō*: Yanagita Kunio's Japan." In *Mirror of Modernity*: *In vented Traditions of Modern* Japan, edited by Stephen Vlastos, 133–43. Berke ley: University of California Press, 1998.

Hashimoto Yū. *Chūka gensō: Karamono to gaikō no Muromachi jidaishi*. Bense Shuppan, 2011.

————. *Chūsei Nihon no kokusai kankei: Higashi Ajia tsūkōken to gishi mondai.* Yoshikawa Kōbunkan, 2005.

Hashizume Shigeru. *Setonaikai chiiki shakai to Oda kenryoku.* Kyoto: Shibunkaku Shuppan, 2007.

Hayashiya Tatsusaburō. "*Hyōgo Kitazeki irifune nōchō* ni tsuite." In *Hyōgo Kitazeki irifune nōchō*, edited by Hayashiya Tatsusaburō, 221–31. Chūō Kōron Bijutsu-sha, 1981.

Hazard, Benjamin H. "The Formative Years of the Wakō, 1223–63." *Monumenta Nipponica* 22.3 (1967): 260–77.

Heller, Monica. "Code-switching and the Politics of Language." In *One Speaker, Two Languages: Cross-Disciplinary Perspectives on Code Switching*, edited by Lesley Milroy and Pieter Muysken, 158–74. Cambridge: Cambridge University Press, 1995.

Hellyer, Robert. "Poor but Not Pirates: The Tsushima Domain and Foreign Relations in Early Modern Japan." In *Elusive Pirates, Pervasive Smugglers: Violence and Clandestine Trade in the Greater China Seas*, edited by Robert J. Antony, 115–26. Hong Kong: Hong Kong University Press, 2010.

Hirase Naoki. "Shugo daimyo Ōuchi-shi to kaihen no busō seiryoku." *Yamaguchi-ken chihōshi kenkyū* 71, no. 6 (1994): 23–32.

Hobsbawm, Erik. *Bandits.* New York: Delacorte Press, 1969.

Holcombe, Charles. *The Genesis of East Asia, 221 B.C.- A.D. 907.* Honolulu: University of Hawai'i Press, 2001.

Horden, Peregrine, and Nicholas Purcell. *The Corrupting Sea: A Study of Mediterranean History.* Oxford; Malden, Mass.: Blackwell Publishers, 2000.

Horton, H. Mack. "Renga Unbound: Performative Aspects of Japanese Linked Verse." *Harvard Journal of Asiatic Studies* 53.2 (December 1993): 443–512.

Hotate Michihisa. "Chūsei zenki no gyogyō to shōensei: kakai ryōyū to gyomin o megutte." *Rekishi hyōron* 376 (1981): 15–43.

Igawa Kenji. *Daikōkai jidai no Higashi Ajia: Nichi-Ō tsūkō no rekishiteki zentei.* Yoshikawa Kōbunkan, 2007.

Iida Yoshirō. *Nihon kōkaijutsushi: kodai kara bakumatsu made.* Hara Shobō, 1980.

Ike Susumu. "Sengoku-ki chiiki kenryoku to 'kōgi.'" *Chūō shigaku* 27 (2004): 1–17.

Ikegami Hiroko. "Sengoku no sonraku." In *Iwanami kōza Nihon tsūshi.* Vol. 10, *Chūsei 4*, edited by Asao Naohiro, Ishii Susumu, Hayakawa Shōhachi, Amino Yoshihiko, Kano Masaoka, and Yasumaro Yoshio, 89–126. Iwanami Shoten, 1994.

Imatani Akira. "Setouchi seikaiken no suii to *irifune nōchō*." In *Hyōgo Kitazeki irifune nōchō*, edited by Hayashiya Tatsusaburō, 272–88. Chūō Kōron Bijutsu Shuppan, 1981.

Inamoto Noriaki. "Kuki-shi ni tsuite." *Mie-ken shi kenkyū* 1 (1985): 29–50.

Innes, Robert. "The Door Ajar: Japan's Foreign Trade in the Seventeenth Century." Ph.D. Diss., The University of Michigan, 1980.

Ishii Kenji. *Wasen* II. Hōsei Daigaku Shuppankyoku, 1995.

————. *Zusetsu wasen shiwa.* Shiseidō, 1983.

_____. "*Nagoyajō-zu* no atakebune ni tsuite." *Kokka* 77, no. 915 (1968): 31–40.

Itō Kōji. *Chūsei Nihon no gaikō to Zenshū*. Yoshikawa Kōbunkan, 2002.

Iwao Seiichi. *Shinpen shuinsen bōekishi no kenkyū*. Yoshikawa Kōbunkan, 1985.

Kadokawa Nihon chimei daijiten. 47 vols. Kadokawa Shoten, 1978–90.

Kage Toshio. *Sengoku daimyo no gaikō to toshi ryūtsū: Bungo Ōtomo-shi to Higashi Ajia sekai*. Shibunkaku, 2006.

Kalland, Arne. *Fishing Villages in Tokugawa Japan*. Richmond, Surrey: Curzon Press, 1995.

Kanaya Masato. *Kaizokutachi no chūsei*. Yoshikawa Kōbunkan, 1998.

Kanbe Teruo. "Tei Shunkō to Shō Shū: Ōtomo Sōrin to atta futari no Minjin." *Ōita Daigaku Kyōiku Fukushi Kagakubu kenkyū kiyō* 21.2 (1999): 109–24.

Kang, Etsuko Hae-Jin. *Diplomacy and Ideology in Japanese-Korean Relations: From the Fifteenth to the Eighteenth Century*. Houndmills, Basingstoke, Hampshire: Macmillan Press, 1997.

Kariyama Mototoshi. "Sengoku daimyo Mōri-shi ryōnai no ukimai ni tsuite." *Kōgakkan ronsō* 22.6 (1989.12): 50–57.

Kasamatsu Hiroshi. "Youchi." In *Chūsei no tsumi to batsu*, edited by Amino Yoshihiko, Sasamatsu Hiroshi, and Ishii Susumu, 89–102. Tokyo Daigaku Shuppankai, 1983.

Kasaoka-shi shi. Edited by *Kasaoka-shi Shi* Hensanshitsu. Kasaoka-shi, Okayama-ken: Kasaoka-shi, 1983.

Katayama Kiyoshi. "*Bukebandaiki* kaidai." *Suminoe* 226 (Fall 1997): 42–62.

Katsumata Shizuo. *Sengoku jidairon*. Iwanami Shoten, 1996.

_____. *Ikki*. Iwanami Shoten, 1982.

_____. "The Development of Sengoku Law." With Martin Collcutt. In *Japan Before Tokugawa: Political Consolidation and Economic Growth, 1500 to 1650*, edited by John W. Hall, Nagahara Keiji, and Kozo Yamamura, 101–24. Princeton, N.J.: Princeton University Press, 1981.

Kawai Masaharu. "Tagaya-shi no rekishi." In *Tagaya suigun to Maruyajō ato*, edited by Maruyajō Ato Chōsadan, 3–13. Shimokamagari-chō, Hiroshima-ken: Shimokamagari-chō, 1981.

_____. "Kobayakawa-shi no hatten to Setonaikai." In *Setonaikai chiiki no shakaishi-teki kenkyū*, edited by Uozumi Sōgorō, 109–29. Yanagihara Shoten, 1952.

Kawazoe Shōji. "Japan and East Asia." In *The Cambridge History of Japan*. Vol. 3, *Medieval Japan*, edited by Kozo Yamamura, 396–446. Cambridge: Cambridge University Press, 1990.

_____. "Umi ni hirakareta toshi: kodai chūsei Hakata." In *Yomigaeru chūsei*. Vol. 1, *Higashi Ajia no kokusai toshi Hakata*, edited by Kawazoe Shōji, 8–39. Heibonsha, 1988.

Kawazoe Shōji, ed. *Yomigaeru chūsei*. Vol. 1, *Higashi Ajia no kokusai toshi Hakata*. Heibonsha, 1988.

Keene, Donald. "Jōha, a Sixteenth-Century Poet of Linked Verse." In *Warlords, Artists, and Commoners: Japan in the Sixteenth Century*, edited by George Elison and Bardwell L. Smith, 113–32. Honolulu: University of Hawai'i Press, 1981

Keirstead, Thomas. *The Geography of Power in Medieval Japan.* Stanford, Calif.: Stanford University Press, 1992.

Kishida Hiroshi. "*Hakkakoku onjidai bungenchō* ni miru Mōri-shi no Chōsen e no dōin taisei." In *Chūgoku chiiki to taigai kankei,* edited by Kishida Hiroshi, 133–69. Yamakawa Shuppansha, 2003.

———. *Daimyo ryōgoku no keizai kōzō.* Iwanami Shoten, 2001.

Kishida Hiroshi, ed. *Chūgoku chiiki to taigai kankei.* Yamakawa Shuppansha, 2003.

Kitai Toshio. "Sengoku makki Honganji no kōtsū taisaku." *Nihonshi kenkyū* 294 (1987): 1–22.

Kobayashi Hiroshi. "Domain Laws (*Bunkoku-hō*) in the Sengoku Period: With Special Emphasis on the Date House Code, the *Jinkaishū.*" *Acta Asiatica* 35 (1978): 30–44.

Kubota Masashi. *Nippon no gunji kakumei: Military Revolution in Japan.* Kinseisha, 2008.

Kuroda Hideo. "Gyōkishiki 'Nihonzu' to wa nanika." In *Chizu to ezu no seiji bunkashi,* edited by Kuroda Hideo, Mary Elizabeth Berry, and Sugimoto Fumiko, 3–77. Tokyo Daigaku Shuppankai, 2001.

Kuroda Hideo, Mary Elizabeth Berry, and Sugimoto Fumiko, eds. *Chizu to ezu no seiji bunkashi.* Tokyo Daigaku Shuppankai, 2001.

Kyushu Daigaku Kokushigaku Kenkyūshitsu, ed. *Kodai chūseishi ronshū.* Yoshikawa Kōbunkan, 1990.

Lamers, Jeroen. *Japonius Tyrannus: The Japanese Warlord Oda Nobunaga Reconsidered.* Leiden: Hotei Publishing, 2000.

Lane, Frederic. "Economic Consequences of Organized Violence." *The Journal of Economic History* 18, no. 4 (1958): 401–17.

Lee, Ki-baik. *A New History of Korea.* Translated by Edward W. Wagner. With Edward J. Shultz. Seoul: Ichokak, 1984.

Lewis, Martin W. "Dividing the Ocean Sea." *Geographical Review* 89.2 (4/1999): 188–214.

Lidin, Olaf G. *Tanegashima: The Arrival of Europeans in Japan.* Copenhagen: Nordic Institute of Asian Studies, 2002.

Lieberman, Victor. "Transcending East-West Dichotomies: State and Culture Formation in Six Ostensibly Disparate Areas." *Modern Asian Studies* 31.3 (1997): 463–546.

Lorge, Peter. *The Asian Military Revolution: From Gunpowder to the Bomb.* Cambridge: Cambridge University Press, 2008.

Makita Tairyō. *Sakugen nyūminki no kenkyū.* 2 vols. Kyōto: Bukkyō Bunka Kenkyūjo, 1955.

Markham, Albert Hastings. "Introduction." In *The Voyages and Works of John Davis, The Navigator,* edited, with an introduction and notes by Albert Hastings Markham, i–lxxvii. London: Printed for the Hakluyt Society, 1880.

Marra, Michele. *Representations of Power: The Literary Politics of Medieval Japan.* Honolulu: University of Hawai'i Press, 1993.

Maruyajō Ato Chōsadan, ed. *Tagaya suigun to Maruyajō ato.* Shimokamagari-chō, Hiroshima-ken: Shimokamagari-chō, 1981.

Mass, Jeffrey P. "Of Hierarchy and Authority at the End of Kamakura." In *The Origins of Japan's Medieval World: Courtiers, Clerics, Warriors, and Peasants in the Fourteenth Century,* edited by Jeffrey P. Mass, 17–38. Stanford, Calif.: Stanford University Press, 1997.

———. "Jitō Land Possession in the Thirteenth Century: The Case of *Shitaji Chūbun.*" In *Medieval Japan: Essays in Institutional History,* edited by John W. Hall and Jeffrey P. Mass, 157–83. Stanford, Calif.: Stanford University Press, 1974.

Mass, Jeffrey P., ed. *The Origins of Japan's Medieval World: Courtiers, Clerics, Warriors, and Peasants in the Fourteenth Century.* Stanford, Calif.: Stanford University Press, 1997.

———. *Court and Bakufu in Japan: Essays in Kamakura History.* Stanford, Calif.: Stanford University Press, 1982.

Mass, Jeffrey P., and William Hauser, eds. *The Bakufu in Japanese History.* Stanford, Calif.: Stanford University Press, 1985.

Matsubara Hironobu. *Fujiwara no Sumitomo.* Yoshikawa Kōbunkan, 1999.

Matsuoka Hisato. "The Sengoku Daimyo of Western Japan: The Case of the Ōuchi." With Peter Arnesen. In *Japan Before Tokugawa: Political Consolidation and Economic Growth, 1500 to 1650,* edited by John W. Hall, Nagahara Keiji, and Kozo Yamamura, 64–100. Princeton, N.J.: Princeton University Press, 1981.

McClain, James L., and Wakita Osamu, eds. *Osaka: The Merchant's Capital of Early Modern Japan.* Ithaca, N.Y.: Cornell University Press, 1999.

McMullin, Neil. *Buddhism and the State in Sixteenth-Century Japan.* Princeton, N.J.: Princeton University Press, 1984.

Miki Seiichirō. "Chōsen eki ni okeru gun'yaku taikei ni tsuite." *Shigaku zasshi* 75.2 (1966): 1–26.

Milroy, Lesley, and Pieter Muysken. *One Speaker, Two Languages: Cross-Disciplinary Perspectives on Code Switching.* Cambridge: Cambridge University Press, 1995.

Miyamoto Tsune'ichi. *Setonaikai no kenkyū.* Vol. 1. Miraisha, 1965.

Moerman, Max. "Passage to Fudaraku: Suicide and Salvation in Premodern Japanese Buddhism." In *The Buddhist Dead: Practices, Discourses, Representations,* edited by Bryan J. Cuevas and Jacqueline I. Stone, 266–96. Honolulu: University of Hawai'i Press, 2007.

Moon, Hyungsub. "The Matsura Pirate-Warriors of Northwestern Kyushu in the Kamakura Age." In *Currents in Medieval Japanese History: Essays in Honor of Jeffrey P. Mass,* edited by Gordon M. Berger, Andrew E. Goble, Lorraine F. Harrington, and G. Cameron Hurst, 363–99. Los Angeles: Figueroa Press, 2009.

Morillo, Stephen. "Guns and Government: A Comparative Study of Europe and Japan." *Journal of World History* 6.1 (1995): 75–106.

Morimoto Masahiro. "GoHōjō-shi no suisanbutsu jōnōsei no tenkai." *Nihonshi kenkyū* 359, no. 7 (1992): 31–50.

Morohashi Tetsuji, ed. *Dai Kanwa jiten.* 13 vols. Taishukan, 1955–60.

Morris, V. Dixon. "The City of Sakai and Urban Autonomy." In *Warlords, Artists, and Commoners: Japan in the Sixteenth Century*, edited by George Elison and Bardwell L. Smith, 23–54. Honolulu: University of Hawai'i Press, 1981.

———. "Sakai: From Shōen to Port City." In *Japan in the Muromachi Age*, edited by John W. Hall and Toyoda Takeshi, 145–58. Berkeley: University of California Press, 1977.

Murai Shōsuke. *Nihon chūsei kyōkai shiron*. Iwanami Shoten, 2013.

———. "Poetry in Chinese as a Diplomatic Art in Premodern East Asia." Translated and Edited by Haruko Wakabayashi and Andrew E. Goble. In *Tools of Culture: Japan's Cultural, Intellectual, Medical, and Technological Contacts in East Asia, 1000s–1500s*, edited by Andrew E. Goble, Kenneth R. Robinson, and Haruko Wakabayashi, 49–69. Ann Arbor, Mich.: Association for Asian Studies, 2009.

———. "Rettō naigai no kōryūshi." In *Hito to mono to michi to*, edited by Akasaka Norio, Nakamura Ikuo, Harada Nobuo, and Miura Sukeyuki, 3–38. Iwanami Shoten, 2003.

———. *Umi kara mita Sengoku Nihon: rettōshi kara sekaishi e*. Chikuma Shobō, 1997.

———. *Higashi Ajia ōkan: kanshi to gaikō*. Asahi Shinbunsha, 1995.

———. *Chūsei Wajinden*. Iwanami Shoten, 1993.

———. *Ajia no naka no chūsei Nihon*. Azekura Shobō, 1988.

Murray, Dian. "Cheng I Sao in Fact and Fiction." In *Bandits at Sea: A Pirates Reader*, edited by C. R. Pennell, 253–82. New York: New York University Press, 2001.

Mutō Tadashi. "Chūsei no Hyōgo no tsu to Setonaikai suiun." In *Hyōgo Kitazeki irifune nōchō*, edited by Hayashiya Tatsusaburō, 232–71. Chūō Kōron Bijutsu Shuppan, 1981.

Naganuma Kenkai. *Nihon no kaizoku*. Shibundō, 1955.

Nagazumi Yōko. *Shuinsen*. Yoshikawa Kōbunkan, 2001.

Nakai, Kate Wildman. "Tokugawa Confucian Historiography: The Hayashi, Early Mitō School and Arai Hakuseki." In *Confucianism and Tokugawa Culture*, edited by Peter Nosco, 62–91. Princeton, N.J.: Princeton University Press, 1984.

Nakajima Takashi. "Tei Shunkō no rainichi ni tsuite." *Tōyō Daigaku Bungakubu kiyō, Shigakka-hen* 19 (1993): 59–77.

Nakamura Hidetaka. *Nissen kankeishi no kenkyū*. 3 vols. Yoshikawa Kōbunkan, 1973.

———. *Nihon to Chōsen*. Shibundō, 1966.

Nakamura Tadashi, ed. *Sakoku to kokusai kankei*. Yoshikawa Kōbunkan, 1997.

Narisawa Katsushi. "Nanban byōbu no tenkai." In *Tokubetsuten Nanban kenbunroku: Momoyama kaiga ni miru seiyō to no deai*, edited by Kōbe Shiritsu Hakubutsukan, 76–87. Kōbe-shi: Kōbe-shi Supōtsu Kyōiku Kōsha, 1992.

Needham, Joseph, with the collaboration of Ho Ping-yü, Lu Gwei-Djen, and Wang Ling. *Science and Civilisation in China*. Vol. 5, *Chemistry and Chemical Technology*, part 7, *Military Technology; The Gunpowder Epic*. Cambridge: Cambridge University Press, 1986.

Nelson, Thomas. "Slavery in Medieval Japan." *Monumenta Nipponica* 59 (2004): 463–92.

Nihon kokugo daijiten. Shukusatsuban. Shōgakukan, 1974.

Nishio Kazumi. *Sengokuki no kenryoku to kon'in.* Seibundō, 2005.

———. "Sengoku makki ni okeru Mōri-shi no kon'in seisaku to Iyo." *Nihonshi kenkyū* 445, no. 9 (1999): 1–29.

Nosco, Peter, ed. *Confucianism and Tokugawa Culture.* Princeton, N.J.: Princeton University Press, 1984.

Ōbatake-chō shi. Ōbatake-chō, Yamaguchi-ken: Ōbatake-chō, 1992.

Ōji Toshiaki. *Echizu no sekaizō.* Iwanami Shoten, 1996.

Okiura Kazuteru. *Setouchi no minzokushi: Kaiminshi no shinsō o tazunete.* Iwanami Shoten, 1998.

Ooms, Herman. *Tokugawa Ideology: Early Constructs, 1570–1680.* Princeton, N.J.: Princeton University Press, 1985.

Ōta Kōki. *Wakō: shōgyō, gunjishiteki kenkyū.* Yokohama: Shunpūsha, 2002.

Ōtomo Shin'ichi. *Nihon ikkan: honbun to sakuin.* Kasama Shoin, 1974.

Oxenboell, Morton. "Images of 'Akutō.'" *Monumenta Nipponica* 60.2 (2005): 235–62.

Parker, Geoffrey. *The Military Revolution: Military Innovation and the Rise of the West,* 2nd ed. Cambridge: Cambridge University Press, 1996.

Pennell, C. R. "Introduction." In *Bandits at Sea: A Pirates Reader,* edited by C. R. Pennell, 3–24. New York: New York University Press, 2001.

Pennell, C. R., ed. *Bandits at Sea: A Pirates Reader.* New York: New York University Press, 2001.

Pérotin-Dumon, Anne. "The Pirate and the Emperor: Power and the Law on the Seas, 1450–1850." In *Bandits at Sea: A Pirates Reader,* edited by C. R. Pennell, 25–54. New York: New York University Press, 2001.

Pigeot, Jacqueline. *Femmes galantes, femmes artistes dans le Japon ancien: (XIe–XIIIe siècle).* Paris: Gallimard, 2003.

Pitelka, Morgan. *Handmade Culture: Raku Potters, Patrons, and Tea Practitioners in Japan.* Honolulu: University of Hawai'i Press, 2005.

Pryor, John H. *Geography, Technology, and War: Studies in the Maritime History of the Mediterranean, 649–1571.* Cambridge: Cambridge University Press, 1988.

Ramirez-Christensen, Esperanza. *Heart's Flower: The Life and Poetry of Shinkei.* Stanford, Calif.: Stanford University Press, 1994.

Ravina, Mark. *Land and Lordship in Early Modern Japan.* Stanford, Calif.: Stanford University Press, 1999.

Rediker, Marcus. *The Slave Ship: A Human History.* New York: Viking, 2007.

———. "Liberty Beneath the Jolly Roger: The Lives of Anne Bonney and Mary Read, Pirates." In *Bandits at Sea: A Pirates Reader,* edited by C. R. Pennell, 299–320. New York: New York University Press, 2001.

———. *Between the Devil and the Deep Blue Sea: Merchant Seamen, Pirates and the Anglo-American Maritime World, 1700–1750.* Cambridge: Cambridge University Press, 1987.

Rimer, J. Thomas, ed. *Culture and Identity: Japanese Intellectuals During the Interwar Years.* Princeton, N.J.: Princeton University Press, 1990.

Risso, Patricia. "Cross-Cultural Perceptions of Piracy: Maritime Violence in the Western Indian Ocean and Persian Gulf Region during a Long Eighteenth Century." *Journal of World History* 12, no. 2 (2001): 293–319.

Ritchie, Robert. *Captain Kidd and the War Against the Pirates.* Cambridge, Mass.: Harvard University Press, 1986.

Roberts, Luke. *Performing the Great Peace: Political Space and Open Secrets in Tokugawa Japan.* Honolulu: University of Hawai'i Press, 2012.

———. *Mercantilism in a Japanese Domain: The Merchant Origins of Economic Nationalism in 18th-Century Tosa.* Cambridge: Cambridge University Press, 1998.

Robinson, David. *Bandits, Eunuchs, and the Son of Heaven: Rebellion and the Economy of Violence in Mid-Ming China.* Honolulu: University of Hawai'i Press, 2001.

Robinson, Kenneth R. "A Japanese Trade Mission to Chosŏn Korea, 1537–1540." In *Tools of Culture: Japan's Cultural, Intellectual, Medical, and Technological Contacts in East Asia, 1000s–1500s,* edited by Andrew E. Goble, Kenneth R. Robinson, and Haruko Wakabayashi, 71–101. Ann Arbor, Mich.: Association for Asian Studies, 2009.

———. "Treated as Treasures: The Circulation of Sutras in Maritime Northeast Asia from 1388 to the mid-Sixteenth Century." *East Asian History* 21 (2001): 33–53.

———. "Centering the King of Choson: Aspects of Korean Maritime Diplomacy, 1392–1592." *Journal of Asian Studies* 59.1 (2000): 109–25.

———. "The *Haedong chegukki* (1471) and Korean-Ryukyuan Relations, 1389–1471: Part I." *Acta Koreana* 3 (2000): 87–98.

———. "The Imposter Branch of the Hatakeyama Family and Japanese-Choson Korea Court Relations 1455–1580's." *Asian Cultural Studies (Ajia bunka kenkyū)* 25 (1999): 67–87.

———. "The Jiubian and Ezogachishima Embassies to Choson, 1478–1482." *Chōsenshi kenkyūkai ronbunshū* 35 (1997): 203–34.

———. "From Raiders to Traders: Border Security and Border Control in Early Chosŏn, 1392–1450." *Korean Studies* 16 (1992): 94–115.

Rodger, N. A. M. "The Development of Broadside Gunnery, 1450–1650." *Mariner's Mirror* 82.3 (1996.8): 301–24.

Rogers, Clifford J., ed. *The Military Revolution Debate: Readings on the Military Transformation of Early Modern Europe.* Boulder, Colo.: Westview Press, 1995.

Rosenfield, John M. *The Courtly Tradition in Japanese Art and Literature: Selections from the Hofer and Hyde collections.* Cambridge, Mass.: The Fogg Art Museum, Harvard University, 1973.

Rubin, Alfred P. *The Law of Piracy.* Newport, R.I.: Naval War College Press, 1988.

Ruch, Barbara. "Woman to Woman: Kumano Bikuni Proselytizers in Medieval and Early Modern Japan." In *Engendering Faith: Women and Buddhism in Premodern Japan,* edited by Barbara Ruch, 537–80. Michigan Monograph Series in

Japanese Studies, Number 43. Ann Arbor: Center for Japanese Studies, The University of Michigan, 2002.

Ruch, Barbara, ed. *Engendering Faith: Women and Buddhism in Premodern Japan.* Michigan Monograph Series in Japanese Studies, Number 43. Ann Arbor: Center for Japanese Studies, The University of Michigan, 2002.

Sack, Robert David. *Human Territoriality: Its Theory and History.* Cambridge: Cambridge University Press, 1986.

Sadler, A. L. "The Naval Campaign in the Korean War of Hideyoshi (1592–1598)." *Transactions of the Asiatic Society of Japan* 2nd series, 16 (1937): 177–208.

Saeki Kōji. "Ōei no gaikō to Higashi Ajia." *Shien* 147 (2010): 17–37.

———. "Chinese Trade Ceramics in Medieval Japan." Translated and Adapted by Peter D. Shapinsky. In *Tools of Culture: Japan's Cultural, Intellectual, Medical, and Technological Contacts in East Asia, 1000s–1500s,* edited by Andrew E. Goble, Kenneth R. Robinson, and Haruko Wakabayashi, 163–84. Ann Arbor, Mich.: Association for Asian Studies, 2009.

———. "Muromachiki no Hakata shōnin Sō Kin to Higashi Ajia." *Shien* 136 (1999): 101–21.

———. "Jūroku seiki ni okeru kōki Wakō no katsudō to Tsushima Sō-shi." In *Sakoku to kokusai kankei,* edited by Nakamura Tadashi, 31–50. Yoshikawa Kōbunkan, 1997.

———. "Kaizoku-ron." In *Ajia no naka no Nihonshi III: Kaijō no michi,* edited by Arano Yasunori, Ishii Masatoshi, and Murai Shōsuke, 35–62. Tokyo Daigaku Shuppankai, 1992.

———. "Muromachi jidai no kenminsen keigo ni tsuite." In *Kodai chūseishi ronshū,* edited by Kyushu Daigaku Kokushigaku Kenkyūshitsu, 461–80. Yoshikawa Kōbunkan, 1990.

Sakuma Shigeo. *Nichimin kankeishi no kenkyū.* Yoshikawa Kōbunkan, 1992.

Sakurai Eiji. "Chūsei kinsei no shōnin." In *Ryūtsū keizaishi.* Vol. 12 of *Shintaikei Nihonshi,* edited by Sakurai Eiji and Nakanishi Satoru, 112–49. Yamakawa Shuppansha, 2002.

———. "Chūsei no shōhin ichiba." In *Ryūtsū keizaishi.* Vol. 12 of *Shintaikei Nihonshi,* edited by Sakurai Eiji and Nakanishi Satoru, 199–234. Yamakawa Shuppansha, 2002.

———. *Nihon chūsei no keizai kōzō.* Iwanami Shoten, 1996.

Sakurai Eiji and Nakanishi Satoru, eds. *Ryūtsū keizaishi.* Vol. 12 of *Shintaikei Nihonshi.* Yamakawa Shuppansha, 2002.

Sansom, George. *A History of Japan, 1333–1615.* Stanford, Calif.: Stanford University Press, 1961.

Sasaki Gin'ya. "Sengoku Daimyo Rule and Commerce." With William B. Hauser. In *Japan Before Tokugawa: Political Consolidation and Economic Growth, 1500 to 1650,* edited by John W. Hall, Nagahara Keiji, and Kozo Yamamura, 125–48. Princeton, N.J.: Princeton University Press, 1981.

Sasaki Junnosuke. "The Changing Rationale of Daimyo Control in the Emergence of the Bakuhan State." With Ronald P. Toby. In *Japan Before Tokugawa: Political Consolidation and Economic Growth, 1500 to 1650*, edited by John W. Hall, Nagahara Keiji, and Kozo Yamamura, 271–94. Princeton, N.J.: Princeton University Press, 1981.

Sato, Elizabeth. "The Early Development of the Shōen." In *Medieval Japan: Essays in Institutional History*, edited by John W. Hall and Jeffrey P. Mass, 91–108. Stanford, Calif.: Stanford University Press, 1974.

Satō Shin'ichi. *Shinpen komonjogaku nyūmon*. Hōsei Daigaku Shuppankyoku, 1997.

Schwartz, Stuart B., ed. *Implicit Understandings: Observing, Reporting, and Reflecting on the Encounters between European and other Peoples in the Early Modern Era*. Cambridge: Cambridge University Press, 1994.

Scott, James C. *The Art of Not Being Governed: An Anarchist History of Upland Southeast Asia*. New Haven, Conn.: Yale University Press, 2009.

Segal, Ethan I. *Coins, Trade, and the State: Economic Growth in Early Medieval Japan*. Cambridge, Mass.: Harvard University Asia Center, 2011.

Seki Shūichi. "Chōsen Ōchō kanjin no Nihon kansatsu." *Rekishi hyōron* 592.8 (1999): 16–28.

Shapinsky, Peter D. "From Sea Bandits to Sea Lords: Nonstate Violence and Pirate Identities in Fifteenth- and Sixteenth-Century Japan." In *Elusive Pirates, Pervasive Smugglers: Violence and Clandestine Trade in the Greater China Seas*, edited by Robert Antony, 27–42. Hong Kong: Hong Kong University Press, 2010.

———. "Predators, Protectors, and Purveyors: Pirates and Commerce in Late Medieval Japan." *Monumenta Nipponica* 64.2 (2009): 273–313.

———. "With the Sea as Their Domain: Pirates and Maritime Lordship in Medieval Japan." In *Seascapes: Maritime Histories, Littoral Cultures, and Transoceanic Exchanges*, edited by Jerry Bentley, Kären Wigen, and Renate Bridenthal, 221–38. Honolulu: University of Hawai'i Press, 2007.

———. "Polyvocal Portolans: Nautical Charts and Hybrid Maritime Cultures in Early Modern East Asia." *Early Modern Japan* 14 (2006): 4–26.

Shibagaki Isao, ed. *Chūsei Setouchi no ryūtsū to kōryū*. Hanawa Shobō, 2005.

Shibata Keiko. "Kaizoku no iseki to ryūtsū." In *Chūsei Setouchi no ryūtsū to kōryū*, edited by Shibagaki Isao, 251–73. Hanawa Shobō, 2005.

Shinjō Tsunezō. *Chūsei suiunshi no kenkyū*. Hanawa Shobō, 1995.

Silverberg, Miriam. *Erotic Grotesque Nonsense: The Mass Culture of Japanese Modern Times*. Berkeley: University of California Press, 2006.

Smits, Ivo. "Song as Cultural History, Reading *Wakan Rōeishū* (Interpretations)." *Monumenta Nipponica* 55.3 (2000): 399–427.

So, Kwan-wai. *Japanese Piracy in Ming China During the 16th Century*. Lansing: Michigan State University Press, 1975.

Spafford, David. *A Sense of Place: The Political Landscape in Late Medieval Japan.* Cambridge, Mass.: Harvard University Asia Center, 2013.

Spence, Jonathon D., and John E. Wills, Jr., eds. *From Ming to Ch'ing: Conquest, Region, and Continuity in Seventeenth-Century China.* New Haven, Conn.: Yale University Press, 1979.

Starkey, David J. "Pirates and Markets." In *Bandits at Sea: A Pirates Reader,* edited by C. R. Pennell, 107–24. New York: New York University Press, 2001.

Steinberg, Philip E. *The Social Construction of the Ocean.* Cambridge: Cambridge University Press, 2001.

Suda Makiko. "Chūsei kōki ni okeru Akamagaseki no kinō to Ōuchi-shi." *Hisutoria* 189 (2004): 72–106.

_____. "Muromachiki ni okeru Ōuchi-shi no taichō kankei to senzokan no keisei." *Rekishigaku kenkyū* 761, no. 4 (2002): 1–18.

Sun Laichen. "Military Technology Transfers from Ming China and the Emergence of Northern Mainland Southeast Asia (c. 1390–1527)." *Journal of Southeast Asian Studies* 34.3 (2003): 495–517.

Suzuki Atsuko. *Nihon chūsei shakai no ryūtsū kōzō.* Azekura Shobō, 2000.

Suzuki Masaya. *Sengoku teppō, yoheitai: Tenkabito ni sakaratta Kishū Saikashū.* Heibonsha, 2004.

_____. *Teppō to Nihonjin: "Teppō shinwa" ga kakushitekita koto.* Chikuma Shobō, 2000.

Swope, Kenneth M. *A Dragon's Head and a Serpent's Tail: Ming China and the First Great East Asian War, 1592–1598.* Norman: University of Oklahoma Press, 2009.

_____. "Crouching Tigers, Secret Weapons: Military Technology Employed During the Sino-Japanese-Korean War, 1592–1598." *Journal of Military History* 69.1 (2005): 11–41.

Tabata Yasuko. "Women's Work and Status in the Changing Medieval Economy," translated by Hitomi Tonomura. In *Women and Class in Japanese History,* edited by Hitomi Tonomura, Anne Walthall, and Wakita Haruko, 99–118. Michigan Monograph Series in Japanese Studies, Number 25. Ann Arbor: Center for Japanese Studies, The University of Michigan, 1999.

_____. "Chūsei no kassen to josei no chii." *Rekishi hyōron* 552 (1996): 12–23.

_____. *Nihon chūsei josei shiron.* Hanawa Shobō, 1994.

_____. *Nihon chūsei no josei.* Yoshikawa Kōbunkan, 1987.

Takahashi Osamu. "Shinshutsu no 'Murakami Takeyoshi kashoki' ni tsuite." Jō and ge. *Wakayama Kenritsu Hakubutsukan kenkyū kiyō* 3.4 (1999): 41–52; 3.5 (2000): 32–41.

Takekoshi Yosaburō. *The Story of the Wakō.* Translated by Hideo Watanabe. Kenkyūsha, 1940.

_____. *Wakō-ki.* Hakuyōsha, 1939.

Tanaka, Stephan. *Japan's Orient: Rendering Pasts into History.* Berkeley: University of California Press, 1993.

Tanaka Takeo. *Higashi Ajia tsūkōken to kokusai ninshiki.* Yoshikawa Kōbunkan, 1997.

———. *Wakō: Umi no rekishi.* Kyōikusha, 1982.

———. "Japan's Relations with Overseas Countries." With Robert Sakai. In *Japan in the Muromachi Age,* edited by John W. Hall and Toyoda Takeshi, 159–78. Berkeley: University of California Press, 1977.

———. *Chūsei taigai kankeishi.* Tokyo Daigaku Shuppankai, 1975.

———. *Chūsei kaigai kōshōshi no kenkyū.* Tokyo Daigaku Shuppankai, 1959.

———. *Wakō to kangō bōeki.* Shibundō, 1953.

Thomson, Janice E. *Pirates, Mercenaries, and Sovereigns: State-Building and Extra-territorial Violence in Early Modern Europe.* Princeton, N.J.: Princeton University Press, 1994.

Tilburg, Hans Konrad Van. "Vessels of Exchange: The Global Shipwright in the Pacific." In *Seascapes: Maritime Histories, Littoral Cultures, and Transoceanic Exchanges,* edited by Jerry H. Bentley, Renate Bridenthal, and Kären Wigen, 38–52. Honolulu: University of Hawai'i Press, 2007.

Toby, Ronald P. "Review Article: Rescuing the State from History: the State of the State in Early Modern Japan." *Monumenta Nipponica* 56.2 (2001): 197–237.

———. "Three Realms, Myriad Countries: An Ethnography of Other and the Rebounding of Japan, 1550–1750." In *Constructing Nationhood in Modern East Asia,* edited by Kai-wing Chow, Kevin M. Doak, and Poshek Fu, 15–45. Ann Arbor: The University of Michigan Press, 2001.

———. "Imagining and 'Imaging' Anthropos in Early Modern Japan." *Visual Anthropological Review* 14.1 (1998): 19–44.

———. *State and Diplomacy in Early Modern Japan: Asia in the Development of the Tokugawa Bakufu.* Princeton, N.J.: Princeton University Press, 1984.

Tokunō Kōichi. "Setonaikai kaizokushū Murakami-shi no kashindan kōzō." *Hyōgo shigaku kenkyū* 45 (1999): 24–38.

———. "Sengokuki ni okeru kaizokushū Noshima Murakami-shi no dōkō." *Seiji keizai shigaku* 383 (1998): 14–25.

Tonomura, Hitomi. *Community and Commerce in Late Medieval Japan: The Corporate Villages of Tokuchin-ho.* Stanford, Calif.: Stanford University Press, 1992.

———. "Women and Inheritance in Japan's Early Warrior Society." *Comparative Studies in Society and History* 32.3 (July 1990): 592–621.

Tonomura, Hitomi, Anne Walthall, and Wakita Haruko, eds. *Women and Class in Japanese History.* Michigan Monograph Series in Japanese Studies, Number 25. Ann Arbor: Center for Japanese Studies, The University of Michigan, 1999.

Totman, Conrad. *A History of Japan.* 2nd ed. Malden, Mass.: Blackwell Publishers, 2000.

———. *Early Modern Japan.* Berkeley: University of California Press, 1993.

———. *The Green Archipelago: Forestry in Pre-Industrial Japan.* Berkeley: University of California Press, 1989.

Toyoda Takeshi and Sugiyama Hiroshi. "The Growth of Commerce and the Trades." With V. Dixon Morris. In *Japan in the Muromachi Age*, edited by John W. Hall and Toyoda Takeshi, 129–44. Berkeley: University of California Press, 1977.

Troost, Kristina Kade. "Peasants, Elites, and Villages in the Fourteenth Century." In *The Origins of Japan's Medieval World: Courtiers, Clerics, Warriors, and Peasants in the Fourteenth Century*, edited by Jeffrey P. Mass, 91–112. Stanford, Calif.: Stanford University Press, 1997.

Tsang, Carol. *War and Faith: Ikkō Ikki in Late Muromachi Japan*. Cambridge, Mass.: Harvard University Asia Center, 2007.

Tsuji Zennosuke. *Zōtei kaigai kōtsū shiwa*. Naigai Shoseki Kabushikigaisha, 1930.

Tsuruta Kei. "The Establishment and Characteristics of the Tsushima Gate." *Acta Asiatica* 67 (1994): 30–48.

Turner, Victor. *Dramas, Fields, Metaphors: Symbolic Action in Human Society*. Ithaca, N.Y.: Cornell University Press, 1974.

Udagawa Takehisa. "Teppō to ishibiya." *Nihon no bijutsu* 390 (1998): 17–87.

———. *Teppō denrai: heiki ga kataru kinsei no tanjō*. Chūō Kōronsha, 1990.

———. "Ōuchi-shi keigoshū no shōchō to Mōri-shi no suigun hensei." In *Mōri-shi no kenkyū*, edited by Fujiki Hisashi, 438–61. Yoshikawa Kōbunkan, 1984.

———. *Nihon no kaizoku*. Seibundō, 1983.

———. *Setouchi suigun*. Kyōikusha, 1981.

Unno Kazutaka. "Cartography in Japan." In *The History of Cartography*. Vol. 2, bk. 2, *Cartography in the Traditional East and Southeast Asian Societies*, edited by J. B. Harley and David Woodward, 346–477. Chicago: University of Chicago Press, 1987.

———. "Japan Before the Introduction of the Global Theory of the Earth: In Search of a Japanese Image of the Earth." *Memoirs of the Research Department of the Tōyō Bunko* 38 (1980): 40–69.

Uozumi Sōgorō, ed. *Setonaikai chiiki no shakaishiteki kenkyū*. Yanagihara Shoten, 1952.

Uozumi Sōgorō and Matsuoka Hisato. "Itsukushima Jinja shozō *Hogourakyō* ni tsuite." *Shigaku zasshi* 61, no. 3 (1952): 48–61.

Usami Takayuki. *Nihon chūsei no ryūtsū to shōgyō*. Yoshikawa Kōbunkan, 1999.

Uyenaka, Shuzo. "A Study of Baishōron: A Source for the Ideology of Imperial Loyalism in Medieval Japan." Ph.D. Diss., University of Toronto, 1976.

Varley, H. Paul. "Oda Nobunaga, Guns, and Early Modern Warfare in Japan." In *Writing Histories in Japan: Texts and Their Transformations from Ancient Times through the Meiji Era*, edited by James C. Baxter and Joshua A. Fogel, 105–25. Kyoto: International Research Center for Japanese Studies, 2007.

Vlastos, Stephen, ed. *Mirror of Modernity: Invented Traditions of Modern Japan*. Berkeley: University of California Press, 1998.

von Verschuer, Charlotte. *Across the Perilous Sea: Japanese Trade with China and Korea from the Seventh to the Sixteenth Centuries*. Translated by Kristen Lee Hunter. Ithaca, N.Y.: Cornell University East Asia Series, 2006.

Wakita Haruko. "Ports, Markets, and Medieval Urbanism in the Osaka Region." In *Osaka: The Merchants' Capital of Early Modern Japan*, edited by James L. McClain and Wakita Osamu, 22–43. Ithaca, N.Y.: Cornell University Press, 1999.

Walthall, Anne. "Do Guns Have Gender: Technology and Status in Early Modern Japan." In *Recreating Japanese Men*, edited by Sabine Frühstück and Anne Walthall, 25–47. Berkeley: University of California Press, 2011.

Wang Yi T'ung. *Official Relations between China and Japan, 1368–1549*. Cambridge, Mass.: Harvard University Press, 1953.

Wang Yong. "Realistic and Fantastic Images of 'Dwarf Pirates': The Evolution of Ming Dynasty Perceptions of the Japanese." Translated by Laura Hess. In *Sagacious Monks and Bloodthirsty Warriors: Chinese Views of Japan in the Ming-Qing Period*, edited by Joshua A. Fogel, 17–41. Norwalk, Conn.: Eastbridge, 2003.

Watanabe Norifumi. "Chūsei ni okeru naikai tōsho no seikatsu: Iyo no kuni Yugeshima o chūshin toshite." In *Setonaikai chiiki no shakaishiteki kenkyū*, edited by Uozumi Sōgorō, 81–108. Yanagihara Shoten, 1952.

Wheelwright, Carolyn. "A Visualization of Eitoku's Lost Paintings at Azuchi Castle." In *Warlords, Artists, and Commoners: Japan in the Sixteenth Century*, edited by George Elison and Bardwell L. Smith, 87–112. Honolulu: University of Hawai'i Press, 1981.

White, Richard. "'Are You an Environmentalist or Do You Work for a Living?': Work and Nature." In *Uncommon Ground: Rethinking the Human Place in Nature*, edited by William Cronon, 171–85. New York: Norton and Co., 1995.

Wigen, Kären. "Japanese Perspectives on the Time/Space of 'Early Modernity.'" *The XIX International Congress of Historical Sciences*. Oslo, Norway: 2000: 1–18. http://www.oslo2000.uio.no/program/papers/m1a/M1a-wigen.pdf. Accessed 7.23.2009.

Wills, John E., Jr. "Maritime China from Wang Chih to Shih Lang: Themes in Peripheral History." In *From Ming to Ch'ing: Conquest, Region, and Continuity in Seventeenth-Century China*, edited by Jonathon D. Spence and John E. Wills, Jr., 203–38. New Haven, Conn.: Yale University Press, 1979.

Wilson, William R. "The Way of the Bow and Arrow: The Japanese Warrior in *Konjaku monogatari*." *Monumenta Nipponica* 28.2 (1973): 177–233.

Yamada Kuniaki. *Sengoku no komyunikēshon: jōhō to tsūshin*. Yoshikawa Kōbunkan, 2002.

Yamada Nakaba. *Ghenkō: The Mongol Invasion of Japan*. London: Smith, Elder & Co., 1916.

Yamamura Kozo, ed. *The Cambridge History of Japan*. Vol. 3, *Medieval Japan*. Cambridge: Cambridge University Press, 1990.

Yamamuro Kyōko. "Sengoku no chiikisei." In *Iwanami kōza Nihon tsūshi*. Vol. 10, *Chūsei 4*, edited by Asao Naohiro, Ishii Susumu, Hayakawa Shōhachi, Amino Yoshihiko, Kano Masaoka, and Yasumaro Yoshio, 162–91. Iwanami Shoten, 1994.

_____. *Chūsei no naka ni umareta kinsei*. Yoshikawa Kōbunkan, 1991.

Yamauchi Yuzuru. *Setouchi no kaizoku: Murakami Takeyoshi no tatakai*. Kōdansha, 2005.

_____. *Chūsei Setonaikai no tabibitotachi*. Yoshikawa Kōbunkan, 2004.

_____. *Chūsei Setonaikai chiikishi no kenkyū*. Hōsei Daigaku Shuppankyoku, 1998.

_____. *Kaizoku to umijiro: Setouchi no sengokushi*. Heibonsha, 1997.

_____. *Yugeshima no shō no rekishi*. Yuge-chō, Ehime-ken: Yuge-chō, 1985.

Yata Toshifumi. *Nihon chūsei Sengokuki kenryoku kōzō no kenkyū*. Hanawa Shobō, 1998.

Yonemoto, Marcia. "Maps and metaphors of the 'Small Eastern Sea' in Tokugawa Japan (1603–1868)." *Geographical Review* 89, no. 2 (1999): 169–87.

Index

Noshima Murakami family (*continued*)
boundaries of, 30, 96, 122, 224–25, 131–32;
castles, 24, 106–8, 113, 119, 121, 126, 133,
136–40, 236, 241–42; chokepoints and,
24–25, 100, 106, 108, 113, 116, 122, 130,
136–37, 160–61, 163, 174, 185, 224, 235–39,
243, 246, 249; coalitions of, 120, 142, 157,
159, 160, 163–68, 179–81, 185; code
switching and, 14–15, 87, 92fn100, 105–7,
118, 231, 246; crest-pennant system,
123–31, 161, 222; domain, 6, 14, 24, 30, 66,
93–96, 102–3, 105–51, 159, 161, 201, 205,
210, 212, 222, 224, 230–33, 236–44,
246–47, 249, 253; earliest mention, 88, 94;
as entrepreneurs, 19, 69, 97, 106–7, 110,
113–14, 119, 122, 124, 129–30, 209, 231–32,
238–40; as estate managers, 93–94, 97,
128–29; firearms and, 116, 122, 173,
179–83; Futagamijima and, 95–96, 132,
143–44; genealogies, 256–58, 260;
Hosokawa family and, 108, 110, 216; Ikkō
Ikki and, 108, 119, 161, 163, 165–70, 181,
184–85; Imaoka family and, 112, 216;
imperial family and, 257; Innoshima
Murakami and, 92n100, 103, 111–12,
115n45, 157, 166, 170–71, 184–85, 212,
257–58, 260; internecine feud, 113;
Itsukushima and, 108, 111–14, 115n45,
118, 124–27, 135, 163, 258; Jesuits and, 6,
14, 21, 105–6, 110, 123–24, 126–27, 243;
Kizu River battles and, 119–20, 157, 159,
161, 163, 165–71, 173–74, 179–81, 184, 233;
Kobayakawa family and, 108, 165n46, 166,
236–37, 239, 243, 245, 248, 253; Kōno
family and, 95, 108, 111, 114, 166, 174, 236,
240; Korean War and, 24–25n85, 244, 250,
253; Kurushima Murakami family as ally,
96, 111–12, 114, 115n45, 132, 157, 161,
165–66, 179, 184, 233–35, 237, 244,
252–53, 258, 260; Kurushima Murakami
family as enemy/competitor, 92n100, 121,
143–44, 236–41, 258; Kutsuna and, 95,
143–44, 237, 240; laws of, 143–45;
marriage alliances of, 96, 110, 114;
Matsura family and, 126, 254;
mercenarism of, 20, 105–21, 150, 159, 160,
164–70, 184, 215–16, 231, 233–37, 241;
military revolution and, 154, 158–60,
164–65, 170, 173, 180–81; Miyoshi family
and, 108, 119; Mōri family and, 12, 108,
110, 114–21, 130n104, 140n156, 161, 163,
165–70, 174, 179, 181, 184, 223, 232–41,
243, 246, 251, 253–54, 256–58; as naval

warfare specialists, 111, 114–17, 119–20,
159, 161, 163, 165–71, 173–74, 179–81, 184,
219, 231–32, 237, 245, 247, 252–54, 256–58,
260–61; Nomi family, 163, 165n46, 166,
181, 233, 237, 240; oaths and, 117–19,
237–38, 240, 243, 253; Oda Nobunaga and,
108, 119–20, 159, 163, 167, 169, 173,
180–81, 184, 232–38; Ōtomo family and,
111, 116–17, 163, 165, 173, 179, 216, 219,
222; Ōuchi family and, 108, 111–14, 132,
140–41, 205, 222–23, 257–58, 260; overseas
exchange and, 110, 112–13, 116, 132–33,
179, 187, 201, 205, 212, 214–16, 219,
222–24, 260; as pirates, 14, 93, 113, 114,
140, 244–46, 257, 260; poetry of, 139,
166–67; protection businesses of, 66, 88,
96, 102–4, 106, 110–14, 116–17, 120–33,
136–37, 141, 143–45, 214, 224–25, 231, 235,
238–46; religion and, 118–19, 132, 139,
167, 237, 240; reputation of, 66, 105–6,
114, 116, 122, 124, 231, 233, 245; Saika
bands and, 126, 157, 161, 167–68, 180–85;
Sakai and, 112–14, 120, 161, 169; as
samurai, 14, 105, 140–41, 149–50, 153, 231,
241, 246–47, 258, 260–61; shared lordship
and, 93–97; as shipping merchants, 110,
113–16, 119, 122, 143, 150, 224–25,
238–40; ships of, 121, 131–36, 170, 174,
179–81, 244; Shirai family and, 111;
Shiwaku and, 14, 102–3, 108, 110, 113–14,
116–17, 119–20, 122, 126, 128–29, 132,
136, 139, 143, 150, 163, 169–70, 224, 240,
243; siege warfare and, 119, 169, 180–81;
Sue Harukata and, 108, 113–15, 258;
Tokugawa period and, 12, 25, 135, 231,
247, 253, 256; Toyotomi Hideyoshi and,
108, 232–33, 235–50; unification and,
230–32, 244–47; unitary lordship, 105,
110–11, 128–30, 143–44, 150–51;
Yugeshima and, 14, 88, 92n100, 93–94,
128–29, 132, 239
Noshima Murakami Gyōbu shōyū
Takemitsu, 114, 120, 166n55, 184–85, 233,
238
Noshima Murakami Mototake, 254
Noshima Murakami Shōyūgorō Kagehiro,
163, 166, 254
Noshima Murakami Shōyūtarō Motoyoshi,
123, 126, 139, 144, 157, 163, 166–67, 169,
234–39, 245–46, 253, 257n118
Noshima Murakami Takashige, 111–12
Noshima Murakami Takeyoshi, 6, 14, 96,
105–6, 113–27, 139, 141, 143, 157, 159, 161,

About the Author

Peter D. Shapinsky is an associate professor of history at the University of Illinois, Springfield. His research interests include the maritime history of medieval Japan, intercultural exchange in premodern East Asia, and cross-cultural cartography in fifteenth- and sixteenth-century East Asia.